C000176156

THE FRIARS

THE FRIARS

A History of the British Medieval Friars

Kenneth Rowlands

The Book Guild Ltd
Sussex, England

The Book Guild Ltd.
25 High Street,
Lewes, Sussex

First published 1999

Set in Times
Typesetting by
Acorn Bookwork, Salisbury, Wiltshire
Printed in Great Britain by
Antony Rowe Ltd, Chippenham, Wiltshire

A catalogue record for this book is
available from the British Library

ISBN 1 85776 399 8

This book is dedicated to my wife
Rose
without whose forbearance it
would never have seen the light of day

CONTENTS

ACKNOWLEDGEMENTS

Front Cover: *The Mendicant*, painted by G. Gastagola, signed and dated 1874. The painting is owned by Cardiff County Council, who have given the author permission to publish it.

Aerial photograph of Aylesford Friary, Kent. The Prior, who owns the copyright, has given his authority for the photo to be published.

Isomeric elevation and plan of the former Carmarthen Franciscan Friary. The Dyfed Archaeological Trust has given its authority for these to be published.

Projected drawing and plan of the former Gloucester Dominican Friary. English Heritage have given their authority for these to be published.

Photographs of the misericord seats and sarcophagus of Princess Joan in Beaumaris parish church. The rector of the church supplied and authorised the publication of the photographs.

The drawings of the King's Lynn, Lichfield, London and Winchelsea Greyfriars churches are by A.A. Martin, and are taken from *Franciscan Architecture in England*, published by Manchester University Press in 1937. MUP have written to the author to say that the copyright for the drawings has reverted to the author and they have been unsuccessful in obtaining a forwarding address for him. The author has also tried to trace Mr Martin, or his family, but he also has been unsuccessful.

The photographs of various friary remains were taken by the author.

INTRODUCTION

One of the remarkable achievements of the medieval church was its ability to create the kind of institutional framework that could harness the successive waves of revival that swept across the church in Britain and Western Europe between the tenth and fifteenth centuries. By the end of the thirteenth century the parochial clergy and monastic houses were ill-equipped to satisfy the spiritual needs of the people in the way they had in previous centuries. The parochial clergy mostly consisted of a large number of ill-educated priests who were incapable of passing on the teachings of the Christian faith to their people, and monks prayed for the world from the solitude of the cloistered seclusion of their monastic houses. When friars first made their appearance in the early part of the thirteenth century the church was rich and powerful, but was at a very low spiritual point.

The early years of the thirteenth century saw the inauguration of a great experiment in Christian discipleship when a new kind of cleric, the mendicant friar, appeared. Friars were something new in the church and were without precedent in the way they propagated the Gospel. Friars founded most of their friaries in the centres of populations so as to be able to minister to the masses by their preaching and by tending the poor and needy. The new intellectual and social forces of the mendicant movement took a lead in the intellectual life of the universities in the late thirteenth century and the first half of the fourteenth, and had a major impact on the practice of the Christian faith as they decisively stamped their influence on the ecclesiastical and religious life of the thirteenth century. Friars catered for the spiritual, social and intellectual needs of the people and ministered to them whenever they found a need. Friaries were centres for pastoral work in the communities where friars lived close to the people.

We will not be able to understand what motivated people in the Middle Ages if we do not keep their fear of hell and purgatory in the forefront of our minds. Their religion entered into every part of their lives, from birth to death and the hereafter.

When we look at the medieval friars and their religious calling, we look at them over a period of about 300 years from the thirteenth to the sixteenth century. During that period, the motivation of friars changed considerably. The first generation of friars were a radical driving force within the church, and as such were welcomed across Europe. They bypassed traditional ecclesiastical niceties and became an active reform movement within the church. In the first hundred or so years friars were the white heat of evangelism and brought a new intensity of personal religion to the people and into the church. They largely eradicated heresy in Britain by their re-emphasising the teachings of the Christian faith. Friars were looked on as holy men who were doing God's work, men who lived the religious life and observed the sobriety of life, and work of mercy. During the second hundred years or so friars were part of the background of medieval life, men who were better at explaining religion and who undertook social work within the community. They earned the respect of the people by the simplicity of their lives. During the third hundred years or so, while they were still respected by most people, they became a reactionary force within the church, as they fought a rearguard action against the coming onslaught of the Reformation.

The mendicant movement was started by two very different men, St Francis of Assisi and St Dominic, in different circumstances. They were born within eleven years of each other, and they also died within five years of each other. The figure of St Francis has haunted and inspired the church ever since he died in 1226. Francis and Dominic between them, through the movements they founded, activated or reactivated the theme of salvation and Christian living.

Friars, who constituted a part of the medieval religious landscape of Britain, have largely been ignored and get very little mention in history books, and the story of the medieval friars is largely forgotten. Although comparatively small in numbers, they exercised an immense influence on popular religion and in the universities. Some friars went about preaching, others taught in schools and universities, while others cared for the needy. A number of British friars eventually became bishops and a few became cardinals.

Great care has been taken in cataloguing and dating the establishment of friaries in Britain. The date of the foundation of many of the houses is not known, due to the absence of reliable information about the origin and foundation dates. The list of friaries has been compiled from various records, including most Victorian County Histories. Most friaries were founded between 1225 and 1300 and, once founded, nearly all of them survived up to the Reformation.

After a calamitous decline in standard of friars in the fifteenth century, a great chapter of English and Welsh history came to an end in 1538–9 when Henry VIII dissolved all monastic houses, including friaries, in his realm. When the Reformation took hold in Scotland in the mid-sixteenth century, friary buildings were mostly swept away. The numerous friars, with hundreds of years of spiritual and intellectual achievement behind them, were gone. Today there are numerous ruins of monastic houses but very few remains of friaries.

The aim of this book is to give a general history and description of the life, aims and impact of the friars. However, to have an understanding of the friars, it is necessary to look at the background of how medieval religion was practised. The book does not aim to be either comprehensive or exhaustive on the subject, but to give an overall theme, with examples under the various headings. However, it is not the writer's intention to compare or criticise the doctrines and traditions of the medieval church. That is a matter left to theologians.

When the French preacher Lacordaire was campaigning for the restoration of the Dominican Order in France in 1839, he wrote 'If God gave me the power to create a new Order, I am convinced that I should discover nothing more modern or better adapted to our time and its needs than the rule of St Dominic. There is nothing antiquated about it except history'.

I wish to express my thanks to the help extended to me by the librarians in a number of libraries, especially the Blackfriars Library, Oxford. I also acknowledge the help and courtesies extended to me by Aylesford Friary, the Prior of Clare Friary and by the sisters of Elgin Convent. I also wish to express my sincere thanks to Victor Dunstan for his help in checking the proofs of the book and for his encouragement.

1

MEDIEVAL TOWNS

To appreciate the kind of environment in which the friars worked it is necessary to look briefly at the background of town life in medieval times.

Britain was predominantly agrarian, with wool as the main source of the country's wealth. Until the fourteenth century the lords of the manor based their prosperity on the use of serf peasantry, whose status and duties were enjoined by long-standing customs enforced by manorial courts. It is estimated that, in the late Middle Ages, about 95 per cent of the population lived in the countryside.

With the expansion of the towns, the serfs drifted to them in search of the freedom they appeared to offer. The comparative stability and isolation of rural life was not fertile ground for new ideas; but life in the towns, with the relative freedom from customary constraints and the constant stimulus of competition, fostered a more critical mentality and provided better opportunities to exchange intellectual, moral and spiritual ideas.

The ruling class were professional soldiers who were always ready to fight their own, or somebody else's, wars. By contrast, the administrators constituted a comparatively stable bureaucracy with an organisation which slowly evolved to meet the changing needs of the growing middle class in the expanding towns.

The typical layout of a town in the thirteenth and fourteenth centuries consisted of three main elements. Firstly, there was the castle – most towns were fortified – which was the seat of the sheriff, who was the king's officer responsible for the peace of the area and for collecting royal taxes. By the latter part of the Middle Ages, most town castles were manned only during hostilities and many were in a ruinous state. Secondly, there was the market place, which was often the focus around which the town developed; and thirdly, the church, which played a central part in the life of the community to a degree which is hard for us to appreciate today. It is interesting to note that the nucleus of most towns that exist today were already established by the time the friars arrived.

Market towns were often situated at crossroads and were closely linked with rural production, being the distribution and economic centres for the rural hinterland. They were busy places where country people brought their cattle and produce to sell or exchange for the goods and services the town dwellers could offer, places where the limited medieval industrial and craft activities took place.

The newly emerging towns were incredibly small by today's standards and we would consider most of them to be small country towns or even large villages. As commercial prosperity and trading activities grew, urban populations increased and many medieval towns expanded beyond their town walls.

The populations of medieval towns were very small compared with their populations today. Estimates for the population of England, before the Black Death in 1348–9, fluctuate from 2.5 million to 4 million, depending on the research figures to which one refers. Historians differ in their interpretation of the available data on the population of medieval towns, consequently researchers give varying figures. Calculations based on the Poll Tax returns of 1377 give some interesting population information for England. But many did not pay the tax, either through avoidance, destitution, or for other reasons, and children under the age of 14 were excluded from the tax. Therefore, the Poll Tax figures did not reflect the population as a whole but only the tax-paying people in the society of the day.

The population of the whole of Scotland was estimated at about 400,000 in the mid-fourteenth century but there does not seem to be sufficient data for us to quantify the disastrous results of the Black Death in Scotland.

The population of Britain fell by about a third between 1348 and 1377, due to the heavy toll of the Black Death. This decrease reflected not only the loss of life suffered in the plague, but also a dramatic drop in the birth rate in the decade that followed.

The population of England in the Middle Ages was most dense in the wheat-producing areas of East Anglia, south Lincolnshire and the east Midlands. In Scotland, nearly a quarter of the population lived in the area around the Firth of Forth.

The populations of towns were not static and in some towns the population figures fluctuated considerably. Many small towns were founded in the twelfth and thirteenth centuries only to fade away and become abandoned by the late Middle Ages. Other towns were able to sustain their economic prosperity and grow to become centres of trade and administration for their area.

In some towns the population figures fluctuated dramatically during the Middle Ages. In 1226, Norwich, for example, had a population of about 10,000, but by 1360 the population had fallen to 6,000, only to rise again to about 10,000 by 1524. Boston had a population of about 5,500 in 1377 but the population had fallen to 2,250 by 1524. King's Lynn experienced a decline in population from 9,000 in 1350 to 5,000 in 1550.

The population of many middle-size towns remained reasonably constant during the Middle Ages. Cardiff had a population of just under 2,000 from the thirteenth century and up to the end of the eighteenth century, while other towns, Hereford, Ipswich, Shrewsbury and Worcester, had only marginal fluctuations in population.

Some towns experienced decreases. The population of Bridgnorth fell from 1,700 in 1377 to 720 in 1525. At Bristol, the population fell from 12,000 to 7,600, and at Colchester from 5,600 to 4,600. The population of Gloucester fell from 4,250 to 3,000, and at Leicester from 4,400 to 2,800. In 1377 York had a population of about 13,600, which rose to nearly 15,000 by 1400, only to fall to about 8,000 by 1525. Until about the year

1400 York was the second wealthiest city in England but, after suffering a rapid decline in wealth and population, by 1525 the city was only fifteenth in the table of taxable wealth in England. The population of Coventry fluctuated from 10,000 in 1280, when it ranked fifth in size in England, to 8,000 in 1377 and fell to 6,600 in 1521.

In the same period, many towns grew in both size and numbers. The population of Exeter grew from 3,000 to 6,800, Lichfield from 2,000 to 2,600 and Reading from 1,500 to 3,500. The population of Southampton increased from 2,100 to 3,000 in the years between 1377 to 1524. The 1377 Poll Tax assessed 2,357 for the tax in Oxford, although some sources suggest that the total Oxford population was then about 5,000.

By far the largest growth was in the population of London, which rose from 40,000 in 1377 to 70,000 in 1500 and over 100,000 in 1550. By the sixteenth century London had far outstripped its rivals in size and importance, being as large as the next 15 or so provincial towns put together.

The countryside was heavily wooded and much of the lower land was undrained bog and wetland, which made travelling difficult. The vast woodlands provided an abundance of timber for building. Towns were linked by trackways or rivers but travelling along them would have been both arduous and dangerous. Although nobles with their retinues, soldiers, traders and clerics travelled extensively, most of the population did not venture far from their home district. Transport was difficult, roads were tracks which could become seas of mud in winter and transportation by water was the practical way of moving bulky goods around the country. Boats plied the coastal trade, using the numerous coastal inlets and rivers, which were often the lifeblood of towns' trading interest. But travelling by water in small boats always had its dangers, due to changing weather conditions, although it was preferable to lengthy journeys by land over inadequate roads. There were many marauding bands of armed men and the country was not always a peaceful or safe place in which to travel. Men of religion were respected and left unharmed but people who appeared to be wealthy or to have valuables with them were always at risk from robbers.

Violence and the threat of war was always in the background and the protection of the population was the first duty of the town authorities. The importance of military preparedness loomed large in the life of the times and the town communities were obliged to look after the defences of their town. Town walls were built as a defence during times of hostilities but were also defences against roaming bands of robbers. During later medieval times, these walls were often breached for the convenience of the citizens and many town walls fell into disuse. The walls and gates were not only military defences, the walls kept out unwanted traders and the gates served as barriers where tolls were collected on goods coming into the town. In the thirteenth and fourteenth centuries the gates were locked at nightfall and no one could enter until they were opened at dawn, and the walls gave the town dwellers a sense of security during the hours of darkness.

The construction and maintenance of the walls was paid for by a Murage Tax (Latin for 'wall') levied on persons coming into the town to trade, or on the import of goods. It appears that by the fifteenth century the money for repairs to the walls came from rents for rooms in the gateways, from wall towers leased as houses or storerooms and from rents received from the letting of grazing on the ramparts. All able-bodied men, other than those in religious orders, could be called to fight in defence of their town or to help dig the town ditch and repair the walls in times of emergency.

Commercial activities were conducted within the confines of the towns and, as the wealth created by the expansion of trade grew, towns could no longer be kept within the walls and suburbs grew up outside. By the sixteenth century, most towns had developed beyond their walls and into the countryside beyond.

There was a clear social hierarchy and society accepted that everyone had their station in life. Rising in society was considered to be a matter of pride, and demotion in the social scale was shameful. The majority of people expected to remain at the level of society into which they had been born.

The burgesses, who owned the larger houses and ran the

towns, employed journeymen and apprentices. Below them in the social order came shopkeepers with small businesses, who employed workers and servants. Yet lower down the scale came the craftsmen and semi-skilled labourers, who lived in smaller houses in the backstreets. The lowest stratum of society was composed of servants, apprentices and pedlars, who lived in very poor accommodation or in the attics of their masters' houses.

Town trade was predominantly a money economy, although there was a lot of bartering of goods at the lower levels. Towns enjoyed a degree of self-sufficiency and town life was much more sophisticated than rural life. The burgesses and freemen in England and Wales, and the burgher and mercantile classes in Scotland, formed small oligarchies which dominated the towns.

Land in the medieval boroughs of England and Wales was divided into burgages. The tenure of land involved a small annual rent and provision of services to the superior lord of the town.

In Scotland, a burgh was a town with privileges accorded to it by charter, usually, but not always, granted by the king. Scottish royal burghs alone had the privilege of self-government and the right to trade overseas and import goods. It was costly but profitable to be a burgess. It primarily involved the ownership of a toft, or strip, of burgh land within the town, on which a house had been built, and payment of the burghal share of taxation was due.

The cramped conditions of medieval towns allowed only narrow frontages for most burgages or tofts for houses. The living accommodation was usually two rooms deep; the upper storeys were built, or jettied, over streets to gain more room. The burgage or toft was usually a long, narrow plot of land about 18 feet wide and between 20 and 30 feet long, running back from the main street. Medieval towns had a series of such plots laid out in a uniform plan. They were originally large enough for a dwelling place at the street end with a yard or garden at the rear, but during the latter part of the Middle Ages the rear part of the plot was often subdivided for other purposes. Most buildings were built partly of stone and partly of timber, with thatched or slated stone roofs.

The holders of burgages or tofts, as leading citizens of their town, had a number of privileges, and a status, as well as obligations and duties to the communities. Trading inside towns was regulated by the civil authorities, comprised of local merchants. They fixed the price of bread and ale and punished people who gave short weight or sold faulty goods. The flourishing towns had a number of such prosperous merchants whose riches came from trade.

By the fifteenth century most important towns were self-governing communities with their own mayors, councils, town seals and the power of local taxation. The councils were in fact perpetuating oligarchies of wealthy merchants. Most towns appointed a bailiff, usually one of the junior members of the town governing class, to preside over the local courts and collect rents from market stalls and dues from alehouses.

Towns accrued commercial benefits from the trade at weekly markets, when people from the surrounding countryside bought from the local town market that which they could not produce themselves. As the prosperous bourgeois class developed, the lives of the rich contrasted markedly with the poor. The great disparity between extreme wealth and destitution, between the knights, masters, merchants, servants, apprentices and the poor, was made more conspicuous by the crowded conditions of medieval town life.

Streets were narrow and, because there were no proper drainage systems, towns had stagnant ditches and ponds that received the heaps of garbage and effluent. It was the responsibility of individual house owners to remove rubbish from outside their premises but it was nobody's responsibility to remove the rubbish and garbage from the streets. The presence of so many animals in the town must have added considerably to the squalor. Edward III complained that York smelt worse from the dung and manure wherewith the streets and lanes were filled and obstructed more than any other town.

Market days brought a large number of people into the towns both for business and pleasure, and the activities of the markets contributed to the stench of garbage and undrained sewers. In the absence of any system of sanitation or refuse collection, dunghills and other filth accumulated in places, and inevitably fumes and other odious smells arose. The stench from so many different trades and the animals brought into the town for marketing must have been unbearable by today's standards. The level of hygiene does not bear thinking about, though no doubt, people became so used to the smells that they were immune to them. The filth was a constant source of disease and of the numerous outbreaks of plague.

Most towns held annual and occasional fairs, to which merchants from all over the country and abroad brought their goods and animals into the town for trading. When trading was over there was much pleasure-making and drinking and, needless to say, it often turned into riotous behaviour. Disorderly alehouses were a constant problem throughout the Middle Ages. Many houses brewed their own ale and such potent quaffs were the source of much idleness and rowdiness in the towns.

Dorchester was typical of many small medieval towns. In the Middle Ages it was governed by 24 burgesses, the equivalent of today's local councillors, who elected a town bailiff or mayor. The by-laws of 1414 reflected the half agricultural and half manufacturing life of the town. Dorchester had three fairs each year and markets were held on Wednesdays, Fridays and Saturdays. The by-laws decreed that no skinner was to beat skins or hides in the street where human food was sold, manure was not to be left in the market place for more than a week, pig keepers were to keep their charges under control and carcasses of animals that had died were to be dumped out of town.

Town traders formed trade guilds which exercised monopolies for selling their products in the town. The guilds ran their own apprenticeship schemes, and the way into a craft guild was by serving a seven-year apprenticeship in the trade from the age of 14. An apprentice who eventually became a master in his trade became a substantial and important member both of his guild and community.

Traders and craftsmen were reasonably well off and had acceptable standards of living by medieval standards. Below them in status were the hewers and fetchers, the illiterate poor, the beggars and pauper families. They were uncultured, uneducated, illiterate and worked long hours. There was no social service or safety net for poor people, who had to rely on the charity of the more prosperous citizens.

The rolls of criminal cases remind us that murders, thefts and brawls were frequent occurrences in towns, and that gallows, pillories, whipping posts and ducking stools were used against convicted offenders.

Life in the towns was often nasty, brutish and short. A study of medieval skeletons reveals that scurvy, rickets, arthritis and bad teeth produced a life of pain and deformity for many. Winter must have been dreary, when frost, rain and the shortage of fresh food made the cold months a time of real hardships for many.

It was to such towns and people that, for a period of about 300 years, the friars came begging for a living and ministering to people of all classes.

MEDIEVAL RELIGION

In order to understand the background of religion during the medieval period, it is necessary to look at how the Christian faith was practised in the Middle Ages. When referring to church activities during the medieval period, I have used the past tense in this chapter, although some of the activities continue in a modified form in many churches today. My references to the Christian faith are to show how it was practised in pre-Reformation days, and it is not intended to uphold or deny any held truths.

The Church of Rome claimed it had received the teachings of Christ in direct succession from the apostles and it was the keeper of the traditions of the church. The church had a missionary status from the beginning and was motivated by a desire to share the Christian revelation by preaching and teaching the faith. Its mission is best described in the First Epistle of John (1:3): 'That which we have seen and heard declare we unto you, that ye also may have fellowship with us: and truly our fellowship is with the Father, and with his Son Jesus Christ'. The church accepted the doctrinal definitions of the faith made at the First General Council of the church held in Nicaea in AD 325, which was codified in the Nicene Creed, the formal profession of Christian beliefs.

The church emphasised the crucifixion of Christ as the suffering and humiliated divine Son of God who by His death on the cross redeemed mankind from its sins. Jesus Christ arose from the grave and is alive for ever, and the risen Christ made it possible for sinful man to attain a place in heaven after death. As stated in the Byzantine rite for the Feast of the Holy Cross:

> Hail, life giving cross, unconquerable trophy of godliness, door to paradise, succour of the faithful, rampart set about the Church. Through thee corruption is utterly destroyed, the power of death is swallowed up and we are raised from earth to heaven; adversary of the devils, glory of the martyrs, true ornament of saints, haven of salvation bestowing on the world great mercy.

In modern times religion has, for many people, been relegated to going to church on a Sunday but, in the Middle Ages, religion was entwined with every public and private action and was part of society, both individually and corporately, and it touched people at every stage of their lives.

As among today's churchgoers, so there were diverse degrees of spiritual enthusiasm and spiritual insight, but all the laity participated in the life of the church. The influence of the church extended to all aspects of life through its sacraments of birth, marriage and death and by its teachings on public morality. Everyone believed in an eternity, and the fires of hell were a real and nasty possibility, and things done for the church were thought of as insurance policies for the afterlife.

People believed in God and the devil and tended to see life

as a struggle between the forces of good and evil. The Christian faith was the one thing that was sure and certain in uncertain medieval times. It was looked to for guidance, succour in time of need, comfort in times of sickness, help for the poor and a refuge of hope at the time of death. Its ongoing religious observances were a source of comfort in an otherwise harsh life.

The universal Catholic Church presented itself as one and indivisible, it was Christian and Christianity was the Catholic Church. It was an orderly and authoritative system of belief and practice based on the Gospels, encompassing individuals throughout their lives and guiding them to eternity. The church boldly asserted her divine right to lead her people in spiritual and moral progress. All individual Christians had to do was to fashion their lives in accordance with the rules and practices of the church and its beliefs. There was no serious questioning of the teaching of the church and heresy was not a problem in Britain. During the Middle Ages, the church had more influence on an individual than the state did.

Most babies born in Britain in the Middle Ages entered the life of the church when they were taken, a few days old, for infant baptism, or christening, as the sacrament is generally known. Children of about ten years of age were confirmed, a rite that confirmed a person in the faith and admitted them to full participation in the life of the church.

Every Christian was named after someone in the Bible, or a saint, and placed themselves under the special care of the saint after whom they were named. When the faithful got up in the morning and when they went to bed at night, or if they were due to go on a journey or carry out some important work, they placed themselves under the protection of God, the Virgin Mary and their patron saint. Most of the faithful considered going on a pilgrimage at least once in their life. The people had an awareness of sin and felt the need to make expiation if there was to be any hope of salvation. Then, at the end of their life, they left money to pay for a Mass or a series of Masses to be said for them, depending on their wealth.

Death was a simple fact of life. When a person was dying,

the priest administered the Last Rites, heard the dying person's confession and gave the sacrament of Extreme Unction, the holy communion from the reserved sacrament.

They learned by heart some of the basic scriptures and texts used in the services and ceremonies of the church. The Lord's Prayer trained them in the devotional life, the Creed taught them the faith, and the Ten Commandments and the seven deadly sins led to self-examination and penitence. They learned by heart some of the Psalms and knew the calendar of the principal festivals and feasts of the church.

The standards of morality enforced by the church were acceptable to the conscience of the people, and whatever the faults and failings of the medieval church, it set a definite scheme of Christian life and duty and showed how it could be accomplished.

Religion made no scholarly demands on the laity, who had no interest in the intellectual matters of the church; such they left to the men of religion. This did not change until the latter part of the fifteenth century, when there was a renewed laity interest in the theology of the church.

All ranks of the community joined in the picturesque festivals, during which most parishioners took part in the colourful pageantries; this had the advantage of integrating everyone into the daily life of the church. The calendar of the church's liturgical year kept the faithful constantly aware of the principal events of the Gospel and the church's sacred history. People used to record the times of the year by the various liturgical feasts. Feasts in this context did not mean sumptuous meals but periodic religious celebrations. People went to Mass on the important feast days, which were also holidays. There were many such days: Lady Day (25 March), St Peter and St Paul (29 June), Lammas (1 August), Michaelmas or the Feast of St Michael and All Angels (29 September) and All Saints' Day (1 November).

The AD 325 Council of Nicaea also agreed on a method for fixing the movable date for Easter each year. Easter Sunday fell, and still does, on the Sunday following the first full moon after the vernal equinox – that is, the time at which the sun crosses the plane of the equator, making day and night of equal length.

Easter was the greatest festival of the church, leading up to the powerfully dramatic elements in the Easter liturgy. The Easter period began with Lent on Ash Wednesday and lasted for 40 days. Lent, which commemorated Jesus's fasting in the wilderness, was observed as a time of penance and fasting. Palm Sunday, the start of Holy Week, was celebrated with processions, which passed through the west door of the church, and was followed by special church rites centred around the churchyard cross. Other than on special occasions this was the only time the west door of a church was used during the later Middle Ages.

The days leading up to Good Friday, which commemorated the death of Christ upon the cross, were celebrated with great solemnity. Good Friday and Holy Saturday were marked by sombre processions with tableaux representing the main events of the Passion. Holy Week culminated on Easter Sunday in great rejoicing when the church celebrated the resurrection of Jesus. There were numerous acts of worship during the Easter period, when local churches enacted local traditions that had been passed down over the years. The climax of the Easter services came with the lighting of the paschal candle to celebrate the resurrection of Christ, as dawn broke on Easter Sunday morning. The candle was carried around the church as people lit their tapers and candles from it and went in procession singing and exclaiming 'He is risen, Hallelujah!'

The feast of Pentecost, or Whit Sunday as it is more commonly known, was held on the seventh Sunday following Easter Day, to commemorate the descent of the Holy Spirit on the apostles. This festival does not seem to have been celebrated with the same liturgical enthusiasm as were other festivals.

The Feast of Corpus Christi (Body of Christ) was in honour of the Holy Eucharist and emphasised the mystery of the Blessed Sacrament. The festival was a product of the Middle Ages, when the faithful began to show a desire to see and adore the Host, the bread consecrated in the Eucharist. In

1264, Pope Urban IV issued a papal bull making Corpus Christi a feast of the church. A number of Corpus Christi guilds came into being, such as the one formed in York in 1408 with the aim 'To the praise and honour of the most sacred body of our Lord Jesus Christ'. On Corpus Christi day, guilds held an annual festival, which started with Mass in the church. The Host was then carried in the Corpus Christi procession in a monstrance, a receptacle usually of gold or silver, with a transparent container in which the Host was exposed for the people to see. Banners and crosses were carried in the procession, which wended its way in solemn pomp through town or village. It was a time when the Host was shown to the people to see and adore and was looked upon as a substitute for receiving the Eucharist at the Mass. As the Host was carried in the procession, people along the way knelt in worship and made the sign of the cross. The whole community took part in this display of faith and devotion which remembered the passion of the cross.

Christmas (Mass of Christ) was, as now, held on 25 December. The Christmas period extended, and still does for a large part of Christendom, from Christmas Eve on 24 December to Epiphany on 6 January, which commemorated the manifestation of Jesus to the Magi, the wise men from the East who came to do homage to the infant Jesus. A Praesepe, or representation of the child Jesus in the crib, and the scene at Bethlehem were displayed in most churches. In the year 525 a Roman abbot, Dionysius Exiguus, introduced the system of reckoning time as Anno Domini (the year of the Lord) from the birth of Christ, as the church had invested the birth of Christ with a temporal distinction as well as a spiritual distinction. It was not until the eighteenth century that it became customary to designate the preceding era 'before Christ' (BC).

The festival of Candlemas, held on 2 February, celebrated the presentation of the infant Jesus in the Temple. From the second century, candles were lit for ceremonies and for evening prayers, and by the third century, candles were burnt at the tombs of Christian martyrs. The practice of using candles as lights before the relics of the saint became popular during the fourth and fifth centuries and there is evidence from that period that lighted candles were borne in procession around churches and placed around altars. By the twelfth century, candles were being placed on altars as a symbol of the living presence of Christ, the 'Light of the World'. The festival is so named because it was the time when candles for church use throughout the year were blessed. Votive lights flickered before the great rood on the chancel screen, before images of Our Lady and the saints, where the faithful stopped to say a prayer and light a candle.

In the New Testament, the word 'saints' referred to members of the early church who had received the Gospel message and had set themselves apart for God; in other words, the collective body of those who were righteous in the sight of God. During the persecution of the early church there were many who suffered martyrdom for their faith, and as examples of courage and faith, were canonised by popular acclaim. The anniversaries of their deaths were celebrated more in commemoration than mourning; after all, the saints had assured themselves of their places in heaven. By the Middle Ages the term 'saint' referred to those who during their lives had borne witness to God through their sanctity. The Canonisation Code required evidence that the candidate for sainthood had lived a holy life; that miracles had been performed through his or her intercession; and that through him or her a contact was established between heaven and earth. They were admitted to the list of canonised saints and gained the right to be honoured and venerated by the faithful. Some saints, such as St Dominic and St Francis, became a kind of living image of holiness, attracting veneration during their lifetime, and became objects of cults as soon as they were dead. The medieval church laid great stress on praying to the saints, who, in their turn, would present the prayers and petitions to God. They, as holy men and women of the faith, acted as intermediaries between God and his people. To the people of the times, saints were every bit as beloved as are pop stars, football or TV personalities today.

Churches were dedicated to one or more patron saint in the belief that the saint or martyr would give the church his or her patronage and assist the church in its spiritual work. The patron saint of the church was also the patron saint of the community and was especially venerated by the people of the parish. Friars' churches, as did other churches, had patronal days for their own patron saints. They were days of special rejoicing which commemorated the birthday of the saint in whose name the altar was dedicated. The patronal day was a day of feasting and jollification, and such occasions gave ordinary people time to relax and have some enjoyment as an interlude in their otherwise harsh life.

The cross, which has been the most widely recognised symbol of the Christian faith from early times, was displayed in differing sizes in all churches and most homes. In the fourteenth century the figure of Christ was added to the cross, which then became a crucifix. The figure of Jesus stripped and nailed to the cross with his head bowed, represented 'Christ in Agony' and remembered His suffering and death on the cross. A plain cross, without the figure of Christ, represented the empty tomb and Jesus as the risen Christ, the heavenly king of glory.

Christians made the sign of the cross on their body during certain points in the liturgy and frequently during their private devotions. The sign of the cross was made with three fingers touching the forehead, touching the heart area and the right shoulder and then the left shoulder. This sign was usually accompanied with a verbal 'In the name of the Father, Son and Holy Spirit'.

Some people, no doubt, repudiated their religious duties, but the gate of penitence was always open to them and the church could provide atonement for their rumbustious and violent lives. However bad or scandalous some may have been in their private lives, most had genuine respect for those who were seen to be living the holy and austere life of the faith.

THE BIBLE

In AD 382, Pope Damasus I commissioned St Jerome (342–420) to make a new translation of the Bible from the Greek and Hebrew originals. Jerome completed the work, which is known as the Vulgate, or vulgar common speech, Bible, in AD 404. For over a thousand years Christian leaders adopted the fundamental attitude that the Vulgate Bible was inspired by the Holy Spirit and should not be altered.

The understanding of the scriptures was considered to belong exclusively to the priesthood by virtue of the special grace given to them by God when they were ordained. It was believed that lay people did not possess this grace, and to read the Latin scriptures without it would be injurious to them because they would mistakenly think they understood the great truths of scripture. The church would not risk private translations of the scriptures and any attempt to translate the Bible into English, or any other language, was considered an abasement of the Word of God. This attitude was widely held throughout Christendom. The 1229 Council of Toulouse forbade lay people even to own copies of the Bible.

Because of the cost of producing bibles by hand, which would have taken years rather than months to produce, there were very few complete texts of the Bible until the invention of the printing press in the latter part of the fifteenth century. As a result, the great majority of people knew very little about the Bible, which was a highly venerated but closed book. Bibles were looked upon as treasured possessions, which were often encrusted with jewels and other elaborations and paraded as objects for adoration which were safely kept, but rarely read. The fruits of scriptural studies were passed down to the people through lessons and sermons.

The division of the Vulgate Bible into chapters was undertaken by Cardinal Hugo in the thirteenth century. The Old Testament was first divided into verses by Rabbi Nathan in 1448. This was adopted in a Latin edition printed in 1528, which also employed a similar method for dividing up the New Testament. In 1555 another Bible was issued by Robert

Estienne of Paris, in which the same verse division was used for the Old Testament, but a different one was provided for the New Testament. The Geneva Bible published in 1560 followed the arrangement adopted by Estienne and was the first English Bible broken up into verses, as is the present method.

Following the invention of the printing press there grew a ready market for books on personal devotion and theology. By the early sixteenth century there was an increasing number of laity who were literate and able to read and study the Bible and its scriptural text for themselves.

While William Tyndale (1494–1536) was serving as tutor in the household of Sir John Walsh, of Little Sodbury, Gloucestershire, he scorned the ignorance of the local clergy because of their lack of knowledge of the Latin scriptures and he resolved to translate the New Testament into the vernacular. He wrote, 'I had perceived by experience how that it was impossible to establish the lay people in any truth except the scripture was plainly laid before their eyes in their mother tongue, that they might see the process, order and meaning of the text'. His highly literary English translation of the New Testament was printed in Cologne in 1525 and, in the following year, the first printed copies of the New Testament in English were being surreptitiously circulated in England. Tyndale's translation was to become the basis of the Authorised, or King James, version of the Bible, although his New Testament didn't legally reach the hands of the people until 1537, when, by order of Henry VIII, a copy was placed in every parish church in his realm.

Miles Coverdale (1488–1569), an Austin friar, preached a sermon against images in 1528. He then left the Austin Order and fled to the Continent, where he translated the Bible into English. In 1535, it became the first Bible in the English language to be printed in England. Coverdale followed Luther's example in segregating the apocryphal books of the Old Testament from the canonical books in the Hebrew text and inserting the apocryphal books as an appendix at the end of the Bible.

In 1610, the Douay Bible, an English translation from the Latin Vulgate text, was completed by Roman Catholic scholars in Douai, Northern France, which was the centre for exiled English Roman Catholics during the sixteenth and seventeenth centuries. The Apocrypha is still retained as an integral part of the Douay Bible.

The Scottish version of the New Testament was begun by Matthew Nisbet, but it was not completed or printed and the Geneva version of the scriptures was used in Scotland.

CHURCH HIERARCHY

Popes

Popes rested their claim to be head of the church on earth on their representing a higher power and administering a higher law than the rulers of earthly nations. They took their authority from St Peter's great confession recorded in the Gospel of St Matthew (16:15–19) where Jesus said to His disciples, 'But whom say ye that I am?' And Simon Peter answered and said, 'Thou art the Christ, the Son of the living God'. And Jesus answered and said unto him, 'Blessed art thou Simon Bar-jona: for flesh and blood hath not revealed it unto thee, but my Father which is in heaven. And I say also unto thee, that thou art Peter and upon this rock I will build my church and the gates of hell shall not prevail against it. And I will give unto thee the keys of the kingdom of heaven: and whatsoever thou shalt bind on earth shall be bound in heaven: and whatsoever thou shalt loose on earth shall be loosed in heaven'.

The Pope, as God's vicar on earth, was recognised as the spiritual father of the faithful and the central and supreme religious arbiter, under God, of the Catholic Church. The church was governed by the Sacred College of Cardinals, who were the popes' chief advisers and who collectively formed the Curia, the papal court and government of the Catholic Church. Its members were appointed by the Pope and they in their turn elected a new pope when the Holy See was vacant. They kept firm control of the Catholic Church's beliefs and clergy. The Roman Curia was considerably increased in size between the eleventh and fourteenth centuries due to the volume of ecclesiastical business which had been reserved to it. They built an ecclesiastical organisation of great efficiency.

The range of subjects referred to Rome for a decision was remarkable. It is staggering just how many mundane matters such as wills, appellant business concerning property and matrimonial laws, in addition to the large amount of ecclesiastical business, were channelled through bishops and archbishops to Rome. The system was cumbersome but it worked and it had no equal in medieval Europe.

The church in Britain was an integral part of the Western church, obeying the canon laws of the church as expressed in papal codes.

The Great Schism of 1378 to 1429, during which rival popes reigned in Rome and Avignon, divided the mendicant orders in the same way as it divided the church as a whole. The mendicants had no choice in the matter as it was a political decision made by rulers of the various countries. English kings followed the Roman Obedience and Scottish kings followed the Avignon Obedience.

The Great Schism undermined the prestige and power of the papacy and put more power into the hands of the bishops. The papacy did much to recover what had been lost, often supporting the friars as agents in its attempt to regain its former supremacy. Thus were the papacy and friars brought closer together, to their mutual advantage.

Archbishops

The church was divided into provinces, with an archbishop as head of each province. Britain was divided into two archbishopric provinces, Canterbury and York. St Augustine (d. 604) was the first archbishop of the church in Britain and Egbert (732–66), a Northumbrian, was the first archbishop of the Province of York when it was formed into a separate province of the church. However, it has been claimed by some that there was an archbishop of York as early as AD 314.

During the earlier part of the Middle Ages, the archbishops of York claimed that Scottish bishops were under their authority and the archbishopric's territory extended into much of Scotland. In 1192 Pope Celestine III made the church in Scotland a 'Special Daughter' of the Holy See, dependent on the Pope, with no subjection to the Archbishop of York. The church in Scotland cherished its independence and was continually alert against interferences from York. In 1225 Pope Honorius III, refusing to give the church in Scotland the status of a province with its own archbishop, allowed the Scottish church to hold regular provincial councils. Each council was to choose one of its bishops as 'Conservator of the privileges of the Scottish church' and he was to act as such until the next council meeting. St Andrews, which was the premier see in Scotland, was not elevated into a metropolitan see with an archbishop until 1472, when Pope Sixtus IV issued a papal bull to that effect. In 1487, Pope Innocent VIII made the Archbishop of St Andrews the Primate of Scotland, enjoying the same rights in Scotland as the Archbishop of Canterbury did in England.

Bishops

Archbishoprics were organised into dioceses, territorial areas entrusted to the pastoral care of bishops. Bishops were regarded as successors, in the Apostolic Succession, of the apostles Christ appointed to guide the church. There were 21 dioceses in England and Wales during the medieval period. Eighteen of them, including the four Welsh dioceses, were in the Province of Canterbury and three (Carlisle, Durham and York) in the Province of York. Dioceses varied considerably in size. The Canterbury, Chichester and Rochester dioceses covered comparatively small but well-populated areas. The Exeter diocese covered all of Cornwall and Devon, while the huge diocese of Lincoln extended from the Thames to the Humber River. The diocese of York comprised the whole of the county of York and the archdeaconate of Nottingham.

There were 11 dioceses in Scotland but most of them covered

large areas of mountainous land and were poor, with few churches or resources. The dioceses of St Andrews, Dunblane and Glasgow covered the more prosperous central belt of the country. The boundaries of the St Andrews diocese were, for a number of reasons, extremely complicated and were intermeshed with detached territories. The diocese of Orkney, along with the diocese of the Isles, was under the authority of the Archbishop of Trondheim in Norway for most of the Middle Ages.

Dioceses were headed by bishops who were, in the main, learned men. They had authority over all parish churches, non-parochial churches, chapels and clergy in their diocese. They also had episcopal control in their diocese, over abbeys and priories that had not been granted exemption from episcopal visitations. Friaries were exempt from episcopal jurisdiction, but more of that later.

A cathedral was a church in which the bishop set his seat as the chief pastor and teacher in his diocese. Because he was Father-in-God to his people, the cathedral was the mother church of the diocese and the centre of church life in the diocese, maintaining both study and worship.

Bishops had no responsibility for running a cathedral and did not usually attend its services. Each cathedral had its own chapter, headed by a dean, to administer the affairs and possessions of the cathedral, and clergy to maintain a regular round of services which reflected its dignity as the mother church in the diocese. It was the centre of diocesan church life and its main purpose was to maintain a regular round of worship of the highest standard possible in and for the diocese.

However, bishops had the responsibility of maintaining a supply of sufficiently educated men in their dioceses to serve as priests. In order to carry out this duty, most dioceses had a school attached to the cathedral, for training young men for the ministry of the church. These schools were the forerunners of the public schools that are still attached to most cathedrals.

Bishops alone had the authority to ordain priests, through whom the sacraments of the church could be made available to the faithful. Only bishops could consecrate the holy oil used in baptisms, confirmation and the Last Rites.

The *Pontifical Manual* laid down how bishops should be consecrated at their induction service. It was important that the consecration procedures were strictly followed, otherwise the consecration could be invalid. At the consecration of a bishop, three bishops had to lay hands on him at the same time before he could be confirmed into his office as bishop of the diocese. The 'laying on of hands' was considered to be an important part of the rite as it signified that the consecration of the bishop was in the long line of succession of bishops from St Peter and symbolised the passing from one generation to another, in direct line from the early apostles, the power and authority of the Holy Spirit. Three bishops were deemed necessary for the rite, in order to avoid malpractices developing over a period of time.

The *Pontifical Manual* also laid down the various duties of bishops, such as the order of services for ordaining men to the priesthood, the consecration of churches, altars, churchyards and objects such as chalices and items used in the Mass. It also stressed that bishops should set an example to their clergy and laity by giving alms, showing hospitality and living holy lives.

Administering the confirmation rite of admitting a baptised person to full membership of the church was also one of the duties of a bishop, but it was carried out in a very casual way. Due to the lack of organisation it was not the practice of bishops to hold confirmation services at definite times or places but bishops usually administered confirmation to those who presented themselves to them as they travelled around the diocese. Bishops were known to administer confirmation to people while still on horseback. There was no special preparation for the rite, it being assumed that everyone understood the significance of confirmation.

Medieval bishops were not only prelates but also local magnates with feudal obligations to the King. As feudal lords, they held their lands from the King in return for undertaking knight-service for him. They belonged to the King's Council and often their work was not concerned with spiritual matters but with the duties of the high secular offices they held under the crown. This frequently distracted them from concentrating on their spiritual work, which often brought them into protracted conflicts with their people. Many medieval bishops and senior clergy lived lives of luxurious indolence governed by maxims of worldly ambition rather than the cure of souls in their charge. This resulted in the neglect of their episcopal duties and many ambitious men saw a bishopric as a post which gave them prestige and power.

However, the medieval bishops were, on the whole, able and responsible leaders, administrators, builders and patrons of the arts. But bishops were a formidable body whose ill will even the most powerful magnates had cause to fear.

The church was open as a career for all ranks and classes of people and was the one way in which men in medieval times could climb the social ladder. Thomas Wolsey, born at Ipswich in about 1473, the son of a grazier and innkeeper, reached the positions of both Lord Chancellor of England and a cardinal of the church.

When free from other duties, a bishop made progress tours of the churches and other religious establishments in his diocese, so as to keep in touch with the working of the ministry in the churches entrusted to his pastoral care. An episcopal visit started with an official welcome of the bishop at the door of the church, followed by a sermon given by him. His examination of the clergy allowed them, in their turn, to draw to the bishop's attention matters that required his consideration. He would get an overall view of the church and would issue instructions to rectify any problems he found during the visit. Thus it was ensured that the churches and religious establishments were functioning in accordance with the canon law. The heavy cost of such visits by the bishops, who travelled with a large retinue of servants, was paid by the churches or establishments being officially visited. As a result, although people welcomed visits from their bishop, they hoped he would not visit them too frequently.

Parish Priests

Monks and friars living in monastic and friary communal

establishments were known as 'regular' clergy, for they took vows to observe a rule, wore distinctive clothing and belonged to a community. Collegiate churches had communities of priests who went about their priestly duties in towns but lived in communities, following similar monastic lives to those of monks, and were known as regular canons. Priests who served a parish church and were engaged in active parish ministry were known as secular clergy. In this sense, 'secular' means non-monastic.

The basic parish had a resident priest who had the responsibility for the 'cure of souls' of the people who lived in the parish. They had control over religious events in their own parish but were not allowed to take part in religious activities in another parish, unless authorised to do so by the resident priest of that parish.

By the time the friars came on the scene in the thirteenth century, there were about 10,000 parish churches in England and Wales and up to 1,100 in Scotland, but there was only a small pool of competent priests to serve these churches. The more capable clergy were absorbed by the cathedrals or the greater town churches, where spiritual and doctrinal standards were markedly higher than in rural churches. The educated elite who entered the religious life mostly went into the monastic life, where they had the opportunity to further their studies.

There were poor educational facilities for training the large number of priests required to serve the thousands of local parish churches in the countryside. Candidates for the priesthood merely had to show that they understood enough Latin to read their service books and, it appears, as long as there was a priest in charge of every parish, regardless of the standards and qualifications of the priest, the hierarchy was generally satisfied. It would have taken a considerable amount of money, and a much more efficient organisation, to have brought the general clergy to anywhere near the educational standards of today's clergy.

Before being allowed to carry out priestly duties, a novice priest had to be ordained by a bishop laying his hands on the ordinand's head and anointing him with holy oil. The 'laying on of hands' was, and still is, a pivotal element in the ordination of a priest.

The number of candidates who were ordained for the priesthood in the Middle Ages shows how easy it was to be accepted. In 1370, there were 374 candidates ordained in Worcester Cathedral and a further 613 in 1377. If these figures for ordination were reflected across the British dioceses, they would have produced an extraordinary number of ordinations. It must therefore be assumed that some dioceses did not hold ordinations. It was also the period when the church was making up its numbers of clergy, following the devastating losses suffered during the Black Death.

The educated priests who were usually qualified for the more lucrative appointments in the church were drawn from the younger sons of the nobility.

Rural parochial priests, who formed the great majority of the ill-paid lower clergy, were largely recruited locally from the ranks of peasant stock and the lower middle class. They were not scholarly men but they generally knew enough to teach their people and, because they came from the free peasantry, understood the problems of village people. Such priests often lacked the special vocation and calling required for the priesthood and had no expectations of promotion to a higher post in the church. Once a priest had been appointed to a rural church, he tended to stay in the same parish for many years, sometimes for the rest of his ministry.

Many of the parish clergy were badly educated and consequently were unable to convey to their parishioners the church's teachings. The celebration of the Mass was their chief duty and most of them could follow the *Ritual Manual*, which prescribed the religious ceremonies and rituals for infant baptism, marriage, the Last Rites and other such rituals.

Few of the clergy possessed a bible, or even part of a bible, and as a result they were not able to expound the scriptures or give systematic instruction in the Christian faith, and still less able to combat heretical opinions. They went through the formal services of the church, such as the Mass, but some rural priests were so backward they did not understand the mysteries of the sacraments performed in Latin at the altar.

Few people, other than clerics in the teaching ministry of the church, had a deep knowledge of the Bible or the theology of the church. Although the medieval church was a large organisation, it did not hold what we would call ongoing seminars to instruct the clergy, who lived in spiritual isolation and without contacts in the church at large, except for the annual diocese synods. Due to the priests' lack of training, sermons were rare in most parish churches, most secular clergy having neither the ability nor inclination to preach. But people in medieval times went to church to adore the presence of Christ in the Mass, not to hear sermons or learn about the faith.

The relationship between some parish priests and the people they served was at times difficult. Many priests were held in little esteem but were, nevertheless, deemed to be an essential part of the rural community, though their poor standards resulted in apathy in the church. By the late Middle Ages, there was a strict regard for ecclesiastical discipline and respect for the spiritual hierarchy. However, there was little understanding of the spiritual calling of the faith; it had become an outward show, and the spiritual aspects of it had been generally forgotten. This was ultimately to trigger the Reformation.

Secular priests wore distinctive garb which made them recognised as a separate class in society. There was a desire to make worship in the church as beautiful and reverential as possible and this was partly achieved by priests using special vestments when celebrating the Mass. As we shall see, everything in the medieval church was symbolic, and the symbolic interpretations attached to the priestly vestments served the purpose of keeping the mind of the faithful focused on holy things during the Mass. It was therefore important that the vestments themselves, whether elaborate or plain, didn't lack the beauty and dignity becoming for garments set aside for use in the worship of God. The eucharistic vestments included an alb, the simplest of the vestments, which was derived from the commonest garment worn in ancient times. It was white, as a symbol of purity, and was normally made of wool, for warmth.

A chasuble was worn over the alb. This was originally a circular piece of cloth with a hole in the middle to allow the head through, like a South American poncho. Later the chasuble was altered by cutting it down the middle so that it could be put on like a cloak. It represented the seamless garment of Christ and the purple robe put on Christ by the Roman soldiers at the crucifixion. The stole, a long strip of linen worn by the priest, was originally a napkin for cleaning the sacred vessels after they had been used in the Mass and represented the priest as the servant of God. There were many additions and variations on the basic vestments and the colour of the priest's chasuble used in the Mass varied according to the festival season.

Many parish priests gave of their best with their limited ability but that ability left a lot to be desired. Dominic saw that there was a connection between an ignorant clergy and the spread of heresy and the need for a clergy able, above all, to preach and teach the faith. There were, of course, many priests who were competent and devoted shepherds of their flock, men who were godly and saintly and who ministered faithfully to their people week by week. They were the precious gems of the church and Chaucer found the most attractive religious characters among their ranks.

LANGUAGE

In 1066, the Normans brought the Norman French language to England for administrative and legal purposes. The court and ruling classes used Norman French, while the general population used Anglo-Saxon, Celtic or other local languages or dialects. By the fourteenth century the English language, which was the ancestor of modern English, began to assert itself and in 1362 an Act of Parliament decreed that Norman French was no longer to be used in English and Welsh law courts.

Clerics were the educated class and were employed in many senior administrative posts, and they, naturally, used Latin for all top-level official work. It was the only language of correspondence and records across the Western church and was the common language of scholars of all nationalities. This had the advantage of unifying the church across the many language barriers and considerably eased communication.

Latin was used for public worship in all Catholic churches throughout Europe and travellers were able to follow the Mass and other church services in whichever country they were. The use of the vernacular was allowed in the bidding prayer at the Mass and in the preliminaries of the marriage service. The major part of the Mass and the reading of the epistles and gospels were said and read in Latin and were therefore incomprehensible to the congregation. Due to long usage, however, people knew the general outline of the Latin Mass and other services. The use of Latin meant that although people had an understanding of the principles of the faith, they had little comprehension of its inner meanings. This ignorance added to the apathy and superstition which overtook much of the church in the latter part of the Middle Ages.

CELIBACY

Until the late eleventh century, clergy were permitted to marry and have families. There were many instances of the son of a priest being appointed to the parish in succession to his father. The practice of celibacy was a gradual development. The church hierarchy became persistent in requiring a celibate priesthood so that priests would be more responsive to the needs of the church and able to put their whole energy into their calling. A priest who was encumbered with a wife and family and had the domestic responsibilities of family life, they reasoned, was not as free to be moved if the church authorities required his services elsewhere. In 1079, Pope Gregory VII decreed the celibacy of the priesthood and in 1123 the Vatican Council declared the marriage of all in sacred orders to be invalid. This order took a while to filter down to the rural priesthood and it was not until well into the twelfth century that celibacy became the practice. The marriage of the clergy then became a sin and wives became concubines in the eyes of the church. In a number of instances, celibacy remained an aspiration rather than a reality, and a number of priests, especially in rural areas, remained married. It was not long before the coming of the friars that the whole of the priesthood became celibate. From that time until the Reformation, the marriage of those in holy orders was contrary to ecclesiastical law.

MILITARY ORDERS

A brief mention must be made about the crusades in the eleventh and twelfth centuries because they had a marked effect on the church. The crusades were seen as a moral conflict between Christians and the infidel, between good and evil. There was an amazing response to the call for a crusade to capture the Holy Land from the infidel. Jerusalem was captured by the crusaders in 1099 and this was followed by the setting up of the Christian kingdom of Jerusalem.

Monks and clergy were forbidden by canon law to have any part in the shedding of blood but, during the crusades, the Knights Templars and Knights Hospitallers were dedicated to fighting the infidel. They considered it a sin only if they killed a fellow Christian; it was not a sin, in their eyes, to kill the infidel while fighting the crusades. By the time the friars came into being, the Knights Templars and Knights Hospitallers were powerful military and religious organisations.

The Knights Templars, or Knights of the Temple of Solomon, were an international order formed circa 1118 as a military order to guard the Church of the Holy Sepulchre and to protect pilgrims to the Holy City. The order was introduced into the British Isles ten years later. However, in 1308 Edward II complied with the papal request that all Knights Templars in his realm be apprehended and their property taken into the hands of the King. The Templars were disbanded by apostolic authority of Pope Clement V in 1312.

The Knight Hospitallers, or Knights of the Hospital of St

John, were founded in Jerusalem in 1113 to care for poor, sick and weary travellers and to provide escort for pilgrims to the Holy Land. The order was introduced into England the following year.

As both orders were linked to the crusades, they gained a high prestige in the land and became richly endowed and wealthy organisations. Both orders had their preceptories, or houses of knights of their order, in Britain, where they lived in monastic communities but were free to carry out their knightly duties. The knights were fully professed monks who had taken the religious vows of poverty, chastity and obedience, though, being wealthy orders, they found the vow of poverty difficult to keep.

PARISH CHURCHES

Today we tend to think of churches as places to be used on Sundays and other special occasions. In medieval times, and even later, the parish church was the most important building in the community and the scene of activity throughout the week. It was the house of God and therefore it was treated as a holy place, but the solidly built stone church buildings were used both for worship and as the forerunners of village halls. The church sprang to life on the great feast days, when most parishioners attended their church.

The actual foundation dates of most medieval churches remains conjectural but the network of parishes was virtually complete by the mid-thirteenth century. Originally, the numerous parish churches in the countryside were founded by landowners for Christians on their estates, and the church building was often considered to be the property of the founding family. Having been built on the landowner's land, the church was often adjacent to the manor house of the parish. The parochial parish boundaries date from around the twelfth century and often corresponded with boundaries of secular estates described in tenth and eleventh-century charters. Parish churches were usually, but not always, sited at the northern end of the village, as it was believed that spiritual powers attacked from the north.

During the earlier part of the Middle Ages towns were divided, for religious purposes, into a number of small parishes, each parish being served by a church and parish priest. These, often small and poor, churches were founded by landowners on their urban estates, which often consisted of a cluster, or a street, of houses. In circa 1100, there were about 100 such parish churches in London, 39 churches in York in addition to the cathedral, Holy Trinity Priory and St Mary's Abbey. In 1100, Lincoln had 35 parish churches, which increased to 46 by the end of the thirteenth century. Bristol and Stamford each had 20 such churches. Winchester had 47 at the end of the thirteenth century, which was reduced to 30 by 1500. When the Dominican friary was established in 1335 and an Austin house established in 1387 in Thetford, the town had a comparatively static population of about 4,000. It had 20 churches, a Clunic priory and a Benedictine nunnery. When the Austin friars arrived in Huntingdon in about 1258, the town had 15 parish churches. Many other towns had a similar number of religious establishments, commensurate to the size of the town.

However, during this period, English and Welsh towns each had one principal parish church, which was usually sited in a central place in the town and therefore near the market area. During the later Middle Ages towns took pride in their central church and competed with each other on beautifying and embellishing them. The work of beautifying the house of God was an ongoing practice and was considered a corporate act of worship. A few towns, however, such as Ludlow, had but one large parish church to serve the town.

As the Middle Ages progressed, many of the smaller town churches became impoverished and the patrons received no income from them to support a priest. Such churches were allowed to decay and were subsequently abandoned and the parishioners assigned to other churches. Such reductions greatly reduced the number of town churches and as a result there were fewer but larger churches in the towns.

In Scotland a church is, of course, known as a 'kirk', the word kirk being derived from the old Norse *Kirkje*. To avoid repetition, further references to 'church' will include the Scottish kirk. Unlike south of the border, Scottish burghs usually had a single large burgh kirk, which was the centre of all kinds of religious and civic activity. In the fourteenth century, Perth had a small monastery, a nunnery, five hospitals run by religious orders and two friaries, in addition to its parish kirk of St John's.

A majority of medieval Scottish churches were plain rectangular buildings with no structural distinction between choir and nave. The separation of the choir and nave was clearly defined internally by a timber screen, or rood loft.

Nearly all of the numerous parish churches we see in the countryside in England and Wales began their existence as small rectangular buildings, each with a small nave and a chancel which terminated in a semicircular apse projection. The high altar was sighted in the apse at the east end of the church. The division of a church into a nave and chancel, divided by a chancel arch, first appeared in Britain in the eighth century, but the familiar long rectangular chancel, with the altar placed against the eastern wall, became unique to British churches during the thirteenth century. Medieval Continental churches retained the apse at the east end.

The church building's primary function was as a house for divine worship, and the churches bear some relationship to the liturgical uses for which they were intended. Liturgical practices were not static and as the mode of worship changed, church buildings were changed to meet the requirements of current liturgical usage.

Most parish churches were added to between the thirteenth and sixteenth centuries by enlarging the nave and building north and south aisles to the nave, extending the chancel and adding to the height of the tower. The naves and aisles were enlarged to make more space for the secular and social activities of the parish as well as for the increasing number of parishioners. Transepts were added to many larger churches, to increase the space for processions and to accommodate altars for the ever-increasing number of obituary masses. However, there was a great reluctance to demolish the original church towers, therefore a number of churches which were enlarged retained their original tower, even though the tower was heightened. Many church towers in prosperous towns were topped with a crown of intricate stonework, which symbolised the crowning glory of the Christian faith.

Medieval people did not have the means of knowing the times to go to services so churches had bell towers, or bell-cotes, with bells to call people to worship. The world was a quieter and calmer place then, no traffic noise or other human activity to muffle the sound of the bells, which were audible over a wide area of the countryside or town. The sound of church bells carried a long way and could at times be heard two or even three miles away, depending on the direction of the wind.

The times of the services could not be rigid for there were no clocks to go by. Many churches had a scratch sundial, which was divided by radial lines into periods called 'tides', hence came the old saying that 'Tide and time waits for no man!' These sundials were used by the priest as the timepieces, weather permitting!

The chancel was the only part of a medieval church which was consecrated. Under church law, the maintenance of the chancel area was the responsibility of the recipient of the parish tithes. Where the church had a residential rector who received the tithes, the chancel area was properly maintained by him. Where the nominal rector of a parish was a distant religious house, it showed little concern for the maintenance of the choir areas of churches for which it had responsibility. By the late Middle Ages, a growing sense of civic pride, of which the local church was a prime focus, induced the communities to rebuild or enlarge the choirs of their local church on a grander scale, at the expense of the parishioners.

The day-to-day maintenance and state of repair of the rest of the church building – nave, tower and porch – and any necessary enlargement and embellishment, was the responsibility of the parishioners, who were also responsible for maintaining the churchyard and providing places within it for the burial of the dead.

The main entrance to British medieval churches was usually on the south and warmer side of the building. Inside the open porch, there was stone seating where the parochial church council, which was in effect the local authority for the parish, met to discuss parish business.

A recess in the wall at the entrance of the church contained a stone stoup, a basin which contained Holy Water. On entering the church, the faithful placed a finger in the Holy Water and made the sign of the cross upon themselves.

The first thing one would notice on entering a church was the awesome but colourful interior. Christians through the centuries had decorated and furnished church buildings with objects of beauty and colour, to teach and remind people of the essential Christian beliefs. The interiors of churches were alive with colour from wall paintings, the colourful vestments of the priests, painted images, altar hangings and the metal work of the altar cross and candlesticks. The interiors of many churches in the fifteenth century were made lighter by installing the, then, newer perpendicular windows, which gave considerably more light.

Infant baptism was universal and the font used for baptising babies into the faith was sited near the entrance of the church, symbolising the babies' entry into the Christian Faith. By an order of 1236, all fonts which were not in use had to be covered and locked to prevent witches coming at night and stealing the Holy Water. The ordinance of baptism was the prerogative of the parish priest and a mark of his parochial status. Fonts are often the oldest remaining object in many churches, pre-dating many medieval church buildings.

The nave of the church was used by the public, and the church chancel was the liturgical area used by priests. An elaborately designed wood or stone rood-screen was mounted directly in front of the chancel arch. Rood-screens were introduced into the churches in the fourteenth century, when the rituals associated with the crucifixion were elaborated. The screen was surmounted by an image of the crucified Christ, with the accompanying figures of the Virgin Mary and St John on either side of Him. These figures were veiled during the period of Lent, and decorated with greenery during festival times. The word 'rood' is from an old English word meaning 'cross'. Many medieval churches still have the narrow stairs built into the wall or pillar of the tower which once led to the gallery above the rood-screen, but nearly all the roods were dismantled during the Reformation.

The chancel was entered through the rood-screen. The sanctuary at the east end of the chancel, which contained the high altar, was the area where God was worshipped in fullest splendour. It was always in an elevated position at the east end of the chancel so that the faithful had to lift their eyes to the high altar. In this part of the church the vestments, embroideries and fittings were objects of beauty and colour and the best the church and its people could afford or obtain. The altar area was considered to be the most holy part of the church and would only be approached with great reverence. Often the roof over the altar area was distinguished by an elaborately decorated ceiling or canopy.

There was always a strong odour of incense emitted from gilded censors burning near the altar or being swung by the priest while he was performing the religious rites at the altar. The incense symbolised a sweet-smelling savour rising from the church and ascending to heaven. The priest, clothed in the eucharistic vestments to which we have previously referred, performed the liturgy of worship, especially the Mass, at the altar. However, the average person had little comprehension of the rituals that were being performed at the altar. On the south side of the altar was a recess for a triple sedilia (seat), where the officiating priests sat during the singing of the Creed and Gloria. On the wall near to the sedilia was a piscina, a recessed stone basin with an outlet leading to the outside ground so that any consecrated wine drained away and entered the earth. Although they are not now used for their original purpose, they can still be seen in most medieval churches.

On Sundays and saints' days parishioners met together for Mass, but there was not the hushed calm in the church that is expected today. During the Mass there was a lot of noise and movement in the church and the Latin service being led by the priest at the altar was virtually inaudible. When the sanctuary bell rang to indicate that the Host was being elevated by the priest, people stopped what they were doing, turned to the altar and genuflected; that is, bent one or both knees as a sign of reverence for the Blessed Sacrament.

There were frequent comings and goings to churches, with their constant round of services and small processions. It gave a perception of the busy ongoing life of the church in a way which is hard for us to grasp these days. The church knew how to encourage people to rejoice in the faith at festival times as well as to be thoughtful and serious about things eternal, even if it did not instruct the laity in theology.

Churchgoing was a social occasion as well as a religious duty. Country dwellers who lived isolated lives all week were able to have their meagre experience of social life in church, where they met neighbours, indulged in gossip and exchanged pleasantries. Small groups met in a corner of the church, children played in the aisles and dogs made a commotion until they were chased out by the dog-whipper.

Because the nave of the church was not a consecrated area, it was used for all kinds of activities, sacred and profane. In the absence of suitable buildings for secular business, naves were used for many parish purposes, much as the village hall is today. There might have been a number of barrels of beer stored under the church tower to keep cool in the summer months, or a pile of weapons kept in another corner of the church in case they were required for military action. The medieval year was filled with festivals, feasts and ceremonies, special occasions marked by feasting and jollification which took place in the nave of the church, along with various other parish activities. People who lived some distance from their local church spent the entire day there, enjoying eating their bread and cheese and drinking their beer with their neighbours in the nave of the church.

No doubt some people tried to bring more reverence and order into the church but it was accepted that the church building was in part a public storehouse and focal point for parish social activities, as well as being a house for prayer and the sacraments.

Medieval people did not consider there was anything improper about conducting business in church. Wills and other legal documents were drawn up in the church's porch, with the parish priest often acting as notary. The nave was near to the altar and any agreements made there were considered as binding before God, which provided a guarantee of fair trading and honest dealing. Disputes about the ownership of cattle, land and such like were settled in the nave of the church.

As the nave was considered to be community property, courts of justice were convened there when there was no other suitable place available in the village. Until buildings such as town or burgh halls were built in the later medieval times, many civic gatherings took place in naves of town churches; even parliaments met in some of the larger churches.

Medieval people considered it natural to go into a church and have a quiet time of devotion at any time of the day. Churches were seldom closed and were considered to be second homes where people could enter at any time for private devotion.

Very few graves in medieval churchyards were marked in any way and most churches were surrounded by an open expanse of grass. This was used for putting up market stalls and playing games during festival times, when all the villagers would help brew ale, bake bread and cakes and plan sporting competitions and games. The sums raised from the fêtes were used for the needy.

Thus did the local churches continue as the centres of religious life until the storms of the Reformation beat upon them. When the Reformation came, the roods were demolished, statues and images, altars and altar furnishings were destroyed, walls whitewashed and the tithes of the church diverted to courtiers. The medieval parish churches are but a skeleton of their former and original glory. They have been dressed up in a new but reverential manner to meet the changing needs of the times, but they are a visual history of their parish through the ages.

PARISH FINANCE

The Old Testament practice of giving a tenth to God or His representatives was observed by the patriarch Abraham, who gave a tithe of his spoils to Melchisedec the priest. It was also observed by Jacob, who vowed he would give to God a tenth of all that God gave him.

Until the tenth century, clergy were financed by voluntary gifts given by the pious faithful. As part of the reform of the churches in the tenth century, payment of a tithe to the church became a legal requirement. During the medieval period few people, other than the merchant classes, used money and there were no cash collections during church services as we have today. A tithe (in England and Wales) and a teind (in the north of England and Scotland) was one-tenth of all of the villagers' produce, and its payment became a tax enforced by law which was paid until the Reformation. The paying of tithes was modified after the Reformation and their payment was phased out over a long period. In 1891, Parliament passed a law that only landowners in England and Wales had to pay tithes. It was not until 1936 that Parliament passed the Final Tithe Commutation Act, abolishing the compulsory payment of the tithes which had first been introduced in Anglo-Saxon times.

As long as the parish priest had his permanent benefice, or church living, which yielded an income, the priest's financial position was assured. Parishes were endowed with a plot of cultivated glebe land granted to the parish priest for his material support during his tenure of office. The land was originally intended to be large enough to support the parish priest but most glebes proved to be insufficient and he had to rely on his income from tithes. Priests usually lived in clergy houses built on glebe land near the church. The rector of the church was the priest who was entitled to receive the tithes of the parish.

The relative wealth of parish churches attracted the attention of monastic houses and cathedrals and was to become a favoured means of providing funds for monastic communities. The right of patronage, or advowson, the right to choose a rector and present him to the bishop for installation in a church, was generally regarded as belonging to the family or successors of those who had founded the church. These families had a strong belief in the efficacy of the prayers of monks and nuns and were ready to support them in their activities. Around the twelfth century, landowners who owned the advowson rights of a parochial church or kirk found it convenient, as an act of piety and for the good of their soul, to grant their advowson rights to religious organisations. The appropriation of a church by a religious organisation meant that the parish church with its tithes and endowments passed to a monastery or another religious establishment. Religious houses all over Britain came into possession of appropriated churches, and by this method the parish funds of numerous churches were devoted to monastic use.

It was, perhaps, natural that the monasteries and cathedrals that became patrons of local churches strove to extract the maximum advantage from the parochial tithes, dues and endowments. The ambitious building programmes of many monastic houses and cathedrals were expensive to maintain and most of the larger religious establishments needed the finance from a number of appropriated parishes to pay for the work. St Albans Abbey, Westminster Abbey and Kilwinning Abbey (Ayrshire) each had the tithes of 16 churches, Coldingham Priory (Berwickshire) had 18 churches, while Norwich Priory Cathedral took the tithes of 87 churches.

By 1500 about one-third of parish churches in England and Wales had been appropriated by monastic houses, who also owned about one-third of all land. In Scotland, the proportion was vast and about four-fifths of all parish teinds were appropriated to monasteries, cathedrals and collegiate churches.

Where a church was appropriated to a monastery, the monastery became the corporate rector of the parish and appointed a vicar, or substitute, to look after their parishioners. Vicars appointed by monastic houses were given a place of residence, usually a house with the glebe land, and were allocated a small portion of the parish tithe. The bulk of the income went towards the finances of the mother house. The vicar's portion of the tithe was often barely sufficient for subsistence and certainly not sufficient to attract competent persons. As we have seen, this resulted in a low standard of person being attracted to many of the poor livings, which could only offer a pittance because the mother houses received the benefits of the tithes.

As income from benefices varied enormously, the richer parishes, mostly found in towns, attracted plenty of candidates, but the poorer parishes found it difficult to attract competent priests.

The advowson has been described as the curse of impropriation because the wealth and talent of the church gravitated towards the monasteries and cathedrals. When we see the splendour of the great medieval churches, it is only fair to reflect that most of them were built by the money taken from parishes.

MONASTIC HOUSES

From an early period in church history, men and women, moved by the desire to live a religious life, found it impossible to do so in a world in which there was so much violence and sin. They therefore retired from the world and, with like-minded persons, dedicated themselves to live the monastic life and be bound by its strict rules.

The monastic life was a disciplined life and those who sought admission to it were required to pass the first year as a novice, to test their perseverance and suitability, before they could take the vows binding them to observe its rules. The cultivation of obedience and humility was the foremost virtue of a novice. Monks and nuns considered that monasteries, where they lived enclosed lives, cut off from secular life and isolated from the outside world, were the best places to serve God. Their lives involved total poverty for individual members but they accepted the necessity for the monastery collectively to acquire corporate land and wealth.

Among the people, the monastic life inspired considerable affection, but it was not part of the local community. Monks and nuns were people who had chosen to dedicate their lives to God, to the exclusion of the ordinary things of life such as marriage and material success. They considered their denial of worldly contacts enabled them to concentrate on the worship of God and give Him the devotion He deserved. They gave themselves wholly to the enjoyment of communion with God, and the spiritual kingdom was as real to them as the temporal kingdom was to the laity. Those who served in monasteries were considered to be soldiers of the Kingdom of God and were just as necessary as the soldiers who served earthly kingdoms.

Monks and nuns turned to God by means of prayer and secured their passage to heaven, and also at the same time enjoyed a foretaste of its pleasures on earth. By their renunciation of individual property, they regarded themselves as beacons of prayer in a sinful world, fighting the forces of evil from inside their enclosures as they prayed for the rest of mankind. From the early days of the Christian church, down to the sixteenth century, the monastic life was considered a perfectly natural vocation.

The monastic foundations were primarily concerned with the offering of worship to God through the celebration of the Mass and the recitation of the Canonical Hours daily throughout the year.

In AD 985, England possessed 30 monastic houses and by 1215 the number had increased to 222 houses for monks and 75 for nuns. The massive expansion of monastic life in Britain started after 1066, at a time when the monastic ideal was rapidly spreading across Europe. The twelfth century was the golden age of monasticism, when numerous new houses were founded and the monastic orders attracted vast numbers of recruits of ability. It was a time when a host of rich donations and benefactions were lavished on the monasteries.

It has been estimated that as late as 1500 there were about 10,000 monks and 2,000 nuns in England and Wales.

An abbey was largely an autonomous and self-contained group of monks under the leadership of an abbot. A priory was generally a dependent house of an abbey and under the leadership of a prior. The Cistercian Order was organised as a family of priories across Europe, dependent on their loyalty to the Cistercian mother house at Citeaux Abbey, Burgundy, the home of the order.

The monks collectively formed a body known as the chapter, which was corporately responsible not only for the administration of the house and its possessions, but also for providing an unbroken round of religious services.

Monastic houses built up substantial estates as they received property and land, as well as churches, for their income. Benefactors considered monasteries places where monks and nuns could be set apart for the lifelong and irrevocable practice of the Christian life, at a level of excellence judged to be impossible outside such a community. The monastic life was held by many to be the most perfect life. Donors and recipients alike shared in the belief that the prayers of the monks were much more effective than those of a humble parish priest. Prayers would be offered by holy men for the souls of their founder and his family, and such prayers would blot out the sins of the donors, who hoped that the perpetual remembrance and intercession of the monks might avail them at the bar of eternal mercy. It was for such a service that the gifts were both given and received.

Most monastic houses followed the rule of St Benedict, which in turn followed the psalmist's words in Psalm 119:164: 'Seven times a day do I praise thee because of thy righteous judgements'. This set a pattern of chanting prayers and praises to God seven times a day, for which no congregation was necessary. The seven services were known as 'hours' of the work of God. A sequence of services made up of psalms, prayers, anthems and readings, starting with nocturn at 2 a.m. and ending with compline at sunset. The time between was punctuated by five other services. Between the services there was time for spiritual, intellectual and manual activities.

The Benedictine Order is the oldest monastic order in the West and the 'Rule of St Benedict' was the governing code which laid down simple and practical guidelines for the monastic life and became the basis of the daily routine in all Benedictine houses. The rules were not intended to make the life of a monk harsh but were framed to be within the grasp and capability of the ordinary man and woman. So that monks had no need to wander outside the curtilage of their house, the rules prescribed that, if possible, a monastery should be so arranged that all necessities such as water, mills, gardens and various crafts were situated within the monastic enclosure. In order to be self-sufficient, Benedictine houses were complete with church, cloisters, accommodation, infirmary, kitchen, stables, brew-house and barns, all within a walled enclosure. Access to the abbey precincts was controlled by a gatehouse.

The monastic way of life provided a context in which a spiritual life could develop peacefully in the discipline of the cloister, far removed from many of the temptations of normal life. The perfection of monastic observance came to be seen as the closest likeness of paradise on earth.

Monks and nuns spent most, or all, of their life in one community. If they left their parent house to take up other duties in the church, it was customary for them to return to the house of their first profession in order to end their days there. Their days were planned for them and their clothes and food provided out of a common fund. Their little world was restricted to the few acres surrounding the monastery and within its protective wall, which gave them privacy. The outside world became almost a foreign country which they seldom visited.

Monasteries were not inclined to minister to the people outside their house but neither did they close their eyes completely to the secular society around them. They emphasised the importance of hospitality to travellers, stressing 'let a guest be received as if he were Christ'. Entertaining guests imposed a heavy financial burden on houses, especially if they were in towns or on main travel routes, when they were expected to provide shelter and hospitality to strangers and travellers, both rich and poor.

Benedictine houses owned a number of urban tenements in towns and therefore had an input into the lives of the towns-people who lived close to the abbey, and who were never free from abbey control. As a result, abbeys often came into conflict with local people over various borders, river weir and fishing rights. The monks and officials of the monastic houses with whom the local people had to deal appeared to have greedily appropriated all they could get and seemed to be more concerned about the wealth of their house than with spiritual matters. Such abbeys provoked envy and criticism.

Cistercian monks advocated both austerity and manual labour and settled in places remote from the society of men. They, through their servants, cultivated their own lands and became efficient sheep farmers and wool producers. They kept large flocks of sheep and herds of cattle on estates, which they controlled from outlying granges where they stored their crops, and became more like farmers than monks. In due course, such activities ensnared the interest and energy of the Cistercian monastic communities, which became not unlike modern corporations.

The Cluniac Order placed great emphasis on offering to God the best they could afford; the result was that their services became very long and their buildings and furnishings ever more opulent.

The original fervour of the monks was maintained for a few generations and then the 'old Adam' of selfishness asserted itself in one way or another. By the fifteenth century, the enthusiasm and piety that had existed among them had given way to greed. Respect had gone for these people who withdrew from the world but took the rent and tithes of the people. Geraldus Cambrensis (Gerald the Welshman) (1146–1220) wrote in his *Itinerary* that 'The Benedictines in their original state were wholly admirable, but later they acquired vast wealth which led to gluttony, indulgence and corruption. The Cistercian Order clung tenaciously to its original vows of poverty and holiness but, there again, blind ambition crept in and took possession of it, making it insatiable in its quest for more and more land'. He may have been harsh in his comments but they had more than a grain of truth in them. Most monastic houses proved to be able administrators and, in most cases, good landlords, but that was not the purpose for which they had been founded.

By the fifteenth century, monastic houses had lost a lot of their religious influence and were regarded by the people as opulent corporations whose members lived comfortable lives and were more concerned with levying fees and enforcing the payment of rents due to them than in their spiritual lives. The monks, who had vowed personal poverty, often belonged to wealthy corporate communities, and some of the larger abbeys acquired more worldly wealth than was necessary for their needs or good for their reputations.

Spiritual stagnation and a descent into worldliness came to the monastic life, although there were still a number of houses and individuals that held fast to the ideals of monasticism. David Knowles, in his *The Religious Orders in England*, tells us that when, in 1421, Henry V addressed 360 leaders of the Benedictine monks in the chapter house of Westminster Abbey, he recalled to them the primitive observances of their order and reminded them that his royal ancestors and other founders had made their benefactions from a sense of value of the prayers of men of an austere and regular life. The old religious orders had been left behind by the new social needs and ideals fostered by the growth of the new intelligentsia.

When monks by their austerity and devotion obeyed the medieval ideal of true religious life, they were regarded with respect and exercised influence, but when they ceased to be models of austerity, they lost the source of their strength. Their wealth, which was a symbol of their power, became the source of their weakness and hastened the waning of the monastic appeal. Estranged from the poor, their vows of poverty eluded them, and in seeking their own spiritual welfare they failed to meet the needs of the time.

During the Middle Ages, the patronage of the great tended to focus on one particular order, which for a generation or so enjoyed their beneficence, before losing their appeal in the face of newer and stricter expressions of religious zeal. In Britain, the Benedictine Order was favoured by the first generation of Norman barons; by the middle of the twelfth century the Benedictines had given way in the esteem of the people to the Cistercian monks. By the thirteenth century, the monks had given way to the friars in the esteem of the people.

2

START OF THE FRIARS

By the beginning of the thirteenth century the church had done little to adjust itself to the intellectual and economic changes which were influencing the thoughts and lives of people. There was widespread criticism of it in Western Europe and there were calls from within the church for reforms. Though the agrarian population was unquestioning as to the role of the church, the urban population, through its wealth and commerce, became a new power in the land. This in turn made them a more independently minded class of people, people who questioned the ability of the clergy to effectively lead them in the faith.

In 1179, bishops, abbots and heads of religious orders met in council in the Lateran Basilica, the cathedral church of the popes as Bishops of Rome. The Lateran church, where so many ecclesiastical assemblies were held, was built by Constantine the Great, the Roman Emperor who adopted the Christian faith in AD 312. The papal headquarters was moved from the Lateran church to St Peter's, Rome, following the return of the popes from their Avignon exile. The Lateran Council, in reacting to the abuses within the church, laid down a rigid division between church and state; no laymen were to own churches; the clergy were not to take on secular occupations.

The early part of the thirteenth century proved to be a turning point for the church; a wave of enthusiasm swept across Europe for a new form of religious vocation which identified the service of God with service to man. Not all the events were organised by the church and some were actively opposed by it. This was the era in which the mendicant orders came into being. They first sprang from the zeal of two very different, but enthusiastic, men who saw that the spiritual needs of the people were not being met by the monastic or secular clergy.

The mendicant friars were a radical breakaway from the monastic traditions of the past. They broke from one of the basic principles of traditional monasticism by abandoning the seclusion of the enclosed cloisters in order to engage in an active pastoral mission to society. At first, they needed neither abbeys or benefactors, nor even a summons to attract them to a town. They brought a new vitality to the faith as they took their message and enthusiasm to the rich and poor, to universities, castles, village greens and towns. In their early years, they lived out the Christian message which they were preaching and teaching and which was to regenerate the life of the church.

Alas, as with so many organisations, their initial enthusiasm gave way to a settled way of life. This in turn gave way to a reactionary and obscurantist movement whose actions led to its downfall in Britain in the sixteenth century.

The word 'mendicant' comes from the Latin *mendicare*, meaning 'to beg', a name given to the friars due to their vows of poverty. Members of the mendicant orders were known as 'friars' which means 'brothers', as in the French *frère*.

Friars belonged to organisations called 'orders'. All orders, other than the Trinitarian Order, were founded in differing circumstances during the thirteenth century. Each order had its own objectives and rules, but they were to become less distinguishable from each other as time went by.

Orders	*Year the Order was Founded*
Dominican	1216
Franciscan	1223
Carmelite	1226
Mercenaries	1235

Orders	*Year the Order was Founded*
Crutched Cross	1248
Sack	1251
Austin	1256
Servites	1256
Pied	1257

The Trinitarian Order was formed in the previous century, but was incorporated as a mendicant order when they adopted the friars' way of communal living.

The second Church Council of Lyons, held in 1274, considered that the number of mendicant orders were proliferating too rapidly and suppressed all but the Dominican and Franciscan Orders and the small Crutched Cross Order, which was mostly concerned with a ministry to the sick and infirm. The Carmelite and Austin Orders were later reprieved from the decree. The other lesser mendicant orders were forbidden to recruit new members, resulting in the slow withering away of the Pied and Sack friars.

The Order of the Blessed Virgin Mary for the Ransom of Captives was popularly known as the Mercedarian Order, from *Merced*, Spanish for 'mercy'. The order was founded for the ransom of Christian captives when St Peter Nolasco and 13 noblemen took the three religious vows, poverty, chastity and obedience, in Barcelona Cathedral in 1218. The order added a fourth vow, that members would act as hostages, if necessary, to free Christian captives from the Moors. The order was approved by Pope Gregory IX in 1235, who gave them the rule of St Augustine to follow. It was responsible for the liberation of up to 70,000 prisoners, 2,700 of them in the founders' lifetime. The order did not reach Britain.

The Order of the Servants of St Mary, known as the Servites Order, originated in 1233 when St Bonfilius and a group of Florentine cloth merchant companions left their trade for a life of poverty and penance. They lived in a small abode and oratory dedicated to St Mary, in Florence. They did not intend to found an order but their numbers grew and in 1256 Pope Alexander IV approved them as an order of friars living in strict corporate poverty. This order did not reach Britain either.

There were a number of less prominent orders established across Europe, each with one or just a few houses. Information on most of them is very slight and they did not attract many recruits.

Each of the four main mendicant orders started with separate origins and distinct characteristics. The Dominican and Franciscan Orders started off with much in common and worked along similar lines. Their first houses were founded in university towns, episcopal centres and commercial towns. The Austin and Carmelite Orders founded their first houses in remote areas, but soon followed the example of the two older orders and established themselves in the towns. The period of rapid growth of the four orders scarcely extended more than 80 years, when their houses became centres of an organised Christian ministry.

The antecedents and circumstances of the origins of the Dominican and Franciscan friars were different but the orders came into existence almost simultaneously, in the early part of the thirteenth century. Within a quarter of a century, both had blossomed into orders of great influence, academically as well as pastorally, and were well established throughout Britain and Europe. It is generally accepted that the orders complimented each other, for without the Dominican example of good organisation, which the Franciscans followed, the Franciscan Order would not have survived. If it had not been for the spiritual instincts of the Franciscans, the Dominicans would have remained a relatively small order dedicated to the task of combating heresy. Whereas the unworldly Francis was a spiritual leader, he was not an organiser and resisted efforts to organise and regulate his followers too precisely, the more practical Dominic saw that an effective organisation was essential if his order was to flourish. The contrasting spirit of these two remarkable men was impressed on the societies they formed. The pure devotion of St Francis aimed at self-renunciation with incessant evangelistic work, whereas the austere zeal of St Dominic was inflamed by the need of a new power to combat heresy. The Franciscans were dedicated to taking the Christian message to the people, especially to the sick and needy. The Dominicans were dedicated to preaching and teaching, to rooting out heresy and proclaiming the Christian truths. While contesting every inch of ground occupied by the other, they became increasingly interlocked in their aims and practices.

The Austin and Carmelite Orders started as fragmented groups of hermits who had been brought together under their respective order. Their new rules brought them from their previous hermit way of life into cohesive groups which enabled them to have an effective ministry within the church.

The Dominican and Austin friars followed the 'Rule of St Augustine'. St Augustine (354–430) lived most of his life in the city of Hippo Regius in the Roman province of North Africa. A man of wide culture and powerful intellect, he searched through philosophers for the meaning of life. In reading the works of Cicero and Plato he found nothing about the redemption of man, so he turned to the New Testament and especially to St Paul's epistles. One day in AD 387, he was reading the thirteenth chapter of the Epistle to the Romans and was so impressed by what he read he was converted to the Christian faith.

In AD 388, Augustine returned to Hippo with some friends and they founded a monastery. He was a prolific writer and theologian and in about 397 he wrote his *Confessions*, which described his pilgrimage to Christianity. He became bishop of Hippo, a leader of Christian thought and a doctor of the church. In about 423, St Augustine wrote a document of only a few hundred words, which he sent to the convent where his sister was, to settle the affairs of the house. This became the 'Rule of St Augustine', a brief set of rules and principles for a common-sense way of life for those living in a community, but they lacked specific regulations for the monastic life. They were used extensively from the eleventh century onwards and taught the love of God, love for one's neighbour, humility before God and man, chastity, obedience, study of scriptures, care for the sick and how to live in a community. The rules were followed by many religious orders through the centuries, including the mendicant orders, which served them as a basis for their way of life.

The Austin friars' logo was a bible and a heart pierced by the arrow of God's love, and their motto, *Tolle Lege* (Take up and Read), which is derived from Augustine's conversion when reading the New Testament.

The friars' organisations became an integral part of medieval Catholicism and the centralised church, and were international orders which transcended frontiers. No national barriers prevented them from going where they had a calling or were invited to settle and, because they had been authorised by the Pope to undertake their special duties, they worked in a more or less freelance manner within the dioceses and had no direct responsibilities to the spiritual hierarchy of the dioceses.

Each order had its own 'Cardinal Protector' who represented and acted as guardian of the order at the Papal Curia, the central administration governing the church. Each province of an order had its own 'Conservator of Privileges', usually a bishop, appointed to protect the order in disputes with other religious bodies in the province.

Each order developed by stages, an organisation with its own form of government that gave it its own special ethos and character, but the constitutions were based on the constitution of the Dominican Order. In the course of time they tended to become more and more assimilated through conscious, or unconscious, imitation of each other.

Each order was headed by a Minister-General, who was directly responsible to the Pope and, so as to be near the centre of the church's decision making, resided at the papal court in Rome. Each order had a General Council, the ruling body responsible for regulating and maintaining a common standard of efficiency and competence in the order's houses.

The General Councils passed legislation and their policy matters and decisions were passed on to the Provincial Chapters of their order. The Provincial Chapter was in charge of administration and personnel matters within its province and the Principal Ministers resided in the largest or principal house in the province.

Provincial Chapters received amalgamated reports from the districts, which had been made up from the visitation reports from the various houses in the districts. The reports included information on the education requirements, finance and discipline within the province. The Provincial Chapters received legislation and instructions from their General Council and passed them down to the districts.

Provinces were subdivided into districts, for convenience of organisation, which generally consisted of a group of six to eight houses. These districts, although known by different titles by their respective orders, had the duty of ensuring that each house within their district respected and fulfilled its obligations and avoided recurring problems such as gambling and drunkenness in their houses.

The prior of each house was responsible for the economic and external affairs of his house. The material and spiritual quality of their house, its raison d'être, depended on his leadership, as he guided, trained and directed the friars under his charge and all the activities of the friary were under his control. As St Augustine's Rule reminded the friars, 'Your superior should not take pleasure in ruling you, but rather in serving you with all charity. While the honour you may pay him exalts him in your eyes, let fear prostrate him at your feet before God. Let him correct the unruly, encourage the faint-hearted, comfort the sick and be patient to all'. Smaller houses feared the loss of outstanding priors when they were transferred to another, larger house or advanced to a higher post, as it could inflict great loss on the house. In many houses the prior was aided by a sub-prior who took charge of internal discipline and deputised in the prior's absence.

The General Councils of the mendicant orders ensured there were systems of regular judicial visitation and inspection of houses in their order and that visitations were carried out by a superior officer who had been authorised to do so. Such visits started with the community gathering in the chapel for a Mass; a sermon was given by the visitor, who then addressed the brethren in the chapter house. These were followed by an inquiry into the life of the community and the general standards of the house. During the visit every member of the house had a separate examination by the visitor, allowing each friar to draw attention in private to items he considered needed rectifying. This enabled the visiting inspecting friar to report on the efficiency and conduct of the house and to correct and chastise those responsible for indiscipline and obstinate or wilful behaviour. The visitors also made enquiries about students who showed promise for further education.

Unfortunately, the visitation process was designed to root out faults great and small, and therefore tended only to highlight reprehensible deeds and faults in the houses. Good conditions were taken for granted and their praiseworthy work went largely unrecorded. It may have been considered that each house was expected to set an ongoing high standard and it was therefore not necessary to highlight and report on its good points.

The binding feudal institutions that had developed in Britain were not developed in Ireland until the twelfth century. Ireland was a loose federation of Gaelic-speaking rural communities controlled by a small group of clan patriarchs, or local kings. Over all lay the shadowy authority of the high king of Tara, though he did not exercise any real power or central authority. Other than a few coastal settlements, there were no towns of Irish foundation from which the countryside could be organised. The Tuath, the local chief's lands, were the units of administration, with the chiefs living in a ringed fort within the Tuath. Most of medieval Ireland lay outside the pale, that is, beyond the limits of English authority from Dublin. Ireland was organised on a rural and tribal basis, which served tribal areas rather than towns. Because they served the needs of a differing community, they have not been included in this work, although their ministry and organisations were basically the same as their British and Continental brethren. However, most Irish houses were poor and education was a drain on their resources.

Mendicant friars were known as the 'First Order'. The 'Second Order' of mendicants consisted of nuns, who, unlike their male counterparts, lived in enclosed communities.

Each order of friars had its own 'Third Order', or confraternities of lay people, both males and females, who lived under the direction and in the spirit of the order to which they were attached. They were pledged to lead a pious life in their own homes and were bound to a performance of devotional exercises and charitable works by following a simple rule for their way of life. They were part-time friars who lived ordinary lives in the world but under the strict rules of personal religion. The confraternity members differed from the brothers in their respective orders by their absence of vows and lack of community life.

Confraternities had their own altars in friars' churches and members had the right of burial in friars' churchyards. Mass was said daily in the confraternities' chapels and members carried out works of piety and distributed alms to the poor. Members paid subscriptions to support their chosen friary.

DOMINICAN FRIARS

The Dominican Order of friars was founded by Dominic De Guzman (1170–1221), a reserved, intellectual priest born into the illustrious house of Guzman's of Calaruega, in old Castile. Dominic was enrolled at the age of 25 as a Canon Regular of the Augustinian Order by Bishop Diego, at Osma Cathedral in Spain. Within nine years, he was appointed Sub-Prior of the cathedral.

Dominic accompanied Diego, his bishop, on a journey to Rome. On their return journey in late March or early April 1205, the bishop and Dominic encountered three Cistercian abbots in Montpellier. The abbots had been commissioned by Pope Innocent III to oppose the Albingenses heresy, which was committed to the dualist doctrine that this material world is evil and that it was made, not by God, but by an evil anti-god and only the spiritual world was good. It was a heresy widespread in the Languedoc area on the Mediterranean coast of France. There were a number of such heresies in medieval times, but they did not intend to be precursors of rival churches to the universal Catholic Church. They had no differences with Catholicism but, rather with the way it was practised. The three abbots had been travelling with the pomp and trappings of high ecclesiastical dignitaries and a large retinue of servants; consequently, the people they confronted regarded them as an affront to the simplicity of the faith. The abbots in their turn despaired of any success in their mission. Dominic and his bishop could see the reason for the abbots' failure and answered the complaints about their lack of success with the rebuke: how could they expect success, with all their show and secular pomp? Heresies could not be countered by displays of power and pomp but by zealous preaching and by apostolic humility and austerity. Zeal must be met with zeal, false sanctity with real sanctity, preaching falsehoods by preaching the truth. Sow the good seed, as the heretics sow the bad seed.

Dominic and his bishop saw that to succeed, the church must employ persuasion and adopt a more simple way of life, modelled on the early apostles'. They were aware of the dangers threatening the church, due to the widespread revolt against the papacy and the indolence and ignorance of the lower clergy, who were not equipped to contend with spiritual weapons against those who would not conform to the established doctrines and order of the church. Dominic and his bishop set the tone of their new mission by sending their servants home, and, dressed in the simplest canonical dress, set off on foot on an itinerant preaching tour, holding public disputations with the leaders of the heresy.

Dominic, filled with zeal for a crusade on behalf of orthodoxy in the church, spent the next ten years in the Languedoc area preaching and seeking to reconcile heretics to the church. During that time, his evangelistical fervour drew a number of like-minded brethren to him, whom he trained as preachers and teachers, and they gradually developed a special style of preaching and a mendicant way of life. Dominic travelled to Rome in 1215 to seek papal authorisation for his new Order of Preachers. However, at that time the reforming Fourth Lateran Council of 1,200 prelates was assembling in Rome, headed by Pope Innocence III, who is regarded as one of the greatest popes of the Middle Ages. It was a time when the power of the papacy was at its zenith and its council decrees decisively influenced the life of the church for centuries. The aims of the council as set out in the Pope's letter of summons was to root out vices, foster virtues, correct errors, reform morals, stamp out heresies and strengthen the faith. It had a vision of a reformed and rejuvenated church going forward to the establishment of Christ's kingdom on earth and it also adopted some very practical measures of reform.

The council was perturbed by the proliferation of new orders in the church and passed a decree forbidding anyone to found a new religious order. Anyone wishing to found a new *Religio*, who had a sense of duty and had a respect for the sanctity of the religious or monastic life, should adopt one of the existing religious rules. Following the ban, Dominic returned to Toulouse to consult his brethren and after some consideration, they agreed, as a community, to follow the Rule of St Augustine. Dominic's order was approved by decree at the Council of Lateran in 1215. Pope Honorius III issued a papal bull in December 1216 which designated the Dominican preachers as champions of the faith, entreating prelates to support their preaching efforts and commending the brethren to prelates everywhere. (A 'bull' is an official document issued by the Pope and sealed with a *bulla*, medieval Latin for a seal.) The papal bull did no more than authorise the existence of the order and didn't ratify any specific rule for it. The rules sanctioned by the General Council in 1215 were never confirmed by the papacy.

The order was given the title of 'Brethren Preachers' but, due to the friars' preaching ability, it soon became known as the 'Order of Preachers', which was in turn, popularised to 'Preaching Friars'. They had appropriated the title 'preachers', which had traditionally mainly belonged to bishops. In Britain, they were commonly known as the 'Black Friars' because of the colour of their dress.

In 1217, Dominic and his band of preachers held a meeting in Toulouse, where the first house of their order was established. They decided that the brethren should disperse; four went to Spain, seven to Paris, four stayed in Toulouse and

Dominic went to Rome, where he set up the headquarters of the order. In 1218, Philip Augustus bestowed on the Dominicans the hospital of St James in Paris, whence they obtained the popular name of 'Jacobin Friars' in some countries. They went out with no resources and very few books but they were the vanguard of a worldwide organisation which was to have a considerable impact on medieval society.

Their mission was to combat heresy, to evangelise through education and to uphold the dignity of the church. Everything was subordinate to their teaching and preaching mission. In 1220, Dominic summoned representatives from all his communities to a General Chapter in Bologna. The council agreed to the principle of poverty and agreed to live on alms, unsupported by property or revenue. However, the Dominicans never regarded the rule of poverty in the same light as the Franciscans did and they soon began to disregard the rule, as they accepted land and buildings for their priories.

At the Second General Chapter held in 1221, Dominic tried to resign his position as head of the order, but the brethren would not hear of it. However, he insisted that it was they, not he, who must decide about the constitution of the order, although they took their lead from him. The meeting divided the order into eight provinces: France, Germany, Hungary, Lombardy, Provence, Rome, Spain and England, and determined the guidelines of the order. When the chapter had finished its work, the order was in all essentials formed, leaving only a few administrative details to be added at a later chapter. The order had a more upper-class appeal and the men entering it were well-schooled and intellectually alert. As a result, they required suitable accommodation for studying, teaching and meeting the influential people of society.

The Dominicans were a severely intellectual order, rigidly orthodox and tinged with a sternness inherited from Dominic. They saw the battle for souls as a battle for the mind and so set out to capture the leading theological centres of their time, and soon had strong links with various universities. Dominican friars were soon to be seen everywhere in their black and white dress, preaching, arguing, disputing and wrestling with heresy and unbelief wherever it arose. They were the spearhead of orthodox theology, strong and sure in the confidence that they possessed the truth, as they expounded the Christian message to a people who had previously relied on a faith which mainly comprised of ritual. They were fully equipped for the ministry of the Word and for the direction of souls which must inevitably go with it. Due to their aristocratic manners as preachers and teachers, though, there was a gulf between the Dominican friars and the ordinary people.

The popes referred to them as '*Domini Canes*', the Lord's dogs, who tracked down heresy and 'barked' at any straying sheep, to drive them back into the fold.

The Dominican Order was the first Christian order where members gave up manual labour as one of the duties of religious life, and to put study and preaching in the forefront of their religious duties.

Dominic died in Bologna on 6 August 1221 and was canonised in 1234. When he died, the order which he had founded buried him with great sadness and affection, and then went on with the job he had given them. He is regarded by many as one of the senior saints of the church and is held in high regard by the traditional church.

Within 50 years of Dominic's death, about 470 Dominican houses had been established across Europe. There were 35 in Spain, 52 in France, 52 in Germany, 32 in Tuscany, 46 in Lombardy, 30 in Hungary, 36 in Poland, 28 in Denmark, 40 in England, 5 in Wales, 9 in Scotland, with others in Ireland and other countries. By 1300 the number had increased to 557 Dominican houses and about 15,000 members, an average of 27 per house.

Dominic was a legislator of genius and the creator of the constitution of the order, which was formally passed in 1228. The constitution, known as the 'Book of Custom', abandoned the rigorous details regulating monastic life. From its commencement, the order was made up entirely of members of the clergy. The Dominican friars, who allied learning with apostolic zeal, had no qualms about organising themselves into an order with a strong central authority. As primarily a teaching and preaching order, they recognised the need for an efficient organisation through which to channel their intellectual energy, and to enable them to penetrate the universities, the principle targets in their mission to teach a higher standard of theology. By placing a great deal of their effort into the universities, they aimed to teach sound theology which would filter down through Dominican students to the commonalty.

The arrangements made for governing the order were complex but effective. It had its own constitution and a strong and effective leadership, but the government of the order was based on election and representation in which all officers were elected by a simple majority of authorised voters. All officers, from the Master-General to the prior in charge of a local priory, were elected to their post and were accountable to their electorate for their conduct during their period of office. All Dominican friars vowed to obey their superiors.

It was a fully centralised order governed by a General Council, the supreme legislative authority of the order. The council could, and often did, call to account, punish, suspend and even depose officers. However, it was tempered by the relative autonomy at local level. The Master-General, who held his office for life, or until his resignation, was elected by all the Prior-Provincials and two representatives from each province, in an enlarged session of the General Council. He was called the servant and master of the order and was answerable for his stewardship to the General Council, which had the power to correct or depose him.

The annual meetings ran in three-yearly cycles, two years when the General Council was composed of the Master-General and one representative from each province, and the third year when it was composed of the Master-General and the Prior-Provincials, who were accompanied on their journey to the General Council and, in the meetings by a *socius*, a companion. Until 1410, the General Council meetings, which were held on the Feast of Pentecost (Whitsun), rotated annually among the various countries. Also in 1410, the frequency of General Council meetings was reduced to once in every two years and, by 1553, once in every three years. Prior to 1300, there were only 13 provinces in the order and the General Council probably consisted of only a small body of officers.

The order was divided into provinces, each with their own Provincial Chapter headed by a Prior-Provincial. Houses of the order in England, Wales, Scotland and Ireland were part of the English Province headed by the Dominican Prior-Provincial of England, who was elected by a special provincial meeting which consisted of the heads of the visitations in the province and the prior of each constituent house. The General Provincial Meetings consisted of the Prior-Provincial and the Prior-Visitation of each visitation in the province. The Prior-Visitations were accompanied by a companion who had been elected by their visitation to accompany them and who sat in the meetings on equal terms with them. The provincial annual meetings had overall control of the houses within their province and made regulations relating to the promotion of friars within their province. It elected the province's representative for the General Council meetings. Their constitution decreed that the power to authorise a new house was the prerogative of the General Chapter, and its location within the province was left in the hands of the Provincial Chapter, who petitioned the General Chapter for the necessary licence.

Provinces were subdivided into districts, known as 'visitations', for the ease of administration and to facilitate journeying to and from council meetings. Each visitation was headed by a Prior-Visitation who dealt mainly with local administrative matters. The English Province had four visitations in England: London, Cambridge, Oxford and York, with separate visitations for Scotland and Ireland.

Although the Scottish and Irish houses were part of the English Province, due to the long distance between the Scottish, Irish and the English houses, they exercised a considerable amount of autonomy and were therefore only nominally part of the English Province.

Following a petition by James III in 1481, the Dominican General Council created a separate Province of Scotland headed by the Dominican Provincial of Scotland.

The Irish Dominicans formed the 'Vicariate of Ireland' which held its own Irish Visitation meetings and enjoyed most of the rights of a province, except direct representation to the General Council. It did not become a separate province in the order until 1536. The Dominican friars came to have 43 houses in Ireland.

There are numerous references to the holding of Provincial and Visitation Chapter meetings in various houses. These meetings were considered to be important occasions and arrangements had to be made for an influx of brethren to the friary where the meetings were to be held. Such occasions were considered to be important for the towns too. In 1344, the Provincial Chapter met on the Feast of the Assumption (15 August) at Canterbury. The friars went in procession through the streets of Canterbury from their friary to St Augustine's Abbey and on to Christ Church Priory Cathedral, where they heard a sermon. They returned, with the monks of both monastic houses, to the friary church, where Mass was said, and after Mass there was an outdoor feast. The Provincial Chapter meetings continued for two more days.

Each house in the order was headed by a prior, who was elected by his brethren at a special chapter meeting of all members of the house.

The Dominicans' 'Second Order' for women had its origin with St Dominic; it was he who had converted nine women from the Albigensian heresy, and, to ensure their steadfastness, formed them into a community. Dominic had accepted from the beginning that women members of the order would form part of their own enclosed order, with their own monastic constitution. When Dominic was dying in 1221, he promised the nuns that their communities would be helped, and from that time convents, or nunneries, for Dominican nuns were established. The order of Dominican nuns began to grow at a phenomenal rate and by the end of the thirteenth century there were many convents of Dominican nuns in Europe, but there were only two such houses in Britain.

The confraternity of lay people who wished to be associated with the Dominican friars was known as 'Tertiaries', or the

'Third Order', or the 'Soldiers of Jesus Christ'. It started as fraternities of men and women who brought themselves together for the advancement of their spiritual lives, and a number of the fraternities sought to associate themselves with the Dominicans in their prayers and good works. Dominic did not consider it necessary to found a new order for these followers but, instead, gave directions that they should seek the experience of God through prayer and actively conform to the faith and Christian practice. The 'Order of Penance', as it became known, formally became an order under the jurisdiction of the Master of the Dominican Order in 1285, but it did not receive papal approval until 1406, when it became known as the 'Third Order of St Dominic'.

FRANCISCAN FRIARS

The Franciscan Order was founded by an extraordinary man; John Bernardone, whom we know as St Francis of Assisi (1181/2–1226), is one of the church's most prominent servants of Christ. He was the son of an affluent cloth merchant in the Umbrian town of Assisi, in central Italy. Nicknamed 'Francesco', or Frenchman, by his father, due to his love of all things French, he was born 11 years after St Dominic. He was an intelligent young man who enjoyed the delights of the world and loved the local high life. Due to the benevolence of his father, he was able to wear smart clothes, attend numerous parties and became a leader of the smart society of the town. He was by nature a meek and compassionate person who had a real concern for the poor and afflicted; he hated suffering in any form and was especially compassionate towards lepers.

On 24 February 1206, Francis was praying in the little ruined church of St Damian, outside the walls of Assisi, one of the places he was accustomed to go for a time of quiet prayer, when he heard a voice saying three times, 'Francis, go and repair my house, which you see falling'. Francis thought the call referred to the old church of St Damian and went home and took a horse load of clothes from his father's warehouse and sold them to defray the cost of repairs to the church. The priest in charge of St Damian's refused to take the money and Francis's father insisted that he return home or renounce his share of his inheritance. Francis replied that being now a servant of the church, he was not subject to the secular power; so his father took his complaint to the Bishop. Francis was summoned to the Bishop's palace, where the Bishop informed him that he must give back anything which belonged to his father, since it was not right that the church should benefit from money it was not entitled to. After the Bishop's speech, Francis stripped off all his clothes and renounced the world. The Bishop procured the cast-off clothes of one of his servants, and, thus arrayed, Francis set out on his great adventure into the unknown. From that time, he saw himself as married to 'Lady Poverty', and turned to a life of poverty, compassion for the sick and needy, and prayer. He went out, following the command of Jesus to His disciples: 'Take nothing for your journey, neither staves, nor scrip, neither bread, neither money: neither have two coats apiece. And whatsoever house ye enter into, there abide, and thence depart'. (Luke 9:3–4)

For two years or more he continued his restoration of ruined churches and his ministry to the lepers, supporting himself by going around Assisi with a beggar's bowl, to the great indignation of his family.

Francis then devoted his life to a literal observance of the commands Christ gave to His apostles and took unto himself the apostolic life of poverty, wandering from place to place, telling people about Jesus and His kingdom, ministering to the sick and needy. He went along the highways and byways, calling on men and women to repent and to be absolved from their sins. He did this with such energy that people were deeply stirred. Some thought he had gone mad but others began to think of him as a saint and prophet. He had no plan or programme and he did not seek disciples, but his love for the crucified Christ, his intense love for the church and his tender concern for all God's creatures attracted others to join him as companions and disciples.

Francis the solitary became Francis the leader of a band of

disciples. When the number of his followers had increased to 12, Francis made rules for them to follow. About April 1209, he journeyed to Rome and submitted to Pope Innocent III a primitive set of rules based on a few texts from the gospels and some practical details to guide the little band of brethren on the life of poverty and simplicity. After some hesitation, the Pope gave the rules his verbal approval. The text of the primitive rules is not known, but it is believed they were based upon the three vows of religion: poverty, chastity and obedience, with the emphasis on poverty. In 1224, Pope Honorius III granted the first formal charter to the order, confirming a stricter rule than that which had been drawn up by Francis. The small group preached simple sermons exhorting people to love God and to repent for their sins, as they served the poor, sick and forgotten members of society. Francis told his followers, 'Do not be afraid to be called beggars, for Christ himself declared that the poor are blessed. Do not be ashamed to beg for your bread: Christ himself begged for a drink of water from the Samaritan woman'.

He forbade his followers to preach in any place without the bishop's permission, but when permission was sought, it was readily given.

The early Franciscans were homeless wanderers who were content to go wherever they thought they were needed, but they soon found it convenient to have lodgings of some kind, and small houses were given by well-wishers, as more or less permanent places to go to. They depended for their livelihood partly on alms of the faithful and partly on their own manual work in the fields, for which they might receive food and shelter, but they were strictly forbidden to accept money, a commodity which Francis regarded as untouchable. If they failed to get work, they took their begging bowls from door to door, sleeping in churches, barns and shacks. Francis taught that only those who had themselves stood barefooted in the market place asking for alms could have any real compassion and understanding for the poor and needy, and their voluntary destitution identified them with the most deprived sections of society. They became missionaries to the towns through their encouragement and sermons. They had a compassion for the poor, the lepers, the beggars, those who were condemned to a life of hardship and misery. They were men who showed love as they preached to the poor, depending entirely on their sympathy, and left when such sympathy was withdrawn.

Less than three years after the foundation of the order, the small group of followers had multiplied so rapidly that they developed into about 60 houses of friars. In 1217, the brethren held an assembly at the tiny church of Portiuncula, a building near Rome, lent to them by the Benedictine monks of Subasio, where the decision was made to launch the brethren on a universal mission. Parties were sent to various countries, provinces were defined and Provincial Ministers were appointed to establish the new provinces. The rapid increase in the number of his followers was phenomenal and in 1221 about 3,000 friars attended a chapter meeting of the new order. Many were men from the educated classes and of genteel birth who saw that their mission was to take the Christian message of repentance and service to all levels of society, but especially to the poor and destitute, who were entirely outside the sphere of any ecclesiastical influence.

Those who joined the order were expected to sell their possessions and give the proceeds to the poor before taking their place in a community of friars. The association of brethren had become a religious order which worked to bring back a much needed simplicity to Christianity.

Enthusiasm and self-sacrifice were the powerful agents which ensured the success and favour of the early Franciscans. They did not depart far from the teachings of their founder and lived the life of the poor among whom they ministered.

The efforts to carry forward a new zeal and understanding of the Christian faith among ordinary people was spearheaded by one who had not received an ecclesiastical education. Francis was not in holy orders when he began his mission and was only made a deacon of the church by Pope Innocent III in 1209. A deacon is the lowest order of the threefold church hierarchy: deacon, priest, bishop. St Polycarp (AD 80?–166), one of the more illustrious early apostolic fathers, wrote, 'Deacons are the servants of Christ and not of men'. Nothing could have been more true when referring to Deacon Francis.

He imitated Christ with all his heart and soul and merged himself in Christ as he shared the reality of the cross as completely as possible for a human being. On 14 September 1224, while praying on Mount Alverna in the Apennines, Francis experienced the supreme moment of his earthly life, when he saw a compelling vision of the crucified Christ. After the vision disappeared, the stigmata, marks resembling the marks of the nail wounds of Christ, appeared on his hands and feet. He endeavoured to conceal the stigmata but at the time of his death, two years later, his miraculous wounds were still there and were seen by many. There have been many explanations put forward as to the appearance of the stigmata; some explain their appearances on the body of St Francis as the physical effect of exalted meditation, combined with an intense love and compassion for Christ. He was canonised less than two years after his death, showing how greatly he was loved and how his work was admired within the church. He was revered by his compatriots as a man who had a burning love for his crucified saviour and whose life imitated Christ more closely than any other Christian since the days of the early church. He was considered by many to have been the only perfect Christian, due to his example of devoutness of faith and humility before God and man.

Francis called his followers 'Little Brothers' and from this they were known as 'Friar Minors'. They willingly accepted this secondary title as it expressed the humility of the Franciscans, who considered they were the least of all the orders of friars. They were also known as the 'Grey Friars', a name derived from their garment which was made from a coarse woollen cloth of a nondescript colour.

In the beginning, the order recruited persons who were not in holy orders, as well as those who were, but by the 1240's only those who had been ordained into holy orders were admitted.

In adopting the rule of corporate poverty, and refusing to

accept endowments or property, they discarded the impedimenta of the monks and were able to travel about on foot, in poverty and humility, begging their bread from door to door and spreading the Gospel of Jesus Christ. The early friars relied on God's protection and the help of Our Lady, rather than on their own prudence, and believed that God would provide for the needs of His servants, in accordance with the scriptural promise: 'Whatsoever house ye enter, first say "Peace be to this house" and if the son of peace be there, your peace shall rest upon it: if not, it shall turn to you again. And in the same house remain, eating and drinking such things as they give: for the labourer is worthy of his hire. Go not from house to house'. (Luke 10:5–7).

There was a steadfast refusal by Francis to leave the spiritual level for that of the external. Humility, simplicity, poverty and prayer were the four foundations on which Francis built, and each was worked out on the literal obedience to the recorded sayings of Christ. It was this uncompromising challenge which drew a large number of people to follow him into the hardships and dangers which such a way of life would inevitably contain. He seems to have stopped short of the rigid application of his principles, which would have forbidden the possession of any property, churches or accommodation.

The problem of maintaining an intense level of poverty and yet being an organised religious order with a rule of its own and with its own officers, was one which caused Francis worry and distress. The ideals were workable for a small group of itinerant friars but when their numbers grew rapidly, they ceased to be itinerant friars. The attempt to reconcile absolute poverty with the practical needs of a pastoral ministry involved the Franciscans in an increasing agility of conscience. In order to survive, friars' houses, regardless of their size, needed to be in a community in which the citizens were not poor; the more affluent the people, the more they would be able to give financial and material support to the friars. The theory and practice of the principle of poverty became a stumbling block; it was unadaptable as the order grew. The friars had to face the realities of an organised rule and way of life, with all that it entailed, such as discipline and observance of decrees aimed at safeguarding the positive expressions of the religious life.

It was one thing to be an itinerant friar in the warmer climate of Mediterranean countries but life was much harsher in Britain, especially in inclement weather. As their numbers grew, permanent shelter became a necessity. The rapid increase in numbers required larger houses and, as persons of quality entered the order, it made the provision of more acceptable accommodation inevitable. Permanent establishments became necessary for their organisations, both for training novices and for the provision of facilities for friars who went to universities.

The theme of poverty became an issue that had a troubled history in the Franciscan Order, and brethren had different interpretations of the rule. Most of them wanted to follow a less rigid observation of the rule than that taught by Francis. They considered that with the ever increasing number of recruits, the order should be administered in a more organised manner, with an appropriate organisation to cater for the churches, accommodation and gifts.

When Francis knew he was dying, he asked to be buried at the site where condemned criminals were executed. He was unable to take a full part in the 1226 General Chapter meeting, and instead, in August 1226 he left a valedictory instruction to his followers: 'Let all the brethren beware of accepting churches, houses or anything else provided for them, unless they conform to holy poverty, to which we are vowed in our rule, always lodging as strangers and pilgrims'. It was to no avail!

Francis died on 3 October 1226, aged 44, but the exact location of his grave was kept secret for fear that the relics might be stolen. His astounding popularity brought in both funds and people, many of whom worked without pay, to build a massive church over his burial site. This was precisely what Francis had forbidden. After many attempts to find it, his grave was located in 1818 and its surroundings were expanded into a vault-church. Alas! the Basilica of St Francis was badly damaged by an earthquake in September 1997.

The ideals raised at the height of religious exaltation could not be sustained when it became necessary for the order to organise itself effectively. There were those who realised that St Francis had started something which was going to continue to grow; what had begun as an association of brothers had become a religious order and some measure of control and organisation was essential.

The early Franciscans were forbidden to touch money, but this rule did not last for long as many believed it to be quite impossible to live without money, and many houses wanted to manage their own affairs. The spirit of the rule was easily circumvented by friars employing officers to act on their behalf, or people would place money in their cowls and the friars' servants would take it out. They also avoided touching money by counting it with sticks.

In 1230, a majority of the followers of St Francis voted to ask the Pope to give a ruling on the vexed subject of poverty. In response, Pope Gregory IX issued a papal bull which was a compromise solution, declaring that Francis's verbal valedictory to his followers did not have the force of law. Communities of friars could have *nuntiuses*, or Spiritual Friends, who would act as trustees authorised to act on behalf of the friars, to receive, hold and administer gifts of money, property and other bequests that were lavished upon them. The problem of ownership was overcome by the legal device of vesting the ownership of the friars' land and buildings into the hands of the community of the town, or trustees, for the use of the friars. Following the Pope's ruling Provincial Ministers ordered that copies of Francis's valedictory testament be burnt.

In the course of time these legal fictions were sometimes forgotten and this destroyed a fundamental principle of Francis's teaching. The Franciscans had to bend St Francis's rule in order to survive as a great order of friars, but the papal compromise of 1230 was the start of the Franciscans' inevitable retreat from Francis's uncompromising ideal of holy poverty. The order also gave up Francis's hostility to learning and they were to follow the Dominicans as scholars and theologians.

One of the ironies of the Franciscan quest for poverty is that it proved attractive to the rich, who were moved to shower wealth and possessions on the order.

In Britain, all land, buildings and other such gifts were held in trust by the Spiritual Friends, who were in effect the authorities in the towns in which friaries were situated. The Franciscans' land, buildings and possessions in England and Wales were held by the town magistrates and burgesses, and in Scotland by the town bailies and burghers, who were the Spiritual Friends, or custodians, of the friars' property. In a number of instances, benefactors gave plots of land to the town communes to build Franciscan houses. The friars were able to purchase provisions through a third party, their Spiritual Friends, from funds they received for that purpose. The friars, of course, would have administered the funds brought in from begging.

This compromise allowed the friars, through their Spiritual Friends, to possess the buildings and other necessities for their work, but not to own them. In a number of instances, the Spiritual Friends legally owned the friars' property under a deed of gift, but it is reasonable to assume that they considered they were acting on behalf of men of God and no doubt acted scrupulously in the performance of their duties.

In 1279, Pope Nicholas III issued a bull reviving Pope Gregory IX's rule on Franciscan property. The new bull asserted that according to the teachings and example of Christ, there was a distinction between individual and common ownership, and granted the brethren the moderate use of things necessary.

Within a century of the founding of their order, Franciscans were no longer accepting the life of absolute poverty, but the aims of the Franciscans remained noble and pure to the ideals of service as practised by St Francis.

The unworldly Francis had resisted efforts to regulate too precisely for his followers and was more concerned about the harmful effects of forming them into a cohesive group than in the value of a good organisation. The transformation from a small group into a company of thousands necessitated a reorganisation of the young order so that the bonds of discipline and authority could be strengthened. The Franciscans inevitably became institutionalised as they made the rules more precise, and their initial fervour waned.

Much of the Franciscans' structure of government was based on that of the Dominicans. At the head was the Minister-General, who was assisted by a General Council in which the legislative power of the order was vested. It consisted of the Minister-General, Provincial Ministers and elected representatives from each of the provinces. Though the representatives were qualified to be present at the General Council meetings, the Provincial Ministers alone had a voice in the election of a Minister-General. The General Council met every three years. The Franciscans stressed that the governors of the order were the servants of the order and the Minister-General, who was left with executive powers between the three-yearly meetings of the General Council, was the servant of all men.

The Franciscans attached great importance to the temporary nature of the offices in the order. Provincial Ministers were elected by the Provincial Chapter, but Custody Ministers and Wardens of local houses were designated by the Provincial Ministers.

The order was territorially divided into provinces, each province being headed by a Provincial Minister, the English Province being headed by the Provincial Minister of England. The Provincial Chapter meetings, which were held every year, consisted of the Provincial Minister, Custody Ministers, Wardens and one elected representative from each house in the province. The constitutions of the Provincial Chapters were not fixed by the order, but it was left to each Provincial Chapter to make its own constitutions, which left them a lot of leeway.

The Provincial Chapters kept an oversight on finance, discipline, education and the establishment of new houses in their province. There are a number of references of the Provincial Chapters removing priors from their houses, on disciplinary grounds.

In England, the province was first divided into four regions, but these were afterwards increased to seven, known as custodies: Bristol, Cambridge, London, Newcastle-upon-Tyne,

Oxford, Worcester and York. Each custody contained seven to nine friaries. The Worcester Custody covered North Wales and the north-west Midlands, while the Bristol Custody covered South Wales and south-west England.

The Franciscan English Province originally included the custodies of Scotland and Ireland. Franciscan friars first entered Ireland in 1231–2, when they settled at Youghal, County Cork. From there the order rapidly spread across Ireland until eventually there were 63 Irish houses. The 'Vicarate of Irish Franciscans' was divided into four, and later into five, custodies. They enjoyed most rights of a province, except direct representation in the General Council. A decree of 1484 established them as an independent province, but it was revoked in 1491. It was not until Henry VIII destroyed the Franciscan English Province in 1538 that the independent Irish Province came into being.

The Scottish houses were allocated to the Custody of Newcastle for much of the time. As did the Dominicans in Scotland, the Scottish Franciscans tried to break away from the Custody of Newcastle and the Province of England, and had a protracted struggle to obtain an independent Scottish Province. In 1231–2 the Scots set up their own province under a Scottish vicarate, but in 1239 the province was suppressed. The Scots again set up a Scottish vicarate from 1260 to 1279 and from 1329 to 1359, when the Scottish vicarate was again suppressed and Scottish houses were once more incorporated in the Custody of Newcastle. The Scottish Franciscans finally severed connections with the English Province during the Great Schism of 1378–1429, and the Scottish Franciscans remained an autonomous vicarate until the Reformation.

The Franciscan Order spread across Europe and beyond to Syria, the Holy Land and further east. They became, and still are, the largest and most popular religious order in the Roman Catholic Church. It is estimated by some researchers that by 1300 there were 30,000 members of the order, but some consider that even this figure is a conservative estimate.

As did the Dominicans, the Franciscans attracted women followers. One of Francis's earliest converts was an 18-year-old noble lady named Clara Sciffi, who was born the daughter of rich parents in Assisi in 1193 and was brought up in some luxury. As a young girl she listened to Francis talking to God in his prayers and was captivated by his words. She felt a longing to know more about this God of love and mercy which Francis spoke to with such inspiring enthusiasm. Clara felt God was calling her to dedicate her life to Him, through following the ideals of Francis. Despite protest from relatives and friends, she cast off her family ties and vowed to follow Francis in the practice of poverty and in the imitation of Christ. The brotherhood was still in an early stage and Francis may well have thought that some way would be found whereby a woman could be attached to the community and assist in the practical work of nursing the sick and needy and caring for the lepers.

In 1212, St Clare of Assisi, as she became known in Britain, was the founder of the sisterhood of St Clare, known as 'Poor Clares'. This order of contemplative nuns formed the 'Second Order of St Francis' and took their inspiration from Francis. Clare and her companions worked alongside the friars ministering to the sick and destitute in the towns, and soon other women were attracted to the work of Clare. Francis assigned to Clare and her sisterhood the restored church and house of San Damiano situated just below the walls of Assisi, which he begged from the bishop. Houses of the Poor Clares multiplied, but, because it was contrary to custom for women's communities to live without assured revenues, Pope Innocent III granted them concessions from poverty which allowed them common ownership of goods and property.

Francis soon came against the pressure of social convention and the disapproval of the church hierarchy for his collaboration and work with women. In 1219, Cardinal Hugolino, patron and protector of the Franciscans, gave Clare and her disciples a strict rule of enclosure based on the rule of St Benedict, and the Poor Clare nuns thus became an enclosed monastic order of the traditional type. This finally brought to an end any hope which the sisters might have had of being allowed to minister to the poor.

St Clare died in 1253 and was canonised two years later. In 1956, Pope Pius XII proclaimed St Clare patroness of television, not for giving out news or entertainment, but because by her loving and prayerful concern for all, she was a window on the world.

The Clare abbesses had no organisational or official means of meeting together to discuss their problems and their Franciscan Provincial Minister was expected to look after them and see that all was well in their houses.

The Poor Clare sister, or Minoresses as they were often known, devoted themselves to praying for the friars, contemplative prayers, saying the daily canonical hours, and manual labour. The order is still strong and has about 800 houses throughout the world.

St Francis founded the 'Third Order Secular of St Francis' for the laymen who came to him longing to be allowed to follow his discipline and leadership. He assigned them a way of life by which they retained their social position in the world, but took religious vows which did not require them to join a religious order. Whereas the Dominican Third Order was militant, that of the Franciscans was penitential.

They desired some corporate form of religious life and their rules, drawn up in 1221, were based on that of the parent order. The rules of the Franciscan Third Order required members to adhere faithfully to the Commandments of God, attend frequently the sacraments of Penance and Mass, and to practise poverty by avoiding the extremes of cost and style. They should be moderate in eating and drinking, and obedient to divine, ecclesiastical, civil and domestic authorities. Members of the Third Order highly valued the privileges of being allowed to be buried in a Franciscan habit, which, they believed, would hasten their path to heaven.

Investiture into the Third Order was through a solemn religious act of dedication to God, in which the candidate promised to observe the Gospel of Christ. This was followed by the blessing of the scapular (two rectangular pieces of cloth joined by a cord and worn under secular clothes), after which they were given letters of confraternity by which they became members of the order. These letters gave the recipient all the privileges of association and were highly regarded by their owners.

The Third Order had a chapel and an altar reserved for them within their respective friary church, for the confraternity's religious functions.

Many of all levels of society belonged to it, and even today the Third Order counts millions of members throughout the world, all striving to follow the example of St Francis.

FRANCISCAN FRIARS OBSERVANTS

As time progressed there were those in the Franciscan Order who wanted a more relaxed and less demanding way of life than their earlier brothers, while others hankered for the austere way of life of primitive Franciscanism and its literal observance of the Gospel. As the popularity of St Francis increased, he was venerated but his ideals were forgotten, or explained away with a medieval astuteness.

Within 25 years of Francis's death, the order he had inspired was rent with controversy over his teaching on poverty. This was to erupt into a bitter and protracted dispute and the schism that, far from healing, became worse and was to become a permanent and tragic feature of Franciscan history.

During the fourteenth and into the fifteenth century there was strife in the order between those who wished to follow the simple life of poverty, free from statutes and decrees, as lived in the early days of Francis. They became known as Franciscan Spirituals. Although there were few of them in Britain, the Continental brothers formed themselves into small groups or lived as hermits, and broke away from the order, following the simple life of Francis, which they considered was the only true Franciscan way of life. However, after persecution within the order in the mid-fourteenth century, they ceased to be a faction of any significance.

The history of the order in the fifteenth century is taken up with the question as to whether it could hold together as one, or would have to be divided into two. The debate continued within the order as to whether Christ and His apostles owned the goods they used and whether they renounced all ownership, both private and corporate. There can be little doubt that there were many hot debates in some houses between conservative and progressive members of the community.

The decline in religious life and discipline in the fifteenth century created in many friars a desire to return to a purer observance of the rule. Efforts to satisfy this yearning marked the beginning of the Observances movement. Numerous small groups on the Continent, with the permission of their superiors, retired to remote hermitages, there to observe the rule in its primitive severity. The impulse for reform was felt on the Continent and houses were assigned to the Observants.

There were papal efforts to bring unity between the two groups, but most friars were unwilling to accept the fact that the order was in need of reform. Following the failure of the papal effort, the Observances movement was recognised within the order. In 1445, Pope Eugenius IV issued a papal bull which authorised the Franciscan Observants friars to choose two Vicar Generals, one for the Italian Province and one for the Northern Province (areas outside Italy). The Franciscan Observants became a separate body within the order and claimed to be the authentic custodians of the rule of St Francis. The policy of the Observants friars contained nothing new; their only desire was to recreate the conditions under which the first friars lived in the days of their poverty and insecurity, and set up again the ideal of evangelical perfection. They did much to encourage the devotional and contemplative life. The new order quickly spread through Italy and France, but there is no sign of it arousing much interest in Britain; it did not reach Scotland until 1463, and England until 1482. In 1517, Pope Leo X issued a papal bull which finally divided the Conventual Franciscans (adherence to the traditions of the order) from the Observants Franciscan (fundamentalist), each with its own Minister-General, its own customs and its own jurisdiction.

St Bernardine of Siena (1380–1444), a powerful preacher who became Provisional Vicar General of the Italian Province in

1438, was devoted to the Holy Name of Jesus. His devotion was not a new thing in the church, but he contributed greatly to its spread, and he devised a symbol to help people to appreciate its theological basis. This was the symbol 'YHS' set in the midst of a blazing sun. During his sermons Bernardine displayed the symbol in gold letters on a board, as an aid to help the faithful to appreciate the basis of the name of Jesus. The cult of the Holy Name spread rapidly and its symbol began to appear in churches, homes and public buildings. The symbol was a translation of Jesus from the Greek 'IHSOUS', and the Hebrew 'YESHUA'. In Western Europe the Latin symbol 'IHS', being the first three letters of the name of Jesus in Greek, was used. This symbol can still be seen in many churches.

The Franciscan Observants refused to possess permanent buildings but made use of buildings which were loaned to them, but which they never owned, even indirectly.

AUSTIN FRIARS

The friars of the 'Order of Hermits of St Augustine', usually shortened to 'Augustinian Friars', were popularly known in England as 'Austin Friars' to distinguish them from Augustinian Canons. They trace their antecedents back to their days as congregations of recluses in Italy and 'Hermits' remained as part of their title after they had ceased to be hermits. The order was formed by the amalgamation of hermits who lived in the Lombardy and Tuscany regions in the northern and western parts of central Italy. In 1223, five houses were united in a loosely organised brotherhood and they were joined five years later by eight additional houses. There is no certainty that any of their early constituent houses were of any great antiquity and only a few of the earlier hermitages are known to have possessed records reaching into the first years of the twelfth century. At first, each hermitage followed the eremitical tradition quite independently of other hermitages, but they were under the control of the local bishops who did not hesitate to depose the superior of a hermitage if a bishop had not supervised or confirmed his election.

The principal aim of the hermitages was for their members to retreat from the world in order to attain a full union with God. In the mid-thirteenth century, the powerful impact of the mendicant ideal upon the religious consciousness was strong and the hermits of Tuscany, complying with the desire of the church, requested the Pope to unite them under a fixed rule. In 1243, Pope Innocent IV prescribed the Rule of St Augustine and charged Cardinal Annibaldi to undertake the task of unification. In 1244, the Cardinal withdrew the hermits from episcopal jurisdiction, bound them to the Rule of St Augustine, gave them a new constitution modelled on the Dominicans and placed them under the authority of a Prior-General. In 1249, the leadership of the new order resolved, under papal guidance, to organise themselves into an order of mendicant friars. Their first houses were in thinly populated areas and away from large towns.

Within ten years, they had departed from their solitary life and formed themselves into an order which possessed privileges similar to other mendicant orders, and the number of houses in the order increased to 61. In 1256, the papal act was confirmed by the papal bull '*Licet Ecclesiae*' of Pope Alexander IV, which called the Austin friars from the eremitic way of life to active life in towns, but the change from the contemplative to the active life was not effected without serious opposition. After that date, they organised themselves along the lines of other mendicant orders. The youth in the order had to be trained in the new ways, but it was not until the end of the century that the fruits of the order's education policy could be harvested. The first General Chapter meeting, held in Rome in the same year as the papal act and referred to as the 'Great Union', consolidated the groups into the 'Order of Hermits of St Augustine', bound to one observance under a Prior-General. The Austin mendicant vow of absolute poverty originally agreed upon was relaxed by Pope Alexander IV in 1257, so as to permit goods to be held in the name of the community when it was deemed necessary.

As we have seen, the 1274 Church Council of Lyons under Pope Gregory X abolished all mendicant orders except the Franciscans and Dominicans, but permitted the continuance of the Austin and Carmelite Orders only until it would be decreed otherwise. Thus the two orders lived under the threat that they might be suppressed at any time. Fortunately for the two orders the anti-mendicant policies of the council were not continued by Pope Martin IV, and especially by the first Franciscan pope, Nicholas IV, who proved to be a friend of the mendicants. In 1298, Pope Boniface VIII modified the threatening decree when he amended it to read 'We will that the Austin and Carmelite Orders continue as fully approved', and there the struggle for their survival ended. In 1326, Pope John XXII extended the '*Super Cathedram*' to both orders, thereby giving them the same privileges as the two senior mendicant orders.

The Austin friars pursued both the contemplative and active aspect of monastic life, as they looked back longingly to their former days. Within the framework of their constitution, they harmonised their daily lives of apostolic work among the people with the pursuance of the contemplative life. The friars' activities included worship, prayers, study of the scriptures, and especially preaching and teaching, along with pastoral care in the community. From an obscure origin, the community became an order of scholars and preachers, and one of the four main orders of medieval friars.

It was a centrally directed order devoted to the Pope and the need to preserve orthodoxy within the church. The constitution placed the General Chapter, headed by a Prior-General, as the ruling council of the order. The legislative power of the order rested in the General Chapter and the executive power with the superiors within their jurisdiction. The Prior-General and the heads of each province, limit and house were elected.

The order was divided into provinces, each headed by a Prior-Provincial, but little is known about their duties and jurisdiction. The work of the Provincial Council was greatly impeded by the rights of individual houses, which were considerably greater than for the local houses of other orders.

However, the Prior-Provincial was entrusted with the government of the province; he had to give his consent for the admission of novices and the appointment of the first prior to a house, and supplied the initial funds for new houses. Provincial Chapters were held every year, then from 1432 every two years, and every third year after 1453. The order differed from its sister orders in that two visitors were elected at the Provincial Chapters, who were obliged to visit each Austin house in the province and could impose prescribed penances when they found the rules were being broken.

During the period when the order was being founded, Henry III ruled England and large parts of France, and the Prior Provincial of the English and French Province covered all the Austin houses in the King's realm on both sides of the English Channel. The first record of an English Province as a separate organisation occurs in 1265.

For easier management of houses, provinces were divided into districts called 'limits', headed by a Vicar-Provincial. The English Province was divided into four limits: Cambridge, Lincoln, Oxford and York, each limit consisting of a group of friaries.

The Austin friars came to Ireland from England soon after they received their rule in 1256. At first they were a separate limit of the English Province of their order but, in 1305, were formed into an Irish Province and became a self-governing province with 22 friaries. Most of their houses were staffed with native Irish friars who spoke the Gaelic tongue and therefore could get close to the people they served.

A prior was the head of a friary. The local autonomy allowed for each house to recruit its own candidates, but the candidates had to be approved by the Prior-Provincial. Each novice admitted to vows became affiliated to the house that admitted him, which also obliged the house to provide for his education, daily sustenance and care in sickness and old age.

The order showed concern for their novices by endeavouring to give them the finest education, and followed the two senior mendicant orders into the scholastic world, establishing a strong presence in both Oxford and Cambridge universities.

The order considered theology, which they diligently studied, the queen of the sciences. In their intellectual pursuits, the spiritual life of the Austin friars was based on the Scriptures, the teachings of the church and the teachings of the saints, especially those of St Augustine. They were unwavering in their devotion to the Pope.

The Austin friars, as did friars in other orders, had a strong devotion for Our Lady and invoked her protection under the title of 'Mother of Grace' and, from the fifteenth century, 'Mother of Good Council', now expressed as 'Our Lady of Good Council'.

By the beginning of the fourteenth century the Austin Order had about 350 houses and about 8,000 members in Europe.

During the fifteenth century there was general religious decline in the church, including the Austin Order, and as a result, a movement dedicated to the restoration of pristine observance of the rules developed within the order. This resulted in the 'Austin Observants' friars breaking away and establishing their own houses on the Continent, but they did not establish a house in Britain. If a brother in one of the British houses wished to join an Observants house of his order, he joined an Observants house on the Continent. In 1431, an English Austin brother was given permission to spend three years at the isolated Woodhouse friary, after which he went on to join a stricter Observants house in Italy.

Martin Luther was a member of the Austin Observants friars. As a representative of seven houses of the Austin Observants group in Saxony, he objected to other houses of the Saxony Province being invited to the congregation, lest they dilute the reforming principles of the Observants. He was unsuccessful in his objection and, in 1511, went to Rome to appeal against the decision of the Saxon Province, but, being unsuccessful again, he returned to Germany. He later turned against the Austin Observants friars and began to evolve his own ideas of reform. While some Austin friars in Germany followed his lead, others were among his strongest opponents. But more about Luther further on.

The Third Order of Austin Friars started with the gradual

association of the faithful laity with the friars. The association developed into the Augustinian Third Order for women, which in 1400 was approved by Pope Boniface IX. In 1470 a separate branch for men was approved by Pope Paul II.

CARMELITE FRIARS

The origin of the 'Order of Our Lady of Mount Carmel' is obscure, but it grew from a community of European hermits who settled on Mount Carmel, near Haifa, overlooking the Mediterranean Sea. Mount Carmel was the scene of Elijah's struggle with the priests of Baal 3,000 years ago when he prayed for rain and called down fire from heaven (1 Kings 18:37–38). From very early times, Mount Carmel has been a favourite resort of Greek anchorites who regard themselves as the spiritual sons of Elijah the prophet.

The hermits on Mount Carmel lived alone or in small isolated groups, led by their desire for the ascetic life of strict abstention, fasting and long periods of silence. In about 1156, some crusaders settled on Mount Carmel and a group of about 11 brethren established a society of hermits, calling themselves the 'Brothers of Our Lady of Mount Carmel'. They applied to Patriarch Albert of Jerusalem for a written 'Rule of Carmel', which he gave them in 1209. The group increased in numbers and, in 1226, the rule was confirmed by Pope Honorius III, but it was moderated in 1247 by Pope Innocent IV, on their petition that they were no longer hermits. The rules entailed a strictly contemplative life which involved very little in the way of a communal living. The rules show they were governed by a prior and the brethren were leading an eremitical life. The rules also gave them a liturgy which followed the rites of the Church of the Holy Sepulchre in Jerusalem. By 1220, they had loosely organised themselves into groups of individual cells, each group having an oratory dedicated to the Blessed Virgin. Life on the mount was simple and the rules of the order were straightforward.

The fall of Jerusalem to the Saracens in 1187 and the decline of the Latin kingdom made it difficult for the Carmelite hermits to remain on Mount Carmel in safety, and for a long time the community debated what they should do and where they should go. They had divided opinions as to what extent they should allow any new influences, following their move from the mount, to change the character of their traditions. When in 1238 they finally decided to leave Carmel, they were fortunate in finding friends who took the hermits with them on their return journey to Europe. Some settled in Cyprus, Italy and France, while others continued their journey to England, under the benevolence of Lord de Grey. Carmelite friars returned to the mount in the seventeenth century and a community of them is still there.

In 1247, the order was fortunate in that the General Chapter held in Aylesford, Kent, elected an Englishman, Simon Stock (d. 1265) as Prior-General of the order. He came from Kent and was among the first Englishmen at Mount Carmel to join the Carmelites. It was a difficult time in the history of the order, which was passing through a crisis due to attacks from without and disunity within; but, under Stock's strong leadership, the General Chapter modified the rule of their order, which permitted them to plant Carmelite houses in towns and engage in the apostolic mission after the manner of other mendicant orders. Though never formally canonised, Stock was venerated by the Carmelites as a saint. He died in Bordeaux in south-west France and was buried there. In 1951, his relics were removed from their resting place and taken to Aylesford Friary, where they are now encased in a modern reliquary shrine.

The order was approved by Pope Innocent IV in 1250 and organised on the lines of the Dominican friars. Like the Austin Order, it managed to survive the 1274 Council of Lyons, which abolished all mendicant orders except the Dominicans and Franciscans but granted provisional approval to the Carmelite Order. As we have seen, in 1298 Pope Boniface VIII extended unconditional approval to the order. In 1326, Pope John XXII granted them all the privileges and exemptions of mendicant orders, thereby completing the gradual process by which the Carmelites became a mendicant order.

Although they established their first houses in thinly populated areas, within a few years the strain of isolation became apparent. Following the death of Stock, there was a reaction against the purely contemplative life and the younger recruits pressed for the order to adopt an active roll of study and preaching, after the example of the other mendicant orders. By the end of the century the Carmelites had established themselves in a way of life that differed very little from other mendicant brethren. They supported themselves by begging and gifts but were allowed to hold their property in common. However, many brethren maintained a love for the solitary life and chose to dwell in their more remote houses.

The Carmelites were devoted to the Virgin Mary and dedicated all their churches to her. When Carmelite friars made their profession, they vowed their lives to God and Our Lady, and it was in her honour they offered their lives to God.

It seems that every mendicant order sought inspiration from the life and ideals of an individual. The Dominicans looked to St Dominic, the Franciscans to St Francis and the Austin friars to St Augustine. The Carmelites chose the Prophet Elijah for their ideal and teacher and strove to realise in their own lives the example set by him.

From their origins as unlettered laymen living the hermit life, they became clerics and literate friars who ministered to the community, with an emphasis on study and preaching. By the end of the thirteenth century they had an input into both Oxford and Cambridge Universities, where many of their brethren became eminent in the intellectual and university world.

The order was headed by a Prior-General and divided into provinces. The English Province, which met annually, was headed by the Provincial Master of the English Carmelites. It was divided into four districts called 'distinctions': London, Norwich, Oxford and York, each headed by a Provincial Prior. Scotland and Ireland were also distinctions within the English Province. The Carmelites came to Ireland some time before 1272 and, in 1309, the General Council of the order meeting in Genoa established Ireland as an independent province which eventually had 28 houses. In 1321, the Carmelite friaries in Scotland achieved partial independence when they were formed into a vicarate. At the next General Chapter meeting, held in Barcelona in 1324, the Scottish houses were constituted into a Scottish Province.

Their houses were headed by a warden and each warden had to write an annual report on his house, which he took to the Distinction Chapter meeting. The Distinction Chapter passed the reports from the houses in its jurisdiction to the Provincial Chapter, who compiled a combined Province report which was forwarded to the General Chapter. This medieval system of reports appears to be the prototype for such report writing in today's Civil Service.

In 1432, the Carmelite friars were authorised to eat meat three days a week and the regulations for fasting and abstinence were later further modified. The fifteenth-century relaxation of the Carmelite rules and the decline in religious observance led to a division in the order, as in other mendicant orders. The 'Shop' or 'Conventual Carmelite' friars wanted to follow a more relaxed rule, while the stricter branch of 'Barefooted', or 'Observants Carmelite', friars wished to return to the early ideals of the order. In 1462, the Observants Carmelite movement was given a constitution which allowed it to establish its own houses. There were no Observants Carmelite houses in Britain, but, no doubt, there was agitation for reform within the order in Britain. If a brother in one of the British houses wished to join an Observants house of his order, he joined such a house on the Continent.

By 1300, the order had about 150 houses in Europe, and during the fourteenth century the number reached nearly 300 houses.

From the thirteenth century onwards, there are instances of women taking the vows according to the Carmelite Rule. However, it was not until John Soreth, Prior-General of the Carmelite Order, requested Pope Nicholas V to issue a bull, which he did in 1452, that the order was given permission to receive women into the 'Carmelite Second Order'. They lived in enclosed convents and were dedicated to praying for the friars of the order and for all who were engaged in the work of saving souls. The Carmelite Second Order was not a strong movement and had no houses in Britain.

According to tradition, in answer to the fervent prayer of Simon Stock, the Virgin Mary appeared to him and, giving him the scapular of his order, said, 'This shall be a sign to you and all Carmelites: whosoever died wearing this shall not suffer eternal fire'. As a consequence of the vision there arose the 'Scapular Devotion'. The 'Confraternity of the Scapular', which is known as the 'Third Order of Our Lady of Mount Carmel', was founded by John Soreth, Prior-General of the Carmelite Order. In 1452, it was approved by Pope Nicholas V and, in 1476 the order was confirmed by Pope Sixtus IV. Soreth drew up a rule for the order, based on that of the friars, a rule aimed at honouring the Blessed Virgin with special devotion, cultivating the inner life of lay members and leading them in works performed in the service of God. Members professed the private vows of obedience and chastity in accordance with their state of life. The Third Order supported the brethren of the First Order with finance and in their work.

At the time of their joining to the Third Order, members were given a small brown scapular as a visible sign of their affiliation to the order. It consisted of two small rectangular pieces of woolen cloth joined by tapes passing over the shoulder and worn under secular clothes or attached to their clothing like a badge. The small scapulars were frequently embroidered and had a picture of Our Lady or a saint on them. Due to the Third Order's devotion to the Virgin Mary, the scapular became very popular and those who wore the scapular saw it as a sign of their devotion to Mary. The Scapular of Carmel is still popular in the Roman Catholic Church.

SACK FRIARS

The 'Friars of the Penance of Jesus', also known as 'Friars of the Sack', were given the sack name because of their dress, a coarse cloth which resembled a formless sack. Little is known about the order, which had its origins in Marseilles, southern France. The order, which followed the rule of St Augustine, was approved by Pope Innocent IV in 1251 and confirmed by Pope Alexander IV in 1255. In 1257, the order reached England and established a house in London, and in 1271 Queen Eleanor, wife of Henry III, gave the friars new quarters in the city. In the following year they established houses in Norwich and Cambridge; their Cambridge house was situated where the Fitzwilliam Museum now stands. In 1277 there were six brethren in their Cambridge house and the numbers increased to twenty by 1289. In 1261, they established a presence in Oxford, where they built an oratory, and in 1264 the King gave them Oxford's St Bodoc's Church, and its neighbouring houses, for a study centre. The order established its own English Province and was expanding quickly, opening four new houses in 1274, the year the Council of Lyons forbade minor mendicant orders to admit new members. The order had 16 houses in England and one in the parish of Holy Trinity, South Berwick, Berwick-upon-Tweed, then part of Scotland. All their houses, with the exception of Bristol, Chester and Worcester, were concentrated in the eastern part of England.

The order became popular in a short time and in 1274 had over 100 houses across Europe. The main functions of the order were teaching and preaching.

Their English Province was headed by a Vicar General, who at the time of its brief existence resided in their King's Lynn house.

The Friars of the Sack was the largest of the orders in England forbidden by the 1274 Council of Lyons to receive new recruits or new sites. The existing houses were allowed to remain until they were extinct or until 1317, when any surviving members were to join a house of one of the four principal mendicant orders. There were still nine brethren in their Canterbury house as late as 1289. Their Newcastle-upon-Tyne house at Wall Knoll, which had three brethren in 1299, was taken over in 1307 by the Carmelites, who moved from another site in the town on condition that the sole surviving

Sack friar was given subsistence for life. In 1343, their vacated Stamford house was taken over by Austin friars.

There is an ecclesiastical-style building facing the parish church in Rye which is reputed to have been part of the friary buildings of the Sack friars. The building, which is now a private residence, is built of stone and is one of the few buildings to survive the disastrous French raid of 1377 when the town was almost completely destroyed by fire.

PIED FRIARS

The 'Friars of the Blessed Mary', known as the 'Pied Friars', was a small order and one of the orders affected by the Council of Lyons decision in 1274 to phase out smaller orders. The word 'Pied' is an allusion to the black and white magpie colouring of their habits. The three houses of the order in England, Norwich, London and Cambridge, ceased recruitment and the order died out by the early fourteenth century. There were about 20 Pied friars at Cambridge in 1279, the peak of the order's activities, down to two in 1319. In about 1307, Edward II gave the abandoned Pied site in Norwich to the Dominican friars, who built a new and larger church on it.

CRUTCHED CROSS FRIARS

The origins of the 'Order of the Holy Cross', or 'Crutched Cross' friars, is uncertain but they are known to have existed by the middle of the twelfth century. In 1169, Pope Alexander III gave them a fixed rule of life and a constitution. Holy Cross hospitals were established prior to the coming of the friars, but in the thirteenth century the order showed the characteristic of the mendicant orders and was classed as exempt friars, that is, exempt from the rule of mendicant poverty. As the order was dedicated to running hospitals, they were not affected by the 1274 decision of the Council of

Lyons which prevented minor orders from further recruitment. By 1300 the order had about a dozen houses, confined to Belgium, France and England, but by the fifteenth century the order grew to about 60 houses, more than half of them in Holland and the Rhineland.

It was not a strong order in Britain, where they had about 11 mostly small, establishments. Only five houses remained at the time of the Reformation. Their Colchester house, which was founded prior to 1235, seems to have been the first house of the order in England. In 1392, the hospital and its lands were granted by licence of Richard II to the town bailiffs, probably due to the poverty of the house. Towards the end of the fifteenth century Crutched Cross friars claimed that the hospital had formerly belonged to them and they managed to regain possession of the house, which survived until the general Dissolution. The house was outside the town, in what is now Crouch Street. The London house of the order, which was founded in 1298, had 20 friars in 1314, 15 in 1317, 13 in 1346 and six in 1538. It was favoured by the citizens of the city, who as late as 1520 gave aid for the rebuilding of their church. In 1342, the friars arrived in Oxford, where they acquired a site near Merton College but, due to opposition in Oxford, the friars appear to have left by 1362. Their Donnington house (Berkshire) was founded, or perhaps refounded, in 1393 by Sir Richard Aberbury, who directed that inmates of the hospital should go to Mass every day and say 60 Paternosters (The Lord's Prayer) and the same number of Ave Marias (Hail Mary's).

The brethren wore a black, or brown, habit with a red cross on the breast. The word 'Crutched' refers to the cross worn on their habit.

In 1137, Bishop Henry de Blois of Winchester founded St Cross Hospital, Winchester, for 13 poor men so reduced in strength as to be rarely or never able to raise themselves without the assistance of another. The wonderful group of early medieval buildings, which can still be visited, though used for similar purposes as those of the Crutched Friars, were not linked to the order.

TRINITARIANS FRIARS

The 'Order of the Most Holy Trinity for the Redemption of Captives' is better known as 'Trinitarian Friars'. The main archives of the order have not been preserved but the order was probably founded in 1197 and confirmed by Pope Innocent III in 1198, or soon after. The order was devoted to promoting the Holy Trinity and dedicated to raising funds for the ransom of Christian pilgrims and crusaders held captive in Islamic lands.

During the crusaders' wars, Moslems in North Africa, the Holy Land and in parts of Spain held Christians captive in conditions of slavery, but they could be ransomed. The hermit, John de Matha (1160–1213) was among those who pitied the miserable plight of the Christian captives and slaves. He is said to have been inspired to undertake his mission after being moved by a vision of a white stag with a cross between its horns. Tradition says that he, with a fellow hermit, Felix de Valois, formed the 'Order of the Trinitarians', or 'Mathurins' as it was known in parts of Europe, to systematise the procedure for ransoming Christians. Trinitarian friars travelled extensively on their various missions of mercy, raising funds from various European countries and carrying them to Moslem ports in exchange for prisoners. They provided the released prisoners with spiritual and physical aid to help them adjust to their freedom. The first shipload of captives, who were ransomed from Morocco, returned home in 1200, two years after the founding of the order. The order had an international mission and quickly spread to other countries. John de Matha died in 1213 and was later canonised as a saint of the church.

Although they were not a mendicant order, they observed the rule of St Augustine and the religious vows of poverty, chastity and obedience. They were closer to Canons Regular, but their order was classed as an exempt mendicant order and, though they lived the life of friars, they were exempt from the obligations of mendicant poverty. They observed the Divine Office services in their churches.

Unlike mendicant orders, they were allowed to accept

endowments and other such gifts because the cost of their work would not have been met by alms alone. Their income was equally divided three ways: to maintain the order, to support poor pilgrims or travellers and to bribe or persuade the Moslem captors to part with their prisoners.

Friars of the order sometimes acted as hostages to the Moslems until more funds arrived from Europe. It has been estimated that about 90,000 people were ransomed during the first three centuries of the order and up to 140,000 people were ransomed between its establishment in 1198 and 1855.

The order continued to exist after the initial need had passed, following the end of the crusades, and its role in Britain changed from ransoming people in Moslem hands to that of caring for the sick. The order was suppressed in Britain at the time of the Reformation.

The order was governed by a Minister-General and General Chapter consisting of the Minister-General and the Provincials of the order. The English Province was headed by the English Vicar-Provincial. Although there were ten houses in the English Province, the province was comparatively poor. This could have been due to the English houses having been poorly endowed and having to divide their income three ways, with only a third of their income being used for the maintenance of their houses. A number of the English houses had the advowson of churches.

Their houses were minor friaries with a hospital dedicated to the Holy Trinity attached to them. The hospitals were modest in size and had a hall linked to the nave of the friars' church, with the inmates' beds lined up along the walls of the hospital hall: the friars' church being separated by a dividing partition between the two sections, at the east end. Each house was headed by a minister, who at times was referred to as the prior, and had a complement of the minister, three priest-brethren and three lay helpers, but the complement was revised in 1267 to a minister, five brethren and five helpers per house.

Trinitarian friars wore long white gowns gathered at the waist with a belt. They wore scapulars on top of the gowns, white sleeveless outer garments which hung from the shoulders, and white cowls or hoods. On solemn occasions they wore black capes with black hoods. A cross with the horizontal bar in blue and the vertical bar in red was affixed to the front of the scapular and to the left side of the cape.

3

START OF THE MENDICANT WORK IN BRITAIN

The new mendicant orders were used by the church to reinforce the efforts of the secular clergy and bring a new vitality to the spiritual life of the people, and during the Middle Ages the friars' movement became an integral part of the life of both church and nation. Most friars' houses were established in major towns so as to be near the poor and needy and where sizeable congregations were at hand to listen to their sermons.

The religious enthusiasm of the new orders flowed into new channels as friars put into practice the teachings of the early church. At first they were well received, not only in Britain but across Europe, and their early years were the golden age of the mendicant movement. It was an era when often highly educated men clothed themselves in worn-out religious habits and lived meagrely on the alms of the poor. It was a time when they were very close to the hearts of the people in love and affection.

We must keep the medieval preoccupation with service for God, salvation, the fear of hell and, later, the fear of purgatory, in mind or we shall fail to understand the background of medieval religious life. Without that it is difficult to appreciate what inspired men to set aside the pursuit of power and riches and willingly take to a life of poverty and austerity.

In the first decades friars were content with simple accommodation and suffered great hardship. In some towns, the accommodation provided by their lay friends consisted of dilapidated, unhealthy dwellings in the poorest parts of town.

Unknown and without aid, they depended for their day-to-day benefactions on the goodwill of the laity, and, although this was often given, there were times when they had little to eat and nowhere to reside.

The Franciscan friars in particular lived, by their own choice, in the slum areas of the towns. There they visited the sick, poor, lame and the blind, giving them succour and preaching the love of God in a way poor people understood. Living out their Christian ideals, the friars made a very favourable impression on all classes of the population and the townspeople opened their arms to them and provided them with lodgings or donated money for their needs.

As comparative latecomers to the crowded towns, they took such sites as were offered to them and had often to be content with places that were cramped and insanitary. It was not long before these were enlarged or abandoned in favour of new, more open sites. Many of the original plots donated to the newcomers were empty sites adjacent to town walls, with the walls serving as boundary precincts for friaries. In Gloucester, for example, the Dominican and Franciscan houses were sited on spare land adjacent to the town walls. They were also given a surprisingly large number of undesirable sites on, or near, river banks or on marshy and unhealthy ground on the outskirts of towns, which had later to be abandoned due to dampness or the liability of flooding. There are numerous references of intermittent flooding of friaries. Some houses, of which Dunwich, Shoreham, Yarmouth and Winchelsea are examples, were built near the seashore and were eventually covered by the sea.

Friaries were founded in various ways, either by the initiative of the friars or at the invitation of prominent townspeople or the nobility, often with the encouragement of the local bishop. When the order's Provincial Chapter approved the foundation of a new house, a small group of friars would be sent to the town to establish an oratory, or private chapel, which then formed the nucleus of a community and from where they could start their spiritual ministrations among the people. In the thirteenth century, the great and lowly were willing and eager to provide friars with lodgings and money with which to build. However, a house would not have been successfully founded without the help of the wealthy townspeople or men of note in the surrounding countryside. In some instances, local landed families or prosperous merchants invited friars to settle in their town and either provided land or funded the building of a friary. In a number of places, a donor gave the site, another paid for the church buildings, while a third party paid for the conventual buildings. Most Dominican houses were fortunate in being supported by the generosity of noble benefactors from the beginning.

In towns that wanted a community of friars to be established, the burgesses gave sites as an encouragement for them to settle there. In 1245, the Franciscan friars were encouraged by the burgesses of Shrewsbury to settle in the town and, in 1255, the Austin friars were also invited to settle in Shrewsbury. This repeated itself in a number of towns in which there were no local noblemen or bishops to encourage the friars to settle in towns. Soon patronage flooded in from all ranks of society.

The original buildings were probably simple structures of wood, wattle and daub, where a few hardy friars lived, prayed and carried out their spiritual duties. These often poor and small structures were added to as funds became available. Excellent timber was to be had from the vast woodlands in the countryside, but in areas where timber was at a premium buildings were constructed of rough stonework. The early friary churches were plain and utilitarian, without ornamentation, and the domestic buildings were equally plain and functional, even spartan.

Soon the little preaching halls did not suffice and larger churches became imperative and, as the prestige of the friars grew, they were given more desirable sites within the towns.

The term 'patron' of a friary was generally applied to an important person, or successive members of a family, who either gave or procured the site for the friars, or those who paid for the buildings. Many, if not most, gifts of land came from noblemen or landowners who were closely linked to the town, and families of the founders often came to regard the friary as their property. They could not, of course, have a say in the spiritual side of the house, or in the running of the house, even when the family gave regular alms to it over a long period.

In 1216, Henry III (1207–72), who at the age of nine was crowned in Gloucester Cathedral, succeeded his father, King John. Henry survived the troubled times at the beginning of his reign and, by the end of it, England was enjoying a prosperity and peace unknown when he was a child. At the end of his days, though, he had little peace in his personal life. He is described as usually mild, affable, scholarly, artistic and a devout son of the church. He was responsible for rebuilding Westminster Abbey, other than the Henry VII Chapel. He reigned in an age when kings wielded absolute power over the lives and property of their subjects.

In his young days, Henry saw what people without faith were capable of perpetrating and feared that, if they remained ignorant of Christian virtues and faith, they would degenerate even further.

Henry was instrumental in obtaining many sites for the friars and was generous in his gifts of timber and contributions towards the cost of establishing friars' houses. Edward I (1239–1307) and, to a lesser extent, Edward II (1284–1327) were also generous patrons of the friars.

The religious history of Scotland is quite different from the religious history of England and Wales. Alexander II of Scotland (1198–1249) was said to be comradely to his fellow soldiers, humble towards the aged, modest towards the common people, compassionate to the wretched, liberal to the poor and kindly to the religious. He founded Elgin Cathedral in 1224, when the seat of the Bishop of Moray was transferred there from Spynie a few miles north of Elgin. His reign coincided with much of Henry III's reign and he, as did Henry, helped the Dominican and Franciscan friars to establish themselves in his realm. Tradition asserts that Alexander met St Dominic in France in 1217 and ascribes the King's partiality to the Dominicans to that meeting.

Most founders were identified with just one friary in a town but a few noblemen established two or more houses in the town they controlled or in which they had a major interest. Many of their gifts of land were accompanied by gifts of timber, stone, lime, or funds for the buildings. For instance, Henry III co-operated with a knight in the founding of the Oxford Austin friars' house. He also gave land for a church for the Yarmouth Dominican friars, and a local family paid for its erection. Lord Berkeley gave land for the Gloucester Dominican house and Henry III gave generous gifts towards the building work. Lord Berkeley also founded a Franciscan friary in Gloucester and his family remained connected with it until the dissolution of the house in 1538.

Many trading and wool towns had houses of two or more orders. By 1300, as the tide of mendicancy reached its zenith, it had established about 144 houses in England, nine in Wales and 20 in Scotland. By the end of the Middle Ages, 28 towns in England, one in Wales and three in Scotland had both Dominican and Franciscan houses in them, and 14 towns in England contained houses of all four orders. Oswestry, which in medieval times had a population of between 2,000 and 3,000 people, was one of the few towns without a mendicant house.

Six mendicant houses established themselves in both Oxford and Cambridge.

FOUNDING FRIARIES

The church strictly governed the founding of new ecclesiastical establishments and there are numerous references to inquisitions being held before a licence to build was issued, to see if the new church would have any effect on neighbouring churches. In the earlier years of the mendicant orders, Provincial Ministers gave permission for the establishing of new houses, but, later, Pope Boniface VIII (1294–1303) demanded that papal permission be obtained before new mendicant houses were establishments.

Bishops were generally glad to welcome these new evangelists, who came to bring new life and vigour into their dioceses, and friaries were established in all English cathedral towns except Durham, Ely, Rochester, Bath and Wells. It is possible they were not established in Rochester due to the town being easily served from the Canterbury and London houses. The Franciscans tried to establish a house in Durham but were opposed by the cathedral authorities and the house endured for less than a year. There seems to have been no attempt to open friars' houses in the cathedral towns of Ely, Bath and Wells.

Relations with the older monastic orders were not generally so happy, as monks resented the coming of the friars and did their best to prevent them from settling in towns which they controlled, or had a major interest in, possibly because they saw friars as competitors for the support and alms of the town. When Agnellus of Pisa, the first leader of the Franciscans in England, sent friars to establish a presence in Coventry, Chester and Winchester, they had great difficulty and opposition from the monks in the towns. Monastic orders generally tended to regard friars with suspicion, and abbots, with the authority to enforce their will, did not hesitate to use their power to stop friars establishing houses in their towns. The following larger abbey towns in Britain are notable for not having houses of friars in their towns.

Arbroath	Abingdon	Barnstaple	Cirencester
Dunfermline	Evesham	Glastonbury	Hexham
Malmesbury	Melrose	Pershore	Peterborough
Romsey	St Albans	Shaftesbury	Sherborne
Tewkesbury	Whitby		

The Dominicans tried to establish a house in Bury St Edmunds in 1233 but the papal legate Otho, who was at St Edmundsbury Abbey at the time, discouraged the friars from settling there. The Franciscans later established themselves just outside the town, but more on that further on. Kelso had the Roxburgh Franciscan house nearby. The Benedictine communities at Abingdon, Peterborough and St Albans were hostile to the friars and kept them out. In 1342, the Pope gave consent to the Bishop of Salisbury to found a house in Sherborne but the abbot of Sherborne Abbey would not permit the Austin friars to establish a house in the town. However, not all abbeys were hostile; the monks of Reading Benedictine Abbey gave the Franciscans land on which to build their house.

The East Coast, East Anglia, the Midlands and the central belt of Scotland were well populated with friars' houses.

In about 1300, Boston, which had four mendicant houses, was a prosperous port second only to London in sea trade, exporting wool, hides and leather to the Continent. The early part of the fourteenth century was a busy period for church building in the town but, although it was an important port, the first house of friars, Franciscans, was not established until the late 1260s. The Dominicans arrived in 1280, the Carmelites in 1293 and the Austins in 1317. The delay in opening houses in the town may have been because it was served by friars from Lincoln. In 1309, at about the same time as the citizens of Boston were contributing towards building friaries, the town started work on building its impressive parish church. Robert Chamberlain led a gang of disguised monks in a wild riot in Boston in 1287, when the new Dominican house was badly damaged by fire. During the latter part of the fourteenth century and during the fifteenth century the winding River Witham became badly silted up, which resulted in severe floods in the town. Consequently, trade suffered a serious decline and Boston became a distressed town. The four friars' houses, established in more prosperous times, endured considerable hardship as a result.

When Dominicans and Franciscans established early houses in Norwich, both in the same year, 1226, the town had its royal castle, cathedral, industry and an estimated population of 6,000 to 7,000 people. Norwich was chiefly famed for worsted and woollen cloth, but it was also the chief market town in one of the richest and most populated counties in England.

In Yarmouth, which exported woollen cloth to the Continent, there was a burst of enthusiasm for the mendicant orders when the Carmelite, Dominican and Franciscan friars each established a house in the town between the years 1267 and 1276.

Dominican friars settled in Lancaster in 1260 and Franciscan friars settled in Preston, also in 1260. At the time they were the only towns in the large, but then thinly populated, area of the County Palatine of Lancaster.

A number of friars' houses were established in towns with populations of 2,000 or less. A Franciscan friary was established in 1257–8 in Richmond (Yorkshire), which then had a population of only about 300, of which only 67 paid tax. In 1257, Henry III confirmed Guildford as the county town for Surrey but, even with its wealth and status, the population was not more than 1,000. In 1275 a Dominican house was opened in the town, the only house of friars in Surrey.

It is surprising there were no houses in Dover, the main gateway to and from the Continent. However, the lack of friars' houses in such a busy port may have been due to the number of religious hospices in the town, catering for the traveller. It is possible that friars from Canterbury, 16 miles away, rendered a ministry to the people of Dover.

Not all attempts to found mendicant houses were successful. There are a number of references to frustrated efforts to establish houses, and some houses that were established, did not survive for long.

During medieval times, Wales was ruled by the kings of England but the Principality was not politically united with England until the 1535 Act of Union. However, due to a mixture of conquest and peaceful penetration, Wales became unified with England in ecclesiastical matters. Other than the Llanfaes Franciscan house, Anglesey, and the Bangor and Rhuddlan Dominican houses, other friaries in Wales were founded in Norman plantation boroughs. The Welsh border towns of Chester, Shrewsbury, Ludlow, Hereford and Gloucester were well served by friars' houses.

There were very few monastic houses and no mendicant houses in the vast mountainous and coastal areas of Scotland north and west of the Glasgow – Perth – Inverness line, for some reason unknown to us.

Other than those for Franciscan Observants, most of the houses established in the fourteenth century, and later, were modest establishments of secondary importance.

Friars left few registers and cartularies; those for English and Welsh houses were destroyed during the suppression of the houses in 1538–9. Nearly all the friary archives in Scotland were either destroyed or dispersed when the houses withered away in the middle of the sixteenth century. Due to the loss of so many records, there is no accurate information on the origin of a number of houses. Many dates given for the establishment of mendicant houses are exact dates of their foundation, but in other instances the date given is the earliest recorded date of the house. In some cases this may be the year of its foundation, but in a few instances the house may have been in existence for some time.

With the rush of new and enthusiastic members joining the new orders, the orders appear to have established houses in important towns and later sent out a nucleus of brethren to establish daughter houses in nearby towns. With this in mind, we will look at the establishment of houses on a regional basis, with each area being concerned to extend its outreach in its area.

DOMINICAN FRIARS

In his *Annuals of England*, Nicholas Trevet (1258–1328) writes that the Second Chapter of the Dominican Order, held in 1221 at Bologna, sent Dominican friars to Britain to start work there. It happened that while the Chapter was in session, Peter de Roche, Bishop of Winchester, was passing through Bologna on his way home from the East. At St Dominic's request, the Bishop promised to let the friars travel in his suite and to be their guide to his country. They entered Britain on 6 August 1221, when 13 Dominican brothers under the leadership of Gilbert de Fresnoy came in the company of the Bishop. This was the day Dominic died, although they were as yet unaware of his death. When the Dominicans arrived at Canterbury, they were lodged in Christ Church Cathedral Priory, and the Bishop introduced them to Stephen Langton, Archbishop of Canterbury. When the Archbishop learnt that the friars were preachers, he asked Gilbert to preach an impromptu sermon. The Archbishop was so impressed by the sermon and the sincerity of the friars that he took them under his protection and invited the band to settle and expand in England.

The small group of friars did not delay long in Canterbury and arrived in London on 10 August 1221. Three of them remained there and settled in Holborn. Hubert de Burgh gave them a number of gifts and bequeathed to them his mansion near Westminster. Their London house must have soon been enlarged, for the 1250 General Chapter of the order was held in it when about 400 members were present.

The other members of the founding party headed by Gilbert de Fresnoy left London and reached Oxford on 15 August. Oxford appears to have been their destination from the beginning and was to become the scene of some of their greatest British intellectual achievements during the thirteenth century. Their first lodgings were in Little Jewry in the parish of St Aldate's, on a site south of the Town Hall. There, they established a foothold in the academic world and built an oratory dedicated to the Virgin Mary, which served as a chapel for their small community. They soon began teaching in the Oxford schools and attracted students and teachers of outstanding ability. The English Dominicans held their first Provincial Chapter in Oxford in 1230, when the framework of their work and organisation in Britain was probably completed. In 1237, building work started on their new site south of Littlegate, in the parish of St Ebbes, and in 1246, the twenty-fifth anniversary of their arrival in Oxford, they celebrated Mass in their new church.

Any attempt to trace the growth of the province in the successive foundations of Dominican houses is bound to prove unsatisfactory because of the fragmentary nature of the evidence available. However, by noting the earliest known recorded dates for Dominican houses, we get some idea of the order's progress in establishing houses. This is not an exact method for tracing their progress; that cannot be achieved without the information which has been lost to us.

By 1226, the infant order felt strong enough to send a party to Norwich, where they hired a house in the poor quarters of the town, lived simply and the parish church of 'St John the Baptist over-the-Water' was assigned to them for their services. In 1307, they were given the house vacated by the Friars of the Sack, which they considerably enlarged. The Norwich house became one of the most important Dominican priories in the English Province and the nucleus for a missionary outreach into the Midlands and East Anglia. The church was destroyed by fire in 1413 and the Dominicans moved back to their original site while the fire-damaged buildings were being rebuilt. The church was restored on a magnificent scale between 1440 and 1470, with the leading citizens vying with one another in the generosity of their gifts. The new church is the only Dominican church in Britain to have survived complete, although the building is now used as a concert hall.

The Dominicans extended their influence in the Norfolk Diocese by establishing houses in Sudbury by 1248, Dunwich by 1256 and King's Lynn by 1256, which is the earliest mention of the establishment. Henry III purchased a house on the eastern ramparts of Ipswich in 1263, which he gave to the Dominican friars as the nucleus of their house. The number of friars in the house increased rapidly and by 1277 had reached 50. The first reference to the Chelmsford house records that food was provided for 30 friars at the house in 1277. In 1267 two friars arrived in Yarmouth as the nucleus for a house which was sited near the seashore. In 1287 the house was swamped by the sea and the friars built a wall to prevent further flooding. The site is now covered by the town Fire Station.

Sometime before 1233, the Dominicans entered Northampton, and within eight years they had reached out to Derby, Lincoln and Stamford. It has been suggested that the Lincoln house was founded by Bishop Grosseteste, although there is no evidence to support this.

About the end of 1225, the King caused enquiries to be made as to a suitable site in York for the Dominican friars,

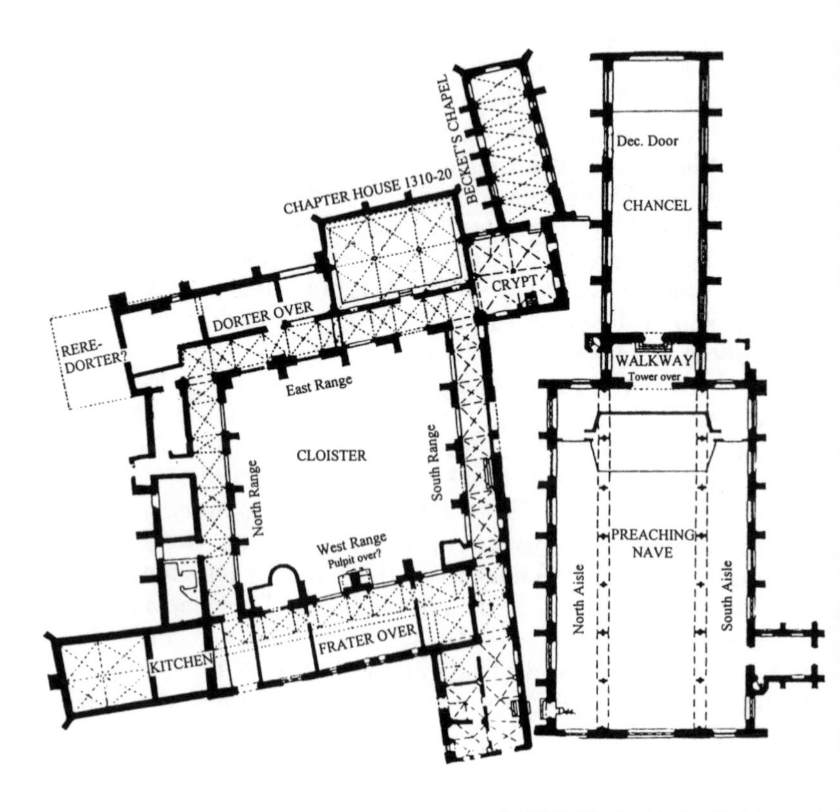

THE NORWICH BLACKFRIARS c. 1450

and the mayor and burgesses recommended an open space adjacent to the city wall which had previously been the site of the Roman baths. In 1226, the Dominicans arrived in the city and were given the use of an ancient royal chapel on the recommended site. The York Dominican house flourished and was full of missionary enthusiasm; it became the nucleus for branching out into towns in the north of England.

Friars from the York house branched out to the fortress and border town of Carlisle in 1233. They reached Beverley in 1240 and, with the support of Alexander II, were established in Berwick-upon-Tweed in 1240, where their first settlement was outside the town. In 1285, they were permitted to purchase the former house of the Sack friars in Berwick, which had been vacated. They reached Scarborough by 1252, where, as were the Franciscans, they were opposed by monks of the Cistercian Order. The monks later stated that the advowson of Scarborough church was held by them and they applied the revenues from the church to the expenses of their yearly Cistercian General Chapter meetings at Citeaux, and the presence of the Dominicans had cut into the revenues of the parish church to such an extent that instead of supporting the General Chapter for three days, as formerly, they now only sufficed for one day. Undeterred by this opposition, the friars succeeded in establishing a large house.

Edmund de Lucy, son of the Earl of Lincoln, resolved to establish a house of Dominicans on his estate, the Honour of Pontefract, and finally chose Pontefract, the administrative centre of his estate, as the site. The friars moved into Pontefract in 1256. They established a house in Bamburgh in 1265. The choice of Bamburgh shows the importance of the town at the time. Later, Scottish raids on the town reduced it to poverty, which must have had serious consequences for the Friary. When the Dominicans settled in Yarm in about 1266, it was the only port on the River Tees and had a thriving export trade in wheat and wool.

The Dominicans established themselves in Newcastle-upon-Tyne in 1239, where their house was built just inside the town wall, by Peter Scott, the first mayor of the town. The friars, having to make their way through narrow crowded streets, found public access to their house difficult and they were soon given permission to make a postern gate in the town wall and, later, to erect a drawbridge over the outer town ditch. The friars' postern gate and a recently replaced wooden bridge are still in use.

There are references in 1283 to friar preachers of Jarrow, but if the house was established, it had only a short existence. There are also references to Dominican houses in Doncaster, Hartlepool and Hull but there does not seem to be any conclusive proof of these houses.

It was not until 1237 that the Dominicans, at the request of the Archbishop of Canterbury, settled in Canterbury and acquired a plot of land by the River Stour, almost certainly the piece of land on which the former guest house now stands. Henry III was patron and founder of the house and between 1237 and 1259 gave gifts of nearly £500, a very large sum in those days, towards the building of the house. Henry, however, gave very little to the Canterbury Franciscan house.

In 1227 or 1228, the Dominicans established an oratory in Bristol, then one of the richest towns in England and for a time second only to London. In spite of opposition from the neighbouring Benedictine Priory of St James, the Bishop of Worcester dedicated their first house in 1230, which no doubt had been given by local burgesses who were pleased to aid the new austere order. It is probable the friars started their first permanent buildings in 1247 when the Earl of Warwick gave them a new site at Lewin's Mead in the town. Henry III gave them numerous grants of timber.

It appears that the Bristol friars started a work in the cathedral town of Exeter in 1232. The foundation was aided and assisted by the Bishop of Exeter, who gave them stone from the town ditch to build their priory. The Dominicans reached the cathedral town of Winchester by 1234, where they were assigned a site near the east gate of the town. In the following year a Dominican friar preached in Winchester, in favour of the crusade to recover the Holy Land, before the King and barons, when the King's brother, Richard, Earl of Cornwall, and a number of knights of noble families took up the Cross for the crusades. In about 1239, the friars branched out from Bristol to Gloucester. Their Gloucester house was founded by Sir Stephen of Harnhill, a local benefactor. Henry III, who was also a major benefactor to the house, gave 20 marks towards the foundation of the house and land on the recently vacated outer bailey of the royal castle. Two years later he gave them a further 41 marks to buy land to widen their churchyard and construct a road to the High Street. They entered Wilton in 1247 and Truro in 1259. The Wilton house was only three miles from the new cathedral town of Salisbury, which was then being built. Edward I gave land for the site of the Salisbury Dominican house, and his queen, Eleanor of Castile, was a great benefactress to the house. The friars soon found that due to the increasing importance and influence of Salisbury and the waning influence of Wilton, Wilton was the wrong location for their work, and in 1281 the Wilton friars moved to Salisbury. The Wilton work was not abandoned: the land and church had been dedicated to holy use and could not be readily secularised. The house remained a preaching station for two or three friars.

Dominicans settled in Hereford in 1246 and built an oratory, but the Hereford Cathedral authorities opposed the settlement on the grounds that the town already had enough claimants for its charity. Bishop Peter de Aquablanca appealed to Pope Innocent IV about the proposed house, and in 1250 the Pope warned the Dominicans not to make themselves a home in the town against the wishes of the higher clergy. However, on the death of the Pope and Bishop, the long dispute with the cathedral chapter was finally healed by the mediation of Edward II, and in 1322 they were given the chapel and buildings of the Knights Hospitallers, outside the town walls. The Hospitallers had taken over the buildings from the disbanded Knights Templars, but due to their having houses in Garway and Dinmore, both about six miles out of Hereford, the buildings were surplus to the Hospitallers' requirements. The dedication of the new priory church was attended by Edward III, accompanied by his son the Black Prince, three archbishops and the chief nobility of the day.

Within 25 years, the order was established in nine English medieval cathedral towns, and in the cathedral towns of Chichester in 1280 and Worcester in 1347.

At the first Dominican Provincial Chapter held in 1230 in Oxford, it was agreed that a community of Dominican friars should establish themselves in Shrewsbury. In the following year the Constable of Shrewsbury, the King's representative, gave the friars 50 loads of lime from the store accumulated for work on the castle. Following the Battle of Shrewsbury in 1403, many of distinguished rank were interred in the cemetery of the Shrewsbury Dominican priory.

Some time before 1236, the Dominicans branched out to Chester and, in 1260, the order established a house in Lancaster. When Robert the Bruce raided and destroyed Lancaster in 1322, he spared both the Lancaster priory and the friars' house.

The Bishop of Winchester attempted to establish a house of Dominicans in Portsmouth in 1225, when he gave them a gift to purchase a house in the town, but this attempt may have failed due to the Bishop's absence from his diocese from 1226 to 1230, which could have deprived it of the necessary support in its early stage.

The Dunstable Augustinian priory tried to prevent the Dominicans establishing themselves in the town, but Henry III wrote in 1259 to the canons of the priory that he held the Dominicans in special devotion as men of the Gospel and ministers to the most holy King. He gave the friars help in establishing themselves there. The monks later accused the friars of exploiting the King's favour and deceitfully entering Dunstable against their will.

A grant of land between Guildford and the royal park, given by Edward I to the Guildford Dominican house in 1275, is the first reference to the house, but it is probable it was founded in 1274 by Queen Eleanor of Provence, in memory of her grandson Prince Henry, son of Edward I, who had died at the age of seven in Guildford Castle while accompanying her. His heart was buried in the newly founded Dominican church. Normally the cloister of a house lay on the south side of the church, but in Guildford it was on the north side, so that the church was nearest the town.

In 1308, Edward II established a Dominican house for 100 friars, at King's Langley, six miles south-west of St Albans, but 45 brethren seems to have been the average number there. Because of its royal connections, it had an income from a quarry, a local fishery and other endowments. The 1536 *Valor Ecclesiasticus* gave the annual income of the house as £122.

In 1318, the Dominicans wanted to open a house in the new town of Winchelsea. The town authorities had previously agreed that the new town should have only one house of mendicant friars and, as the Franciscan friars were already established there, the Dominicans were given a site some distance from the town. It proved to be unsuitable as few people were willing, or able, to travel the distance from the town to the Dominican church. As a result, they were given a new site near the town, but they found it even worse due to flooding from the sea. They were eventually settled on a suitable site in the town in 1358 but the house was considerably smaller than the Winchelsea Franciscan house.

Of the five houses the Dominicans founded in Wales, two were near the North Wales coast, two near the South Wales coast and a house inland, at Brecon, close to the River Usk and beside the town bridge.

The North Wales house at Bangor was founded sometime before 1251, when Bangor was a small but prosperous settlement of about 50 householders clustered around its sixth-century cathedral. The first mention of the house occurs in 1251 with the friars receiving protection in procuring supplies over the River Conway, the regular route into North Wales. The house was destroyed by fire during Edward I's Welsh wars in 1284, or during the subsequent insurrection of Madoc ap Llywelyn in 1286. The King gave the house £100 compensation and the restored church was finished in 1299. The Penmynydd family, descendants of Ednyfed Fychan, the seneschal of Llywelyn the Great, maintained a close connection with Bangor for generations and three members of the family were buried there: Sir Tudor himself in 1311, his son Gronw in 1331 and his grandson, Sir Tudor, in 1367. Sir Tudor's grandson Owain had been accepted into the household of Henry V and on the death of the King, Owain secretly married Catherine, Henry's young widow. The royal line of Tudor descended from this union.

In about 1257, Llywelyn ap Gruffydd, Prince of Wales, founded the Rhuddland Dominican house. The priory was sited near the earlier Norman castle known as Twthhill, which suggests that Llywelyn gave the friars the site of an old Norman castle, possibly to prevent anyone building a castle on the strategic site. During the wars of Edward I, friars from the Rhuddland Dominican house took charge of the English wounded and carried communications between the King and London. The establishment of the friary on the castle site may have been the reason for Edward I choosing a new site in 1277 for his Rhuddlan castle and borough.

The Dominican house at Haverfordwest, founded some time before 1245, was one of the most isolated Dominican houses in Britain, being about 100 miles from their Cardiff house, the nearest house of their order, and 30 miles from the nearest Franciscan friary at Carmarthen. At that time, Haverfordwest was a small town, yet it was important as the capital of the Pembrokeshire English community that gave the county the name of 'Little England beyond Wales'. Because Haverfordwest was in the far western part of South Wales, no doubt the house was used by a stream of friars and other visitors going to and from Ireland. The Haverfordwest English-speaking friars would have received a hostile reception if they went beyond the English part of the county, as the Welsh people to the north and east of them strongly resisted any contact with their English neighbours.

The Cardiff Dominican house, founded by 1242, is generally attributed to the Clare family, from Clare, Suffolk, who were Lords of Glamorgan.

In 1215, William Malvoisine, Bishop of St Andrews, attended the Lateran Council in Rome, when reference was made to the Albigensian and Waldensian heresies and to the

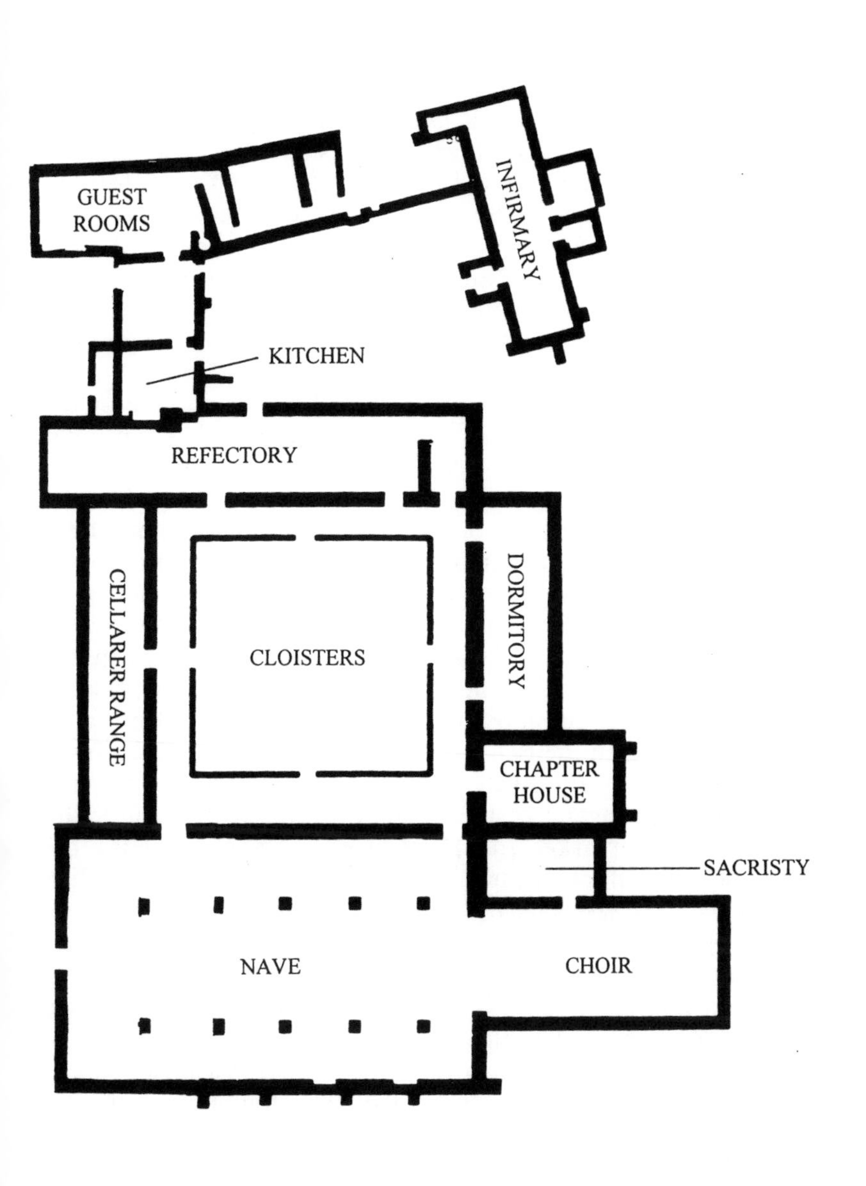

DOMINICAN FRIARY, CARDIFF

Dominican friars. On his return, and having other use for his money, he did not endow a Dominican friary in his episcopal city, though he was later responsible for encouraging Alexander II to support the Dominican friars in their efforts to establish their order in Scotland. The Dominican mission in Scotland followed soon after the 1230 General Chapter meeting in Oxford which authorised the outreach. In Scotland, the King endowed Dominican houses in towns where their evangelistic outreach was likely to be effective, and the Dominicans became the largest mendicant order in Scotland.

The Dominicans stood high in royal favour and nine or ten of their fifteen houses in Scotland were founded by Alexander II. Their first house in Scotland was established in 1230 when the King granted them the royal residence of the Kings Manor, with its large piece of ground, near Cowgate in Edinburgh; Cowgate was simply a narrow road for cows to pass onto the pleasant pastures beyond the town wall. A lane was added so as to give passageway from Cowgate to the High Street. Today, Edinburgh is a large modern city, though when the Dominicans first arrived there it was a small, thinly populated town, but by far the most prosperous in Scotland, due to its trading links with the rich countryside around and its sea trade with northern Europe. Medieval Edinburgh principally consisted of a strong castle on a hill at one end of the town, with the Lawnmarket and High Street leading down the hill for about a mile, to Canon Gate at the other end. The High Street had numerous narrow tenement wynds leading off it.

As the Dominicans rapidly increased in numbers, they were thus enabled to establish houses in several of the royal burghs within a few years. They branched out to Perth in 1231, when Alexander II gave them land just outside the northern part of the town walls, where Perth castle had stood. Various councils of the Scottish church were held in the Dominicans' church. Scotland at that time had no capital, but due to Perth's central position between the Highlands and the Lowlands, Scottish kings frequently resided there and Perth was in effect the capital of Scotland.

The Dominicans established a house in Elgin in 1233 or

1234; and in Sterling in 1233, when the town was strategically important because it was in the centre of communications between the north and south of Scotland.

By 1240, the Dominicans had reached Inverness, as their existence is recorded in the town in that year. The house was founded by Alexander II but it was never large, although the King sent friars from the house as ambassadors to King Haakon of Norway in 1263.

The Dominicans reached Aberdeen in about 1239–40, during the reign of Alexander II. The Aberdeen house had branched out to Montrose by 1275, but the house appears to have been abandoned after it was destroyed by fire and became ruinous following the wars of the fourteenth century. It was refounded as a Dominican house in 1517. As we have noted, a Dominican house was established in Berwick-upon-Tweed in about 1240 when Alexander II gave an endowment to the house. The Dominicans established a house in Ayr around 1242, and in either 1267 or 1287, established another, in Wigtown.

In the thirteenth century, Glasgow was a small town with an important cathedral. The Bishop of Glasgow must have been impressed with the preaching abilities of the Dominican friars, for in 1246 a papal bull granted an indulgence to all who contributed to the building work of the new Dominican church in the cathedral town. No doubt the Bishop saw the friars as a means of injecting a new vitality into the churches in his diocese.

A charter of 1274, regarded by some authorities as spurious, states that the Bishop of St Andrews established a Dominican house in his cathedral town. Nothing appears to be known about the house until 1464, when there are references to a small house or hospice. St Andrews was a flourishing burgh and the seat of Scotland's most important bishopric and the largest cathedral in Scotland, and by the time of the Reformation, St Andrews had become the intellectual capital of Scotland. However, original expectations for the Dominican house were unfulfilled, as in the late fifteenth century only one or two friars were in residence. In the early sixteenth century, the Scottish Dominicans experienced a regeneration, and in 1516 it was agreed that money bequeathed to them by Bishop Elphinstone of Aberdeen should be devoted to rebuilding St Andrews Dominican Friary. A side chapel, which originally projected from the north side of their church in South Street, is a surviving fragment from the building which dates from soon after 1525, when permission was given for the friars to build out into the street, there being insufficient space for the new buildings in their own grounds.

In 1348, Duncan, Earl of Fife, founded a house near his castle at Cupar. The house was in a state of collapse in 1519 and the two remaining friars were transferred to their St Andrews house.

The Dominicans opened a house in Haddington in 1471 but it appears to have had a brief existence. Also in 1471, a house was established in St Monans, where the friars used the parish church, still the town's parochial church, for their services. It was a small and poor house with only a few friars and appears to have been established so that the number of Dominican houses in Scotland would justify a separate Scottish Province. If that is the case, the ploy succeeded, for, as we have seen, a separate Province of Scotland was formed in 1481. In 1519, the house was incorporated into their St Andrews house.

In about 1521, Andrew Abercromby, a merchant, founded and endowed a Dominican house in Dundee on the grounds that there were no houses of the order in the town. It was the last mendicant house to be founded in Scotland prior to the Reformation; it appears that there were only a few brethren there and the house had a brief existence.

By 1300, there were 44 Dominican houses in England, five in Wales and 11 in Scotland, and there were eventually 49 Dominican houses in England, five in Wales and 15 in Scotland.

Only one house of Dominican nuns was established in England and that was founded by Edward II to implement the wishes of his mother. Edward II wrote a letter to Pope John XXII in 1318, and sent it with two Dominican friars to plead the cause in person, seeking permission to change the Guildford Dominican house into a convent which he would endow for Dominican sisters. The Pope withheld his permission, and due to delays and the Black Death, Henry III was not able to fulfil his father's vows until he established a priory at Dartford in 1356, when an advanced party of four nuns from France moved into the new house. The house was intended for 40 nuns. However, in 1381 there were 20 nuns and in 1538 19 nuns were granted pensions. It was an enclosed priory where the Dominicanesses lived within the confines of their house. The sisters ran a school for the daughters of the gentry, thereby following the practice of the order in teaching. The Dartford house was subordinate to King's Langley Priory, and a few friars from King's Langley were attached to the house to serve as chaplains.

In 1517, a house of Dominican nuns was established at Sciennes, about a mile south of Edinburgh old town, when Sisters of the Order of St Dominic were given St John's Kirk with its churchyard, houses and land. The monastery was erected for a house of 30 nuns. In 1556, there were 12 nuns in residence, when they were expelled from the house by the reformers.

FRANCISCAN FRIARS

The history of the Franciscan Order is well documented. Thomas of Eccleston started collecting material in about 1232 for his history of the early Franciscans in England and finished his work in 1258–9. He chronicled that in June 1224, St Francis commissioned Agnellus of Pisa (1194–1236) to establish the Franciscan Order in England. On Tuesday, 10 September 1224, a founding party of nine Franciscan friars, led by Agnellus, was ferried from France to Dover, its passage being paid by the monks of Fécamp Abbey, near Le Havre. The little group, scantily clad in old, patched garments, with nothing on their feet and no possessions of any kind, was the spearhead of the remarkable Franciscan ministry in Britain. The group consisted of four ordained clerics and five lay brothers. Twelve years later Agnellus fell ill with dysentery, died and was buried in the newly built Oxford Franciscan friary church. His reputation for holiness was recognised in 1892 when he was beatified by Pope Leo XIII and the church formally declared Blessed Agnellus worthy of public veneration. He is honoured in the Franciscan Order as a man of outstanding virtue and for his zeal for the primitive observance of Franciscan poverty.

The party left Dover and arrived in Canterbury two days later. A few days after they had arrived in Canterbury, the friars divided into two groups, five brothers remaining in Canterbury and the others going on to London.

The brothers who remained in Canterbury were given lodgings in a small room at the Hospital for Poor Priests in Stour Street, by the warden, Alexander of Gloucester, until they could find a permanent dwelling. Tradition has it that in the evenings, when scholars attached to the hospice school had gone home, the friars went to the schoolroom and sat around a fire they rekindled. They collected the dregs of beer left by the scholars into a pot and, after watering it down and warming it, shared it with each other. Not long after they arrived in Canterbury, the warden gave them a part of the garden of the hospice, which included a small island in the River Stour, and built them an oratory. The dwellings could have been no more than little wattle huts. Unfortunately, the land was low-lying and liable to floods. Here, in the simplest of quarters, they lived for about 50 years, until 1267, when a citizen named John Digges acquired some land for them on the other side of the River Stour, where they built their new church and house.

The four brethren who went on to London dwelt for 15 days with Dominican friars in the city. Supporters then hired a house in Cornhill, where the two brethren who remained in London lived very simply during the winter. They soon gained favour for their sincerity with the citizens of the city, and the community grew fairly rapidly. By the following year the house became too small for the increased numbers and they sought something larger. In the summer of 1225, John Swyn, a mercer, along with other citizens, gave the Franciscans a house they bought in Stinking Lane, near Newgate and among the butchers' shambles. The house was later enlarged by other benefactions. Other brethren soon joined their ranks and within 20 years their numbers had increased to 80.

At the end of September 1224 two of the four friars who had set off for London went on to Oxford and were received with great kindness by the Dominicans, stayed with them for eight days and then lived in a house provided by a well-wisher, in the parish of St Ebbes. Alms sufficient for their needs were probably already forthcoming, as the order did not have long to wait for recognition. They were joined by what were referred to as many honest bachelors and eminent men. It may have been due to the numbers who flocked to their order that they left their first abode in 1225 and hired a house and garden from Richard the Miller, who, within a year, presented it to the city, which held it for the friars. Their Oxford house, which became their first permanent abode in the town, quickly became a lively place and in 1233 there were 40 friars there. From small beginnings, the house flourished, later occupying a large site adjacent to the town walls, and the numbers expanded to over 100 friars.

Within a month of their arrival, the Franciscans had established themselves in Canterbury, London and Oxford: the centre of the church, the capital city and the centre of learning. In contrast, the Dominicans took five years to establish the same number of houses.

Within six years, the founding party of nine penniless beggars became the forerunners of a band of men who were welcomed and supported by the people until the sixteenth century. The friars were everywhere well received and, in an astonishingly short time, novices flocked to the order in great numbers as it attracted many saintly followers who were intent on living the simple life, doing practical work for the needy and earning their keep by manual work or begging. The Franciscans were a new phenomenon in the land and were welcomed and supported as men who had left the settled ways of the medieval church and come down to the level of the poor and suffering. No house or hovel was too poor for them to enter. The example of friars, who lived in the most squalid districts of the towns as they tended to the needs of the less fortunate in society, impressed young middle-class men, who entered the order in large numbers. Today we would regard them as Christian social workers with a Gospel message.

Again, by noting the earliest recorded dates for Franciscan houses, we get some idea of their progress in establishing their houses, and can trace their outreach routes, as far as possible, from their progress in geographical areas of the country.

Three Franciscans were sent in 1226 to found a house in Cambridge, Brothers William and Hugh, who were in clerical orders, and Brother Elias, a novice who was so lame that he had to be carried into the church choir. The house remained so poor that 13 years after its foundation the brethren still had no cloaks. Their first Cambridge house, given to them by the town burgesses, was a disused synagogue next to the jail, but the brethren were disturbed in their devotions by drunks and disorderly people locked up for the night. They stayed in this unsatisfactory accommodation for about 40 years before making a move to more commodious surroundings, when in 1267 they moved into a new site on land, where Sidney Sussex College now stands. They settled in Coventry in about 1234, which was then the third largest town in England.

Two of the Franciscans who settled in Oxford went on to Northampton, which was then an important meeting place, in 1226 and founded a house in the town. When they arrived they were given temporary accommodation by Sir Robert Goblin.

In 1230, the Franciscans acquired land in Lincoln, near the old Guildhall and in 1237 the King asked the citizens to give the friars their Guildhall, promising to give them another place. It seems likely that he gave them the Stonebow, which would have cost him nothing. The Guildhall site was enlarged to about four acres but the site was small. As a result, in order to save space, the church, which still survives and has recently been used as a public library, was built over an undercroft.

During the five years 1225–30, houses were founded in the cathedral towns of Hereford, Lincoln, Norwich, Salisbury,

Worcester and York, and also at the important towns of Bristol, Leicester, Nottingham and Stamford. By 1254 they had founded houses in five more cathedral towns: Carlisle, Chichester, Exeter, Lichfield and Winchester.

The first York Franciscan house was established in about 1230 on a site just inside the town wall, where the wall met the river. The site soon proved too small for the friars' requirements and in about 1243 they acquired a larger permanent site on land adjacent to York Castle. Their premises must have been spacious and well-appointed, since royal visitors stayed there rather than in the castle. The house became important as a regional centre for the order and a number of houses in the north of England were established by friars from it.

From York, the Franciscans reached Carlisle in 1233, the same year as the Dominicans. In 1257–8, they established a house in Richmond (Yorkshire), then a small town with a population of about 300. However, it was a prosperous market centre and seems to have been chosen as the site for the Franciscan house because it was the administrative centre of the widespread but thinly populated Honour of Richmond. The house was sited just outside the town walls and the friars were given permission to make a gateway through the wall, to give easy access for townspeople who wished to attend the friars' church.

In 1239, the Franciscans reached Scarborough, a royal borough dominated by its castle on the hill overlooking the town. When they arrived, Henry III ordered the Sheriff of Yorkshire to provide food to them one day every week. As we have seen, the Cistercian monks of Citeaux, who had the appropriation of St Mary's Church in Scarborough, strongly resisted the establishment of rival organisations in their territory and appealed to the Pope for support. In 1243, Pope Innocent IV instructed Robert Grosseteste, Bishop of Lincoln, to hear the case. When the Franciscan friars appeared before him, one of their number waved aside all legal arguments and renounced their privileges as inconsistent with the Scriptures, which say: 'Resist not evil: but whosoever shall smite thee on thy right cheek, turn to him the other also. And if any man will sue thee at law, and take away thy coat, let him have thy cloak also' (Matthew 5:39–40). He said the friars would rather give up the place than offend the monks. In a letter to the Abbot of Citeaux, Grosseteste wrote: 'We, with your brethren consider that if the friars left Scarborough, it would rebound to your discredit, I have therefore decided that the friars should remain until we hear from you'. However, in 1245, the friars retired to Scalby just outside Scarborough and did not return until sometime between 1267 and 1272, after a protracted struggle. It is not known if the Cistercians offered continual opposition to the Franciscans in the town after their return.

In 1226, Franciscan friars arrived in Norwich, where they were given a house. They set up an oratory, and after receiving a large number of benefactions, they commenced building an imposing church, said to have been 300 feet long and 80 feet wide, with spacious cloisters and conventual buildings. There is some doubt as to the date of the founding of the Yarmouth Franciscan house. Although the earliest references to the house are in 1271, it is generally thought to have been founded in 1226.

By 1236, the Franciscans had settled in Ipswich and from there they spread to nearby Colchester by 1237. They settled in King's Lynn some time before 1230, and by 1277, the Franciscans had established a house in Dunwich, then an important East Anglian town. However, the friars had to abandon their original site due to the incursion of the sea, which eventually washed away medieval Dunwich, and in 1290 they were given another site further inland.

In 1233, two years after the unsuccessful Dominican attempt to establish themselves in Bury St Edmunds, the Franciscans attempted to establish themselves in the town, but the Abbot of St Edmunds Abbey protested and had the friars forcefully expelled and razed their buildings to the ground. The Franciscans, however, persisted, and in 1257 Pope Alexander IV issued a papal bull in their favour. Relying on the papal bull, the Franciscans established themselves on the northern end of the town, but, despite the papal bull, the monks once again drove them out. They then appealed to Henry III, who backed the friars' cause with the civil power, and in April 1258, the friars returned to their site in the town. After the death of Pope Alexander IV in 1261, the monks put their case to Urban IV, his successor. The new Pope ordered the friars to pull down their buildings and abandon the site. The friars obeyed, but a reconciliation between them and the monks occurred in 1263 when the monks gave them a 43-acre site at Babwell, beyond the north gate of the town and just outside its jurisdiction. The Babwell site was the largest recorded for a Franciscan house in England. It is not known why they were given such a large plot; possibly as recompense for past bitterness. Being outside the town, they could not attract much in the way of alms and the land could have been given for them to support themselves by growing vegetables and keeping animals, as well as for the construction of friary buildings.

The Franciscans arrived in Boston over 40 years after they first arrived in England. Their house included a good proportion of German friars, whose services were in demand in ministering to the needs of the port's immigrant community, and many North German merchants were buried in the Franciscan church.

The Reading Benedictine abbey gave the Franciscans a site for their house in 1233, but it was on marshy ground near the river and was inundated with floodwater in the winter. Under pressure from Henry III, the monks gave the friars a new and more suitable site in the town. Henry and Edward I were generous patrons of the house.

The Oxford friars used their manpower resources in establishing themselves in the university and in training friars for their vocation, rather than in taking part in the outreach to other towns.

In 1226, the Franciscans were established in Worcester, and two years later they established a house in Hereford. The Worcester friars were given a new and more central site in the town in about 1237. They arrived in Gloucester in 1230 and Bristol in the same year, where the burgesses of the town were said to have built a house for the friars at their own expense. They were also established in Chichester by 1232 but the date of the arrival of the Franciscans in the town is unknown; it is possible that they first settled in the town in 1225, soon after the order arrived in England. Having established themselves in the town, the Franciscans were originally housed on the site of St Mary's Hospital, but in 1269 they were offered a better site in the ruins of the castle, where they built a new church and house. The choir of their new church still stands and is now a museum.

When they arrived at Dorchester sometime before 1267, they were given a site and allowed to take stones from the castle for their friary buildings. In 1235, the Franciscans were invited to Southampton, where the King gave them a site. Richard Pride, a burgess of the town, paid for the building of the church and Laurence Cox paid for the construction of the conventual buildings.

They established a house in Winchelsea in 1242. During the thirteenth century the Hastings area of the south coast suffered badly from the sea moving large amounts of shingle on the seabed. The old town of Winchelsea was built on a shingle spit running out from the Fairlight Cliffs; during a great storm in 1287, it was virtually destroyed by the sea and had to be abandoned, including its friary. The town was refounded by Edward I, who gave the hilltop site for it, well above the danger of the sea. It was agreed at the time of establishing the new town that only one house of mendicant friars would be allowed within it. As the Franciscans were established in the former town, and no doubt had given the townspeople considerable help during their time of distress, they were chosen as the preferred house of friars and given a central position in the new town. It is not certain whether the Franciscan church was ever completed but the remains of a very large chancel indicates the church was planned on a massive scale, perhaps as a way of thanking the friars. In 1360, the French besieged and attacked the town and destroyed most of the buildings, including the friary, which was later repaired.

In 1338, the Franciscans were assigned a seven-acre site in

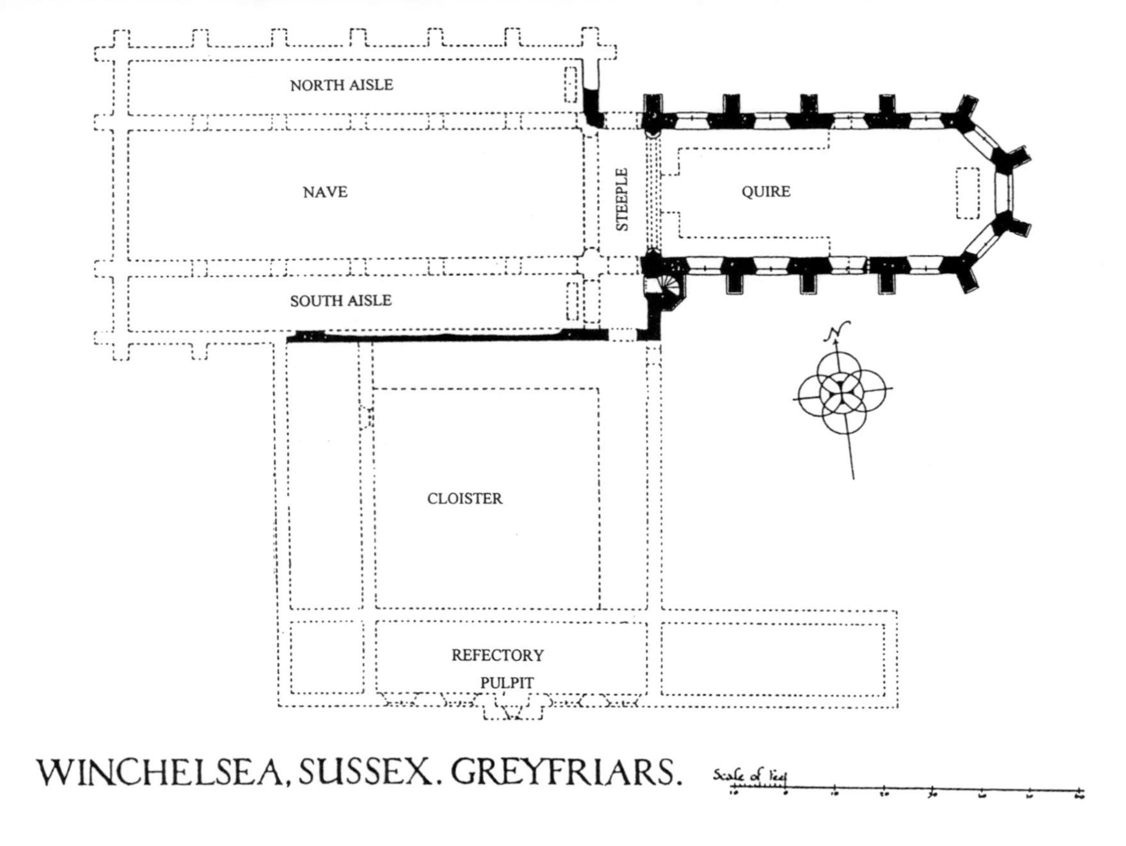
NORTH AISLE
NAVE
SOUTH AISLE
STEEPLE
QUIRE
N
CLOISTER
REFECTORY
PULPIT
WINCHELSEA, SUSSEX. GREYFRIARS.
Scale of Feet

Ware, a small town on the River Lea in Hertfordshire. It was one of only four houses of the order to be successfully established in the fourteenth century. The other three were Aylesbury, Plymouth and Walsingham.

Elizabeth de Burgh, Countess of Clare, wanted to found a Franciscan house in Walsingham as a hospice for poor pilgrims visiting the shrine of Our Lady. The occupants of Walsingham Augustinian Priory, who had full possession of the town, pointed out to the Countess the dangers of the projected Franciscan settlement. They feared the friars would divert alms given by the pilgrims. Their strenuous efforts were unsuccessful, and in 1347 Pope Clement VI, at the request of Edward III, granted a licence to the English Minister-Provincial to acquire a site for a house to accommodate a prior and 12 friars in Walsingham.

In the latter part of the thirteenth century the Franciscans made attempts to establish a house in New Romney, but it did not exist for long. In 1331, a licence was obtained to establish a house in Maidstone, but the foundation was never made.

The Franciscans entered South Wales in 1280, when they established a house in Cardiff, and extended their work to Carmarthen a few years later. Their Carmarthen friary became the most prosperous mendicant house in Wales.

Princess Joan, wife of Llywelyn the Great, Prince of Wales and daughter of King John, died in 1237 and was buried in consecrated ground in Llanfaes, Anglesey. In 1240, Llywelyn built a house for Franciscan friars on the site, as a monument to her and as a place where saintly men could pray for her soul. The small, but prosperous, house was sited near the shore of the Menai Strait and friars from the house served the people of Gwynedd and Snowdonia. After the Welsh wars of 1277 to 1282, when Edward I extended English administration over the Principality, he erected a castle and founded a new town at Beaumaris, about a mile to the west of Llanfaes. In 1319, the existing parish church of Llanfaes was destroyed and the inhabitants of the village were moved to Newborough on the south-west coast of Anglesey. Llanfaes friary was spared and experienced the unusual circumstance of being deserted by the

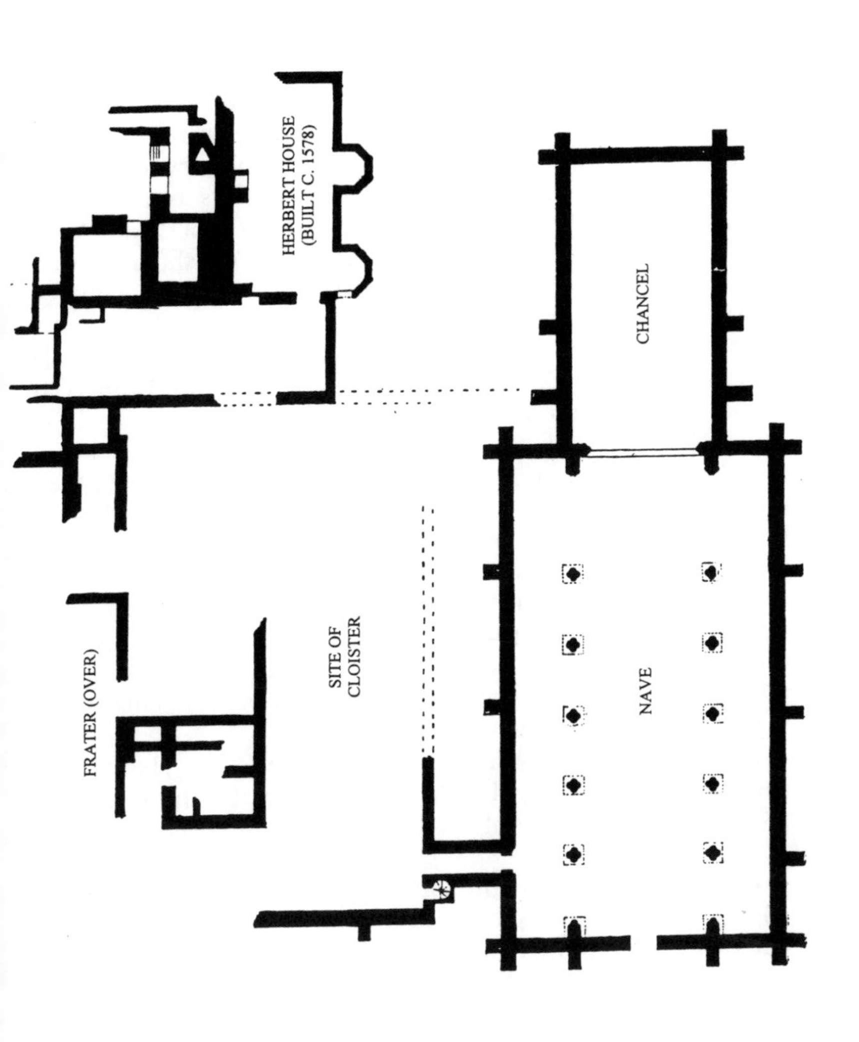

FRANCISCAN FRIARY, CARDIFF

community in which it had settled. The house was not prominent during Edward I's wars but their cemetery was the burial place of many knights slain in the Battle of Menai in November 1282. In 1284, the warden of Llanfaes, along with the prior of Rhuddlan Dominican house, were appointed commissioners to assess the damage sustained by the Welsh church in the wars and to distribute the compensation allotted.

Most local people in and around the Franciscan Welsh houses of Llanfaes and Carmarthen spoke Welsh, and friars from these houses would have used Welsh in their contacts with the people.

As we have seen, Alexander II gave a lot of support to the friars in Scotland. With assistance from the York Franciscan house, he helped the Franciscans to pass into Scotland in 1231, when they entered the town of Berwick-upon-Tweed and founded a house there. He issued a charter which granted them a 'sufficient place' in the burgh to build a church and other buildings, and they received an annual endowment of 20 marks from the town of Berwick.

The Franciscans then pressed on to the Royal Burgh of Roxburgh, in the Border area, in 1233. Royal Burghs were established as trading centres, and Roxburgh, sited as it was on a hill, was an important trading post as well as being one of the principal Border strongholds.

A Franciscan house was established in Haddington sometime before 1242. The friary was burnt by the English in 1355 but was rebuilt, only to be burnt again by the English in 1544.

An alleged charter of foundation dated 1234, although considered a spurious charter by some, states that Alan of Galloway, grandfather of John Balliol King of Scots, with the help of friars from Carlisle, established a house in Dumfries. A Franciscan house was founded at Dundee, sometime before her death in 1289, by Lady Devorgilla, the mother of John Balliol, who later became King of Scots. She may have established the house in memory of her husband, also a John Balliol. In 1273, this pious lady founded Sweetheart Abbey as a labour of love, in memory of her husband, and carried his heart in a casket until her death, when it was buried with her in Sweetheart Abbey. A church council met in the Dundee friary church on 24 February 1310 when senior Scottish clergy declared their support for Robert the Bruce's claim to the Scottish crown. The former burial ground and orchards of the Dundee house are now an open space known as the Howff, in the centre of the town. Its church was said to have had a substantial steeple.

In about 1281, William, Earl of Ross, founded a Franciscan house in Elgin. How long the Franciscans remained in Elgin is uncertain but there is no record of them having been in the town when in 1390 the notorious 'Wolf of Badenock', son of King Robert II, was on the rampage there.

King David I acquired land in Inverkeithing in 1224, where he built a royal palace. A Franciscan house was established near the palace, but, although it is generally agreed that the house was established not long before 1346, its foundation date is unknown. In that year, the bailies of the town remitted to the friars a local tax due to the town for a certain tenement in Inverkeithing, and the local charter authorising it stated that the tenement would in future be free from payments of the tax and other secular burdens. This no doubt refers to the friary buildings. The hospitium, which formed the west wing of the cloisters, is still complete and is used by a number of local organisations.

In 1328–9, during the political disorder in Robert the Bruce's reign, he established a Franciscan presence in Lanark, but it was not until 1346 that a papal bull was issued authorising the erection of the house. James II founded a late house at Kirkcudbright sometime between 1449 and 1456. Most Scottish houses were smaller and had fewer friars than their English counterparts.

By the end of the fifteenth century there were 53 Conventual Franciscan houses in England, three in Wales and seven in Scotland, with about 2,500 brethren. The Elgin, Canterbury, Newcastle-upon-Tyne and Southampton houses are not included in the numbers as they were then Observants houses.

The first house of Franciscan nuns in England was started at Northampton, where, in 1252, Henry III ordered the sheriff to provide the nuns with five habits, but the community did not flourish and within 20 years ceased to exist. In 1286, John de Vescy bought the former house of the Sack Friars in Newcastle-upon-Tyne and tried to found a house of Franciscan sisters. The effort did not meet with success, nor did a later effort to establish a community of Franciscan nuns in Hull.

Only three houses of Poor Clares took root in England. Their large London house at Aldergate was founded in 1293, when a small community of sisters was set up. Due to the generosity of Blanche, wife of Edmond, Earl of Lancaster, brother of Edward I, the sisters soon acquired a good deal of property, from which they drew considerable rents.

In 1294, a wealthy lady named Denise de Munchesney gave the Poor Clare nuns a site at her manor of Waterbeach, six miles from Cambridge, but the site was prone to flooding. The Knights Templars' house at Denney a few miles away started in 1159 as a small community of Benedictine monks and, in 1170, became a house for aged and infirm Knights Templars. The house was vacated by the Templars in 1312 following the suppression of the order. The Countess of Pembroke, founder of Pembroke College, Cambridge, took an interest in the work of the nuns at Waterbeach and when, in 1342, she acquired the former Denney property of the Knights Templars, she transferred the sisters from Waterbeach to better accommodation there. The Countess incorporated her own private apartments in the house, in order to join with the nuns in worship from time to time. It was intended to replace the nuns at Waterbeach with friars but about 20 nuns objected to the move to Denney and remained at Waterbeach. By 1360, the site was desolate, possibly as a result of the Black Death. The Denney house owned four manors and the appropriation of four churches. There were 41 nuns in Denney in 1379 and 35 in 1538, when the house was suppressed. The ruined remains of the Denney Abbey were placed into the guardianship of the Ministry of Works (English Heritage) in 1952.

Maud, Countess of Ulster, established a chantry in Bruisyard, near Framlingham, Suffolk, in 1346, but the chantry priest neglected the services. Maud suppressed the chantry and in 1366 turned it into a house of Poor Clares and 13 sisters from Denney went there to establish the house.

In 1486, James, Earl of Morton, placed a former hospital at Aberdour at the disposal of Franciscan nuns, but it remained a small house with an average of eight sisters. In 1502, James Fotheringham granted St James Chapel, which he had founded in Dundee, to Franciscan nuns for the establishment of a house for a prioress and 12 sisters, but it is doubtful if the complement of the house ever reached that number and the house was closed in 1560.

FRANCISCAN OBSERVANTS FRIARS

In 1463, Pope Pius II wrote to the Vicar General of the Franciscan Observants Northern Province:

> We have learned that, on the account of the devotion of Queen Mary [of Guelders] of Scotland and of that people, at the request of certain merchants, you have sent your brethren to that kingdom in which no houses of Observant's of your order have been built. We therefore grant you power to erect, found and build and likewise to receive in that kingdom three or four houses, or if you can find anyone who would proffer a foundation or erection of this sort.

Bishop Kennedy, cousin of James II, was associated with the Queen in establishing and patronising the Franciscan Observants friars in Scotland.

In 1467, the General Chapter of the Franciscan Observants Order constituted the Scottish Province, headed by a Prior Provincial.

There were probably Franciscan Observants friars from Holland based in Edinburgh prior to 1463, and in 1479 the friary consisted of 12 friars, including the prior. Bishop Kennedy founded a Franciscan Observants house in St Andrews sometime between 1463 and 1466, where friars settled in order to have an influence at the religious centre of Scotland. Franciscan Observants established themselves in Aberdeen in 1469 and two years later they erected a small church, which was rebuilt on a larger scale between 1518 and 1532.

As we have noted, a Franciscan house was founded in Elgin in 1281 but it appears that it was later abandoned. In 1479, Pope Sixtus IV confirmed the erection of a Franciscan Observants house in Elgin, which was built close to the former Franciscan house.

In 1482, the Bishop of Dunkeld received permission from Pope Sixtus IV to found two or three more houses of the order in Scotland. James IV, remembered for his generosity to, and defence of, the Franciscan Observants friars in his kingdom, is credited with founding Observants houses at Ayr between 1488 and 1497, Sterling in 1494, and Perth between 1488 and 1496. A late house of Observants was founded in Jedburgh about 1505, and in 1513 a house was erected for them by the inhabitants of the town. In a letter to Pope Julius II in 1507, the King described the virtues of the Observants friars: 'They stood for the salvation of the soul, they had remedied the neglect of others, they ministered the sacraments and faithfully proclaimed Christ's word'.

The order established itself more slowly in England. In 1454, Henry VI wrote to the Vicar General of the order, asking if he would send a party of Franciscan Observants friars to England, but he replied it was not possible at that time and suggested that he approach the order in France, but nothing came of it.

In 1482, they established their first English house in Greenwich, founded by Edward IV in the year of his death. As there were no English Observants friars to man the house, a party of about 12 friars from the Low Countries arrived in England in 1482, but it was not long before they were joined by Englishmen. The friary is shown in contemporary drawings of the palace as a plain building.

In 1498, the Pope asked the Archbishop of Canterbury and the Bishops of Durham and Ely to choose five of the existing

Franciscan houses where the friars could be removed and the houses handed over to the Observants. In the end they managed to let three Conventual houses become Observants houses: Newcastle-upon-Tyne, where plans were already being made to transfer the house to the Observants, Southampton, where things were somewhat relaxed, and Canterbury, where there was a flourishing and reasonably conscientious community. There was a later proposal to set up a house in Wakefield but it came to nothing. In 1499, Henry VII had an Observants house built adjacent to his royal palace at Sheen, in Richmond (Surrey). The last Observants house in England was founded by Henry VII at Newark in 1507. They had no houses in Wales.

The Franciscan Observants friars established six houses in England and nine in Scotland. At first, the Franciscan Observants houses in England were put under the jurisdiction of the Franciscan Observants Province of Cologne but were constituted as a separate province in 1499.

In 1486, an Observants house was founded in Guernsey, though from the start it was incorporated in the Franciscan Observants Province of France.

Although it was a very small order in Britain, because of royal patronage and their reputation for holy living, the friars had considerably more influence than their numbers would suggest. They were a small but influential order in an age of waning fervour.

AUSTIN FRIARS

Friar Hermits of the Order of St Augustine, or Austin friars, as they were known in Britain, were the smallest of the four major mendicant orders. They were introduced into Britain by Richard de Clare, Earl of Gloucester, head of one of the most powerful medieval families in England, and they were attracted to England by the favourable disposition of Henry III towards the mendicant orders. Friars of the order, almost certainly Italians from Tuscany, arrived in England on 3 September

1249 and received a welcome from Henry III, who informed them that they could stay in his land and that good would be done to them by everyone.

In 1249, de Clare gave the Austin friars a site at the foot of his castle in Clare, Suffolk. Clare Friary, which was rebuilt by Elizabeth de Burgh in the fourteenth century, became the parent house of the Austin Order in Britain. Following the dissolution of the house in 1538, a country house was built on the site of the west range. Clare Priory House, as it was known, was vacated, and, on the Feast of Our Lady of Good Council in 1953, was purchased by Austin friars from Ireland. Austin friars have, after an absence of four centuries, returned to their parent house, which now has a community which uses it for residential training and educational activities. The former infirmary of the friary is now used as their church.

Their second house was established in 1250, when a group of hermits from Tuscany settled in Woodhouse, a remote uncultivated hillside site two miles west of Cleobury Mortimer, Shropshire. The location was well suited to the hermits' early ideals of contemplative retreat, although they must have found it much colder there than in Tuscany.

The brethren who settled in Woodhouse must have soon made a good impression on the local people, as in 1254 they received a request from the people of Ludlow, a town about ten miles from Woodhouse, for them to establish a house in the town. They were first given a house in Dinham, near the castle, but they were soon given a large open space on the eastern outskirts of the town, where their friary was subsequently built. A stream which provided a water supply for the friary ran through the friary grounds, and the friars dammed it in places so as to provide a fishpond for the house.

In 1253, Austin friars established their London house on the site where the Dutch Church is, near the Stock Exchange. It became a large and important house of the order. After the Reformation the church was used by a Protestant congregation until it was destroyed by a bomb in an air raid in 1940.

It appears that the Austins formed a temporary settlement at Crosshill on the north side of Shrewsbury but the location was unfavourable. Following a petition to the Austin friars from the burgesses of Shrewsbury, to settle in their town, Austin friars from Crosshill and Woodhouse settled there in 1255. In the following year they were given a plot of Crown land near Welsh Bridge, between the town wall and the river Severn. In 1337, the friary was fortified and made part of the town wall defences and was occupied by the town's armed forces at times of war. Otherwise the house was at the brothers' disposal.

As we have seen, in 1256 the Pope called on the Austin friars to establish houses in towns rather than in remote areas.When they established themselves in a town with two or more mendicant houses, other than for Ludlow and Gorleston (Yarmouth), the Austin friars were the last mendicant order to be established in the town.

When in 1265 the separate English Province was established, it consisted of seven houses, all of which were in the first stages of development. One of the new province's first projects was to establish a house for the order in Oxford, so as to provide the best possible education for their novices. In 1266, they established a presence in Oxford, and, a year later, were given land in the town by Bogo de Clare, brother of the founder of the Clare house. In 1268 they settled on the site of the later Wadham College. By 1289, there was a nucleus of Austin friars in Cambridge, where they were given a site, which they were later able to extend, on which the Zoology Museum and Whipple Museum now stand.

In 1256, the Austin friars were established on the outskirts of Tickhill, eight miles south of Doncaster. Here, the ideal of solitude was preserved and the house attracted many who had the inclination for the hermitical way of life. Tickhill castle, built by Richard the Lion Heart, was the administrative centre for the Lordship of Tickhill, and in 1334 the town was second only to Doncaster in wealth within south Yorkshire. It had a population listed for taxation in 1379 consisting of 176 married couples and 109 single people over the age of 16.

About a third of their English settlements were in small towns or remote areas. Their main activities were concentrated in the eastern half of England, with a few houses in the Welsh Marches and the south-west.

The earliest reference to the Huntington Austin house is in 1258, when Henry III gave four oaks towards its building. In 1286, the friary buildings were burnt to the ground and John le Romayne, Archbishop of York, granted an indulgence of 20 days to all who helped in its rebuilding. In 1477, Pope Sixtus IV granted an indulgence of seven years to all the faithful who helped in the upkeep of the Austin Huntington house.

In 1271, friars from Tickhill were able to establish their important house in York. They settled on a cramped site between Lendal and the River Ouse, where the main post office now is. When Richard III was Duke of York, he stayed in the Austin house when visiting York. About 1293, friars from Tickhill established a house in Grimsby. Also in 1293 they established a presence in Kingston-upon-Hull, but it was not until 1317, when they were given a plot of land and received a royal licence to build their house, that a party of brethren from their York house were sent to establish a permanent presence in the town.

The Austin friars expanded their order in the north of England when, in 1291, friars from the newly established house at Newcastle-upon-Tyne were given a dwelling place and land in Penrith to establish a house; but the house remained small. In 1381 the order established a presence in Barnard Castle but the house survived for only a few years.

Some time before 1267, they established a house at Gorleston, on the southern outskirts of Yarmouth. It is strange that they did not establish themselves in the town but perhaps they arrived before 1256, when they still preferred solitary sites. Following the dates pattern, it appears that by 1289 brethren from Gorleston established a house in Norwich, and were in King's Lynn by 1295. Sometime between 1295 and 1299 Austin brethren from London settled in Orford, on the Suffolk coast near Ipswich. Orford was then a thriving little seaport, but it lost its importance when the sea threw up a sandbank offshore.

Austin friars established themselves sometime before 1272, by a busy thoroughfare near the bridge crossing the Mersey in Warrington, the ancient trading post on the River Mersey.

A site in Chichester was donated to them in 1282 but, as the house would have been within the prescribed distance of 1500 feet from the Chichester Franciscan friars' house, they were refused permission to establish a house on the site.

In 1318, Edward II granted the request of Archbishop Reynolds to give to the Austin friars the place in Canterbury that had belonged to the Friars of the Sack, who abandoned it in 1314. The location, however, proved unsatisfactory and the Austins bought a piece of land in St George's Parish. The advowson of the parish was held by the monks of Christ Church Priory and the Austins had to agree to pay every tax due on their property.

The order arrived in Winchester sometime before 1300, when they were given a site outside the city walls, but it is possible that they arrived in the town as early 1252. Pope Clement VI instructed the bishop of Winchester, in 1343, to grant a licence to the Winchester Austins to accept a house in the city given them by Sir Oliver Bohun, but the Bishop, for some unknown reason, opposed the move. Three years later, the Austins received the Pope's consent to proceed to the new site without the consent of the Bishop.

The order attempted to spread into the south-west of England. Townstal church, whose advowson was held by Torre Abbey (Torquay), was the parish church for the flourishing port of Dartmouth. However, the church was on a hill and some distance from the town, resulting in the parishioners in the town having a tiring climb every time they went to church. The burgesses of Dartmouth built a church near the waterside without the permission of the Bishop and, in 1331, two Austin friars were invited to minister there. As episcopal permission had not been obtained, Bishop Grandison of Exeter forbade the friars to use the church, and, in 1347, the friars abandoned the site. St Saviour's Church, Dartmouth, was built on the site of their church a decade or so after the friars had left. After their failure in Dartmouth, the Bishop of Exeter offered the

Austin friars a site in Barnstable, when, in 1348, they tried to establish a house in the town; but unfortunately the outbreak of the Black Death that year hindered their attempt. The prior of the Clunic priory in Barnstable was hostile to the new undertaking.

Also in 1331, they began a work in Droitwich, their only Austin house in Worcestershire, and not far from their early houses at Woodhouse and Ludlow.

The Austins were given eight acres in Northallerton in 1340 to build a house, but if the house ever came into existence it may have come to a premature end due to the ravages of the Black Death.

The Austins were given the site of the former Sack friary in Stamford in 1342, and the house gained importance through its school of rhetoric and philosophy.

In 1364, Pope Urban V authorised the establishment of four houses, providing each house could maintain 12 brethren. In the same year, Austin friars from Canterbury established a house in Rye, the only Austin house on the south coast. Their first site was on East Cliff, but in 1377 French marauders burnt the friary and town of Rye. The friars' misfortune proved to be a blessing, for in 1378 they were given a better site within the town. The church of the new Rye house still survives and is now used as a saleroom.

In 1375, the Austin friars were assigned 12 acres of land near the market place in Atherstone, six miles from Nuneaton, Warwickshire, in order to save the parishioners a burdensome walk to their distant parish church at Mancetter. At that time Atherstone was a small town, but it was situated on Watling Street, the Roman road which ran from London to Shrewsbury and beyond. In 1524, the town had an approximate population of 600 occupying 135 houses. It remained a small house and it is doubtful if it ever achieved the compliment of 12 brethren. The chancel and octagonal tower of the present Atherstone parish church are parts of the friars' church.

Newport (Gwent) was the third of four houses authorised by Pope Urban V. This was their only house in Wales; 1377 is the earliest recorded date for it but it was probably founded before then. In 1387, John of Gaunt brought the Austin friars to Thetford, where he built a church and conventual buildings for them. In addition, they were given St John's church on the other side of Thetford, which they repaired and used as a chapel for the hospital they maintained there. The Thetford house was the last Austin house founded in medieval England.

Their Berwick-upon-Tweed house was possibly founded before the death of Alexander III in 1286, and was the only house of the order in Scotland. It was a small house in 1299, with six friars who received alms from Edward I during his stay in the town.

James IV, who had become acquainted with the Reformed Austins, petitioned Pope Julius II that St Laurence Hospital in the Royal Burgh of Haddington be suppressed and converted into an Austin Observants house. The hospital was suppressed, but a letter of 1514 from the King to the Pope stated that the friars did not take possession of the house.

In 1503, James gave a royal gift of £14 towards the establishment of an Observants house near his royal palace in Linlithgow, but this project also failed. James then asked Pope Julius II to authorise the transfer of the five remaining nuns from Manuel Priory, south-west of Linlithgow, so as to allow a foundation of Austin Observants friars to use the house. The request was granted in 1511, but it remained a house of nuns as there were still four nuns in the house in 1552.

By 1300, the Austin English Province had 21 houses in England (including Berwick) and, by 1500, they had 33 houses in England, one in Wales, but none in Scotland. They did not take over the Newark and Southampton houses from the Franciscan Observants until 1534. The total lands of the Austins in Britain did not exceed 350 acres.

CARMELITE FRIARS

The Carmelite friars arrived in England at the end of 1241 with Lord de Grey who was returning from the crusades with Richard, Earl of Cornwall. After being presented to the King, they divided into two small parties. Early in 1242, one party went with William de Vesci of Alnwick Castle, who gave them a site in Hulne, near Alnwick, Northumberland. The other party went with Richard de Grey, who gave them a site in Aylesford, near Maidstone.

The party that went to Hulne in 1242 arrived at an isolated place in the comparatively peaceful times before the wars of the Scottish succession. During and after the wars, Hulne Friary was exposed to Scottish cattle raiders and other marauders, and the friars had to defend their house by a strong battlemented curtain wall which was reached by steps from the enclosure. In about 1488 a tower-house was added by the Earl of Northumberland for the defence of the brethren in time of peril. Because of its secluded situation, the house was mainly used by friars who wished to follow the contemplative and ascetic way of life. The life was harsh and rigorous and the brethren spent much of their time in their cells in silent prayer. The small unadorned narrow windows in the remains of the long but narrow church speak of the simplicity of the life of the brethren.

The second party established themselves in Aylesford, also in 1242, and under the leadership of Simon Stocks the house became the head house of the Carmelite Order in England. Following the dissolution of the friary in 1538, the church was demolished and parts of the cloister range were converted into a country house. However, this is one of the happier outcomes, for, in 1949, the site was purchased by the Carmelite Order, who have re-established a friary on the site. It is now a thriving and lively community and the mother house of the worldwide Carmelite Order.

They were also given a remote site, sometime between 1242 and 1247, at Lossenham, near Newenden, Kent, but due to its isolation it remained a poor house.

The first Carmelites were offered isolated or unsuitable sites and as many as a quarter of their friaries moved from their original sites to new and better sites. Between 1243 and 1247, they were given a site in Bradmer on the north Norfolk coast, but it proved to be unsuitable and, in 1253, they moved to nearby Burnham Norton. During the fourteenth and fifteenth centuries the house had a thriving community with an average of 15 friars. The gatehouse, a rough outline of their church and the boundary wall can still be seen at the Burnham Norton site. It was the last Carmelite house founded in the province before the revision of the rule of 1247 allowing the Carmelites to settle in towns.

With their houses tucked away in sparsely populated areas, the Carmelites found themselves out of reach of the goodwill of would-be benefactors, and the realists among them were aware of the potential of towns, especially university towns, as a source of recruitment. Their later houses, except Maldon and Blakeney, were sited in regional towns, but recruits did not flock to the order in the same manner as they did to the early Dominicans and Franciscans and there were bigger gaps between establishing a house and establishing daughter houses.

In 1247, with their new-found freedom following their licence to settle in towns, they established their London house on a site running from Fleet Street down to the River Thames. It was one of the largest houses of their order in Britain.

As did other orders, they made access to university education a priority. In 1247, a small party settled in Chesterton, a mile or so north of Cambridge. Sometime between 1251 and 1256 they were given a site at Newham on the western side of the River Cam, and took up residence there in 1256. The site suffered flooding in winter and students were not able to come to the friars for study, nor were the friars able to go to Cambridge to obtain supplies. The Carmelites petitioned the King in 1290 for permission to accept a gift of a house in Cambridge where they could build anew. The were given permission to accept the land between what is now King's College and Queens' College, and in 1292 they moved to their new site.

Also in 1256, the Carmelites were given a house in Stockwell Street (now Worcester Street), Oxford. When, after his defeat at the battle of Bannockburn in 1314, Edward II was fleeing from the Scots, he vowed to the Blessed Virgin Mary that if he escaped he would found a friary. In fulfilment of the vow,

Edward made preparations to establish a Carmelite house in Oxford by housing 24 Carmelite friars in the Manor House of Sheen (later called Richmond Palace) from 1315 to 1318, while he made preparations for a dwelling-place for them in Oxford. In 1318 the King gave them Beaumount Palace in Oxford, the palace where Kings Richard I and John were born in the previous century. The palace did not have a chapel so they used one in the side aisle of the church of St Mary Magdalen until their own chapel was ready. In 1328, the mayor and bailiffs of Oxford were commanded to remove harlots and other women of bad character from houses in the neighbourhood of the Carmelite house and were instructed to prevent the nearby houses being let to such people in the future.

They established houses in Lincoln by 1260 and Stamford by 1268. Their Stamford house must have been of considerable size, since Edward III held one of his Great Council meetings there. Carmelite friars from these houses went on to establish a house in Boston in 1293.

Friars from Hulne established a house in Berwick-upon-Tweed by 1262, but after the momentous years between then and about 1335, nothing is known about this house for nearly two centuries. In 1262, Carmelites also from Hulne established themselves in the Wall Knoll site in Newcastle-upon-Tyne, and in 1307 they were permitted to move to the vacated Sack Friars' house to the west of Newcastle castle.

Friars from Aylesford reached Sandwich by 1268, and were established in Shoreham by 1317; in 1326 they obtained the former Shoreham house of the Knights Templars. However, due to the incursion of the sea, they had to move again, and in 1480 they leased the alien Sele Benedictine Priory (Upper Beeding) from Magdalen College, Oxford. Magdalen College had obtained the property after the decline of the priory, the last Benedictine prior being deposed for converting the house for his sole use.

A party of Carmelites settled in York sometime before 1253. Their first site was at the north end of Gillygate, outside the town walls, but in 1295 they were given a new site near St Helen's Church, Stonegate, near the King's Fish-pond. By

1316 their new house was large enough for a Parliament to sit in the church.

They established a house in Bristol in 1256, which had an active outreach work. In about 1261, the Carmelites built an oratory in Bridport, Dorset, but, due to the hostile attitude of the Bishop of Salisbury, they were not allowed to enlarge their site and the house was dissolved a few years later. The Bristol Carmelites established houses in Winchester and Gloucester by 1268 and were in Plymouth by 1296. They settled in Marlborough in 1316, when the mayor of the town and the warden of the castle gave them a site on the High Street. A Carmelite house was started in Taunton in about 1341 but, probably due to the death of its founder in 1345, the work on the house was not completed and it was not established.

The Carmelites attempted to establish a house in Coventry in 1287 but the attempt was blocked by Archbishop Pecham on the grounds that the house would be within the proscribed distance of 1,500 feet from the Coventry Franciscan house. However, a licence was issued in 1342 for the approval of a donor to grant the Carmelites ten acres of land in Coventry for a house of Carmelite friars. The east claustral range, with its cloistered walk, chapter house and vaulted rooms on the ground floor and the dormitory on the first floor, still survives.

There does not appear to be any clear pattern for the progress of establishing Carmelite houses in the East Anglian and Midlands areas where the order was strong. However, the Norwich house, which was established in 1256, is an exception; it became a distinguished house. Carmelites from Norwich established a house in 1293 in the remote sites of Maldon, ten miles east of Chelmsford and a mile from Beeleigh Abbey, who strongly objected to the establishment of a house of friars in their town. Between 1304 and 1316 they established at Blakeney, about 16 miles east of Burnham Norton on the north Norfolk coast, where they built a chancel onto the parish church and used it as their chapel. Local Blakeney landowners gave the friars 13 acres of land near the church and they built their conventual buildings on the outskirts of the town, on the site of Friary Farm. At that time the town was a flourishing seaport, chiefly dealing in the sale of fish, and no doubt many of the friars' activities were with the fishermen. A medieval list of items in Blakeney parish church included a *mappa mundi*, a map of the world, an interesting possession at a time when the town was a seaport.

In 1270, a decision was taken at the Provincial Chapter to found a house in Ipswich and building was started on a site in the centre of Ipswich in the following year. However, it is possible that Carmelite friars had settled in the town before then. The precincts of the friary were extended by taking in tenements during the next 120 years.

The Carmelites established a house in Ludlow in 1350, nearly 100 years after the Austin friars were first established in the town. As this was just after the traumas of the Black Death, they may have been invited into the town as an expression of the town's gratitude for help given by Carmelite friars during the plague. There must have been numerous clashes of loyalties and ministry between these two similar friars' houses in a small town and its surrounding rural area.

The order had one house in Wales, at Denbigh, which was founded between 1343 and 1350, when it was colonised by friars from Chester. Welsh was the language of the local people and the friars serving the town and area would have had to use Welsh in their communications with the townsfolk. Reginald de Grey was to have founded a Carmelite house in Carmarthen but the project was never started.

The order made slow progress in establishing its ten houses in Scotland. They entered Scotland in 1262, when the Bishop of Dunkeld, who probably had some contact with the order in its early days, gave them a chapel in Tullilum on the outskirts of Perth for their first house in Scotland.

In 1273, the Carmelites were invited to settle in Aberdeen, where Reginald le Chen made a series of grants to them until their buildings were completed. They reached Banff between 1321 and 1324, when Robert the Bruce granted them the church of St Mary's in the town. Banff was granted its charter in 1324 by Robert the Bruce and it is possible that the Carmelites were invited to the town as part of its charter. The house, which was sited near the harbour, may have been established in order to give spiritual aid to seafarers.

Sometime before 1293, Carmelite friars from either York or Appelby settled in Irvine, Ayrshire. In 1335, Edward III stayed in the house and gave it a pittance for 20 friars. The first reference to the Carmelites in Luffness occurs in 1293. A small house was established in the Royal Burgh of Inverbervie, a small costal town some ten miles south of Stonehaven. Some authorities claim that the charter purporting to record the establishment of the house in either 1358 or 1388 is not genuine, and that the house was probably established sometime before 1443.

Queen Margaret (1046–93), consort of Malcolm III, gave an endowment to enable ships to give free passage across the Firth of Forth, to pilgrims and the poor, and to establish a hospice in Queensferry for travellers. In 1330 – the date is disputed by some – Sir George Dundas gave the Carmelites the hospice site in Queensferry. It appears the site was given to the Carmelites for them to man the hospice. The Franciscan Inverkeithing house was at the other end of the Firth of Forth ferry and it seems both houses were used as hospices for travellers crossing the Firth. Their church, which was rebuilt in 1441, is a unique survival and is the only medieval Carmelite church still in regular use in Britain. The remaining buildings consist of the chancel, tower and south transept of the 1441 church. It survived destruction at the time of the Reformation, due to the building being handed back to the Dundas family in 1560. However, it is a pity the roof of the church has been retiled with tiles completely out of character with the building.

In about 1401, Sir James Douglas granted the church and grounds of the Blessed Virgin Mary, Linlithgow, to the Carmelites for the establishment of a friary.

A Barony Charter of 1451 was granted to Kingussie, which is beside the River Spey, below the Cairngorns and nine miles south-west of Aviemore. In about 1500, George, Earl of Huntly, invited the Carmelites into the town as part of his plan to establish the new town of Kingussie.

As late as 1520, the Edinburgh town council gave the Queensferry friars a site at Greenside at the foot of Carlton Hill, Edinburgh, for a house, but the friars could not gain possession of the site until 1525. However, due to friction with Holyrood Abbey, the house ceased to exist after about ten years or so.

By 1300, the Carmelites had founded 28 houses in England, none in Wales and four in Scotland, and by 1500 they had 37 houses in England, one in Wales and ten in Scotland.

TRINITARIAN FRIARS

There are references in 1200 to a religious house on the site of Hounslow parish church, which was transferred to the Trinitarian Order sometime before 1252. In 1296, the Hounslow Trinitarian friars were granted weekly markets and an annual fair, and in 1313 Edward II confirmed the gift of the advowson of East Bedfont church and over 80 acres of land to the Hounslow house for the financial support of the hospital. They later received numerous other gifts in land and in kind, and by 1535 it was a comparatively wealthy house with an income from rents and a mill of about £80 per annum.

A Trinitarian house was established in 1224 at Moatenden, near Headcorn, Kent; being on a road to the Kent ports, it was ideally sited for a hospital and reception centre for pilgrims. In 1286, the order acquired a house outside the East Gate, Oxford, and later acquired land within the wall. However, all the Oxford Trinitarian friars died during the Black Death and the house was not reopened. In 1245, a leper hospital was founded in Easton Royal, five miles south of Marlborough, and when it was vacated in 1261 it became a Trinitarian house. It may have been established on this remote site as a hostel on a long-forgotten pilgrim highway. The house was destroyed by fire in 1493 and not rebuilt, but some brethren continued to occupy it.

In the latter part of the twelfth century, William de Lucy signed to go on the fifth crusade but, for some reason unknown to us, was unable to go. He therefore decided to endow a religious hospice at Thelsford, a mile from his home at Charlecote. For centuries Charlecote was the home of the Lucy family, who in 1945 presented it to the National Trust. Sometime before 1240, it might have been as early as 1224, the Thelsford house was reorganised and became a Trinitarian hospital, which had an uneventful history. The house received considerable gifts of land and had the advowson of four local churches.

In the thirteenth century, Knaresborough was a small market town of only about 90 houses and an adult population of about 250, but it had a strong castle which was one of the principal royal strongholds in the north of England. Robert Flower (1160–1218), son of a mayor of York, took up the life of a hermit and went to live in a cave by the River Nidd in the vicinity of the Knaresborough. Robert's brother, Walter, believed that the rough accommodation was too lowly for a member of a prominent York family and had the chapel of the Holy Cross built near the cave. When Robert died in 1218, he was buried in the chapel built into his cave and his tomb became an object of veneration by pilgrims. In about 1252, Trinitarian friars built a church near the town, dedicated to the Holy Trinity, to accommodate Robert's remains. Although Robert was never officially canonised by Rome, he was renowned across Europe throughout the Middle Ages as a saint and his new grave attracted a large number of pilgrims who left numerous gifts. The friars also received valuable gifts of land and the advowson of four or five parish churches, and were able to build their house and hostel adjacent to their church. In 1318, the house, along with most of Knaresborough, was pillaged by Scottish raiders who, following the battle of Bannockburn, forayed deep into the northern parts of England, but the house was rebuilt. A plaque on a farm building on the site of the former hospital, near the river and a mile or so outside the town, states that the Trinitarian house supported 12 friars. No doubt this refers to both the friars and layworkers of the house.

Walter and Agatha le Bon appear to have had no son, and

in 1270 they handed over, in the presence of the Bishop of Exeter, their house and extensive garden in Totnes, so that a chapel might be erected in the name of the Holy Ghost and St Katherine. In the following year Trinitarian friars were established in the house, the Trinitarian Honslow house being responsible for appointing the warden for the house. In 1508 the Bishop of Exeter obtained a licence from Henry VII to suppress the Totnes house and give its lands to the vicars choral of Exeter Cathedral.

In 1307, the Carmelites moved from their Wall Knott site in Newcastle-upon-Tyne to the site of the former Sack friars in the town. The vacated Wall Knott site was taken over by Trinitarian friars in 1361.

The last Trinitarian house founded in England was established in Ingham, Norfolk, in 1360, when Sir Miles Stapleton obtained a licence for Ingham parish church to be rebuilt, with the nave of the new church remaining parochial and the chancel, separated from the nave by an open work screen, becoming monastic. The Trinitarian friars who occupied the monastic side of the church followed the Rule of St Victor, a sixth-century hermit who lived in Plancy, Central France, and whose cult was especially popular in the twelfth century. The Trinitarian prior, or minister, had the care of the monastic side of the church, and his sacrist had the care of the parishioners. It remained a small establishment. The church still survives and is now the parish church.

At the time of the dissolution of the order in England, the Hertford, Easton Royal, Newcastle and Ingham houses had been abandoned.

The Trinitarian friars in Scotland were known as Red friars. There were a number of unauthentic foundations of the order in Scotland, where it appears some Trinitarian houses were never established on a permanent basis. This might have been due to their receiving insufficient financial support to enable them to survive. Because of the obscurity of the Scottish houses and the lack of documentation on the order, the list of Trinitarian Scottish houses is incomplete and their number is not known. However, it is generally accepted that seven Trinitarian houses achieved permanent establishment in Scotland.

The first mention of the Peebles Trinitarian house occurred in 1296 when the master of the house swore fealty to Edward I. However, there is a tradition that Alexander III had a church in honour of the Holy Rood (Cross) built in 1262, following the discovery on the site of an impressive and venerable fourth-century cross associated with St Nicholas. Much of the Peebles church still survives and is now an Ancient Monument in the charge of Historic Scotland. It is a simple rectangular building with no division between the monastic choir and the aisleless nave. The monastic and infirmary buildings were ranged around the three sides of the cloister, with the church on the fourth side. The bell tower, which also served as an entrance porch to the church, was added at the west end of the church in the fifteenth century.

In about 1240–48 the minister of Berwick Trinitarian house was given the custody of a new house at Dunbar and he was to provide for divine worship in the church, but it remained a small and poor house.

In 1250–51, the Red friars were granted the newly built hospital of St Mary's at Scotlandwell, by David de Bernham, bishop of St Andrews. It was sited on the eastern side of Loch Leven, adjacent to a health-giving well, the waters of which, it was claimed, helped cure the sick. The well site has been cleared and is now celebrated for its medicinal waters.

The Trinitarian house at Houston, midway between Haddington and North Berwick, was founded in about 1270 by Christiana, widow of Sir Roger Murbary.

The date of the founding of their Aberdeen house is uncertain and little is known about it. It first appeared in records in 1273.

The foundation date for Fail, or Failford, is unknown but it is first recorded in 1335, but some authorities state it was founded in about 1252.

In 1300, there were eight Trinitarian houses in England and three in Scotland. In 1500, there were 11 houses in England and seven in Scotland. There were no houses of the order in Wales and just one in Ireland, at Adare, County Limerick.

4

FRIARY BUILDINGS

A friary is by definition a friars' church with a range of accommodation sited around a cloister. However, Dominican establishments were called priories but, to avoid repetition, they are referred to as friaries here.

Friars' houses were not places where the lives of members of the community were normally spent; rather they were resting places between journeys, sleeping places for men whose activities often took them away.

The foundation of new mendicant houses in the early days was a simple matter; ordinary houses or temporary wooden buildings sufficed. The Second Franciscan General Council decreed that their churches should be poor and humble and that their other buildings should be of wood, or wattle with clay, and that costly buildings were to be destroyed. Receiving stone-built churches was originally contrary to the Franciscans' rules. Friars were strictly forbidden to have excesses in vaulting or flamboyant and elaborate masonry. In 1236, the Southampton burgesses, out of goodwill towards the Franciscan friars in their town, provided them with a stone cloister, but Agnellus, the English Provincial, heard about it and ordered that the cloisters be destroyed because the stone structure was contrary to the rule of St Francis. A stone cloister built by the citizens of Shrewsbury for the Franciscans was also pulled down, in face of considerable opposition from the townspeople. In London, Agnellus found that the friars had built their dormitory with stone walls, so he had these pulled down and replaced by simpler ones of clay. At Reading he was prevented from pulling down a

GREYFRIARS LICHFIELD

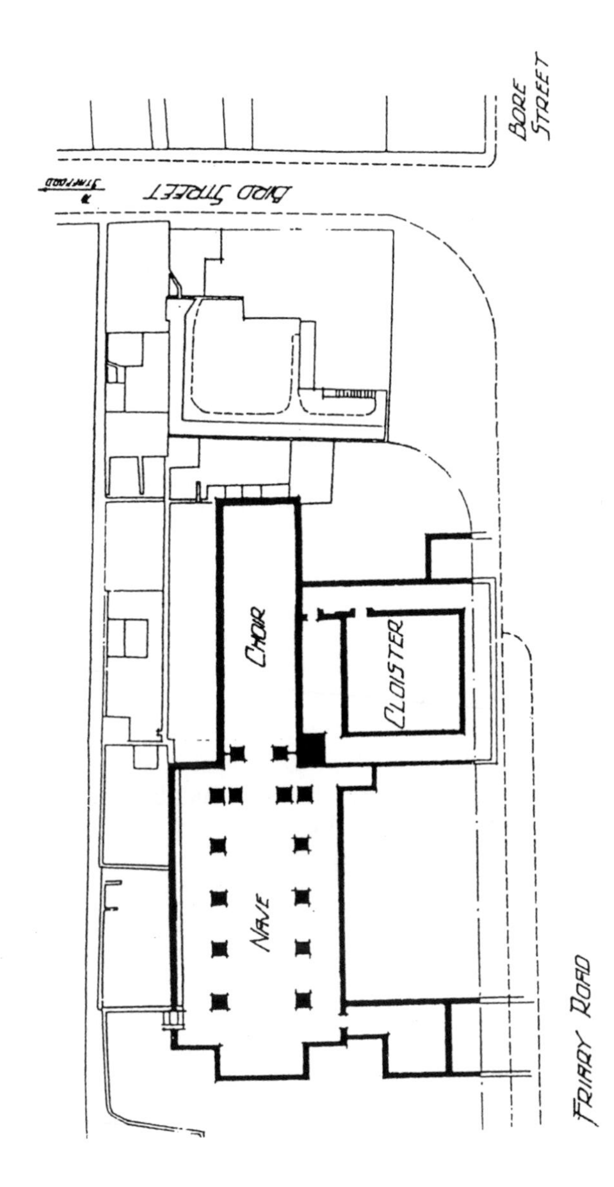

chapel of the Franciscan church, as it had been provided by the King.

Inevitably, as time went by, friars became more fixed in a locality, and the old, temporary lodgings were abandoned in favour of buildings specially constructed as religious houses. The rules of austerity in buildings were relaxed as the plea of necessity began to assert itself over the early rules. The rapid growth in the numbers of brethren required larger houses and larger sites; also, as persons of quality entered the orders, friars considered it fitting that more honourable provision and accommodation be made for them. Donors were permitted to erect stone churches for the friars, and gradually the original hovels gave way to more comfortable buildings.

The rough outline of Burnham Norton Carmelite church, which was built of stone, can be seen, but the lack of surviving evidence of conventual buildings which must have stood on the site suggest that they were made of timber which has either rotted away or been carried away and reused elsewhere.

The constitution framed by St Dominic ruled that no Dominican church should have walls more than 30 feet high, but larger crowds necessitated bigger churches with good acoustics, and the rule didn't last long.

Most of their early churches were long, rectangular, aisleless buildings without a structural chancel, with a roof running the whole length of the church. The Lincoln Franciscan church is a good example of such a building.

The first friaries occupied little land but, as it became necessary to enlarge houses, it also became necessary to enlarge their original sites. In accordance with Dominican and Franciscan rules, they were not to acquire land save for the house itself. The precincts of friaries were gradually extended piecemeal during their period of expansion by taking in tenement after tenement and small plots of land adjacent to the cartilage of their houses. There are numerous references to friars obtaining licences to divert ancient rights of way that ran alongside their land, either to enlarge the site of the friary or to make a roadway from the town to their church. Most friaries gradually acquired between three and ten acres of land for their house and accommodation buildings, but secular buildings were not allowed to be erected within the curtilage of a friary.

However, the precincts of some friaries were small. The precincts of the Newcastle-upon-Tyne Franciscan friary was 3.5 acres, their Lincoln house had four acres, their Shrewsbury house had four acres, their important Oxford house only had nine acres and their large London house was enclosed within a four-acre curtilage.

As the friars became increasingly popular in the latter part of the thirteenth century, they became an integral part of the life of the community. This brought them considerable financial support, which enabled them to build larger churches and accommodation.

There were about 250 friaries of differing sizes in Britain at the end of the fifteenth century. The aims of the friars generally rendered it essential that their houses be in or near towns and, as a result, at the dissolution of the houses, or when they were dissolved, many sites were acquired for redevelopment, which resulted in the rapid spoliation of the buildings. Few buildings, or even fragmentary remains of them, have survived and relatively little is known about a number of the houses, especially the smaller ones. In some instances even the location of the former friary is not known. A few friary buildings, or fragments of buildings, have survived, to give us an idea of the layout. The buildings of the Gloucester Dominican friary retain much of their original plan, with its clusteral rooms around the cloister and parts of the roofs of all four cloisteral ranges. Fortunately when redevelopment took place on a number of sites, archaeological excavations were carried out which traced details of the layout of the buildings; this, coupled with cartographic evidence, has increased our knowledge of friaries.

At first, the friars' churches were built with the utmost simplicity, but the general public did not allow friars to continue to erect such austere buildings and by the end of the thirteenth century, friars, and their patrons, paid scant attention to the original directives. This was partly due to the

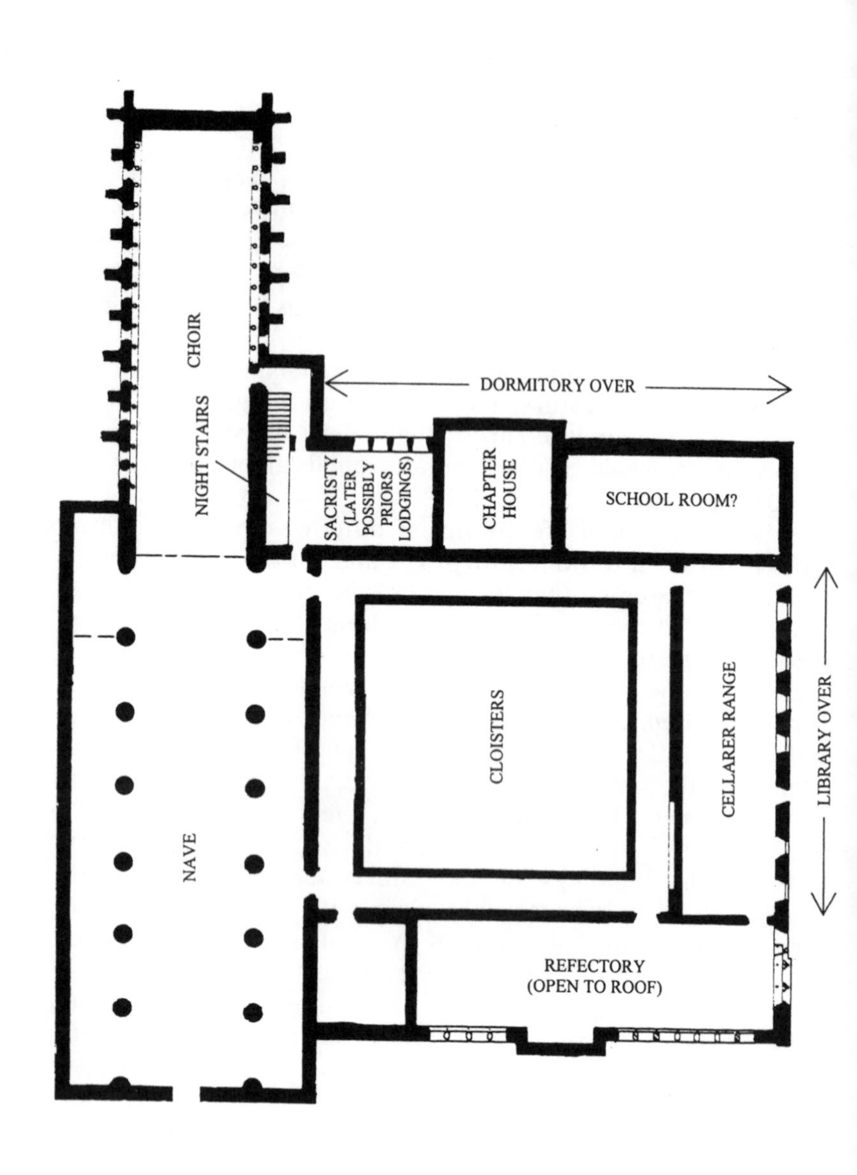

DOMINICAN FRIARY, GLOUCESTER

unforeseen necessity for larger church buildings and partly due to the fact that benefactors who were paying for the various building projects were often more concerned about the visible evidence of their good works and expected to see impressive results for their money, and therefore could dictate the style of new work without reference to past ideals. They had different views from St Francis and St Dominic and considered that the greatness and beauty of God should be mirrored in the places where He was worshipped; but they had to bear in mind the ideal of poverty, which had to be reflected in the simplicity of architecture. The type of church which evolved to suit their requirements was both imposing and spacious, as can be seen from the former Norwich Dominican Church, which, shorn of all its colour and ornamentation, shows how impressive such a building could be.

Their later churches were planned on the auditorium system, making the length and width nearly equal so that no one would be far from the pulpit. As a result, they tended to become barn-like preaching halls, known as hall churches, with large aisled naves of equal width and height, unencumbered by pillars or screens. But tradition dictated that the naves were a little wider than the side aisles. In hall churches, the roofs of the aisles were the same height as the nave, and a clerestory upper range of windows shed light into the nave. The Early English style (1150–1300) was characterised by pointed arches, lancet windows and simple tracery. The Decorated style of architecture (1300–70) was characterised by geometric window tracery and floral decoration in churches other than friaries. The Perpendicular style of architecture (1370–1550) emphasised the vertical, with large windows which gave light and a sense of space. It has been called the architecture of light, and the Victorians, who were great church builders, copied the hall style of the Gothic church in large numbers in the new industrial towns.

The Scottish Statute of 1467 enacted that every homeward-bound Scottish vessel should bring one ton of material for kirk-work in the town to which the vessel was freighted. This bears witness to the prevalence of church and kirk building during that period.

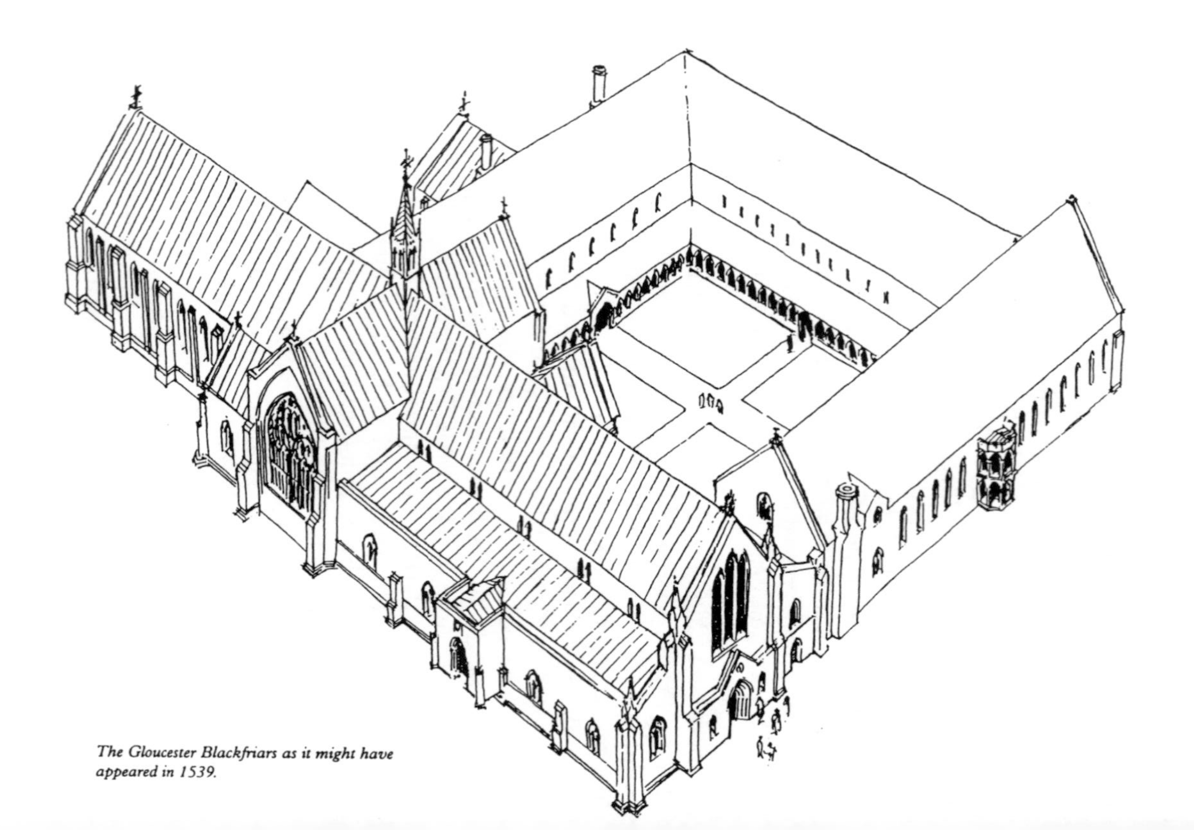

The Gloucester Blackfriars as it might have appeared in 1539.

After the middle of the fourteenth century, other than for building activities due to destruction following a fire, most of the mendicant building activity consisted of the replacement of Early English and Decorated-style windows by the larger Perpendicular windows. This can be seen in the remains of the Dominican church in Gloucester, where the pointed windows on the north side of the church have been replaced by Perpendicular windows. Building activities also included the erection of bell towers over the walkway, and chantry chapels within their churches. Some friary churches were enlarged at the expense of local gentry and merchants. Some families used their local friary as their family burial place as well as a friary church. The advantage to the friars in such an arrangement was that the families would give ongoing support to their 'family' friary.

The friars' building activities were taking place at the same time as magnificent churches and cathedrals throughout the land were being built to the glory of God and as acts of communal worship. Churches were not only religious buildings but were outward and visible signs of the piety of the town or burgh. People of the thirteenth century believed that they did not build their churches for men, but as sanctuaries for God. So conscientious were medieval workmen when building churches that even work in the upper part of the churches that could not be seen clearly by the people was of a very high standard. The builders reasoned that the all-seeing God could observe their workmanship.

Friaries were built by gangs of workmen supervised by master masons, with the help of specialist craftsmen who worked on stone, iron, lead and glass. The hired gangs left their identification marks on the stonework, enabling the master masons to identify and check the quality and quantity of work. The bells were cast as close as possible to the tower where they were to be hung. Most medieval churches were built with the manual help of the community, who dragged wagons filled with stone from quarries to the church site as a labour of love for the church and as an act of penance for the remission of sins.

Firm foundations are the most important feature of a building, but many cathedrals and monastic towers were built on insecure foundations or supported on piers consisting of a rubble core surrounded by a thin stone facing. As a result, builders were often dismayed to see arches crack and become distorted. Bearing in mind the primitive equipment, facilities and technology, the non-existence of schools of architecture and the absence of standard reference books on architecture to guide craftsmen on wall stresses and loading, medieval church edifices are a miracle of ingenuity.

As mortar took about six months to dry, churches were built horizontally in layers. The medieval custom was to build them from east to west, so as to bring the choir into use as soon as possible. The rest of the church was built bay by bay westward. British and Irish friaries were usually built to a standard plan, which was generally adopted, with modifications, across Britain and which was similar, but on a smaller scale, to priories and abbeys. When the church was complete, work started on the construction of the domestic buildings, which were grouped around the cloister, a range of buildings forming a square, usually sited on the south side of the church so as to gain shelter from the cold and to have the advantage of the brighter daylight from the south.

Most church building work was done piecemeal, depending on the degree of ongoing enthusiasm and a satisfactory flow of money. The availability of patronage often determined how quickly the building work could be completed and donors often left proof of their generosity in the form of inscriptions on, or near, the parts of the work for which they had paid.

The gradual development of the Northampton Dominican church extended from 1233 to 1301, while building work on the Shrewsbury Dominican church started in 1239 and took 20 years to complete. The Canterbury Franciscan church was started in 1267 but the church was not consecrated until 1325. Building the first Norwich Dominican church on the former Pied friars' site started in about 1327 and took 18 years to complete. Work on rebuilding the Norwich Carmelite church commenced in 1340 and was completed in 1382, although the work would have been interrupted due to the outbreak of the Black Death. It was said to have been equally as imposing a structure as the surviving Norwich Dominican church. The site of the rebuilt Aylesford Carmelite church was dedicated in 1348 but was not ready for consecration until 1417.

Gorleston Franciscan church was 100 feet long by 24 feet wide, with a square tower 100 feet high. The nave of the Cardiff Dominican church was 120 feet long and the choir was 60 feet long. The total length of Elgin Franciscan Observant church, which is still standing, is 110 feet long by 26 feet wide. This appears to have been the average size of Franciscan churches in medium-size towns. The footings of the Lichfield Franciscan church, which have been well preserved in a lawn, are 110 feet long by 60 feet wide and the chancel was 95 feet long and 28 feet wide.

Friars' churches in some larger towns were on average 200 feet in total length. The Coventry Carmelite church, one of the longest friary churches in the land, was 300 feet in length. The total length of Norwich Dominican church is 265 feet, the nave 77 feet wide and the chancel 30 feet wide.

At the other end of the scale, the nave of Llanfaes Franciscan church was only 51 feet by 28 feet. Brecon Dominican church was 95 feet by 26 feet and the choir was 65 feet by 26 feet. The Franciscan church at Carmarthen was a small building 80 feet by 30 feet, with a single aisle. However, it had a tower with two bells and a steeple.

All religious buildings had to be dedicated and consecrated to the service of God before they could be used for religious purposes, and the consecration of a church was carried out with elaborate ceremonial. It was a great occasion in which the merchants and craftsmen, led by those who had given contributions towards the building, furnishing and ornaments of the church, joined the friars and other local clergy as the Bishop performed the elaborate rite of consecration.

An order of consecration for churches used by Bishop David de Bernham in Scotland has survived and outlines an elaborate ceremony that must have lasted several hours. The Second Council of Nicaea in AD 787 insisted that relics of the saints were to be used in the consecration of a church. The Bishop and his clergy, dressed in sacerdotal vestments, went in procession, chanting psalms and carrying relics of a saint or saints. The procession moved to 12 consecration stations inside the church and 12 on the outside of the building, as the Bishop solemnly anointed each station with holy oil. This was followed by an invocation of saints, beginning with the Holy Trinity, the Virgin Mary and the angels. The proceedings culminated in a consecration prayer and sermon, followed by Mass, and then the long service was concluded with an apostolic benediction. The consecration stations were marked by carved or painted consecration crosses.

Friars' churches had to be consecrated in a similar manner before they could be used for divine worship.

Small clay and wattle churches gave way to commodious town churches full of life and vitality. The following descriptions of friars' churches indicate how they would have been in the fifteenth century when the friars' activities were at their peak.

CHURCH NAVE

Friary churches were divided into two principal parts, a spacious preaching nave and the chancel. 'Nave' comes from the Latin *navis*, translated into 'ship', so called due to the wooden roof structures of medieval churches resembling wooden ships turned upside down.

Many of the naves of their churches were spacious and were able to hold the large congregations who came to hear the friars' sermons, to house the increasing number of altars used for mortuary Masses and to accommodate the increase in the number of people being buried in them.

When we enter a medieval church today, there is an atmosphere of hushed calm and solemnity which is accentuated by the plain or plastered walls and the wooden seats and fittings. The nave of a medieval church was a theatre for worship, and worship was a time for joy and singing, a time when people were glad to be in the house of the Lord.

By the fifteenth century, the naves of friary churches were built as high as reasonably possible in order to improve the auditorium acoustics of their hall churches.

There was no seating for the congregation then, but by the late Middle Ages there was a move towards providing seating, which was resisted by the church hierarchy. Seating was installed in the nave of Lichfield Franciscan church, but in 1531 the cathedral chapter ordered it be removed, hoping to stop citizens going to the friars' church.

The scene in the interior of a friary church in the fifteenth century, when altars and images abounded, was one of bright, almost garish, colours, which were brought to medieval worship, with its love of pageantry and its sensuous appeal. In the days when there were few books and most folk were illiterate, wall pictures were a valuable teaching medium and the interior walls of friars' churches, and other churches, were covered with such paintings, but the range of colours was limited. They were mostly red and ochre, which were earth colours easily dug up. Black was provided by soot. Some walls in sacristies and chapter houses were also painted in the same manner. Rooms in the one remaining range of Beverley Dominican friary retain good fragments of fifteenth-century polychrome wall decoration.

St Basil (329–79), an early Doctor of the Church, suggested in a sermon that painters could give St Barlaam more honour by making pictures of him, than Basil himself could do with words. Wall paintings, along with statues and stained-glass windows, were used in churches as 'poor men's bibles' and as visual aids to promote a spirit of devotion in worship, very much as we give children picture books before they can read. Pictures in stained-glass windows and statues of Jesus, the Blessed Virgin Mary and the saints were considered as aids to worship, rather than images to be worshipped.

The average span of life in the Middle Ages was much less than now and people were aware that death was never far away. This concern was depicted in 'doom' wall paintings of the last judgement. Doom is Anglo-Saxon for 'judgement' and doom paintings were common in churches throughout Christendom, including friary churches. They were painted over the chancel arch of parish churches, and, although friary churches didn't have a chancel arch, doom paintings were probably painted on the east wall of their naves. However, there are no such paintings surviving in British mendicant churches. The paintings illustrated that God was no respecter of persons and His judgment was for all, irrespective of their station in life. They depicted the resurrection of the dead on the Day of Judgment, with angels escorting the blessed to heaven and devils gleefully dragging the wicked to the mouth of hell. People knew the meaning of doom paintings and the fate that awaited them if they did not live a Christian life. One such outstanding painting can be seen over the chancel arch in St Thomas's Church, Salisbury.

Wall paintings also depicted biblical events, scenes from the crucifixion, emblems of the passion, the enthronement of Christ, the enthronement of the Virgin Mary, the four evangelists, saints and Old Testament prophets. The colourful pictures, painted directly onto church walls and pillars, were not necessarily of great artistic merit.

BURIALS WITHIN CHURCHES

Until the thirteenth century, few people other than the founders were offered burial within a church but, from then on, it became common practice and a regular source of income for the church or friary. By providing the service of burial within their churches, friars hoped to gain financially by gifts associated with the burial and the expectation of further patronage from the family. The popularity of the friars is revealed in the extensive list of aristocratic and prominent citizens buried in friars' churches, despite the requests being invariably opposed by the secular priest. Wills specified in which part of the church the testator desired to be buried, as county knights and persons of high rank sought the much-coveted privilege of being buried in a friary church, rather than in their parish church. In so doing, they sought the benefit of the friars' prayers and considered that because of the friars' relative austerity, their supplications were more likely to draw down the benevolence of God's rules than those of local priests. Though friary churches were not intended to be burial places, they became extensively used as such.

As a result of the burial of so many noble and famous people within friary churches, there were sepulchral slabs, alabaster tombs with painted and gilded effigies, recessed tombs, monumental tombs with effigies of knights and their ladies on top of the tombs and inscribed brass tablets laid into the floor of most friary churches. So great was the number of people wishing to be buried in mendicant churches that tombs had to be tightly packed into side aisles, where every possible space was used. The space near walls was at times extensively undermined by the improper practice of constructing vaults for interment within the area of the walls, thereby weakening the structure.

Tombs were not only posthumous signs of the importance of persons during their lifetime, but also reminders of mortality.

Many citizens chose to be buried in the church or precincts of the London Franciscan church, where no less than 765 burials have been recorded. The church was largely paved with their inlaid gravestones. The impressive list of the most powerful personages in the kingdom who were buried in the church included Queen Margaret, second wife of Edward I, and Queen Isabella, wife of the murdered Edward II.

The London Dominican church was also popular for burials. Queen Eleanor of Castile, the first wife of Edward I, was buried in Westminster Abbey in 1290, but her heart was buried in the London Dominican church.

A list drawn up in about 1500 of persons interred within York Dominican church contains about 60 names, the earliest being Robert de Neville, Baron Raby, who died in 1282.

In 1305, Joan of Acre, the second daughter of Edward I and

wife of Gilbert de Clare, was buried in the chapel of St Vincent which she had erected on the south side of the sanctuary in the Clare Austin church. The dilapidated monument can still be seen in the scant remains of the church.

In 1386, the 'Fair Maid of Kent', mother of Richard II and wife of the Black Prince, was buried in a mortuary chapel next to the choir in Stamford Franciscan church. The Despencer family had a mortuary chapel in the Stamford Dominican church and Sir Hugh Despencer directed in his will of 1400 that the chapel, where his uncle was interred, should be made longer and a marble memorial placed there for his father and mother and another memorial for his wife and himself. In 1402, Edmond, Duke of York, was interred beside his wife, the daughter of King Peter of Castile, in King's Langley Dominican church.

Owen Tudor, grandfather of Henry VII, who was taken prisoner at the battle of Mortimer's Cross in 1461, was beheaded in Hereford market place and buried in Hereford Franciscan church.

The Duke of Buckingham, who was killed at the Battle of Northampton in 1460, was buried in the Northampton Franciscan church. Richard III, who was killed at the battle of Bosworth and whose body was carried from the field trussed across a horse's back, was buried in the Leicester Franciscan church. Sometime later Henry VII built a fine tomb for him with an effigy in alabaster. At the time of the dissolution of the friary the tomb was destroyed and Richard's remains were thrown into the River Soar.

In 1298, William de Beauchamp, Earl of Warwick, was buried in the church of Worcester Franciscans. A large amount of money was spent on his funeral, which included a magnificent procession through the streets of Worcester. It must have been an outstanding occasion, though a Worcester chronicler complained that the Beauchamp family was traditionally laid to rest in Worcester Cathedral and strongly resisted a member of the family being buried in the friary.

CHANTRIES

It was usual for late-medieval wills to make some provision for the testator's soul. They did so by arranging for a chantry so that Masses would be said for them and the good of their soul. Such temporary chantries were common in the late Middle Ages.

A chantry was an endowment for the singing of masses for the soul of the founder or others designated by him. The deed of foundation of a chantry usually required that daily Mass be celebrated for the souls of the founder, his family, predecessors, successors and all Christians. Most chantry masses were said by chantry priests at side altars within churches.

In 1369, the executives of a will carried out the testator's intention of founding a chantry in Aylesford Carmelite church where a friar should celebrate Mass daily for the souls of the founder, his wife, children and friends. In 1400, a typical chantry was established in Beverley Franciscan church for the souls of Thomas Kelk and his son, John. The 12 burgesses of the town were responsible for seeing that the services were performed and the fees due were paid in accordance with the chantry agreement.

By the middle of the fourteenth century, bishops and senior nobility wanted more than a temporary chantry and founded chantry chapels. A chantry chapel was in effect a private chapel built within a church, where masses were said for the founder and his family where they would be remembered in intercession before God, long after they had departed this life. The tomb and effigy of the founder were usually erected inside the chantry chapel but there are instances where the founder, for various reasons, was buried elsewhere, but the chantry chapel was still used for masses for his soul.

These enclosed chapels were small, elaborately ornamented stone structures with an altar at the eastern end, where the chantry priest could sing masses, and a tomb chest lying westwards. They were called 'chantries' because they were places where priests chanted the numerous private masses. In using a chantry chapel, the officiating priests had unlimited use of an altar dedicated for the ongoing private masses for the founder. It also ensured that the various priests chanting masses at other altars in the church did not disturb one another.

Most chantry chapels were prepared under the supervision of the founders during their lifetime. The structure was intended to be a permanent memorial to the founder, who devoted much thought to the structure and lavished as much elegance, elaborate embellishment and heraldic symbolism on it as possible.

A bishop had to issue a licence for such a structure to be built within a church, but, no doubt, this was easily obtained. Each chantry chapel had its own service books, chalice, vestments and other altar ornaments for the celebrant. Men in holy orders, such as bishops, not only left finance to maintain their chantry but also provided the vestments, altar pieces and missal which they themselves may have used.

Endowments for chantries, in the form of rents from small properties, were mostly given during the lifetime of the founders. The patronage of the endowment rested with the heirs of the founder, but the appointment of a soul-priest for the chantry could be subject to the approval of the aldermen of the town or burgh, who were responsible for seeing that the terms of the bequest were fulfilled. Few details of chantry endowments have survived, but one such chantry in Tickhill parish church owned nearly 50 acres of land, eight cottages and a barn, while another chantry in the same church owned 13 acres, one house and five cottages, which provided income for the chantry. There were a number of instances when the endowment was not enough to cover the ongoing cost of the chantry, or the buildings providing the rents fell into disrepair. Then, a chantry was abandoned through lack of funds.

Most chantry chapels were housed in cathedrals, abbeys and larger churches. There were 11 chantry chapels in Lincoln Cathedral. The best set of chantry chapels surviving in Britain is to be seen in Winchester Cathedral, but Tewkesbury Abbey might dispute this as they have some outstanding early chantry chapels. In 1107, Robert Fitzhamon, a kinsman of William the

Conqueror and founder of Tewkesbury Abbey, died and his body was buried in the abbey chapter house while the church was being built. In 1241, his body was transferred to a very fine chantry chapel sited near the abbey's high altar. A beautiful chantry chapel, which took 16 years to complete, was erected by Isabel le Despenser as a memorial to herself and her two husbands, who were buried in the same church in the 1230s and who were both named Richard Beauchamp. Her first husband was Richard Beauchamp, Earl of Worcester, and her second husband was Richard Beauchamp, Earl of Warwick.

There were a number of chantry chapels in friars' churches, especially in the larger churches, where friars said obituary masses and received the benefit of the chantry endowments.

It would appear friars recruited men whose sole purpose was to perform the duties of soul-priest, and this resulted in men of lower quality entering the mendicant orders; but we shall look further at the ongoing results of chantries in friary churches. Few chantry chapels were founded after 1450. Chantries in English friary and monastic churches were, of course, destroyed when the houses were dissolved, while the others in parish churches were suppressed in 1547.

At the time of the dissolution or abandonment of the friaries, most of the tomb monuments were destroyed, but a few monuments of royal and other personages were transferred to other churches. The remains of James I of Scotland were buried in the Perth Dominican church, but later transferred to St Johns Church in the town. The tomb of Edmund Tudor, father of Henry VII, who was buried in the middle of the chancel of the Carmarthen Franciscan church in 1456, was removed to St David's Cathedral. The stone coffin of Princess Joan, consort of Llywelyn the Great, who was originally buried at Llanfaes friary, which was founded on her death, finally came to rest in Beaumaris church. Sir Rhys-Ap-Thomas, one of Henry VII's principal supporters at the battle of Bosworth and at his accession to the throne in 1485, had a special affection for the Carmarthen Franciscan church, where many of his kinsfolk were buried. Following a serious illness in 1525, he spent his last days in the friary and was received into the order. He was buried in the Franciscan church, in the habit of a Franciscan friar. At the time of the dissolution of the friary his tomb was moved to the local parish church of St. Peter's. The promise of sure salvation to all dying in the habit of the order, even though only assumed on their deathbed, was adopted by all the mendicant orders.

The church of the Trinitarian friars at Easton Royal, Wiltshire, was the burial place for the hereditary wardens of Savernake Forest. The monument of the last pre-Reformation forest warden was left abandoned in the ruins of the building until his son rescued it and had it re-erected in the parish church of Great Bedwyn. An alabaster table tomb of Sir Thomas Fitzwilliam, who died in 1497, was brought from the former Tickhill Austin friary to Tickhill parish church.

At the time of the dissolution of the friaries a number of tombs were broken up and used as stone quarries. A fine incised slab of marble with a life-sized likeness of a merchant named Wisselus Smallenburgh, who died in 1340 and was buried in Boston Franciscan church, was found in a cottage wall on the site of the former friary. It was handed to Boston parish church in 1897 and now lies in the north-west floor of the church.

THE LADY CHAPEL

From the time of the early fathers of the faith, Mary as the Theotokos (God-bearer) and Virgin Mother has been the subject of special veneration by Christians and has occupied a unique place in the church. She surpassed all others, except her son Jesus, in dignity and authority. In the third century, St Hippolytus spoke of Mary as being free from defilement and corruption and in the fourth century St Ambrose spoke of her as a virgin, immune through grace, from every sin. Also in the fourth century, St Ephrem wrote a prayer to her in which he called her 'Most holy lady, mother of Christ, alone most pure in soul and body, whom of all the graces of the Most Holy Spirit, innocent and free from sin as Eve was before the fall'.

St Thomas Aquinas said there were three kinds of worship. At the highest level there was 'Latria', which is the adoration and worship due to God the Lord of all beings and to Jesus Christ alone. Then below that there was 'Hyperdulia', which is the special veneration and devotion accorded to the Virgin Mary, who, being overshadowed of the Holy spirit, believing and obeying, brought forth the Father's Son. Then there was 'Doulia', which was a lower form of devotion and honour given to the saints of the church.

The church came to regard the Blessed Virgin Mary as the most powerful intercessor and merciful intermediary between the sinner and God. She was seen as forever seeking to placate the wrath of her son, the divine Judge.

The cult of the Blessed Virgin Mary was becoming increasingly popular in the 1200s. It was at this period that 'Ave Maria' or 'Hail Mary', the invocation based on the angel's salutation to Mary in St Luke's Gospel, came into popular use. This simple and moving expression of devotion, easily learnt by the unlettered, became one of the most widely used prayers in the Western Church. The enthusiastic veneration of Mary increased, when, in the same century, the new order of Cistercian monks, led by St Bernard of Clairvaux, dedicated all Cistercian churches to the Blessed Virgin Mary. In the 40 years or so from 1112 to 1153, when St Bernard died, over 340 Cistercian monasteries had been founded in Europe, all dedicated to the Blessed Virgin Mary. The Cistercian's devotion to the Blessed Virgin made an enormous contribution to the increasing devotion of the church to Mary.

Such devotion of the Blessed Virgin Mary was not practised in British churches, other than monastic houses, before the end of the twelfth century, when it was introduced by returning crusaders, who had become familiar with it in southern and eastern Europe. This brought an increasingly widespread popularity of the Virgin; churches built Lady chapels onto the eastern ends of their churches, or aisles dedicated to the

Blessed Virgin Mary. Those which could not afford an extension or did not have room for enlargement dedicated side chapels to the Blessed Virgin Mary.

In Mary, the church found the embodiment of what was most tender and compassionate in Christianity. Devotion to Our Lady became increasingly popular, partly because she was a figure towards whom the most humble could feel a warm affection, a figure of compassion to whom all sufferers could relate to. She was held as an example and an ideal to be followed, especially by women, because of her exemplary life and her sympathetic language, which deserved respect and devotion. Throughout the Middle Ages the reverence in which Mary was held steadily increased and became a major factor in the medieval church. The church held to the principle '*De Maria numquam satis* – one can never say enough about Mary', and, she is 'Full of Grace'. Hence, the church ascribed a whole litany of graces, liturgical feasts and devotional practices in honour of the Blessed Virgin Mary.

Clergy and laity came in large numbers to the Lady chapels to meditate on Our Lady and her mother St Anne, seeking Mary's intervention with her son Jesus.

When the doctrine of the Immaculate Conception was confirmed by the Catholic Council of Basel in 1439 (it became a dogma in 1854), the adoration of the Virgin enjoyed increasingly widespread popularity and she occupied a central place in the life of the church.

The altar frontals of Lady chapels had stripes of alternate crimson and cream woven in silk and powdered with embroidered lilies and pomegranates in honour of Our Lady. Images of the Blessed Virgin Mary were found in every monastic, parish and friary church. These images and sculptured groups of Mary the Mother of God holding the Christ child on her knee depicted the Coronation of the Virgin. Her images were dressed with the regalia of 'Mary the Queen of Heaven' in later medieval festivals. Many Lady chapels contained images of *pieta* (Latin for 'piety'), the Virgin Mary supporting the dead Christ in her arms after He had been taken down from the cross.

All mendicant orders were enthusiastic advocates for the devotion and honouring of Mary as the Queen of Heaven. The friars in their deep affection for Mary highly venerated her, and all friaries had either a Lady chapel built onto the church or an altar dedicated to her. Friars and laity went to the Lady chapel for meditation on the Blessed Virgin Mary and sought Mary's intervention with her son Jesus on many problems affecting everyday life. They prayed to her because they believed she would pass on the prayers of the faithful to her son Jesus, and that their prayer through her would be more powerful with her son.

The Carmelite friars, from devotion to her, dedicated all their friaries to the Blessed Virgin Mary and, as we have seen, the order established the confraternity of the Scapular, which actively encouraged devotion to Mary. The Dominican friaries also had a special devotion to Our Lady and, as preachers and teachers, they enthused the medieval church with a renewal of its devotion to her. The Haverfordwest Dominican church had an image of the Virgin Mary with a 'miraculous taper' which gave a feeble light or glow. The Sandwich Carmelite church had a fair image of the Blessed Virgin Mary, while the Northampton Carmelite church was said to have had a renowned image of her. The Northampton Austin church and Norwich Austin church were said to have had outstanding images of Mary. The Doncaster Carmelite church had an image of Our Lady, and numerous gifts were offered as thank-offerings for her answers to prayer.

In the fifteenth century, friars in their devotion and enthusiasm for the Virgin Mary went to extremes and multiplied the pronouncements about Our Lady and credited her with a degree of authority which in conventional theology she did not have. During the history of the medieval church, one generation taught about Mary from scriptural and apocryphal text, while the next generation elaborated and embellished upon them. By the fifteenth century there were many strange flights of fancy in the over-exaltation of the character and role of the Virgin Mary. The reformers claimed that the medieval church had turned the veneration due to Mary into a cult that could not be justified from Holy Scriptures.

STATIONS OF THE CROSS

Devotion to the 'Passion of Christ', which became widespread in the twelfth and thirteenth centuries, was promoted by veterans of the crusades, who erected tableaux in their local churches representing various places they had visited in the Holy Land. When the Franciscans took over the custody of the Holy Places in Jerusalem in 1342, they saw it as part of their mission to promote devotion to the sites of the suffering of Christ. They organised a devotional walk which followed Christ's journey from the Antonia Fortress, where Jesus appeared before Pilate, and on to Calvary, where he was crucified. In so doing, they retraced the route and events of the day Jesus was crucified. In the days of Christ, Calvary was outside of Jerusalem's city walls.

Stations (From Latin *statio* – stand still) of the cross were erected by the Franciscan friars in their churches and by the fifteenth century other churches followed their lead and erected them as an aid to devotion. Initially there were between eight and twenty stations of the cross but fourteen became the standard number when they appeared in manuals of devotion in the sixteenth century.

ORGANS

Reference is made in 1458 to repairing two pairs of bellows for the great organ at York Dominican church, and, there are a number of other references to organs in inventories made at the time of the dissolution of friaries. It is not known if these primitive organs were used solely for the friars' private services in the choir, or if they were used when there were congregations in the nave of the church. They would not, of course, have been used for community hymn singing, as we do today.

ROOD SCREENS

As we have seen, rood screens were introduced into the churches in the fourteenth century when the rituals associated with the crucifixion were elaborated. It is generally considered that the teaching of the rood, or crucifix, was introduced into the church by the mendicants, especially the Dominicans, in the fourteenth century. Although no mendicant roods have survived, it would be surprising that, having introduced them to the church, they did not possess them in their own churches, in order to emphasise in a symbolic way the nature and importance of the crucifixion of Christ. Friary churches would have had a rood screen near the east end wall, or the chancel arch, of the nave. The existence of rood screens in English Dominican churches may be inferred from the frequent mention of them in inventory lists. William Bateson was probably referring to the rood when he asked, in 1504, to be buried before the high crucifix in the London Dominican church. In 1511, Richard Maynar willed that he be buried before the rood loft in the Warwick Dominican church.

GUILD CHAPELS

Medieval guilds were formed in every town by people who grouped themselves together in a variety of fellowships for religious and craft purposes. The religious guilds' main purpose was to guide members in the way of religion and, in particular, to foster devotion to their special religious causes. Some guilds brought members together in common devotion to Our Lady. There were Paternoster (The Lord's prayer) guilds, St Christopher guilds and guilds for various saints.

As with all medieval organisations, craft guilds took a corporate part in the religious life of the times and held numerous religious services in chapels set aside for them in the churches, where masses were said for past and present guild members. Guild members attended services two or three times a year, when they came together to pray for the souls of departed members. They kept their own Bede-roll, a list of departed members for whose souls prayers were asked. Each fraternity had its own patron saint, its own altar and its own chaplain to officiate at the guild's services. Friars welcomed guild associations in their churches; they united them with the community and brought in additional financial support as guilds rented halls in friaries for their general meetings and other festivities. Friars, in their role as chaplains of guilds, officiated at the guilds' religious services and masses.

THE WALLED PASSAGE

By the fourteenth century, many Franciscan churches in Britain had a distinction, not found anywhere on the Continent, of having a walkway that separated the nave from the chancel, with a slender bell tower or bell turret over the walkway. The walkway, or walled passage as it was sometimes known, not only divided the nave and chancel of the church, but also formed an entrance passage which led directly to the street, a symbol of the friars' close contact with the people.

Prior to the erection of bell towers, people were called to services by the use of hand bells or by a bell in the bell-cote placed above, or near, the walkway. The General Chapter of the Franciscan Order meeting in 1260 forbade their friars to adorn their churches with bell towers; in addition, a papal directive of 1261 granted mendicant houses permission to have one bell only, but as the friars' church bell had to vie with competing church bells, the directives soon fell into disuse.

During the fifteenth century there came a renewed fondness for building church towers, which was evident in friary

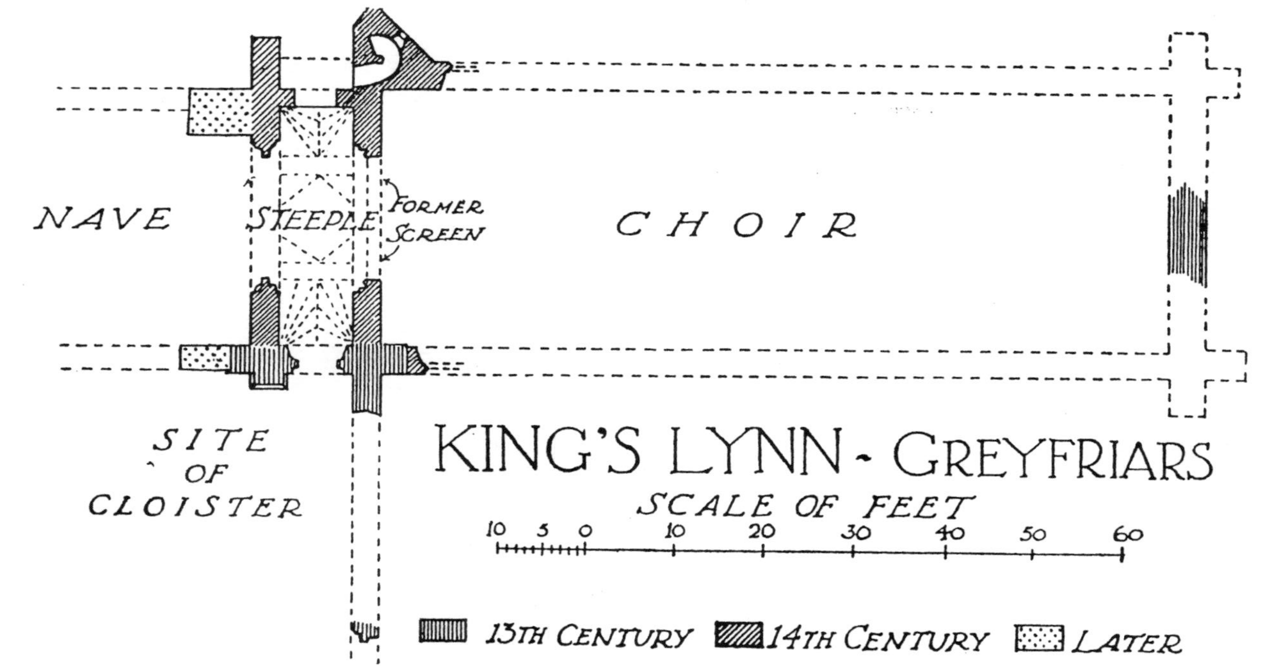

NAVE
STEEPLE
FORMER SCREEN
CHOIR
SITE OF CLOISTER
KING'S LYNN - GREYFRIARS
SCALE OF FEET
10 5 0 10 20 30 40 50 60
13TH CENTURY
14TH CENTURY
LATER

churches from the substantial towers which were constructed over, or as part of, their walkways. A number of friary towers contained a stone or brick hexagonal or octagonal lantern. The tower of the Richmond (Yorkshire) Franciscan church, which contained additional accommodation, still stands on four tall narrow arches and has an openwork parapet surmounted by 12 elegant pinnacles. It stands in splendid isolation, however, for nothing else remains of the former church.

In the fifteenth century church towers with spires became fashionable additions to churches. Spires tapered upwards to a point and could be seen clearly from a long way off. They were expensive to erect and were not built as ornaments to the church but, as with most things in medieval churches, to give a message; pointing silently to the infinite and eternal, 'Look up to God, for your redemption draweth nigh', was their message.

There developed a rivalry between towns, and within towns, about which church had the highest tower or spire; it was thought that it bore witness to the devotion and pride of the town. Fine towers with their spires could take as long as 15 years to erect.

Some spires on friary churches were of a great height. The octagonal steeple, the sole remaining structure of the King's Lynn Franciscan church, has survived as an aid to navigation to shipping coming in from the sea lanes and up the Great Ouse. The octagonal spire on top of the Coventry Franciscan church tower, which still stands in the city centre although the church has been destroyed, is 230 feet high. The Bristol Carmelite church spire reached 200 feet and the Dundee Franciscan church was said to have had a substantial spire, while the Chester Carmelite church spire was reputed to be of great height and beauty. The typical Dominican tower was shorter and more compressed.

CHURCH CHANCEL

Many friars' churches had no direct access from the nave to

the chancel and friars entered the chancel through a door in the walkway. The chancel was generally an elongated rectangular building on average of 100 feet by 60 feet. Chancels in British churches, including friary churches, were square-ended, unlike Continental churches, which usually terminated in an apse. Winchelsea Franciscan church was an exception in that its chancel was terminated by an apse, as was the side chapel of St Andrews Dominican church.

Early British churches were built on an east-west alignment, with the altar at the east end, whereas the churches of mainland Europe were built with their altars at the west end of the church. According to the Venerable Bede (673?–735), this anomaly is due to advice given in AD 601 by Pope Gregory the Great in a letter to St Augustine on how missionaries should deal with the temples for idols they found in Britain. He wrote: 'The idols are to be destroyed but the temples themselves are to be sprinkled with Holy Water and altars set up in them. For if these temples are well-built, they must be purified from the worship of demons and dedicated to the service of God'. Pre-Christian Britons were sun worshippers, and, in consequence, built their temples facing the rising sun. The advice given was to be patient with the pagan practices as long as fundamental issues were not compromised. The missionaries therefore allowed converts to the Christian faith to continue having their places of worship facing east and their altars sited at the east end of the chancel. In time the British church came to accept that the east end of the church, which faced towards Jerusalem, was the proper place for an altar.

The chancel area was used by the community for the sacred offices of the brethren, the one place in a friary which was beautified within the constraints of their order. The roof of the chancel was the only roof in the friary to have ornamentation, and contrasted with the plain roof of the nave.

The floors were covered with clay tiles usually about five inches square and three-quarters of an inch thick. There are numerous references to broken floor tiles being found on former friary sites. Some tiles have designs forming elaborate mosaic patterns incised into the clay and others with patterns picked out by an infilling of white clay in the lines of the design, giving a two-colour effect.

The carpenter's art was displayed in the construction of choir stalls, which occupied the western half of the chancel. The stalls had 'misericord' seats, so called from 'to have pity'. They were hinged seats which could be put down for those parts of the offices that were performed sitting, but raised during the long periods of standing during the services. The carved ledge projecting from the underside of the hinged seat was used by infirm and aged friars to ease their standing position when they were required to stand. Even in poorer houses, such as the Franciscan church at Llanfaes, Anglesey, the misericord choir stalls were of a high standard of workmanship. The choir stalls from the Llanfaes Franciscan church were transferred to nearby Beaumaris parish church, where they are now used by the church choir.

There was a choir stall for each friar attached to a house, and, as we shall see, a number of houses had between 30 and 50 friars, and some of the larger houses had 60 or more brethren. The size of the chancel was reflected in the number of stalls and many churches had double rows of stalls to cater for the number of brethren in the house.

Mass has been celebrated by the Catholic and traditional churches from early days and it still forms a central part of Christian worship. Mass comes from the Latin '*Ite missa est* – Go in peace', and the benediction word '*missa*' has become the name by which the service is known. Masses were considered the most effective form of intercession that could be offered to God, and Mass, celebrated at the high altar, was said for all Christians. In the early church, Mass was a simple breaking of bread and taking of wine, but it later became enshrined in the growing splendour and ritual of the medieval Mass.

Friars were members of religious communities and were expected to say the daily office. They said Mass at the start of every day as they recited the daily offices, a principal focal point of their day. They sang hymns, psalms and litanies, said prayers and chanted the sacred canticles. Some were sweet and joyous, reflecting the joy of the faith, while others expressed

e south side of Ingham Parish Church. The Ingham Trinitarian Community used the ncel of the church (on the right) as their chapel. There are some traces of cloister arches the north side of the church.

King's Lynn Franciscan church. The octagonal tower is the only remaining structure of the church.

Lincoln Franciscan church.
church survives above
undercroft.

Coventry Carmelite friary - the surviving eastern cloister wing. The dormitory was on the first floor, over the cloister and ancillary rooms.

e chancel of the thirteenth-century Chichester Franciscan church. It is now used as a nch of Chichester Museum.

hospitium of the former Inverkeithing Franciscan friary. It was used as a place of shelter travellers using the Firth of Forth ferry.

St Andrews Dominican friary - a fragment of the former friary which was rebuilt in ab
1514.

Newcastle-upon-Tyne Dominican friary. The postern gate from the friary and through
town wall, leading to a wooden drawbridge over the town ditch.

Hereford Dominican friary. The fourteenth-century preaching cross is the only surviving friars' preaching cross in Britain. Behind it is a range of the former friary.

verley Dominican friary. The surviving building, which was probably the domitory and :ary, is now used as a youth hostel.

Beverley Dominican friary - wa
paintings in the surviving buildin
which was probably the domito
wing of the cloister.

The fourteenth-century infirmary block of the former Clare Austin friary. It is now used
the chapel for the refounded Austin friary.

Richmond (York's) Franciscan church - the fifteenth-century bell tower, which is the sole remaining part of the former friary.

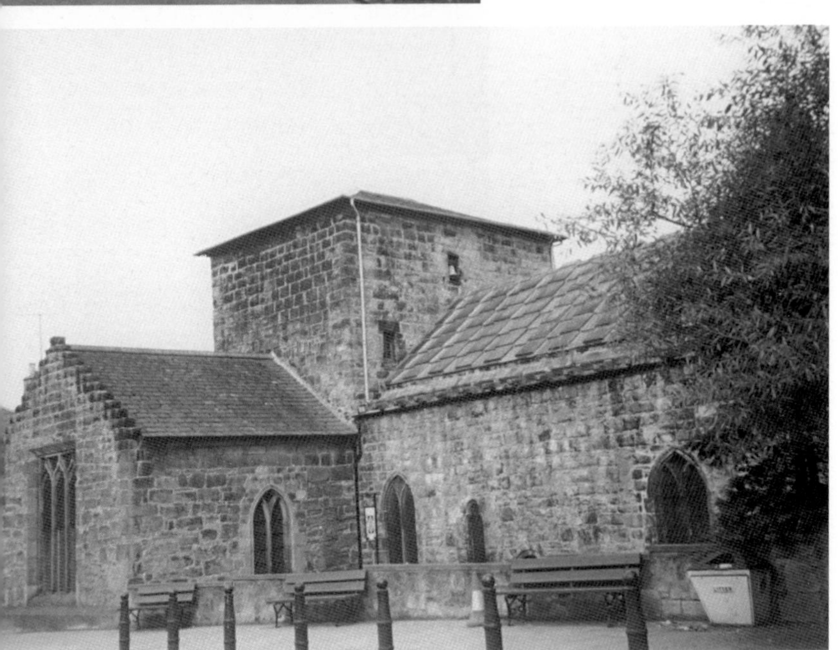

eensferry Carmelite church - the kirk of the former friary, now used as the parish kirk.

Burnham Norton Carelite friar
gateway of the former friary, w
the west wall of the church in
background.

The grave of Robert Grosseteste, Bishop of Lincoln, in Lincoln Cathedral.

A modern rosary.

'he nave of the Gloucester)ominican friary church .lustrates how large their ›reaching halls were.

Peebles - the ruins of the Trinitarian (Red) friars kirk.

Perth Dominican friary - a plaqu on the wall of a building on the sit of the friary.

Doom painting in St Thomas's Church, Salisbury.

ye Austin Church. The church as in the upper part of the uilding, which is now used as a ottery.

The chancel arch and chancel of the Winchelsea Franciscan church. It is not known if th
nave was ever built; if it was, it would have been a very large church for a small town.

Rye Sack friary. This is the so
remains of a Sack Friars' house i
Britain. It is not known if this wa
the church or a wing of the cloiste

ıe courtyard of the refounded Aylesford Carmelite friary, Kent. The Pilgrim Hall with the ɾee dormer windows at the top of the photograph is the former late thirteenth-century guest ɔuse used by pilgrims on their way to Canterbury.

cotlandwell Trinitarian (Red) friars. The friars served in a Trinitarian house built adjacent to ıe health-giving well of St Mary's. The well is still used by some people for its curative ıalities.

Misericord choir stall se
transferred from Llanfa
Franciscan church to Beauma
parish church after the friars' chur
was closed.

The sarcophagus of Princess Joan, wife of Llywelyn the Great, transferred from Llanfaes friary to Beaumaris parish church after the friars' church was closed.

rtherstone parish church, with the town market-place in front of it. The chancel of the rmer Austin friary is on the right, with the medieval friary's octagonal tower dividing the rmer friary building from the Victorian nave.

Cloister and well at the Elgin Franciscan church.

The former frater building of the Canterbury Dominican friary.

The gateway into the Dunwich Franciscan friary enclosure. The larger gateway was the ma
entrance to the enclosure, the smaller gateway was for pedestrian use.

sorrow while reflecting on the passion of the crucifixion, depending on the season of the church calender. Whereas monks were dedicated to a life of prayer and chanted their offices, friars adopted a brisk chant in order to get through their prayers more quickly so that they could get on with their other daily tasks. The Dominican constitution directed that the offices were to be said with brevity and clarity, to avoid friars' studies being hindered. The prior or warden of a friary had authority to grant dispensations from canonical observations whenever it seemed expedient, in order to enable the friars to carry out their duties. The mendicant friars later introduced the custom of saying Mass instead of chanting it, which was the practice in the church.

The sanctuary was the raised area at the east end of the chancel where the main altar was situated. Everything in the sanctuary area was designed to heighten the friars' consciousness of the holy things of the faith. In the early days of the church, the underground tunnels in the catacombs of Rome were used for burial and Christians used the flat tops which covered the tombs of martyrs as the tables for Mass. Since those early days, traditionally, Catholic masses have been said on flat stones used as altars. Altar tops were marked with five crosses, for the five wounds of Christ.

From early times, bones of Christian martyrs were sealed in the altar tables and officiating priests bowed down before an altar and kissed it out of respect for the martyr. Friars, as did other clergy, bowed before the altar when coming into the chancel, whilst saying the Lord's Prayer and the Creed, and on certain other occasions.

The altar had to be consecrated with holy oil by a bishop before it could be used for the celebration of Mass. If, by chance, an act of violence happened in which blood was shed in the church, the altar could not be used again until a reconciliation service with salt, ashes, water and wine had taken place. As we shall see, this occurred in some friars' churches.

The sanctuary was the central point of the friars' devotional life, the place where they celebrated the Mass and offices of the church and where they met for corporate prayers. The senior friar led the Mass, or at times a visiting friar would be invited to be the celebrant. The celebrant dressed in the Eucharistic vestments previously described. During Mass, the altar was covered by a white linen cloth and a cross was placed on the altar. Many friars' churches had jewel-encrusted altar crosses donated to them, but if the house did not possess such a cross, they used one made of baser metals.

The Host, (from the Latin *hostia* – victim) as the consecrated unleavened bread was (and is) called, is the wafer used in the Mass. The Roman church believe that when the officiating priest pronounces the words of consecration, the bread and wine changed into the Body and Blood of Christ and Christ offers Himself to God for the living and the dead. This is known as transubstantiation, a change in substance.

The clergy and laity took the Mass in both kinds, that is, in bread from a platen and wine from a chalice. However, the practice of restricting the bread and wine to the clergy, with the laity only receiving the bread, dates from about the twelfth century. In 1415, the General Church Council of Constance formalised the practice when it considered that, as the consecrated bread was the body of the living Christ, the laity were receiving Christ, Body and Blood, in the bread.

At the altar, the celebrant elevated the Host in a monstrance, a transparent receptacle, so that all attending the Mass might have an opportunity to see and adore the Host. A tabernacle was suspended or placed on a ledge above the altar to hold the pyx, or small receptacle in which the Eucharistic Host was reserved for the sick and dying. After the Mass had been held, the tabernacle was draped with a cloth and the altar cleared of its cross and ornaments.

CLOISTER BUILDINGS

By the fifteenth century, friary buildings tended to follow a set pattern in providing good residential accommodation for friars. The principal domestic buildings were usually placed around the cloister, or internal corridor, which provided protective communication and shelter between the main buildings. It is hard today to visualise the bustle of daily life which once flourished within the cloisters; in their heyday, some friaries had 30 to 50 friars housed in the domestic range. The open space enclosed by the cloisters was used as gardens for culinary and medical herbs. As we have seen, friary cloister walks were usually incorporated in the lower level of the cloister ranges, the corresponding outer halves of the lower level being divided into a variety of storerooms. The whole of the first floor was occupied by the principal living apartments: dormitory, refectory and guest rooms. This had the advantage of economy in building materials and served to reduce the ground space needed in the congested towns. It can be seen in the surviving eastern range of Coventry Carmelite house; the chapter house and two storage rooms are sited off the enclosed cloister at ground level and a large dormitory is situated on the first floor above.

A number of the larger friaries had a small open court, or irregular yard, between the cloister wall and the wall of the church so that daylight coming in through the nave windows would not be obstructed by nearby cloister buildings. Such an arrangement existed at the Norwich Dominican, London Carmelites and Walsingham Franciscan houses, among others.

The sacristy, or vestry as it is now known, was a room adjacent to the chancel area, in which friars prepared themselves for services. It was either the first room leading off the right-hand side of the cloister, or a room attached to the chancel, which gave friars direct access from the sacristy into the chancel. The sacristy was under the control of the sacrist, who was responsible for the care of the church's fabric, furnishings, vestments, altars and church services. Books, liturgical vestments, altar vessels and other valuables the house possessed were kept in the sacristy, the most secure room in the friary.

In medieval times, people did not consider that their muniments, jewels and other treasures could be kept safely in their own homes and regarded houses of religion as the safest places to keep valuables. Such items were often deposited in friaries, where they were placed in the sacristy. However, at times there seemed to have been problems. In 1268, a merchant who had deposited wine and other goods in the Boston Franciscan house complained that the goods had been removed. In 1278, the King, on hearing that Robert de Chause, Bishop of Carlisle, had, before his death, left a deposit in the Carlisle Franciscan house, ordered his steward to go to the friary and take back the debt the late Bishop owed him. In 1305, robbers entered the London Carmelite house and, aided by a renegade friar, bound the prior and brethren and made off with £400 belonging to a knight who had deposited the sum with the friary. The renegade friar and robbers were later caught and hanged.

A friary chapter house was a rectangular room off the eastern range of the cloister. There, the brethren regularly assembled to hear readings and discuss the management of the house and to be assigned to their tasks and duties. It was where brethren confessed their faults and misdemeanours and, when necessary, were admonished.

The dormitory was the most used and most important of the domestic rooms. It was here that the hardships of the common life were felt most keenly. There was no chance of privacy in the earlier friaries, and the ill nature and inconsideration of fellow friars were ever-present possibilities; it was a room where they had to exercise patience, kindness and forbearance. The plain barrack-like dormitories, with straw-filled palliasses placed upon bedsteads along the walls, gave way in the fourteenth century to box beds in individual cubicles or cells. These allowed friars more privacy for meditation, study and sleep. Originally no one, except academic masters and the Master-General of an order, had a chamber of their own but by the fifteenth century senior officers and some priors and wardens had their own chambers. A late fifteenth-century room in the east range of Gloucester Dominican house previously referred to appears to have been fitted out as a prior's lodging.

Neither the church nor the domestic quarters were heated during the winter months and the cold was undoubtedly one of the chief hardships the friars had to endure. The intense winter cold, in bare dormitories with the wind sweeping through the cloisters, would have made life hard. As a counterbalance to this, medieval people were much more accustomed to the rigours of the weather than we are.

Meals were served, except on the vigil of certain festivals, in the refectory, or eating hall, twice a day, the main meal at midday and a light meal at about 5 p.m. There were, of course, no watches or clocks and brethren were summoned to their meals by handbells. At the ringing of the bell brethren washed their hands at the washing trough at the entrance to the refectory, entered the refectory two by two and sat on long wooden benches, with their backs to the wall. It was not customary in the Middle Ages to sit on both sides of a table. Friars in poorer houses, where food was not plentiful at times, would often have wondered from whence their next meal would come. With nothing on the table to eat or drink, they would be forced to scour the town for the necessities of life. The refectory, like the monks' refectories, contained a pulpit in a recess near a window, where one of the brethren read aloud from the Scriptures, sacred writings and a chapter from their constitution, during mealtimes.

Everyone had to be silent at the table; those who broke the rule at mealtimes were allowed to drink only water for one meal and received a beating.

They ate very simple food; their diets were not exciting by our standards and consisted of cabbage, peas, beans, onions and leeks in soup, or pottage, into which they dipped their bread. Such, with corn, milk, cheese, butter and eggs, made up the normal medieval diet. The friars, like the poor, ate little meat. Fish, of course, was eaten on Fridays and the numerous fast days when meat was forbidden. They, along with the ordinary people, drank ale, a staple drink, which they watered down when finances were low.

They ate their meals with knives, spoons and fingers. Excavations at the Bristol Franciscan site revealed nine wooden bowls and platters and two wooden spatulas, which have survived intact. These were an essential part of domestic equipment in a friary.

Because of the risk of fire spreading quickly to any connecting buildings, kitchens were usually near the refectory, but in a free-standing building apart from it. Kitchens had large fireplaces with baking facilities but few cooking utensils, other than cooking pots, caldrons and a few knives and wooden spoons to prepare the limited range of food. Some kitchens had a tank cut out of a large stone, in which live fish could be kept until required for cooking. This method of keeping fish fresh was used extensively over the centuries.

The west range of the cloister, where the provisions of the house were kept, was the province of the cellarer.

LIBRARIES

Until the thirteenth century, monasteries played a major part in writing and copying books and manuscripts on a wide range of subjects, principally theological and devotional works. When the friars were established, they took the monks' monopoly away when they started writing, copying and collecting such books.

As we have seen, Dominican friars were intellectuals who aimed to excel in the academic world. They intended, through preaching, to be a teaching order which proclaimed the principles of the Christian faith and they therefore placed great emphasis on study. This resulted in their houses accumulating a large number of books. Friars in other mendicant orders were also trained in the art of preaching and developed, by reading and study, a love of theology, history and the customs of the church.

Earlier mendicant houses had few books and those they had were usually kept in presses, or bookcases, placed either in the dormitory or sacristy. The only thing friars wanted to acquire in quantity was books and, as time went by, they gradually accumulated a large number. In the fourteenth century, Richard de Bury complained that the friars were buying up all the best books that came on the market and contrasted the size and range of their libraries with the poverty he found in other parts of their friaries. As they developed, most friaries set aside a room as a library for the large number of books and manuscripts they bought or were given. The Austin Gorleston house had a library, built in 1429, which was 100 feet long by 30 feet wide, wainscotted throughout and furnished with desks and settees.

There are numerous references in medieval wills of books, the proud possessions of their owners, being left to friars. Books were sometimes deposited in friary libraries for safe keeping or on loan but for some reason never found their way back to the owners.

A single vellum leaf, written in the late thirteenth century and used in rebinding a fifteenth-century book, gives us a picture of the early days of Ipswich Franciscan friary, when brethren brought their own service books with them to the friary, or persuaded wealthy patrons to provide books for the choir and general reading, or arranged for the purchase of a single book at the cost of two or three benefactors.

Paper began to be used in the early fourteenth century. Prior to the invention of the printing press, books were laboriously copied by hand and so were valuable and had to be kept in safe storage. By the fifteenth century, libraries developed the practice of attaching a chain from the book to the library shelf, to prevent them being removed. The books could only be removed by the use of a key held by the friar in charge of the library, and were then read in cubicles within the library. Hereford Cathedral has the best chained library in Britain. It contains about 1500 books, including some 20 books that have survived from the Hereford Franciscan House, each secured to a shelf by a chain.

The larger mendicant houses accumulated considerable libraries, including the important libraries at the Cambridge Franciscan, Lincoln Carmelite and Exeter Dominican houses. Surviving catalogues are interesting, in that they indicate the extent of friars' libraries. A 1372 catalogue listed 656 books in the York Austin house, a studium of advanced theology. The catalogue included Psalters (Book of Psalms), lectionaries (collections of scriptural readings), missals (text and procedure for celebrating Mass), breviaries (books of psalms, hymns and prayers), book of hours (books for private devotions), books on theological treatises, religious poetry, sermons, English and Scottish history and medicine. The catalogue also included 200 volumes of Latin classics which had been bequeathed to the house.

Oxford Franciscans had two libraries, one for the students and the other for the rest of the house. Their libraries were enlarged when Robert Grosseteste, Bishop of Lincoln, left his library to the Oxford Franciscans because of his close friendship with Adam Marsh, the first Oxford Franciscan Regent Master. Oxford Austin house had a fine library, which was continually being added to during the fifteenth century. Canterbury Franciscan house had a well-stocked library, with books on the Scriptures, history, natural science and literature. Some of these books found their way to the British Museum, the Bodleian Library in Oxford and the Hereford and Lincoln Cathedral libraries.

Oxford and Cambridge friaries had floating populations of student friars and there was a big demand for books in the plainer text, and books, or even a few pages from books, were hired out to students. Friaries who sent students to the universities provided them with the necessary funds to hire books and other such items.

Friars had an advantage when studying, in that they could use the facilities of their continent-wide orders and formulate their ideas with mendicant brethren across Europe. About 1245, Humbert de Romans, the Dominican Provincial of France, produced a standard Dominican lectionary, a book containing passages appointed to be read at divine services in Dominican churches. A copy of the book was in every Dominican house.

Until about 1300, books and manuscripts were written on parchment, usually the skins of sheep, cut into folio size. Then the parchment was cut and folded, the scribe pricked the pages down each side of the page with an awl or pointed knife, then using the prickmarks as a guide, he ruled straight lines across the page with a piece of bone. The scribe wrote on a high sloping desk, which enabled him to keep the pen more or less horizontal and thus avoid making blots.

Their libraries were a source of income for friars. Some friaries had a scriptorium for copying, often with great artistry, religious and non-religious manuscripts for the rich and educated classes who could afford to pay for the work. Most of the earlier manuscript books were written by scribes using sharpened goose or swan quills on parchment and bound into folio-size volumes. Handwritten books were usually beautifully illustrated in colour, depicting groups of people and birds or animals. Copying and illuminating manuscripts took many hours to complete, but time did not have the same importance it has today. Beautifying anything connected with religion, including books and manuscripts, was done to the glory of God. The Hulne Carmelite house had a valuable library with books illustrated with medieval symbolism in which animal illustrations carried subtle symbolic meanings. They were messages in themselves but most of us today would not appreciate the symbols.

John Sifer, a Guildford Dominican friar, worked in Sherborne Abbey for over 25 years on a lectionary commissioned by Lord John Lovel, who presented it to Salisbury Cathedral. The book was beautifully illustrated with groups of human figures, birds and animals.

John Capgrave, an Austin friar at King's Lynn, compiled an encyclopaedia on the lives of the saints which is still one of the basics for research work on saints.

In the fourteenth century, knowledge of the classics was spread by the teachings and writings of the friars, some of whom peppered their theological works with classical references. Friar John of Wales wrote *Communiloquium*, a handbook on moral instructions, which was smattered with classical allusions.

Readers seldom had an index of books to which they could refer, but the Franciscans attempted to create a catalogue of books held by some religious establishments, including their main libraries. The general lack of cataloguing made the job of systematic study more difficult. Because some books were frequently used, friary librarians had an ongoing programme of repairing and rebinding worn and tattered copies, as well as adding books to their library.

The book of hours was the only book on religion that was widely used by the laity in the fourteenth century, but by the fifteenth century many smaller and cheaper books in Latin and English were produced, as some of the lesser gentry and middle classes began to take an interest in reading.

In the 1470s, William Caxton (1422–91) learned the art of movable-type printing in Cologne and returned to England in 1476. The following year the first book, *The Game and Playing of Chess*, came off his printing press in Westminster. From then until his death in 1491, the list of works that passed through his presses was remarkable. Printing presses made the production of books considerably cheaper and books were no longer found only in the libraries of religious or educational establishments but became available to the educated and middle classes. A great number of pious works in English and Latin poured off the movable-type presses. Of the 79 books printed by Caxton up to 1490, 29 were works on morality, spiritual improvement or enlightenment. During this period devotional works centred around the lives of saints were much sought after as aids to personal devotion.

This ushered in an age of spiritual renewal which took the form of personal piety, but alas, did little to reform the church. However, it brought a renaissance of classical scholarship and greater attention to biblical text, and the educated classes started to look more closely at the Holy Scriptures for themselves. With the steady output of the printed work came a stream of books on popular theology, causing the laity to re-appraise their beliefs and increase their understanding of religious matters.

During this period, friars played a major role in defending the traditions and teachings of the church. They used the invention of the printing press to print books and tracts to counter new teachings coming from the Continent. The number of books held in the friars' libraries since the development of the printing press increased considerably and friars regarded their libraries, with all the knowledge they contained, as treasures beyond price; but the same books were classed by sixteenth-century reformers as being tainted with the heresies of Rome and fit only for burning. Alas, nearly all books in the friars' libraries perished when the houses were closed at the Reformation. What a lost treasure!

LITTLE CLOISTERS

Where sites permitted, friaries had a little cloister, adjacent to the north-western part of the cloister buildings, which contained the infirmary for the house. If a brother fell sick or became senile, he received ongoing assistance from the house. Brethren who were ill received a special concession: they were allowed linen sheets and feather beds! Friars also looked after their brethren in good health by bloodletting, a process regarded as the panacea for all ills, as it was believed that bleeding released the fluids thought to determine the emotional and physical dispositions. Individuals underwent bloodletting four times a year, after which they rested for a few days, while maintaining a limited religious routine.

PREACHING CROSSES

During the fourteenth century, outdoor pulpits, or preaching crosses, were erected in areas near the entrances to many friary churches. One such open-air preaching station was erected in 1365 in the preaching yard just outside the Nottingham Franciscan church. A preaching cross erected in 1350 outside the Hereford Franciscan church has survived. It stands on steep steps, has a parapet of openwork panels which provide the sides of the pulpit and a slender stone pillar in the centre, surmounted by a cross. It was restored in 1865 and is the only remaining friars' preaching cross in

Britain. It can be seen at the rear of the Coningsby Hospital almshouses in Hereford.

WATER SUPPLY

A remarkable achievement of all orders of friars was the construction of water systems to provide a good supply of fresh water, not only for themselves but also for the communities who lived in the vicinity of their houses. They were concerned about the supply of water for drinking and washing, as well as water to carry away waste. Citizens were often encouraged by the friars to support their water projects for the joint benefit of the town and friary. The source of supply was often situated some distance outside the town and they constructed aqueducts over long distances. There are a number of references to conduits built to take water supplies direct to the friars' houses, indicating that friars had a good understanding of water engineering. The flow of water used in the kitchen and for washing had to be upstream of the sewers and drains of the town and this, at times, influenced where some friaries were sited in relation to their town.

In 1290, the Southampton Franciscan friars secured the grant of a spring from the Lord of the Manor of Shirley, and in 1311 they extended the use of the water to the townsfolk by allowing the burgess to duct the water, through a pipe, to a stone basin from which the citizens could help themselves. Citizens in the area of the Bristol Austin house received a 'never failing flow of clean water' from the friary. The Bristol Franciscans' water supply came from a conduit which continued to be in use until the early part of this century. Newcastle-upon-Tyne Franciscans had the joint use with the town of a stone water conduit, while in 1283 the burgesses of Scarborough gave a spring outside their town for the use of the Franciscan friars. This was on condition that the town should have the joint use of the conduit when it was constructed. The burgess of Gloucester gave the Franciscans a water supply from Robins Hill, about two miles outside the town, while the

Carmelite friars in the same town obtained their supply from a spring outside their enclosure. About 1301, the Lichfield Franciscans obtained an independent supply of water from Aldershaw springs, about a mile and a half south-west of the town, and piped the water to the town; the system was still being used in the mid-nineteenth century. The Perth Dominican friars were granted a water supply from the King's mill, via a conduit from the mill. In the late fourteenth century, Aylesford Carmelite house, which had a piece of land containing a number of springs, was given a licence to make a subterranean piping system from the springs to their house. Cambridge Franciscans built a conduit from a well near Madingley Road, to their house. The conduit passed into the hands of Trinity College, where it still supplies water for the fountain in the Great Court.

Some friaries were sited near springs or other supplies of water. The Elgin Franciscan house had a well in the middle of the cloister; it is still in the cloister of the Convent of Mercy on the site, where it is fed by an active spring.

A few friaries, such as the Aylesford and Hitchin Carmelites and the Woodhouse Austin friaries, had moats surrounding their houses.

FRIARY CHURCHYARDS

During medieval times, Christians, which included most of the population, were buried in ground that had been consecrated by a bishop. It was considered a horrendous thing for a Christian to be buried in unconsecrated ground and only those guilty of hideous crimes, or non-Christians, were so buried.

Illustrious men of the mendicant orders were buried in the chancels of the friars' churches, the cloisters or chapter house. Other friars were buried in their mendicant clothing in the friars' own cemetery on the north side of the church. Franciscan friars were buried with a leaden cross with an absolution inscribed on it laid across their chest. No doubt other orders used similar obituary crosses.

In 1227, the Dominicans acquired the privilege, and in 1250 the Franciscans obtained the same privilege, of permitting anyone who had chosen a friary church or burial ground as their last resting place to be buried in the church or cemetery, and as a result the laity opted in increasing numbers for burial in the friars' churchyards.

The Dyfed Archaeological Trust excavated the site of the small Carmarthen Franciscan friary between 1983 and 1990, prior to the site being redeveloped. The excavations recovered about 250 skeletons from within the cloister alleys, chapter house and church choir. The nave of the church was not included in the excavations and no doubt it would have contained many more burials. The remains were reinterred in consecrated land in the town and the Latin rites of the medieval church were used for the reinterment.

The Royal Commission for Ancient and Historical Monuments of Wales, who co-operated in the Carmarthen excavations, estimate there were about 10,000 burials in the friary graveyard during the 250 or so years of its existence. As in all medieval churchyards, the graveyard became full over a period of time and bones from earlier burials were uncovered in later burials and placed in charnel houses, their removal making room for newer graves. Many thousands of people over the years were buried in the graveyards surrounding our ancient parish churches and the charnel houses were often full with the remains that had been dug up. Burial grounds in many churches were being used in pre-Norman times and it is possible that tens of thousands of people were buried in them over the years and their remains later removed. This also applied to the friars' churchyards; had it not been so, they would soon have become full and no further burials would have been possible in them. This practice went on in parish church graveyards until the nineteenth century, when municipal cemeteries came into use.

5

THE FRIARS

In about 1300 AD, approximately one in every 150 of the population in Britain was in religious orders. However, the mendicants were only a small group in the large religious establishment.

Looking at friars over a period of 300 years or so during the Middle Ages, we see a change of calibre in recruits during that time. The irrepressible earnestness, piety and idealism of their early days, days in which service to God was their principal aim, could not, because of its very nature, continue indefinitely.

A variety of men became friars: men of religious conviction, intellectuals, good honest men, even erratic and some rather odd people. By the fifteenth century, some of them fell far short of the high standards of the holy life of their earlier brethren. However, most friars were diligent and conscientious men who considered they were doing the work of God. The zeal and freshness that had once commended them may have waned, but their admirers continued to outnumber their critics until within a decade or so of the Reformation.

Once the friars had established a house in a town, their work was ongoing and mostly unrecorded, but it was an essential and integral part of medieval life. Their lives were gruelling but they won the respect of the people and had a high standing in the community. There were long periods when nothing noteworthy took place and the friars' lives, and service to the people, continued in an uneventful and peaceable way. They had great prestige in the communities they served and were generally looked upon as friends, even if, later, the communities ceased to respect their methods of raising money. In

Wales there were a number of favourable references to the friars in the early poetry, indicating that they were well known and respected in Welsh popular life.

As early as 1243, Matthew Paris, a monk from St Albans and an English chronicler, complained to Pope Innocent VI:

> When noblemen and rich men are at the point of death, whom they knew to be possessed of great riches, they in their love to gain diligently urge them, to the injury and loss of the ordinary pastors, and extort confessions and hidden wills, lauding themselves and their own order only, and placing themselves before all others. So no faithful man now believes he can be saved, except he is directed by the councils of the Preachers [Dominicans] or Minorites [Franciscans]. Desirous of obtaining privileges in the courts of kings and potentates, they act the part of councillors, chamberlains, treasurers, groomsmen, and mediators for marriages; they are the papal extortions; in their sermons, they either are flatterers or most cutting reprovers, revealers of confessions or impudent accusers.

His comments demonstrate the impact of the mendicant orders in just a short period of time. No doubt Matthew Paris represented the feeling of his Benedictine community of St Albans, who were thoroughly hostile to the friars and saw them as upstarts who carried out their religious duties in a proficient manner.

The best-know 'friar' is Friar Tuck, the jovial cleric of Robin Hood fame. Many of the Robin Hood stories are based on historical fact and the stories are centred around Robin Hood's struggles with the Sheriff of Nottingham and King John, who tried to seize the crown during King Richard's captivity in Germany in 1193–94. John died in 1216. However, the first Dominican friars did not arrive in England until 1221 and the first Franciscans in 1224. If the historical stories are based on the outlaws' struggle with John, then there was no Friar Tuck in the band of merry men. If Friar Tuck was one of the band of outlaws, they could not have been engaged in a struggle with King John. Legend tells us that Robin Hood died in 1246 and was buried in Kirklees Priory, near Brighouse. It appears that the King John part of the story was added to give the tales a better storyline.

Friars were well known in the towns and countryside which they frequently traversed to preach, work with the sick and needy, and carry out their function as confessors.

Only an enthusiastic minority of men adopted the friars' way of life, partly priest and partly monk. In doing so, they considered they were serving God by their lives and took it as their duty to glorify God by their teaching, preaching and service to the community. No doubt some were tempted to become friars in the belief that their calling was the fulfilment of complete union with God and that it would help them to enter heaven more easily.

Friars were incorrigible chatterers, for without their ability to converse they would not have been very successful in their calling. They were versatile Christians who were at ease with the wealthy and influential but could also work with merchants and the poorest in society.

Whereas monks were known by their place names, friars were known by their family names, and ordination lists show many of them were recruited locally.

From the records of the times, we get a few glimpses of the sweet nature of some individual friars. With their poverty and holiness, they were free from the form of poverty which consisted in wearing sad countenances and appearing to the people as men who fasted. We read of the constant prayer and vigils that lasted the whole night. Francis always impressed on his followers that cheerfulness was a sign of a clean heart and a great defence against the devil. A feeling of mutual affection pervaded Salisbury Franciscan house during the priorship of Brother Stephens, who was said to be of such sweetness, geniality and compassion that he would allow no one to be made sad. Eustace de Merc, the second prior of York Franciscan house, always showed to others the sweetness of angelic affection, but subjected himself to fasting, vigils and self-inflicted stripes to the extent that he endangered his health.

An earlier Gloucester prior was described as being of such abstinence and rigour towards himself, and such sweetness and sociality to those under him, that he was believed by all to be angelic in kindness.

It was impressed on the early Franciscan friars that it was important that they should have the demeanour of men who had renounced the world and devoted their lives to the service of Lady Poverty. Agnellus of Pisa said that there were three things which brought special honour to the order: bare feet, ragged clothes and a hatred of money.

RECRUITMENT

Those who were moved to embrace the religious life in the thirteenth century were not short of choices. During that century a spiritual revival swept through intellectual society and educated men turned their backs on rational reasoning, abandoned their birthright way of life, and joined the new religious force within the church. Why did such men join the mendicant orders and undertake the hard and uncertain way of life? Mostly sons of county gentry or wealthy town citizens, they were men with spiritual convictions who wanted to do the will of God as they saw it. They were men who devoted their lives to the Christian faith without thought of self-advancement and were willing to live as beggars for Christ's sake. Their life as friars provided them with some security, prestige and few responsibilities in that uncertain age, but it was a disciplined life and, if one did not have a calling for it, it could have become arduous, even unbearable.

Yet it is amazing that so many gifted men from the elite of society were willing to give up so much to live the mendicant life. Such educated brethren could, possibly, have held well-paid posts within the church, as priests in rich parish churches, canons or archdeacons. However, they turned their backs on all those options in order to become beggars and to serve God. This they did through personal devotion to Jesus and a compassionate identification with his sufferings. It was a hard life, but one they had chosen.

The way of life of the friar offered a challenge to the fervent aspirations of men in search of spiritual perfection. They were men with enthusiasm for the perceived truths of the church and the protection of the church. They lived in the certainty of their faith and in the confidence of God and His promises that He would provide for their needs. Without these strong convictions in the providence of God, they would not have been able to fulfil their ministry to the people. Many friars experienced very tough times in their service to the church and to their God, but they saw themselves as vehicles through which God could work.

The mendicant way of life offered the expression of individuality even though it was a disciplined life. Some no doubt showed their love of God by fasting, vigils and long periods spent in prayer, but they also had a strong conviction that service to others was in itself a form of prayer.

The first of the friars, with their heroic abandonment of material considerations, were undoubtedly men who had a very strong conviction in the Christian faith and whose aim was to take the Gospel to the people in a humble and compassionate way. They were outstanding servants of God who, by their compassion for their fellow men and their love of God, became, as a body of believers, some of the most outstanding men produced by the church.

Well-to-do families, who gave most financial support to the friars, were fearful of their sons becoming friars, as they would not like to contemplate their sons begging and mixing with the poor and destitute. When the Franciscans first arrived in Northampton in 1226, Sir Richard Gobion gave them a temporary house in the town. However, when his son announced his intention to join the friars, Gobion ordered the friars out of the house. He eventually relented when he saw his son's sincerity and the friars' humility. In 1235 he gave the friars a new site where they were able to build a permanent house.

Early on, adult recruits flocked to the orders, and later, boys over 18 were recruited as novices, educated and given a training for their vocation; but there were seldom more than two or three vacancies for novices a year in most houses. The minimum age for entry into the Franciscan order was fixed in 1260 at 18 years of age, but in 1316 it was reduced to 14.

Unlike earlier religious orders, the requisite for admission into the mendicant orders pointed to the better educated, or to those who were able to profit the brethren by their labour. Among the qualifications for acceptance into the orders were that the applicant should be of whole body and prompt in mind, not unlawfully begotten, of good name and fame, and competently learned, not bound in matrimony, honest and teachable, particularly in doctrinal matters, not suspected of error and considered suitable to the mendicant way of life.

In the mid-fourteenth century, Richard Fitz-Ralph, Archbishop of Armagh, maintained that nearly all the students in Oxford University had friars as their confessors and that the friars used their influence to entice these young men to enter the mendicant orders.

The Dominicans recruited men from university circles and the upper middle classes. In order to be propagators of the Gospel, preaching friars had to possess a strong character, an air of authority and charm enough to be able to persuade and move their congregations. When some monks wished a thirteenth-century novice to join them instead of joining the Dominican order, he justified his choice by replying: 'I do not read that Christ was a black monk or a white monk, but that he was a preacher'. Candidates seeking admission to the order were examined by three brothers. The successful postulants were then brought to a chapter meeting and asked what they sought. The postulants replied 'God's mercy and yours'. They were then asked if they were married, serfs, if they were suffering from any hidden disease or if they were professed to any other religious order. If, following acceptable replies, and being deemed suitable, they were accepted as novices and allocated to a house, where they filled one of the vacant novice places.

Other orders had similar practices, and candidates were

admitted to the orders only after being interviewed by their respective chapter meeting and the order being satisfied that the novice came with the right motives and the willingness to accept the way of life they had chosen.

The Austin and Carmelite Orders tended to draw men who wanted to serve the community but also hankered for the ascetic way of life.

The Rule of St Augustine prescribed a noviciate of one year before a recruit was ready to make his profession to an order. Mendicant orders followed this rule and entrants completed a year as novices then, after their training, they made their solemn priestly professions. They freely took perpetual vows of priesthood and vows to their order, which included obedience to their Provincial-Superiors and Minster-General. Religious vows were not promises of resolve but promises made to God and therefore were binding acts of religion.

When novices made their priestly vows, they were professed as ordained priests and full members of their community and order during the ceremony of laying on of hands, which we have already noted. The road was open to them, as it was to all priests, to the higher offices of the church. Many bishops and a number of archbishops came from the ranks of mendicant friars, such as the 20 Dominicans who were chosen to fill vacant sees in England during the fourteenth century.

The Dominican and Franciscan friars were not bound to a particular friary but were professed to a province within their order. Austin novices could join a house only in the district of their home town and were affiliated to that house and could not normally be moved from it, and a prior could not transfer his men to other houses. In new foundations, the Prior-Provincial could either rely on volunteers or assign men as he saw fit. It was not until 1540 that the Austin Order changed the rule whereby a friar was affiliated to a province.

CHARACTERS

Dominican friars were stereotyped as learned and serious

brethren who had shown by their aristocratic manner that they considered that their order had the best-trained and most competent preachers and were the elite of the ecclesiastical establishment. As preachers, they tended to mix with the governing class in the communities and had nothing like the same affinity with the ordinary people as did their fellow mendicant brethren.

Franciscans were stereotyped as jolly friars who lived by their wits and tongue, and earned the nickname of God's Jesters. Because they tended to go out among the ordinary and poor people, they were much more popular and had a closer affinity with them. The people, in their turn, came to respect these men of God who were much less austere in their dealings, and Franciscans became the trusted confidants and friends of the communities.

While friars were allowed by the popes to receive members from monastic orders, other orders were forbidden to receive friars. Within a decade of the Franciscans arriving in England, Walter, a monk of Dunstable priory who had taken monastic vows, and John, who had not, left the priory without permission and took the habit of the Franciscans in Oxford. John of Reading, Abbot of Oseney, near Oxford, entered the London Dominican house. Ralph de Maidstone of Hereford resigned his bishopric in 1239 so as to become a Franciscan friar. After changing his bishop's robes for the coarse clothes of a friar, Ralph was later said to have been among the brethren who carried water, sand and stone for the rebuilding of their Oxford house. No doubt he would have seen this as part of his heavenly work.

It was lawful for a friar to change from one mendicant order to another but it was discouraged. In 1284, the Austins strongly objected when the Oxford Franciscans accepted one of their members without the permission of his superiors.

NUMBERS OF FRIARS

There are few fixed points, and no reliable sources, for the number of friars in Britain in any period during the Middle Ages. When researching the number of brethren in the mendicant orders during the medieval period, it is noted that the various estimates differ somewhat. The writer has taken the average number, in the various estimates he has found, in an attempt to come to an approximate number at any given time.

We can estimate the number in some English houses at the time the King stayed at a friary, between 1277 and 1338, by the amount of alms the King gave to the house to cover the cost of the visit. The number of friars in the house at the time of a royal visit can be concluded from the total of such royal pittances, but more on that further on. From 1338, when the custom was discontinued, there is little information on the number of friars attached to a house. There is less information available regarding the number of friars in mendicant houses in Scotland, although, most Scottish houses were poorer than their English counterparts and had fewer friars As a result, it has not been possible to give any meaningful figures for brethren in the Scottish houses.

There have been various estimates ranging between 4,500 and 5,000 friars in the various orders in England and Wales in 1300. Prior to the dissolution of the houses, many friars fled, leaving about 1,500 brethren still in their houses.

David Knowles, in his *Religious Orders in England*, estimates that by 1256 there were 1,242 Franciscan friars in 49 houses in England and Wales. This gives an average of 25 brethren to a house. Dr Little, in his *Studies of English Franciscan History*, also shows that in 1256 the average number of friars in each Franciscan house in the English Province was 25. Eighty years later, when the friars were numerically at their strongest, this had increased to an average of about 30 Franciscan friars to a house. By about 1300, the larger Franciscan houses had between 40 and 60 brethren, which left many of the smaller houses with between 12 and 20 brethren.

It is estimated that there were about 1,600 Franciscan friars in England and Wales in 1300, increasing to 1,700 by 1348 and then decreasing to about 1,000 in 1500.

In 1260, it is estimated, there were about 900 Dominican

friars in the 35 or so Dominican houses in England and Wales, and about 1,500 in 1300. The numbers rose to 1,700 by 1348 and dropped to about 1,200 in 1450. They then fell to about 800 prior to the dissolution of their houses.

There were on average about 34 brethren to each of the Dominican houses in England and Wales in 1300, falling to about 18 to a house in 1500. Again, some of the larger houses had additional members, while many of the smaller houses had between 12 and 20 brethren.

By 1300, the Austin Order in England had a membership of about 500 brethren. It has been estimated that on the eve of the Black Death there were about 700 Austin friars in England. This number decreased to about 550 by the mid-fifteenth century and was down to about 300 prior to the dissolution of their houses.

The Carmelite order in England and Wales had about 700 friars in 1300, which decreased to about 500 in the mid-fifteenth century and went down to about 300 just prior to the dissolution of their houses.

THEIR MINISTRY

Those who achieved higher office within their order could find themselves allocated to any national area within the order but the less well educated friars generally stayed in the same house for long periods. Each mendicant order looked after their own brethren, and to a zealous friar, his order was the most important thing in this world.

Other than in the Dominican Order, not all friars were preachers and teachers and not all had the same standard of education and training. Friars with potential were developed in the schools of their order and the brighter ones attended university, while their less educated brethren were recruited to carry out the simpler tasks such as alms gathering, attending the sick and saying the numerous masses for the dead.

As we shall see in the next chapter, the Black Death of 1348–49 had a traumatic effect on the people. It has been estimated that the friars lost about half of their brethren during the pestilence, many of them being of the educated classes. The mendicant orders, although they tried to recover numerically from it, never recovered their spirituality. Wadding, the Franciscan annalist, in attributing the Black Death to the decay of his order, wrote:

This evil wrought great destruction to the holy houses of religion, carrying off masters of discipline and the seniors of experience. From this time the monastic orders and in particular the mendicants, began to grow tepid and negligent both in piety and the learning in which they had up to this time flourished. Their most illustrious members being carried off, the rigours of discipline relaxed by the calamities couldn't be renewed by the youths received without the necessary training rather to fill the empty houses than to restore the lost discipline.

The strength and splendour of the mendicants, the flower of the friars, died in the appalling catastrophe.

Following the Black Death, there was a scarcity of vocations, and in their haste to recruit new entrants, the depleted friaries recruited men who didn't have a religious calling for the work and who forgot the poverty of St Francis. Many of the recruits were of an inferior calibre to their earlier brethren, some of them even lacking the necessary qualities of spiritual and moral rectitude. During the latter part of the fifteenth century, indiscriminate recruitment filled the orders with what has been described as 'useless persons'. By the sixteenth century, no standing seems to have been required for ordination into the orders, other than being over the legal age and having the ability to read distinctly and sing correctly. The spiritual effect of the plague on the friars was fundamental.

The Black Death just about stopped further expansion of the mendicant orders and only a few small houses were established after it. Universal poverty followed the plague and this affected the friars, who encountered great hardship, as they lived on transient charity.

POPES' MEN

Popes actively supported the friars in their work. The friars, in their turn, saw themselves as soldiers of the militia of Christ and the mouthpiece of the Pope, their holy father. They knew they had the active support of the popes and, secure under papal protection, they went from strength to strength. They saw the church as a single organisation headed by the Pope and they were the exponents and preservationists of orthodoxy and of the papist view of the church. Popes employed them in both ecclesiastic and secular business and they became familiar with the courts of princes and with the conduct of negotiations. Being trusted by all levels of society, friars were given numerous other miscellaneous tasks such as acting as confidants or carrying confidential messages for kings and nobles. They were tutors for children of the gentry and lecturers in theological schools. In 1322, two friars from the York Franciscan house went to stay with John of Brittany, Earl of Richmond, who had been captured by the Scots. They were to stay with him for as long as he liked, for his recreation and solace. These duties may seem incongruous in view of their rigid religious profession.

Alas, with the papal quest in the second part of the fifteenth century for ever more funds to build St Peter's Church, they became the Pope's instruments in obtaining building funds. The unorthodox methods they used in their quest for funds became the root cause of their fall from popularity with the people, but more on that later on.

FRIARS' ATTIRE

The Dominicans' ministry was a teaching and preaching ministry and, as a result, they mingled with the educated and intellectual in society. This meant that Dominican friars were expected to be better dressed and groomed than friars in other orders. In Britain, the Dominicans were commonly known as 'Black Friars' because of the colour of their dress, a black sleeveless woollen cloth cloak with a cowl headpiece, worn over the shoulders and hanging down to the ankles. The cloak was worn over a white loose-fitting tunic, in the same manner as worn by Augustinian canons. Dominicans were allowed a coat, three tunics and a 'pelliceum', from the Latin *pellicula*, or skin, which suggests some kind of waterproof outer garment. From the start, Dominican friars wore shoes and, as a result, in parts of the Continent they were known as Shod Friars. Tidy dress was thought proper for brethren in their order and stern measures were taken by Dominican provincial chapters to see that the strict rules of dress were observed.

The standard of dress did not have the same significance to the other orders of friars, whose ministry was to all classes of society. The appearance of Franciscan friars was humble, their habits were often worn and patched and they were often hardly distinguishable from the rustic people they served. They were allowed one habit, or garment, which was mostly grey with some brown in it, reaching down to their ankles and girded with a cord. When they went out in cold weather they wore a cloak over their habit. They were not allowed to possess hat, wallet, purse or staff. Their rules, which were drawn up by people living in warmer climates than Britain's, did not allow any footwear, and they, as the poor they served, travelled barefooted even on the coldest of days. The *Lanercost Chronicle*, a general chronicle of events at Lanercost Priory, Cumbria, from 1202 to 1346, tells how the heart of an unfriendly knight was touched by the sight of two Franciscan friars returning from a chapter meeting in Oxford at Christmastime and leaving the marks of blood from their feet as they picked their way along the rugged path over frozen mud and hard snow. The feet of those who did not have footwear were as hard as leather and they could withstand much more hardship than people who habitually donned footwear. They were not to ride, except in a case of absolute necessity. However, during the fourteenth century footwear of some kind was becoming more common.

Austin friars wore a close-fitting white flannel or linen habit when indoors, white symbolising purity. When walking out, they added a black cloak with loose-fitting sleeves and a large black hood, girt with a leather belt, over their habit.

The Carmelite General Council meeting of 1287 decreed that the original striped mantle worn by Carmelite friars be replaced by a white mantle consisting of two pieces of cloth joined at the shoulders and hanging down the back and front of the wearer, in keeping with that worn by ordinary folk. Members of the order were allowed to wear sandals.

Dominican and Franciscan friars wore cords around their waists which had three knots tied on the end of them. The knots were symbolic of the three vows of religion. Austin and Carmelite friars wore leather belts around their waists.

Friars, like others in the religious life, had their hair tonsured, Latin for shaved. Young men being ordained into clerical status had a ritual shaving of the crown of the head as a preliminary to becoming a priest or member of a religious order. After that, the head was shaved fortnightly from Easter to All Saints' Day (1 November) and every three weeks during the rest of the year, leaving a circlet of hair around the sides of the head. Like everything else in the medieval church, the tonsure had a religious significance; it represented the crown of thorns.

FRIARY DUTIES

Information regarding the domestic life of the friars is sparse, fragmentary and seldom intimate. However, it is known that most brethren lived frugally. Friars lived what was in effect a monastic life of individual poverty, a communal life with common refectory, common dormitory and common funds.

When a house was established, it should have had at least the apostolic number of 12 friars, plus a head of the house, which was the minimum number of brethren necessary to maintain an active mendicant house, but most houses were larger communities than required by their constitution. However, the number of friars in some smaller houses fell below the permitted number and it is doubtful if a number of the later Scottish foundations ever reached the minimum number of 13 brethren.

As we have seen, each friary had its own chapter house where the prior or warden presided over the friars' discussion of the business of their house and where individual brethren were allocated duties according to their capabilities. A number of friars had an individual responsibility within their house. The procurator was in charge of financial and personal affairs and kept records of income and expenditure. There was a cellarer, who was in charge of the food, drink and kitchens. The sacristan was responsible for the upkeep of the church, especially of the liturgical services, the vestments and altar vessels. A master of novices was in charge of the novices and the library, although, in the larger houses another friar deputised for him in the latter duty. Some were employed on in-house duties such as illuminating and binding books for the library and for sale. Others would be out on preaching and teaching missions or caring for the poor and sick.

Early Franciscans remembered St Francis's exhortation that they should obtain the necessities of life by manual work as well as by alms. We do not know to what extent manual work was part of their lives, but it is reasonable to suppose that in the early days a number of them took part in labours such as repairing clothes and implements. No doubt the community of friars helped manually in building their houses, a long and slow process. Some of the smaller houses had kitchen gardens, and orchards and pasture land where a few animals were kept, and the husbandry side of the house had to be maintained by the brethren. Work in friaries was not compartmentalised and it was taken for granted that all friars should be prepared to help with the domestic and manual tasks of maintenance of the community and the upkeep and cleanliness of the friary buildings, even though they might normally be employed on more priestly or scholastic tasks. In the larger houses, including by the fourteenth century in Franciscan houses, much of the manual work was done by servants and the less educated brethren. Manual work in Dominican houses was carried out by servants from the start, so that the clerical brethren could devote themselves entirely to study and preaching.

An important duty of every house was the ongoing plying for alms, for otherwise, without some kind of transitory financial support, friars' houses could not have continued to exist. We all know how important it is in our own lives to ensure we have a steady flow of money in order to remain solvent. The friars' communities were no different, but they often lacked continual sources of finance. From the fourteenth century onwards, money problems must have been an ongoing worry in a number of houses, and it became a concern which took up a considerable amount of time.

Friars were independently minded men, and, because of the nature of their work, their activities kept them in the public eye. Whereas the public could see their good works, they could also recognise the bad apples among them, and, unfortunately, they were more inclined to report the doings of a friar who failed to live up to his calling than those who continued a compassionate ministry among the people. I feel this was what frequently happened in the fifteenth century when the friars were being criticised.

Their peripatetic life resulted in many overnight, and longer, stays as they went on their itinerant preaching and pastoral missions. Many people considered it a religious duty to invite passing friars into their homes for hospitality whenever they were staying in their district, but such visits could become a burden to the host. The friars in their turn knew where they would receive a welcome and lodgings during their stay in the area. This was especially so in the smaller towns where they had established an oratory. At times, most of the brethren of a house were out for days on one task or another. and there were many occasions when only one or two brethren would be in the house, although as many of them as possible would return for the evening, or compline, service. As late as 1537, it was reported that there were 25 friars in the town of Winchester, but only three of them, one for each house, remained in their house over the weekend.

All friars, bar the Dominicans, had the ability and freedom

to move about within the hinterland territory of their house. Wandering the countryside from hamlet to hamlet in all weathers, they were seen in barons' halls, in merchants' houses, on village greens or seated at some cottage hearth, delivering the Gospel message wherever a knot of hearers could be found. In such places they were able to speak to the people in their own language and exchange crude jests and honest laughter. The average friar would have had strong feelings about many things, and no doubt ruffled a few feathers in society. There could have been justification for calling them either troublesome, or troubleshooters, depending on the view of the person making the comment.

DISCIPLINE

A decree of the Franciscan 1292 General Council commanded that each Provincial-Minister should have the lives and acts of holy men in his province entered in special registers, and they should also keep registers of grave crimes, creditable accusations and notable excesses of friars and the punishments inflicted on the offenders. These registers were to be preserved in the archives of the province and handed to each succeeding Provincial-Minister. The decree also stated that all the Provincial Acts were to be kept in the same manner.

The constitutions of the orders prescribed a good solid prison for each house with 14 or more brothers. Prison sentences were prescribed for many transgressions. For example, a year in prison was imposed for suppression of letters to and from their superior, or misuse of the seal of the General or Provincial-Minister. Six months was the penalty for stealing, carrying arms or apostasy, but there are very few references to apostasy, which was an unlicensed abandonment of their habit. Forsaking or abandoning their allegiance was an ecclesiastical crime, but the state helped the church to apprehend those who were guilty of apostasy, and those guilty were usually apprehended and returned to their house within weeks.

There were lighter punishments for minor faults, such as

three beatings or three days on bread and water for not obeying a bell promptly or failing to put away clothes and books in their correct place. Four days on bread and water and four beatings was the punishment for those who were accused of a misdemeanour. Francis's advice to all in authority in the order was that they should regard all accusations against a brother with suspicion at first, until the truth was known by an inquiry. An accuser who could not prove his charges was liable himself to receive the punishment which would have been given to the accused.

Others, inevitably, were guilty of disobeying church or civil law and had to be punished. A prior could imprison brethren who came from other houses without a testimonial letter. Those guilty of disobeying church or civil law were punished by their order, and at times friars were sent to another house for discipline.

Grave faults included unseemly disputes and quarrels, speaking ill of brethren, breaking silence, defending one's own or another's wrongdoings, taking money on a journey without permission or grave need, staring at women and breaking a fast of the church. Graver faults included open defiance of one's superiors and hiding forbidden gifts, offences which were punishable by beatings and by seating the offender on the floor in the middle of the refectory, where he was allowed to eat only course bread and drink water.

On occasions, the commands given by a superior were hard or impossible for a friar to accept. His solution to such was to give the superior reasonable objections, followed by obedience, and, if that failed, trust in God.

Despite a number of scandals and cases of misconduct, little is known of the state of discipline among the friars in the decades immediately preceding the Reformation, but we do know that the discipline was more relaxed than in previous times.

Friars, like monks, had one advantage over lay people in that when they were taken sick or were infirm from age they were looked after by the brethren. In old age, or retirement, it was customary for friars to return to the house of their first profession. When they died they were buried in the habit of their order in the friars' burial ground attached to their church.

The spiritual calling of a friar can be summed up in the prayer of an anonymous friar: 'I thank you good Jesus that you have given me to drink in the delights, the works of knowledge, so of your loving kindness you will grant me one day to come to you, the fountain of wisdom and stand forever before your face'.

I am sure most friars would have claimed they were striving to follow the aspirations of St Francis as outlined in his prayer, even if they did not always live up to his high standards.

Lord, make me an instrument of your peace
Where there is injury ... pardon.
Where there is discord ... unity.
Where there is doubt ... faith.
Where there is error ... truth.
Where there is despair ... hope.
Where there is sadness ... joy.
Where there is darkness ... light.

O Divine Master, grant that I may not so much seek
To be consoled ... as to console.
To be understood ... as to understand.
To be loved ... as to love.

For
It is in giving ... that we receive.
It is in pardoning ... that we are pardoned.
It is in dying ... that we are born to eternal life.

6

THE MISSION OF THE FRIARS

Nominal religion played an important role in the lives of the people during the Middle Ages, but by the beginning of the thirteenth century the church had done little to adjust itself to the intellectual and economical changes which were affecting their thoughts and lives. The laity had come to believe that true faith could be found only within the walls of monastic houses and were content to go through the established routine of church services in a mechanical manner, with little awareness of their meaning. This created a strong undercurrent of disbelief and records of church courts reveal that blasphemous jokes freely circulated in the taverns of the time. Because of the lack of teaching the meaning and significance of the Mass, people showed an indifference towards it. The church was growing in size and importance but there was much that was wrong at the heart of it. It was a period when the church had an imperative need of teachers and preachers.

It was during this period that the friars' movements came into being. They touched a receptive cord which had a major impact on the church.

Active faith is of both the head and heart, and friars appealed to intellect and emotion in the church and its people and brought a new perspective to religion. The mendicants' aim was to enlighten people's understanding of the Gospel by proclaiming the Christian doctrines and by education. Their ministry came as a breeze fanning the flames of faith. Friars were certain about their beliefs and they spread their certainties wherever they went. Although the mendicant orders were only a small part of the medieval church, they exercised an influence out of all proportion to their numbers and began a Christian renewal of some magnitude.

Local friaries served as centres of religious organisation in their areas and the early mendicant friars were the church militant and provided the church with one of the most vigorous missionary agencies it ever had. Due to their zeal and dedication, friars achieved a high standing in the community as they won the hearts of the people. They became spiritual guides to the multitudes and had an authority that silenced opposition.

Due to their superior training, friars were able to carry out pastoral work in a more competent manner than the parochial clergy and the people came to trust them with the care of their souls and their spiritual and eternal problems.

At first, relations between the friars and parochial clergy were relatively harmonious and priests were pleased to receive their help, but friars were carefully trained and they far excelled the uneducated and untrained parish clergy in the work of the church. This became the cause of friction between them and the local clergy. Services in mendicant churches were well attended because people were attracted to them by the eloquence and wit of well-prepared sermons. They were so successful that large numbers of parishioners stayed away from their parish churches, preferring to hear the mendicants' sermons.

In 1231, Pope Gregory IX issued papal decree '*Nimis Iniqua*', which declared that friars were free from all episcopal jurisdiction, visitation and taxation, and assured them full rights of self government. However, the constitution of the Dominicans and rules of the Franciscans forbade friars to preach in any diocese where the bishop refused his consent, unless the bishop's objection was overruled by the Pope.

As the clergy saw their spiritual monopoly eroded, they began to resent the popularity of the friars who devoted themselves to the same pastoral work which had for centuries been the preserve of parish priests. Parish clergy considered that they alone were entrusted with the cure of souls in their parish and came to see the friars as interlopers who usurped other people's jurisdiction. The tension between the parochial clergy and friars generally turned on the friars' right to preach, to hear confessions and to bury the dead. In addition, friars were increasingly collecting customary dues which would have rightly fallen to the clergy. This had financial repercussions for the clergy as it diverted alms given for masses, confessions, benefactions and legacies away from them. These inroads into parochial rights and privileges were hotly disputed, for the loss of revenue proved a hardship for medieval parishes at a time when the church hierarchy and the state made frequent tax demands on them.

The clergy had an additional grievance against the friars in that friars were exempt by common law from paying tithes and taxes, but friaries were established in buildings or on land that had previously paid tithes. Obviously, rectors were unhappy about this, and as a result, rectors and mendicant houses often came to local agreements over the payment of donations to rectors. Many friaries voluntarily paid a yearly rent in lieu of the former taxes on their property and there are numerous references to local agreements between the parish clergy and friaries regarding the payment of mortuary fees. The Ludlow Carmelite friars, for instance, reached an agreement with the Ludlow parish priests that any bodies buried in the Carmelite church should be brought to the parish church first and the offerings given to the parish clergy.

The friars, for their part, held most priests in contempt because of their lack of ability and commitment to the faith. They uncharitably referred to the parochial clergy as Dumb Dogs.

The smouldering resentment of the clergy flared up in Paris University in 1254 when the question of the mendicants' rights to exercise pastoral ministry was taken up by the secular masters of the university. The attack was so severe that there were considerable doubts whether the mendicants would be allowed to continue their work. In the November, the ailing Pope Innocent IV was persuaded to recant all the privileges granted to the mendicants, thereby completely undermining their position. The Pope died three weeks later and the new

Pope, Alexander IV, a supporter of the friars, was speedily elected to the papal throne. Alexander's first public act was to restore the mendicants to their previous position. This led opponents to make accusations against the friars. William of St Amour, in his tract *Concerning the Perils of the Last Days*, challenged the friars' rights and took his stand on the supposition that the diocesan and parochial organisation of the church was founded upon the apostles and was a divine ordinance. In this divine direction the secular clergy alone were entrusted with the cure of souls and no one, not even the Pope, had authority to change it. He argued that it was the exclusive role of the superior priestly order to perfect and instruct others. Monks and friars belonged, as did the laity, to inferior orders of those who gave pastoral administration, and therefore, they could not perform the office that belonged to their superiors in the faith.

The Dominican scholar Thomas Aquinas and the Franciscan Bonaventure championed the mendicants' cause, and thanks to Bonaventure's treatise *On the Poverty of Christ*, the mendicants succeeded in procuring the condemnation of St Amour's tracts and invoking the authority of the popes, who had authorised their ministry, and took refuge behind the many papal privileges they had received. The mendicants argued that the Pope was not only the universal bishop but also every mans' parish priest. As such, he could delegate his parochial responsibilities to whom he chose, and he had chosen to delegate them to the friars. The controversy continued with a wave of pamphleteering but, by then, the mendicants had become well established and were not again seriously endangered.

Bonaventure (1221–74) was given his name by St Francis himself. At the age of 36 he was appointed Minister-General of the Franciscans at a time of crisis for the order, which was suffering from poor organisation, complacency and internal division. By his outstanding administration and moderate approach he achieved such lasting success that he is known as the order's second founder.

In 1300, the matter of mendicant rights came to a head when Pope Boniface VIII issued his '*Super Cathedram*' bull. It was a lasting compromise which allowed friars to preach in their own churches and in public places, except at certain times so as not to clash with parish church services. Friars could preach in parish churches by invitation of the parish priest or by the command of the local bishop. However, by then friaries had their own churches designed to accommodate large crowds and facilities for preachers.

PREACHING

The principle task of the friars was to remedy the appalling ignorance of the Christian faith that existed among the people, by popular instruction of the faith and by providing it with a more effective and informed body of preachers. Friars held firm to the traditional doctrines, combated heresy and placed a high priority on lucid and cogent preaching, rather than on ceremonial, but they remained faithful to the ceremonial traditions of the church.

They saw their mission as being one of arousing popular enthusiasm for the great attributes of the Christian faith: peace of mind, penitence and holy joy. In pursuit of this, they argued, disputed, and sought to dispose of error and convince gainsayers. They followed the command of Jesus to His disciples for them to go into all the world and preach the Gospel to all men, and embraced the scriptural edict 'How then shall they believe in Him of whom they have not believed? And how shall they believe in Him of whom they have not heard? and how shall they hear without a preacher?' (Romans 10:14)

As they spoke on the truths necessary for salvation, they concentrated on making the faithful aware of sin and urged them to confess their sins; but their preaching was done more from a moral than a dogmatic point of view. Their aim was to move large audiences and they mercilessly stigmatised those who strayed from those principles, which was, in fact, the major part of the population.

As they preached tirelessly, and with conviction, the message of the Gospel, they came to detest the heretics who threatened the very foundation of the faith and the authority of the church. Consequently they became known as 'the hammer of heretics'.

There was a difference between the Franciscan and Dominican approach to preaching. The early Franciscan friars went out and about, speaking in the common tongue, as they took every opportunity to preach, making simple appeals to love God and renounce sin. People flocked to hear their homilies given from pulpits, in market places or at village crosses. They reached the underprivileged and hitherto forgotten classes as well as the intelligentsia and highest levels of society.

The Dominicans, being a more upper-class order, didn't consider it proper to preach in what they considered unworthy locations. They believed that preaching and teaching about God should be done in a dignified manner and only in buildings dedicated to God. They regarded the soul as more important than the body and thought that concern for souls was more important than works of mercy.

They believed that the whole of a preacher's life should be structured around his vocation. They recognised that preaching was a natural ability, that preachers could not be made, and, when the ability was recognised in a person, it should be developed to its full potential. A Dominican brother over 25 years of age and who had studied theology for one year was allowed to preach, with the prior's permission, within their friary. He had to have read theology for three years and received the authority of the Provincial Chapter, before being allowed to preach within a province.

Prospective Dominican preachers were expected to be fluent and have a ready flow of anecdotes for use in their sermons. It was thought to be of benefit, too, if they had a sonorous voice capable of producing a good sound, a voice that could be heard clearly. They were taught to fit their sermons to their audience, as there was no one kind of sermon suitable for everyone. Consequently, there were sermons for scholars, sermons for merchant classes, sermons for the uneducated and sermons for kings and princes. Except when a sermon was being given to royal or clerical audiences, the vernacular was used.

The Austin and Carmelite friars followed the Franciscans in their ministry, although they cultivated a scholarly basis for their preaching, and, in the fourteenth and fifteenth centuries, produced some outstanding preachers.

We have to jump three or four centuries, to the eighteenth-century Methodist revival, before we find another group of itinerant preachers who travelled the country proclaiming the Gospel in such a manner.

Sermon-making became an art which was taught in their schools. They studied eloquence, the art of rhetorical flourishes in oratory and the art of persuasion. Meaningful sermons require study and preaching friars were expected to be well versed in theology and philosophy. They had to have the ability to find subjects which contained useful thoughts applicable to their audience and to be able to confirm everything they said from the Scriptures.

St Jerome said of novice preachers: 'They disdain to find out what the prophets and apostles really meant. They fitted texts to their own views, forcing reluctant scriptures to serve their own purposes'.

St Gregory the Great said: 'Anyone who speaks the word of God must first consider his own manner of life. Do not let your deeds thwart your words, otherwise, when you are speaking in church, your hearers will silently answer back, "Why do you not put your own words into practice".' Preachers were expected to set an example of the faith that was in them.

Some friars' textbooks and literature on homiletics still survive and give us some background to their sermons. They spoke of God as an authoritative being, of the nature of the soul and the power of divine grace. They warned the haughty that a higher tribunal, before which their ermine robes were no more allowed than the threadbare cloak of a pilgrim, awaited them. They told the burgesses that the gold in their coffers was nothing compared with the treasures laid up in heaven, and countrymen that life was as fleeting as their crops. Teaching the principles of the Christian life, they preached against greed and avarice and reminded those fortunate enough to have wealth of the spiritual value of charity. They exhorted their hearers to penance and warned them against the wiles of the devil.

They were sometimes amusing and flattering in their preaching and the hearers enjoyed many a good story as they were called to repentance and to the renewing of their relationship with God. Preachers were also often outspoken in their sermons, denouncing injustices and moral failings. The friars' vivid portrayal of the fate that awaited the unrighteous made it clear that none, be he king or beggar, could hope to escape the pains of hell or purgatory if he flouted the teachings of the faith.

The orders compiled Bible concordances to provide the sermoniser with a supply of biblical texts, thus ensuring that all friars preached the same universal message.

During Lent and other seasons of the church, friars, with the support of the diocesan bishops, organised preaching missions to outlying villages and small towns. No doubt the outdoor sermons were times for good-humoured banter between the 'bright sparks' and the friars, much as Speakers' Corner in Hyde Park is today, although friars would have been more respected by the people than are the speakers at Hyde Park.

The Dominicans, in particular, organised preaching tours and preaching circuits. Their preachers were accompanied, in accordance with apostolic practice, by a travelling friar companion when they went out to preach. At times the companion was senior to the preacher, though during the journey he carried out duties required by the preacher. No doubt the companion monitored the preacher's performance and sermon. These missions were organised, and, with the sermon, went pastoral care and counselling. On such occasions there were penitents from previous missions who would perform public devotions, or what we would now call public testimonies, before the orator began to speak.

Each Dominican friary divided its territory into districts and assigned friars to preach systematically in places where they were invited in the rural areas. The Pontefract Dominican friars, for instance, established preaching stations in various towns such as at Pontefract, Rotherham and Wakefield. No doubt other mendicant houses followed this pattern but details have been lost.

The King at times used the friars for political purposes, as when, in 1314 Edward II told the York Austin friars to preach against the Scots, and later, Edward III asked the London Austins to preach in support of his war with Philip IV of France and to expound the cause.

By the middle of the fifteenth century there was a new breed of friar who went to extremes in fanciful exaggerated preaching which tended to emphasise the need for indulgences. They, from false piousness, made excessive claims about the efficacity of praying to the saints and the power of religious relics. As time went by, some friars, from excessive zeal, went too far in elaborating the claims of the church. This made them unpopular and was, in the sixteenth century, to prove to be their undoing. However, the influence of the popular preachers in diffusing and forming opinion can hardly be paralleled today save by the press and television.

CONFESSORS

A Roman Catholic Catechism defines the Sacrament of Penance, or Confession as it is popularly known, thus:

Confession is the telling of our sins to an authorized priest for the purpose of obtaining forgiveness. An authorized priest is one who has not only the power to forgive sins by reason of his ordination to the priesthood, but also the power of jurisdiction over the persons who come to him. He has this jurisdiction from his bishop, or, by reason of his office.

Sins committed through human frailty were expiated by good deeds and prayer by a priest towards the redemption of the soul. The confessor, as a representative of Christ in the sacramental form, was seen as exercising the roles of a fatherly judge, physician of the soul and spiritual counsellor. It was accepted by both church and people that Christ gave the power of forgiving or retaining sins solely to the priest of the church. The priests took their authority as representatives of Christ in the confessional from such sayings of Jesus to His disciples as 'Whose soever sins ye remit, they are remitted unto them; and whose soever sins ye retain, they are retained' (St John 20:23).

Ordination empowered a priest to pronounce divine forgiveness for the sins confessed by saying 'By God's authority, I absolve you from your sins, in the name of the Father, Son and Holy Spirit', to which he added 'Go in peace, for the Lord has put away your sins and pray for me, a sinner too'. Confession was an accepted part of the religious life of medieval people, who saw penance as compensation for sins done against God.

All sins of which penitents, after diligent self-examination, were conscious, had to be recounted by them in confession. When sins were confessed to a priest, if he was assured of the real sorrow for the offences by the penitent, he gave the penitent spiritual advice, prescribed an act of penance and gave the person absolution. Many of the faithful had only venial, or lesser, sins to confess, and penances prescribed consisted mainly of fasting, repeating psalms, repeating a number of prayers or giving alms. The act of penance was payment of a debt for sins which had to be paid in this life. It was a voluntary act of self-denial which resulted in the remission of a certain number of days from purgatory, after the prescribed acts were duly performed.

Mortal sins were serious offences committed with the full knowledge and intention to do wrong, but they too could be forgiven if the penitent confessing was truly contrite and performed the imposed penance. Penance for these more serious sins could be long and hard, such as visiting holy places or going on pilgrimages. Sometimes the penance covered long periods, seven, or in some incidents, as long as twenty years. Sometimes the penitent died before the end of the penitential period.

Those who failed to confess to mortal sin were deemed to have committed sacrilege and those who died in a state of unrepented mortal sin would go to hell.

By the tenth century, regular confession to a priest became standard practice. It involved the perception of sin, fear of God's judgment, regret for the sin and satisfaction in the forgiveness. In 1215, the Fourth Lateran Council made auricular confession, that is, confession spoken into the ear, obligatory at least once a year for all adult Christians. The council did not make it clear if this requirement was a human or a divine institution and the question was not resolved until the mid-sixteenth century, when the Council of Trent declared that auricular confession was a divine requirement.

All classes of people were required to open their conscience and make confession, whether pope, king, archbishop or the humblest in the land. There was no problem with the parish priest hearing the confessions of the ordinary laity, but when it came to the rich and influential telling their innermost secrets to another person, even if that person was a priest, it raised doubts of confidentiality. The right to choose their own confessor was a privilege given to the people. The King and nobility thus used more than one confessor, not letting any one person know their total confessions.

Confession introduced a moral consciousness and it encouraged people to scrutinise their lives in search of sin; and, by the use of the confessional, priests became aware of the more intimate lapses of their flock. However, the clergy didn't receive suitable training to undertake what was their most difficult and demanding responsibility. They were governed by *The Penitential Manual*, which contained codes listing offences, together with penalties appropriate to each sin. Most priests felt bound by the manual and did not take into account the circumstances of the transgression. The spirit of correction was more prominent in the manual than that of compassion. However, the penitential judgment of the priest was not intended to be condemnatory or vindictive but rather a liberating and curative sentence, with the aim of healing the wounds of sin.

As we have seen, friars had the advantage of ongoing training, whether as preachers, teachers, working with the sick or as confessors. As with all their activities, mendicants put a lot of thought and effort into training friars nominated to hear confessions. Mendicants compiled manuals on what penances should be give to penitents, and friars therefore escaped the straitjacket of the old penitentials with their graded tariffs of punishment, and laid stress on contrition rather than on punishment. They were seen as representatives of Christ in the tribunal of the conscience and as doctors of the soul who could supply the correct treatment for the sinful condition.

Friars made themselves the chief exponents and practitioners of the confessional and placed greater emphasis on the circumstances of the penitent. This made greater intellectual demands upon the confessor than did the previous system. In order to get an accurate picture of the spiritual problems involved, friars learned the art of both hearing confessions and asking the penitent questions. They were therefore able to appeal to the individual conscience, give appropriate penance and offer spiritual advice, encouragement and inspiration to contrite penitents, rather than just mete out punishment. This resulted in the faithful looking more readily to the friars as their confessors, considering them to be far more competent in this role than their local priests. The friars also became popular confessors, due to what many people considered the lighter penances they gave out. They were also popular as they were mostly peripatetic confessors who didn't know the individual and would perhaps never return.

The confessor was required to maintain the vow of secrecy; this was fundamental to the system of the confessional. It was of prime importance that the penitent had complete trust in the confessor, otherwise people would not confess their sins and the confessional system would fail.

In the early days of the ministry, ordained friars were allowed to hear the confessions of all who came to them. This, of course, upset the parochial clergy, who considered canon law made it clear that it was the privilege of the parish priest to hear confessions and that they should have penitential judgment of all persons within their parish.

In 1281, the Franciscan Pope Martin IV gave friars the privilege of '*Ad Fructus Uberes*', which allowed them to perform all pastoral functions in any diocese, without seeking the consent of the local bishop. This led to a prolonged struggle between friars and those who supported the role of the local clergy. In 1287, despite the local priests' protest, Archbishop Peckham of Canterbury, as protector of the Franciscan Order in Britain, decreed that friars might receive confession and impose penances without the leave of the parish priest. The controversy was finally settled in 1300, when Pope Boniface VIII issued his '*Super Cathedram*' bull, which, as we have seen, was a lasting compromise which settled this controversy, along with other controversies. The compromise allowed friars who had been nominated by their order and licensed by the diocesan bishop to hear confessions within the dioceses. The bull also decreed that anyone wishing to confess to any other than their parish priest should obtain leave from the incumbent to do so. In the following year, the Pope decreed that anyone who made confession to the friars should also confess the same sins to their parish priest. In 1321, the subject was debated, in the presence of Pope John XXII, between John of Billy, a Doctor of Theology at Paris University, and Peter Paludanus, a Dominican friar. The Pope decided in favour of the friars and decreed that friars licensed by bishops were free to hear confession from all who requested it.

Following the Pope's decree, provincial priors selected suitable friars and presented them to the local bishop for his consent for them to act as confessors in his diocese. The number of friar confessors was regulated by the needs of the populace, and bishops made sure that licences were given only to men of ability. The nominated friars, normally those with academic degrees, were the more talented brethren and, as such, became popular confessors. There are numerous ecclesiastical and diocesan records which recorded the names of friars licensed to hear confessions. A bishop could license a friar to act as a confesser in his diocese or in an archdeanery within the diocese. Soon after the papal bull of 1300, fourteen Dominican friars were licensed by the Bishop of Lincoln to hear confessions in the Archdeanery of Oxford, and in the same year the Dominican Provincial Prior requested licences for a further 24 friars. In 1323, twelve Franciscan replacements were licensed in Canterbury to replace friars who had died or had been transferred.

All religious institutions, including friaries, had to have one or more confessors appointed to their house, depending on the number of friars attached to the house. These confessors were usually the local prior or another person appointed by the prior. Those in religious orders were expected to go to confession more frequently. Even though some friars were authorised to hear confessions, they, in turn, had to go to confession and receive penance, or, if they had no sin to confess, receive a blessing from the confessor.

The nobility and members of the royal family used friars extensively as their confessors, and they often became their close confidants and trusted messengers for secret errands. Dominican friar John Darlington was Henry III's confidant and was made a member of the King's council. In 1271 he was appointed Archbishop of Dublin. In 1315, the prior of King's Langley Dominican house was Edward II's confessor. As we have seen, Edward III sent his Dominican confessor to France in 1356 to conduct four sisters from the royal prior of Poissy, near Paris, to Dartford, Kent, where a new monastery had been built for them. Dominican friars were the English kings' confessors up until the fall of Richard II in 1399, but at the end of the fourteenth century, Carmelites began to take the places of Dominican friars as royal confessors.

VISITING THE SICK

In early medieval times there were establishments known as hospitals, so called for the very good reason that they provided hospitality centuries before the word acquired a strictly medical meaning. Some were homes for the poor and sick where they lived communal lives, others gave shelter to the aged and dying. But they were small establishments with only small bands of workers to run them. A large number of such hospitals disappeared during the fourteenth century, when their small endowments became insufficient and contributions dried up.

Since the days of St Francis, friars, especially the Franciscans, showed great compassion for the poor and needy. Whilst a number of the brethren would be concerned with preaching, teaching and reaching out to the leaders of society, others busied themselves serving the sick, lame and destitute, tending loathsome diseases and giving succour to the distressed.

The Franciscans considered it an ongoing part of their service to God and their Christian calling to minister and give practical care and help wherever they could. They did not forget St Francis's compassion for the sick and devoted a lot of effort to their healing ministry. They followed the teachings of Jesus:

I was an hungred, and ye gave me meat: I was thirsty and ye gave me drink; I was a stranger, and ye took me in: naked, and ye clothed me: I was sick, and ye visited me: I was in prison, and ye came unto me. Then shall the righteous answer him saying 'Lord, when saw we thee an hungred, and fed thee? Or thirsty, and gave thee drink? When saw we thee a stranger, and took thee in? Or naked, and clothed thee? Or when saw we thee sick, or in prison, and came unto thee? And the king shall answer and say unto them, Verily I say unto you, Inasmuch as ye have done it unto one of the least of these my brethren, ye have done it unto me (St Matthew 25:35–40).

It was their social work, as well as their preaching, that endeared the friars to the hearts of the people. They, with other religious institutions, were the only social services available to those in need.

Franciscans largely followed the lead of St Francis in showing compassion to the wretched and unfortunate people who suffered from leprosy. In the twelfth and thirteenth centuries, leprosy was endemic, but, fortunately, by the sixteenth century the disease had declined in Britain. Lepers were not permitted to enter towns and were ostracised by society.

Hospitals for lepers were sited outside towns, even hidden away in woods. The lepers, ashamed of their disfigurement and the wasting away of the affected parts of their bodies, ventured outside their compounds only in the dark, hiding themselves by day. We can have only the greatest admiration for the friars, and others, who tended these unfortunate people at considerable risk to themselves.

Franciscans considered that one of their duties was to minister to the sick and dying, as practised by St Francis himself. But work like this received little notice in history, and where it is mentioned, it is usually referring to their greed for legacies; but there are very few recorded instances of friars being found in the chamber of sickness or death solely for the purpose of gathering legacies.

The monks studied primitive medicine from the earliest times. During the twelfth and thirteenth centuries Salerno University, in south-west Italy, was the outstanding medical teaching establishment in Europe. A number of Italian and French monks who studied medicine there later became leaders in major British abbeys and priories. They came with their medical expertise and created a new understanding of medical matters. However, the monks' ministration to the sick was restricted to their brethren, royalty and nobility.

The friars worked with the sick, and this stimulated their study of medicine. They exchanged ideas on pharmacy by sharing information through their Europe-wide contacts, including Moorish and Jewish scholars in southern Spain.

During the thirteenth century, they became the foremost authorities on treating the sick and on minor surgical operations. They took advice from the text of *Aphorisms of Hippocrates*, the work of Hippocrates (*c.* 460–377 BC), the Greek physician, and from other medical books of classical times. The Franciscans in particular practised the ancient art of the herbalists, preparing medicines from natural ingredients.

The friars' widespread interest in medicine is shown by many books on medical matters listed in surviving catalogues of friars' libraries. They show that the medicines they gave to the sick consisted chiefly of herbal remedies. They also relied on certain long-standing beliefs, such as that too much blood caused fever and the best way to treat fever was to bleed the patient.

The Franciscans did not use their friary infirmaries for sick people outside their order but visited them in their homes. The Austin and Carmelite friars followed their example but not with the same degree of enthusiasm. The Dominican friars did not see this work as an essential part of their ministry.

THE BLACK DEATH

Outbreaks of plague were much worse than outbreaks of cholera, and plague was endemic throughout the Middle Ages. The great bubonic plague, or the Black Death as it is generally known, spread rapidly through Britain. In England and Wales it was called the 'Great Mortality' and in Scotland it was known as the 'Foul Death of the English'.

The contagious bubonic plague began in China and swept across Asia and Europe until, in 1348, it crossed the sea from the mainland of Europe. The dreadful malady first entered England at Melcombe Regis (Weymouth) in June 1348. In 1348–49, it reached its peak in England and Wales, and in 1349–50 in Scotland, after which it abated. As it made its ghastly inroads in Britain, it was most fierce in Kent and the East Midlands, although no part of the country was spared the visitation, which ravaged populations in its path.

It is estimated that Norwich lost two-fifths of its population and at least half of its clergy, including nearly all, if not all, of the Norwich Franciscan community, during the pestilence. Oxford lost at least a third of its population, and, it is estimated, up to 60 per cent of the clergy in Lincoln succumbed.

Its affliction was so great and unpredictable that many who felt fit and well in the morning died of the plague by evening. Seldom did only one in a house die; often it took man and wife, together with their children and servants. It is difficult for historians who have studied the fatality figures to assess the number of deaths but it is estimated that the population of London was nearly halved and over one-third of the population of Britain died. In other lands the fatality rate was even higher; no catastrophe in European history has equalled it. Needless to say, at the height of the plague the populace were concerned only with survival from day to day. Ordinary business was brought to a standstill, fields were left untended, crops spoilt and mill wheels ground to a halt. One can imagine the horror of the people as they saw the spectre of death all around them, not knowing if it was their turn next.

As the extent of the plague, and results of its social upheaval, dawned on people, they turned to religion. Weird quasi-religious sects grew up and plague-haunted towns saw the gruesome procession of flagellants whipping and scourging themselves in penitence and fear.

Accounts of the plague tell of the selfless heroism of the clergy as a whole, and the friars in particular, as they ministered to the people. Not only were the friars' houses located in, or near, built-up areas of the towns, but, by the very nature of their calling, friars were exposed to the ravages of the disease. As the plague was deemed a grave emergency, they laid aside their other duties and concentrated on ministering to the sick and dying. As a result, the friars were especially vulnerable and the mortality rate among them was heavy, greater than for the population as a whole. When excavations were being made in London of a pit dug at the time of the epidemic, no less than a hundred bodies were found and they all had lead obituary crosses worn by Franciscan friars on them. It has been estimated the mortality rate among all the British clergy was as high as 45 per cent.

For all their failings, the friars and clergy did not let the people down in their time of greatest need. For a long time after, friars gained great honour and respect among the people for their devoted work during the time of the plague. This can partly explain the continued support of the friars right up to the first quarter of the sixteenth century.

The initial outbreak of the plague was followed by a second, less severe, outbreak in 1361, and there were further milder ones throughout the remainder of the century; but the thought of another catastrophic outbreak was a constant fear which governed people's lives.

After the plague abated, those who survived it, and those born after the pestilence, became concerned with death. Their preparation for death, and the impact and shadow of the Black Death, dominated the scene for the rest of the century and beyond. This took the form of superstition, which, as we will later see, was carried into the life of the church. When considering the gross misuses of religion in the latter part of the fourteenth century and throughout the fifteenth century, one should bear in mind the traumatic effect the Black Death had on the people and their eagerness to do anything they could to avoid a repetition of it. The plague was to have a catastrophic effect on theological thinking for the next generation and beyond. Religious excesses built up from this time which were eventually to lead to the Reformation.

HOSPITALITY

A number of the larger friaries had guest halls able to provide lodging accommodation for travellers but, in the majority of houses, hospitality on a large scale was not possible. Friars found, much against their instinct, that they were frequently being called upon to give hospitality to nobility and royalty. Kings travelled with large retinues and found it useful to reside in a friary, which provided good accommodation, privacy and security for the royal party. Royal visits were an expensive honour, as the high-ranking guests required good food, drink and comfort during their visits. The food eaten by friars would not have been acceptable at the King's table, and the scale of hospitality was proportionate with the importance of the visitor. Edinburgh, Lincoln, London, Perth, Newcastle-upon-Tyne and York friaries were notable for such visits.

Henry III, Edward I and Edward II were frequently accommodated in friaries. In the thirteenth and fourteenth centuries, when kings moved their court to York so as to be closer to any trouble in the north, they usually stayed in the Franciscan house, where they enjoyed the protection of the nearby royal castle into which the King could easily escape and take refuge if the necessity arose. The Newcastle-upon-Tyne Dominican friary must also have been well equipped, for the royal party usually resided there when they stayed in the town. In 1334, Edward Balliol, King of Scots, did homage to Edward I in the friary. Princess Margaret, the eldest daughter of Henry VII, also stayed at the house while on her way to Scotland to become queen consort of James IV.

On 1 December 1315, 30 Dominican friars, 36 Franciscans, 30 Carmelite and 28 Austin friars led the King's procession into Newcastle-upon-Tyne on his return from the north.

In 1301, Robert Bruce, father of the future king of the Scots, stayed at the Lincoln Franciscan house while attending Edward I at a parliament held in the town. Both Edward I, who visited Boston in 1301 before travelling upriver from the town to Lincoln, and Edward II, who did the same journey in 1327, used the Boston Dominican and Franciscan houses to accommodate the royal courts during the visit. In 1395, Richard II stayed at the Oxford Carmelite friars' house on his way back from Ireland. The stay cost the town 22 shillings for fish for the King and 55 shillings for scarlet cloth for his soldiers. Henry IV sometimes stayed in the Guildford Dominican friary and in 1403 he paid the friars 40 shillings for damage done to the house, vessels and gardens whilst he was being entertained.

Scottish kings frequently stayed in the Perth Dominican friary, as in 1436 when James I resided there and the rest of his court was dispersed to lodgings in the town, but more of that later. In 1452, Henry VI and his entourage were accommodated and entertained at the Ipswich Carmelite friary. The Shrewsbury Dominican house must have been in favour with the Earl of March, later Edward IV, who spent Christmas 1460 there and throughout his reign regarded the town with affection. He later sent his queen to Shrewsbury to be delivered of her second son, Richard, Duke of York, and again for the birth of her third son, George. In 1469, she stayed at the Norwich Dominican friary and was one of the many important visitors who stayed there. In 1413, the Duke of Clarence, with his wife and a retinue of 300 horses, stayed in the King's Lynn Austin house. During his visit to King's Lynn in 1498, Henry VII, his queen and many noblemen were received at the town's Austin house. There are numerous other instances of royal and noble visitors being given hospitality at the houses of friars.

THE ROSARY

The origin of the rosary is obscure but it developed gradually over a long period and appears to be derived from the muttering chaplets of the early desert hermits, who recited a series of repetitive prayers using two piles of small stones or pebbles. When they completed a prayer, they placed a stone from one pile onto a second, and when they had moved all the stones from one to the other, they knew they had completed a round of prayers. They then started their series of cyclical prayers over again.

A rosary is a string of beads on which vocal and mental prayers of devotion are counted in a systematic manner. To pray the rosary primarily recalls the mysteries of the Christian faith and brings to mind Christ's death and resurrection. A medieval rosary consisted of 150 beads divided into 15 portions of 10 smaller beads, each decade of beads being divided by a larger single bead. The person performing the devotion of the rosary recited 10 Ave Marias (Hail Marys) counted on the 10 small beads. When they came to the larger single bead, they recited the Paternoster (Lord's Prayer), followed by the Gloria Patri (Glory to the Father) combined with a meditation known as a 'mystery'. This was followed by a further 10 Ave Marias counted on the next 10 small beads and continued until the sequence of 15 lots of Ave Marias, and the meditating attached to each decade, had been completed. The sequence was concluded by saying the Apostles' Creed. The 15 mysteries of the rosary focused attention on the joyful mysteries of the incarnation, the sorrowful mysteries of the sufferings of Christ and the glorious mysteries of the glorified risen Christ. They were a synopsis of the life of Christ and His Mother.

There have been variations on the sequence of prayers and meditations of the rosary over the centuries but the format has remained basically the same. The rosary presented Christian truths comprehensively and graphically, and sanctified those who prayed it. It was believed that rosary prayers made to Mary led to Jesus, the source of all grace.

There have been various debates about the introduction of the rosary into the church. Some consider that the use of the rosary developed gradually as tender devotion to the Virgin Mary and increased in the twelfth century with the desire of the faithful to have a closer participation in the liturgy of Our Lady. According to tradition, Mary appeared to St Dominic when he was working among the Albigenses and gave him a rosary, instructing him to preach and expound the truths of the faith through the rosary. She promised him that much success would attend his mission should he do so. St Dominic was said to have paused when preaching, to invite his listeners to recite the Paternoster and the Ave Maria during his sermons.

The Dominicans would yield to none in their reverence to the Blessed Virgin Mary, in whose honour they adopted the rosary. Just as they were thorough in their training and preaching ministries, so they were thorough in encouraging the faithful in their devotions to the Mother of Jesus. They were in the forefront of encouraging the use of the rosary to strengthen the established faith in Christ as true God and true man, and in focusing devotion on the Mother of God.

In the last quarter of the fifteenth century, Alan de la Roche, a Dominican friar, founded the 'Confraternity of the Most Holy Rosary' in France and the Low Countries. Other such confraternities rapidly spread across Christendom and were formed in many parishes. They were instituted at local level so that the faithful, united by the fraternal charity and prayers of the rosary, would praise and honour the Blessed Virgin and secure her patronage.

While I have used the past tense in describing the rosary,

today there are many Roman Catholics who use it as an ongoing part of their devotion. Confraternities of the rosary still flourish and the Master-General of the Dominican Order is still the appointed leader of the worldwide rosary confraternities.

SANCTUARY

Although not a ministry, the right of sanctuary within a church became an accepted practice in medieval times. It started as a protection for the humble from the vengefulness of private feuds and the cruelty of the penal code. Sanctuary was evoked when a person who had committed a felony endeavoured to escape from the law and possible punishment by entering a church where he could expect, through the compassion of the church, to be sheltered from the law for 40 days. A fugitive fleeing a hue and cry, the ancient way of running a criminal to earth, could claim the right of sanctuary once he grasped the knocker on a church door. He was then considered to have come under the protection of the church and was therefore immune from arrest.

The 40 days period was granted to allow time to try to make peace between the fugitive and his pursuers. The rights of sanctuary were given by the ecclesiastical authorities, provided the person seeking sanctuary took an oath before a coroner that he would submit to a court of Justice or proceed to the next county or a seaport within 40 days. If by then reconciliation had not been achieved, or if the fugitive refused to comply, he could be removed by the legal justices.

There are numerous records of such people fleeing into a church to seek sanctuary while being chased by the lawful civil authority. The civil authorities were not allowed to take the fugitive out of the church by force, without permission of the ecclesiastical superiors. Violation of sanctuary carried excommunication with it.

Once inside the church, the felon was free from the law while he remained in the building. In practice, a great number of those guilty of serious crimes in this way escaped justice, providing they took an oath of obedience to the lord of the jurisdiction. Although the privilege of sanctuary had been hallowed by long custom, it was an illegal, though accepted practice. Felons could seek sanctuary in many churches, not only cathedrals and friaries.

Those who have visited Durham Cathedral may have seen the sanctuary knocker on the main door. Criminals who clung to the knocker could claim sanctuary in the cathedral. However, the original knocker is now kept in the cathedral treasury. A number of other churches still retain their sanctuary ring, such as the handle of the west door of St Margaret's, King's Lynn, and the knocker on the door at the foot of the tower of Boston parish church. The medieval sanctuary knocker from Rye parish church can be seen in Hastings Museum.

In 1312, a breach of sanctuary occurred when two persons seeking sanctuary in Newcastle-upon-Tyne Carmelite church were forcefully taken from the church and beheaded. The culprits, who had broken the rule of sanctuary, were beaten with cudgels. In 1339, a murderer took sanctuary in Grantham Franciscan church and in 1419, Thomas Couper and William Drusthorpe killed Thomas May and also fled to the Grantham Franciscan church, where they received sanctuary. Ten days later the bailiff took them from the church by force and delivered them to Lincoln for trial. The friars appealed to the King in Council against the violation of sanctuary, and a jury was sworn in before the justices. The jury declared that the friary church was a sanctuary and the prisoners were returned to the friars' church to continue their sanctuary. This was an instance of the friars protecting the right of sanctuary within their church.

In 1292, two prisoners escaped from custody in Carlisle during a fire. One claimed sanctuary in Carlisle Cathedral, while the other claimed sanctuary in Carlisle Dominican church. John le Berner committed trespass in 1299 and fled to the Ludlow Austin church, but some of the men of the town dragged him out, put him in chains and jailed him in Shrewsbury. When the King was informed of the breaking of sanctuary, he ordered that the prisoner be returned to the friars' church. In the time of Edward II, John Tynhide was condemned to death by the Salisbury justices for some felonies. On his way to the gallows five Dominican friars from the town forcibly rescued him from the hands of the bailiffs, cut the cords that bound his hands and delivered him from justice. The five friars received a royal pardon in 1318 for this flagrant transgression of the law. In 1334, two killers sought sanctuary in Oxford Austin house, where they were supplied with food by John the Painter, who later took them to the church of St Mary Magdalene, whence they were allowed to escape. In 1338, two Franciscan friars rescued two felons who were on their way to execution in Canterbury. It is not known why the friars rescued the two felons but the friars later received a royal pardon for their action. In 1340, three felons fled to Carmarthen Franciscan friars' church, which was outside the town walls. The Justiciar of South Wales levied a fine of £20 on the burgesses for failing to perform custody. However, they made a successful appeal against the fine, in that they had no responsibility for the custody of robbers fleeing churches outside the town.

In 1354, several Huntingdon Austin friars got into trouble when they helped Richard de Dalton, who had been condemned to death and was on his way to the gallows, to find sanctuary in the parish church of St Andrews. The friars were later pardoned for their action. In 1359, Franciscan friars of York complained that officers of the sheriff, mayor and bailiffs had invaded the friary precincts in order to seize persons who had taken sanctuary in the house. Edward III placed the house under his protection and forbade all persons from infringing any right of sanctuary in future; those who did would be subject to a heavy fine.

In 1471, a Coventry bailiff entered Coventry Carmelite church and arrested a felon. The friars took the mace of office from the bailiff and rescued the man. In 1472, a Shrewsbury Austin friar killed a man in self-defence and sought sanctuary in his own friary. During the scuffle, angry burgesses attempted to drag him out, but the resistance proved so fierce that in the melee, another man was killed in the church. The King intervened to punish the violation of sanctuary and the church was reconsecrated. The friars and citizens were later reconciled by the meditation of the Bishop of Carlisle and the Abbot of Shrewsbury Abbey. In 1487, a man who had confessed to murder took refuge in the Sandwich Carmelite church and was later allowed to leave the realm.

In 1526, the question of sanctuary arose when a man accused of murder took refuge in St John's Abbey, Colchester. He later broke from the sanctuary and went to the Colchester Crutched Cross friary for further sanctuary. The magistrates went to the friary and asked the prior to deliver the man to them in order that Cardinal Wolsey could examine him. The prior refused, saying the friary's privilege of sanctuary was as great as that of St John's Abbey. The magistrates later went back to the friary with a judge, when the prior showed him a transcript of a papal bull declaring the privilege of sanctuary. When asked if he had any grant by the King's ancestors for the liberty, the prior said he had none to show, but he supposed that there was one in the head house of his order. The man confessed the felony before a judge but the magistrate advised him to adjourn the case until Wolsey's pleasure was known.

The practice of seeking sanctuary in churches was not always welcomed by the clergy, who considered it an abuse of the church, or by the bailiffs, whose duty it was to bring felons to justice. The rights of sanctuary became a public nuisance and the action of officers entering a church to make an arrest became increasingly accepted. By the late sixteenth century it came to be reckoned a grave abuse, and the right of sanctuary in England and Wales was abolished in 1624. It lapsed in Scotland after the Reformation.

MYSTERY PLAYS

In the fifteenth century, York, Coventry, Chester and Perth, along with other towns, had their own series of mystery plays. The plays had their origin in church drama, but were taken over by the various town guilds. Many of the plays were enacted in the streets on Corpus Christi day, and on other saints' days, when people packed the streets to see and join in the events. The Perth miracle plays were acted on Corpus Christi day and on the eve of St Obert's day. St Obert was the patron saint of bakers in Perth. The Perth Bakers Guild were accustomed to perform a play in his honour on 10 December each year and it is recorded that the Perth kirk session had great difficulty in suppressing these joyous interludes after the Reformation.

The plays, spoken in the local dialect, covered a wide range of religious themes. They were dramas in which sacred passages of Scripture and allegorical persons from the Scriptures were introduced in the most free and extraordinary manner and used as another method of illustrating the message of the Gospel. The allegories were figurative symbolisms accompanied by joyous music, illustrating morals or Christian truths, and evoked excitement, wonder and fun. The York pageants consisted of about 48 short plays on incidents taken from the Bible, which often had scenes of comedy and mirth to alleviate the solemn gravity or tragic mood of the pageant, as they linked joy with religion. Each play was presented by one or more of the guilds in the town.

Friars of the four orders were closely connected with the fraternities and guilds which organised these dramas. The wheeled platforms were traditionally two-storeyed and canopied, with the lower section curtained off and used by the players as a dressing room. The upper section formed the stage and was decorated with simple props. The wheeled platforms and properties of the York Corpus Christi plays were stored in Pageant Green, adjacent to the Dominican friars' house, while the props and decorations were stored in a number of parish churches in the town.

The Coventry Franciscan house achieved considerable celebrity by the plays, and some of the plays were largely their work. The *Ludus Coventrie* book containing outlines of the pageant plays was believed to have been maintained by the Coventry Franciscan house.

The priors of the Ipswich friaries led the way in organising the 1325 Corpus Christi procession when on May Day they gathered the parish clergy in the church of St Margaret's and agreed with the lay brethren of the guild upon details of ceremonies to be observed in the annual procession of the Host.

Many towns, and even friaries, held their own local religious pageants, when the clergy, friars and townspeople observed the annual procession of the Host. The small Moatenden Trinitarian house in Kent held a solemn pageant and procession on Trinity Sundays.

7

TRAINING FRIARS

Until the thirteenth century, monasteries, cathedrals and church establishments ran most of the schools. Monastic boarding schools were usually situated in the almonries or gatehouses of monasteries, as they were at St Mary's Abbey, York, which had a boarding house for 50 boys in their school. From the thirteenth century onwards there were a large number of small schools where boys were taught to read and write by the local clergy or chantry priest, but they received little more than an elementary education. A number of ordinands for the priesthood obtained their basic education in numeracy and religious training, such as reading Latin, celebrating the sacraments and the church calendar, in such schools, but comparatively little is known about medieval education and it is difficult to determine the standard of teaching.

By the late fourteenth century, grammar was still, by and large, confined to Latin, but schools were beginning to concentrate on the construction of the English language, art, calligraphy for manuscript writing, and chanting. By the fifteenth century, the hunger for books accounted for the growth in literacy in that period, and by the 1500s, general education was available in about 400 academies run by clerics and the church. Many candidates for the mendicant orders would have acquired the rudiments of writing, reading and liturgical singing before entering their orders as novices.

The main purpose of the friars' higher education system was to provide lectures in theology for friaries. The ideal was that each house, however small, should have among its members one theologian whose responsibility was to instruct the rest of the community. Each order developed an early elaborate and efficient three-tier system of scholastic training, but the friars' educational edifices were not ends in themselves, they were considered necessary to achieve their evangelical aims. The curriculum of studies ranged upward, through friary schools, provincial schools and on to houses of general studies in universities. At its base were the friaries' local schools for prospective novices, where the teaching was considered superior to education in establishments run by the secular clergy or laity. Most friaries had such a school.

A solid theological foundation was essential for preachers, and the intellectual element, interwoven with apostolic fervour, was typical of the orders. Through their system of schools, the thirteenth- and fourteenth-century friars were among the most literate group of the age and their educational system produced many distinguished intellectuals.

FRIARS SCHOOL

During their noviciate period, which lasted at least a year, novices wore the habit of the order and lived in with the friars. During that time, they debated, studied and experienced how hard the life of a friar could be, before taking mendicant vows and becoming full members of their order.

The Dominicans accepted the need for the study of theology from the beginning, and it was binding on all novices. 'Study' ran their constitution 'is not the end of the order, but is most necessary to secure its ends, namely, preaching and salvation of souls, for without study neither can be accomplished'.

The Dominican constitution also stated that novices were to be exhorted to be always reading or thinking about something.

St Francis never condemned learning for itself, but he had no desire to see it developed in his order and its pursuit appeared unnecessary to him, since a man could save his soul and win others without it. He feared education could become a source of pride. Yet within 25 years of Francis's death the order had become one of the most learned institutions in the world.

The Franciscans soon found it necessary to train their novices for their preaching and teaching ministry, and at an early stage a friary of any size had a school to teach them and to prepare those who were to proceed to higher education. The schools, which also provided basic education for a limited number of non-oblates, were the bedrock of the academic structure of the orders and promoted a union between the simple life of poverty and the study of theology. In 1251, the Franciscans were said to have had 34 lecturers in England, roughly one lecturer per house. Novices were under the control of the Master of Novices, who was in charge of theological studies, organising disputations and directing the reading of students in his house.

As part of their education, novices were taught by the Precentor in charge of music in the friars' church to know the psalter by heart and to sing plainsong in unison. They were taught the art of chanting or singing the offices for church services.

Great stress was laid on novices having the ability to argue a point and grasp the truths of the faith, so that they could refute heretics and schismatics. The Master of Novices taught the brethren grammar, theology and the art of preaching. He also instructed them in the way of life of the order, encouraged them when they deserved it and corrected them when they behaved carelessly. He taught them to live without private property, to abandon their own will in favour of that of their superiors and to practise voluntary obedience in all things. But above all things, they were taught to meditate on the Passion of Christ.

In 1485, the Franciscan house at Dorchester received a bequest from Sir John Byconic, which stated that the revenues of his mills were to be used to bring boys into the order for their education in good manners and learning, and for books for the choir. The funds were not to be used in any other way, and the brethren so brought in should be educated to the perpetual memory of John and were to be called Byconic's friars. None of them should be called by other surnames.

The Austin and Carmelite friars adopted similar educational systems to the Franciscans'. The Blakeney Carmelite house probably started an education system soon after it was established, as John de Baconsthorpe, who was born in Blakeney in 1290, was educated by the Blakeney friars prior to going on to higher education and eventually proceeding to Oxford and Paris universities. He returned to England in 1329 and later became Provincial of the English Carmelites.

As we have seen, Latin was the language of the universal church and Latin was the language generally spoken in friaries. The boys learned Latin in order to recite the divine office, and learned to identify parts of speech and grammatical forms of Latin in order to improve their knowledge of the language.

Every province had one or more *Studia Solemna*, or houses of advanced learning set aside for study, where brethren from a group of houses studied logic and theology for two years. The mendicants considered small schools of study preferable as students were accommodated more easily, long journeys to and from schools could be avoided and budding professors had more opportunities to complete their required courses.

These advanced training schools provided the necessary philosophical grounding in art courses up to university entrance level, and had ample masters qualified to teach the brethren and groom them for university. The study of Aristotelian logic, which was referred to as 'The Book of the Heathen', formed a large part of the study of theology at the advanced level, but more on that a little further on. These schools also provided training in grammar, philosophy, logic, rhetoric, oratory and the techniques of using speech effectively to persuade and influence people. Students learned mnemonics, the art of improving or aiding the memory, and absorbed knowledge, which enabled preaching friars to retain data for long periods. Students attended lectures and took part in debates, until they became masters of explanation or critical interpretation of biblical text and were ready to go on to university or into the routine work of friars.

Each custody of the Franciscan Order had its own school

of advanced learning. The Gloucester Franciscan house started a school of theology in 1246 when Henry III let a tower in the town wall, near their house, to the friars. In 1336, Pope Benedict XII raised the Franciscan schools at Coventry, Exeter, London, Newcastle-upon-Tyne, Norwich, Stamford and York to the rank of Colleges of Advanced Study.

Dominic never intended his brethren simply to become academics; their task was to preach, and to do this they needed to be well informed and well trained. As a result, the Dominicans aimed to maintain the highest standard of education available in medieval times, and a higher proportion of their friars attended schools of advanced theology. Practical theology was geared to the needs of preaching and refuting errors and, within each Dominican province a number of larger friaries were given the status of Schools of Theology. These schools generally had regular lectures on theology and critical explanation or analysis of the Scriptures, which were open to secular priests. After the dissolution of the Gloucester Dominican friary in 1538, the church was converted into a mansion and the cloistral buildings used as workshops. The substantial remains of the buildings are now in the charge of English Heritage. On the first floor of the south range of the friary there is a large, long and many-windowed room, open to the roof. It was divided into separate carrels, or cubicles, for tutoring purposes and housed a school of theology. Its size indicates the importance the house placed on learning, and is probably the oldest purpose-built library building remaining in the country.

The Austin houses at Lincoln and York became centres for the study of theology in the province and their Leicester and Norwich houses provided schools of philosophy. Their King's Lynn house had 30 friars and 16 schoolboys, which indicates that it not only had an elementary school, but also a school for philosophy and theology.

The Carmelite friars' London house was the school of theology for their English Province. The Carmelite house at Ludlow acquired a reputation for scholarship and produced a number of learned and distinguished men, including three bishops. It is recorded that a number of friars at the Carmelite friaries in Boston, Doncaster, Ipswich and Nottingham became renowned writers and preachers. No doubt there were many others who passed through their schools who were equally renowned in their day, but remain unknown to us.

The Scottish Dominicans had schools of theology in Ayr and Perth; they provided the nearest thing to university training available in Scotland, but they did not survive the fourteenth century. Until the opening of the Scottish universities in the fifteenth century, Scottish friars seeking higher education had to go to establishments outside Scotland.

Training novice friars took a good deal of time and effort but friars considered their teaching role to be essential for the future of their orders; in much the same way, many religious and secular establishments today have an ongoing training programme in their organisations. To become a competent preacher or teacher required years of study, and trainees required adequate food and sturdy health to study effectively. While receiving training, they also required clothing, shelter, books and writing materials, and their education was achieved only at a cost to the parent houses of the trainees. The cost of maintaining the schools was generally paid out of tithes of the collections of the various houses of the order within the orbit of the schools, and the orders spared no effort or expense to enable gifted members to reach the highest academic degrees. Thus, they established pools of well-trained teachers within their orders.

At the end of their three-year course in these schools, students took the arts curriculum necessary for university entrance. The most intelligent, healthy, well-spoken, peaceable students of good report who were selected by their Provincial-Minister could go on to take a degree at either the Oxford or Cambridge university faculty of theology, depending on the quota for the Custody, Distinction, Limitation or Visitation, and the good behaviour and capabilities of the student. Each Visitation within a Dominican province in turn had the right to nominate friars for entrance to university.

UNIVERSITIES

It has been said that without towns, the friars would not have come into existence, and without universities, the friars would not have become prominent. The growth of universities in Western Europe had a profound influence in the Middle Ages, putting Western thinking in the forefront of intellectual development until the twentieth century. The mendicant orders grew up at a time of considerable intellectual ferment, and the Dominican and Franciscan orders entered fully into the debates which absorbed the time and energy of the academic world.

By the late twelfth century, the universities at Bologna, in central Italy, and Paris, were the leading intellectual centres of Europe. Bologna University taught mainly canon and civil law to clerical students who held, or would hold, senior positions within the church. The university did not receive its faculty of theology until 1364. Paris University evolved into a centre of excellence and attracted students studying advanced theology, and in 1231 it received a papal bull recognising the university's faculties of theology, canon law and medicine.

In 1167, Henry II recalled English students studying in Paris, following his quarrel with Thomas à Becket, who had gone into exile in France, and many of the students settled in Oxford. In the early thirteenth century Oxford was just beginning to gain recognition as a *studium generale*, a centre of excellence in education. It is the oldest British university; a place where scholars lived where they liked, but most lived in small communities in halls centred around St Mary's churchyard and largely run by teaching masters for their own students. The students were mostly young men from the nobility and gentry, age 19 and over, who looked to their families or patrons to support them while they were studying. Canon law and civil law were popular as they offered the readiest way to preferment for men destined for the legal system, law courts or administration.

Oxford's fame as a centre of formalised learning developed gradually in the twelfth century as a loose association of masters and scholars under a senior master. It was not until the middle of the thirteenth century, when Walter de Merton conceived the idea of establishing a hostel to enable the students to live together, that Oxford developed an organised college system. The earliest Oxford colleges, Balliol, Merton and University College, go back to about 1260. As each college was separately endowed, or founded, it developed its own rules and privileges for its body of students and masters. As the number of colleges grew, the corporate colleges grouped together under a *magister scholarum*, a master or cleric with a doctorate degree, to form a university which could confer degrees on those who had successfully completed their studies.

So rapidly did the Dominican and Franciscan friars justify their existence in the university that in 1244, when Oxford received its charter from Henry III, the deed of acknowledging it was signed by the Prior of the Oxford Dominicans and the Master of the Oxford Franciscans.

By the end of the thirteenth century both Oxford and Cambridge Universities developed collegiate systems similar to monastic houses, with students studying and living in academic halls governed by rules observed by all college members. Each hall had its own chapel, library, kitchen, refectory, dormitory and cloistered square. This method of development was natural, and the university's earliest halls and colleges followed along the lines of the Oxford Franciscan house. It was the only system of communal living they knew, one which was inspired by the discipline and communal life of monastic houses. Oxford University started work in 1427 on its first major building, the Divinity School, now part of the Bodleian Library buildings, but the school was not completed until 1483. Prior to this the university had no major buildings of its own.

A small party of Dominican friars reached Oxford in August 1221 and were anxious to establish a place in the university where members of their order could be trained in advanced theology. They soon became dominant in the university in the study of theology in its most advanced form, a dominance which they held until the 1400s. They became the leading authorities in the church in teaching systematic theology, as they applied themselves to doctrinal problems. They tended to firm up on the traditional doctrines of the church and disseminated their teachings throughout it.

In 1237, the Oxford Dominicans moved into their 15-acre Littlegate site besides the River Thames and soon began to erect their new church. Work on the church was sufficiently advanced to enable them to enter their new house in 1245, although work on the cloisters and other buildings continued for some years. In 1246, their Oxford house was named by the Dominicans as one of their four *studium generale*s of the order; the others being Cologne, Montpelier and Bologna, to which Dominican students from any part of the world might be sent for training in advanced theology.

In 1250–51, Henry III gave them £10 towards building their cloistral buildings, which were large and self-contained and capable of taking about 90 brethren. The church was consecrated in 1262. Unfortunately, being so near the river, the buildings sometimes suffered from flooding.

The Dominican schools of philosophy and theology attracted many scholars of distinction and produced a constant flow of learned men who could study their subject in depth. A high proportion of those who received bachelor's or master's degrees eventually went on to gain doctorates.

The Dominican house had 70 friars in 1277, rising to 96 in 1305, then 90 in 1317 and 70 in 1377. The reduction in the 1377 numbers might have been partly a result of the Black Death.

When they entered England in 1224, the Franciscans went to Oxford to recruit young men to their order. Their spectacularly successful trawl among the students attracted a number of distinguished recruits, many of whom were already masters, and the original Franciscan distrust of intellectual activities was soon lost as they followed the Dominicans into the scholastic world of the universities. The friars from both orders soon took a leading part in the university.

The Franciscan links with Oxford were strengthened when a lay benefactor bought a permanent house which was to be held in trust by the municipality for the Oxford Franciscans. They soon outgrew their original Oxford buildings, and in 1245 they were given a new site just outside the town wall, on what is now the Westgate Centre. The church was large, with a choir measuring about 98 feet in length, and an exceptionably large north transept, which was used for lectures and debates. In 1244, Henry III allowed them to throw down part of the town wall, and the south wall of the church came to form part of the defensive wall of the town.

The Oxford Franciscan house had 40 brethren in 1233, rising to 84 in 1317 and 103 in 1377.

The Austin friars arrived in Oxford University in 1266, when they established a house in the town. The nave part of the church was 122 feet long and the choir 105 feet in length. Their church and chapter house served as a school of divinity for the university, but the Austins only supplied the buildings and were paid by the university for the use of the facilities. In 1326, the university passed a statute that all students studying for a Bachelor of Arts degree should dispute once and respond once each year, in the Austin church. This became known as 'doing the Austin', which continued until 1483, when the university were able to use their new Divinity School building. Wadham College now occupies the site of the former Oxford Austin house.

The Oxford Austin house had 40 brethren in 1277, rising to 52 in 1305, and 49 in 1377.

The Carmelite friars established themselves in Oxford in 1256, but in 1318 Edward II gave them his palace of Beaumont, which was sited where Beaumont Street is today. This house may well have been the largest house of their order in Britain and many friars who had studied there were noted for their learning.

The Oxford Carmelite house had 54 brethren in the house in 1305, then 45 in 1317, and 57 in 1377.

The Crutched Cross, Sack and Trinitarian friars each had a small house attached to Oxford University, but, apart from the Trinitarians' house, which was abandoned after the Black Death, their houses did not survive for long.

It has been estimated that in 1300 there were about 1,500

students in Oxford University, including about 270 friars. By 1400, the university population was reduced to 1,250, before starting its gradual climb in numbers later in the century, when the number of undergraduates and colleges in the university rapidly increased.

About 1209, there were riots and brawls in Oxford and a number of scholars fled the town and settled in Cambridge, where they established a nucleus of a university, which is said to have brought about the foundation of Cambridge University; but it is possible that students chose Cambridge because teaching facilities already existed there. Cambridge University had the faculties for theology, canon law and arts, to which civil law and medicine were later added. As in Oxford, the arrival of the Franciscan and Dominican friars added stimulation and motivation to the young university. By 1300, Cambridge University was well established and acknowledged as of equal standing with Oxford, and its recognition was confirmed by a papal bull of 1318.

Friars played a dominant role in the development of the academic discipline of theological study. The Oxford faculty of theology had helped to establish the friars' school, but at the sister university at Cambridge it was the friars who helped set up a faculty of theology in the university. Undoubtedly, the thirteenth century was the friars' golden age in the universities, and their pre-eminence as teachers and lecturers placed them in the forefront of the intellectual life of the century.

The Franciscans reached Cambridge in, or about, 1226 and were accommodated by the municipality in an old synagogue and the house of Benjamin the Jew. Their manner of life was such as to make an immediate and deep impression on the academic world, and many scholars and teachers joined the order. Here they lived for over 40 years, and here they held their first school of theology. At that time the university had no faculty of theology and therefore had no secular masters who might be invited to lecture to the friars. The faculty had, therefore, to use lecturers who were themselves friars. In about 1267 they moved to a new site and their new church. By the end of the thirteenth century the theological faculty at the university was a flourishing concern, conducting itself according to the customary methods of the schools. Because of its convenient size, the Franciscan church was used by the university for the ceremony of commencement, and, on Ash Wednesdays, for the ceremonies of admission to Bachelor of Arts degrees. It was also used on St Peter's day, when Master of Arts degrees and doctorates were conferred, followed by the saying of Mass. At the dissolution the premises were granted to Trinity College and were later purchased by Sidney Sussex College. Their Cambridge house had 58 brethren in residence in 1277, and about 75 in 1289 and 70 in 1326.

By 1237, the Dominicans had established a house in Cambridge. Shortly after 1280 Alice, Countess of Oxford, considerably enlarged the building which then had accommodation for up to 80 student friars. There were 55 students in the house in 1326. In 1489, the community numbered about 50, which included the superior, preachers, professors, ministering brethren and lay-brothers. Emmanuel College now stands on the site of the former Dominican friary.

As the membership of the East Anglian Austin houses increased and the academic policy of the order took form, the desire for their own *studium generale* at Cambridge grew; and as the academic aspect of the house became increasingly prominent, the intake of brethren reached about 70 in 1300, then 43 in 1317, and 49 in 1377.

A small party of Carmelite friars arrived in Cambridge in 1247 and proceeded to establish a house in the university and, in due course, their house received friars from all parts of the country.

The Pied friars and Sack friars had houses in Cambridge, but they, like their Oxford houses, were short-lived.

Starting with the reign of Edward I, royal grants of 50 marks a year were given to the mendicant Oxford and Cambridge houses for the advancement of learning, a grant which was renewed at the beginning of each reign.

During his conflict with Simon de Montfort, Henry III arrived in Oxford on 8th March 1264 and made his headquarters in the Dominican friary while waiting for the forces he had summoned to meet him. The King ordered the university to disperse, so that the students would be out of the way of the disorderly soldiery. By 8th April the King's army had gathered and then moved on, to eventual defeat at Lewes.

Simon de Montfort's Baronial Council in 1265 ordered the removal of the developing university at Northampton, in case it injured the interest of the developing Oxford University. In 1333 a number of students, dissatisfied with the conditions at Oxford University, migrated to Stamford and entered schools in the town, but at the request of the authorities at Oxford they were ordered by Edward III to return.

Student and postgraduate canons and monks in universities excelled in the study of ecclesiastical and civil law and, for about 200 years, mendicant friars were practically the only professors of systematic theology. They were the principal exponents and writers of dogmatic, moral and biblical theology books, subjects which were almost exclusively theirs. The major theologians, who gave the universities their verve, came mainly from the ranks of friars at a time when Christian theology played a prominent role in medieval thinking and were in the mainstream of European philosophy. Plain living and high thinking were the settled ways in mendicant university houses.

University statutes provided that none might proceed to a higher faculty, and theology was the highest faculty, unless he first gained a Bachelor of Arts degree. However, the constitutions of the mendicant orders forbade their members to take a degree in arts, as it contained no religious teaching and subjects covered by the arts degree could be injurious to persons in holy orders. In 1253, the friars asked the university to allow the Franciscan Thomas of York to graduate in theology, but the university refused to accept him because he had not graduated in arts and the university statutes stated that no one might proceed to a mastership degree unless he first graduated in arts. The question then arose of presenting friars who had not obtained a Bachelor of Arts degree to a university. A way out of the impasse was found; the universities accepted that by an early custom, friars received graces of exemption from the first degree in the arts requirement and proceeded direct to their Bachelor of Theology degree. In 1317, Pope John XXII wrote an open letter declaring that mendicant friars were allowed to proceed to a Bachelor of Theology degree without having obtained a Bachelor of Arts degree. However, the matter did not appear to have been finally resolved and remained the source of an ongoing dispute between the mendicants and universities.

As we have seen, facilities were given for friars of exceptional promise to receive the fullest possible training. Following three years gaining the necessary philosophical qualifications at their provincial house of advanced learning, the more capable friars joined a university for a three-year course for their Bachelor of Theology, two years on the Sentences and one year on the Bible. At the end of the third year a licence was granted permitting friar graduates who had obtained their Bachelor of Theology degree to lecture and dispute anywhere. Those who obtained such degrees were placed in a pool of teachers and sent to friaries, or a university, where there was a need for their skills. A number of them were given appointments in the royal household or baronial service.

Those who were selected for further education returned to university for four years to study for their Masters Degree in Theology and those who succeeded in obtaining it were eligible to take up a teaching post in higher theology in a university, or to be in line for a senior appointment within their order. Sometimes they were invited to teaching posts in other parts of the church, such as Christchurch Cathedral-Priory, Canterbury, which employed Franciscan friars as lecturers.

The brightest students would return to university for another two years to study for their Doctorate and become eligible for the post of Master Regent at a university. Due to the spacing between courses, they could be in their forties by the time they obtained their Doctorate. The *magisterium* was the highest teaching post a person could reach, its prestige and privileges derived from its importance to the holder's order.

Friar undergraduates had to be over 18 years of age when

they arrived at a university. The course curriculum was centred on the works of Aristotle in the Latin translation, but logic and theology also had an important place. Lecturers read to the students, then a discussion followed. Examinations were judged by disputation, the art of challenging each other with hard questions and arriving at the truth by exposing contradictions in the opponents' arguments or beliefs, and overcoming them.

Neither undergraduates nor graduates had to be concerned about the monetary aspect of their courses; those talented were financially supported by their mother house and provincial organisation. Mendicant students, as did other students, had to deposit a pledge as surety they would complete the course; this was payable by the friar-students' parent house. Educating friars up to a high standard took years and the cost was considerable, adding to the financial burden of houses. This, in turn, added to the friars' reputation for sharp practice in fund-raising, but at times a private benefactor covered all or part of the cost of sending a friar to university.

Each of the four orders of friars developed houses which drew up their own laws for the government of the students and appointed their teachers on their own authority. These schools developed what were virtually separate university systems alongside the secular university, with their degree work dovetailing with the university. They produced men for the church who had the ability to grapple with the most complex theological questions with their numerous ways of reasoning about the methods of investigating divine truths.

As we have seen, theology was foremost in medieval intellectual thought as such knowledge was considered necessary to arrive at an understanding of the Creator and His creation. The Bible remained at the centre of theological study, but, by the thirteenth century, scholars felt a need to present doctrines in a more systematic way. The Dominican and Franciscan schools forced men to think but insisted that all thinkers should arrive at something like the old traditional conclusions.

Peter Lombard, the Italian theologian (1100–60), compiled

textbooks for the study of theology as an academic discipline. They are known as the four *Books of Sentences* (way of thinking) and are a collection of either citations or excerpts from the works of the fathers, or, simply their doctrinal positions. Among its other work, the 1215 Fourth Lateran Council confirmed Lombard's *Book of Sentences*, which became the textbook for candidates for a Master of Theology degree and was used as the fundamental text in theological schools. Lombard proposed that students discuss doctrinal theses which argued for and against a point, and then come to a conclusion in debate. Students took their turn in raising and debating theological questions, while other students responded to the question.

The Franciscans produced some of the outstanding intellectual leaders of Europe in the next hundred years or so, when they took the whole orbit of knowledge as their sphere. It was a period when the English Province supplied the universities with their most erudite members, as the debate on divine knowledge, divine foreknowledge and divine determination went on as they tried to understand God and His ways. They considered that sophisticated disputation and debate could resolve the differences between two opposing viewpoints, rather than insisting that one viewpoint was right. This provided a forum for discussion and argument. They were pioneers in a new intellectual age and contributed to the intellectual ferment of the great philosophical and theological debates of the time. Those entering for their doctorate or master's degree could take up but one problem and develop it in all its ramifications.

In 1230, they invited Robert Grosseteste (1175?–1253), the first Chancellor of Oxford University, to be Regent Master of the school. He was nicknamed 'Great Head' and was considered to be one of Europe's most distinguished thirteenth-century churchmen and intellectuals. He was much impressed by the Franciscans and their ideal of union of scholarship with simplicity of life, and appears to have seen the Franciscans as the group most likely to reform and transform the church. He presided over the school until his appointment as Bishop of

Lincoln in 1235, five momentous years during which their Oxford house acquired a great reputation for thrifty living as they constantly strove after the heights of theological knowledge. A man of Grosseteste's calibre attracted many new students and within a short time the house became an international theological teaching centre as it made incalculable progress in scholastic disputations and in the subtle moralities suitable for preaching. He pointed the Franciscans in the direction they were to continue to go in their university work.

Little of the literature of ancient Greece, such as the *Iliad* and *Odyssey* of Homer, was known to the Western nations. Grosseteste was one of the very few European scholars who was equally versed in Hebrew, Greek, Chaldean, French and Latin. He considered that a knowledge of Hebrew, Greek and Chaldean (Chaldee Aramaic was the common language of the Holy Land in biblical times) was necessary to understand and establish a correct text of the Scriptures. He was also one of the first Europeans to contend that the science and mathematics of the ancient world should be the foundation on which to build contemporary philosophy, theology and biblical explanations. Natural philosophy must be based on mathematics, he taught, because force is always subject to mathematical law.

Grosseteste was also the first English teacher to grasp the philosophical system of Aristotle (384–322 BC), the Greek ethical, metaphysical and political philosopher. Artistotle's fundamental proposition was that theory should be derived from observation of nature and logic, based upon a syllogism. He maintained that this was the essential method of all rational enquiry.

Subtleties of logic and metaphysics became absorbing studies and were the background for assisting students in their explanation of the Holy Scripture. These new scholastic methods, which applied Aristotelian philosophy to the study of the Bible, were considered as rational analysis of the Christian faith and an investigation of the foundation of belief. The rediscovery by the Western world of the philosophical and scientific work of Aristotle caused intellectual ferment and was looked upon as an infallible oracle and guide, and is still important in academic thinking today. Logic and metaphysics still hold sway in some theological colleges and are sources of heated debates between what we might call modernism and fundamentalism in theology.

This was a period when by absorbing the whole body of Aristotelian sciences and metaphysics into theology, intellectuals tried to explain the mysteries of faith in a manner compatible with logic and modify them according to the dictates of reason. It was a time when traditional beliefs were examined in the light of human reasoning and it was thought that God could be explained to the church and presented in systematic ways. It became a conflict between scientific pragmatism and revealed truths, between reasoning and revelation. These often seemingly abstruse matters were arguments about truths that remain unprovable because they are matters of faith.

In 1235, Grosseteste became Bishop of Lincoln. He was succeeded by three eminent secular masters, who presided over the school for the next ten years or so. The Oxford Franciscans at first accepted they would be taught by secular masters, but under the influence of Grosseteste they started their own theological faculty. They then rapidly developed a scholastic structure under Regent Masters of Franciscan friars, closely resembling that of the Dominicans. In 1247, when the school was well founded and had trained a number of friars, they appointed their first Franciscan Regent Master, Adam Marsh. From then onwards all their lecturers were members of their order.

After Grosseteste's death, miracles were recorded at his tomb in Lincoln Cathedral and petitions for his canonisation were sent to the Pope. The petitions were not successful, probably because he had disagreed with the Papal Curia over the appointment of 300 Romans to high posts in the English church and to the lack of interest shown in his piety outside his own diocese.

It has been estimated that by the fourteenth century the Franciscans were nearly 10 per cent of the total Oxford University student population and had changed the university from a training place for lawyers and administrators into a centre for theological and philosophical study. For all the advantages of the close association of the Franciscans with the universities, it would probably have met with the disapproval of Francis himself, who had hoped he had founded a brotherhood of simple, unlettered saints. He did not want his brethren to engage in scholarly pursuits; he thought it would be incompatible with their kind of life. The Franciscans, who had come with a mission to the poor and uneducated, had become a learned and teaching order. The quest for learning had frustrated Francis's ideals; no longer was poverty the chosen way and the aspirations of the literal imitation of Christ were forgotten. However, the order still retained its grass roots ministry at the other end of the social scale.

Roger Bacon (1220–92), born in Ilchester and educated in Oxford and Paris, returned to Oxford at the age of 29, where he was influenced by Grosseteste's ideas. In about 1257, he entered the Franciscan Order in Oxford so as to be able to study at leisure. He became Franciscan Regent Master of Theology, was a scholar, mathematician and scientist, and for centuries was considered one of the greatest geniuses in natural science. He was known as Doctor Mirabilis (Marvellous Doctor). He had a fertile and penetrating mind which was absorbed with the wonders of the mechanism of the universe. He rejected Aristotle's classification of independent science and argued that a study of the natural world, using observation and exact measurements, was the surest way of understanding God and His ways. He believed that the object of all enquiry was to discover the right relationship between God and man. His *Opus Majus* is considered by many to be the greatest scientific work of the thirteenth century and possibly the Middle Ages. He stressed that if one wanted to know the truth, one must seek it by enquiry and experiments; and he emphasised the importance of verifying, by experiments, the conclusion deduced by argument. Bacon became a lonely and persecuted proponent of what would eventually be the recognised method of research; due to his experiments in magic and alchemy he was suspected of heresy and imprisoned.

John Peckham (*c.* 1230–92), a Franciscan friar, studied in Oxford and Paris and lectured in Rome before returning to England in about 1276, when he was appointed Franciscan Provincial Minister of England. He was appointed Archbishop of Canterbury in 1279. He opposed the new teaching, which he felt might undermine the faith of the Christian Church, and composed many learned works on philosophy and theology. He was buried in Canterbury Cathedral, but his heart was buried in the London Franciscan church.

St Thomas Aquinas (1225–74), the Italian Dominican friar, studied the doctrines of the faith and placed them into a regular theological system in his *Summa Theologica* (*Compendium of Theology*) which was universally accepted in the church. His comprehensive system of philosophy and theology, in which natural law was seen as the mind and will of God, was known as 'Thomism' and its maxims became the official doctrines of the Dominican Order.

John Duns Scotus (1265–1308), known as the 'Subtle Doctor', was a theologian and philosopher who lived a generation after Roger Bacon. He joined the Franciscan Order at Dumfries and was one of the few scholars of originality produced by Scotland before 1300. From Merton College, Oxford, he was one of the greatest Franciscan intellectual and original thinkers. He opposed the theology of Thomas Aquinas, and his scholastic philosophy, known as 'Scotism', reasoned that knowledge of God and the universe does not come from harmony of faith and reason, but from what faith reveals to us. He argued that the single power which directed the world through creation is God, and that philosophy and theology are independent. Scotus used complex prose weighed down with difficult technical terms and was anything but explicit in his teaching and writing. Many thought him too clever and tried to ridicule him by turning his surname into 'Dunce'. Such contempt of a great intellectual scholar reflected on the intellectual standards of some of his critics.

William Ockham (*c.*1349), another intellectual figure, stressed the philosophical theory of nominalism, that is, the theory that general or abstract concepts have no existence but as names or words. He belittled abstract thought, denied rational proofs of religion and had little use for metaphysics. He argued that theological doctrines could not be proved by reason and considered that realists had a presumptuous desire to pry into matters that surpassed the comprehension of mortals, and that speculation on the nature and attributes of God was futile. His partisans acquired the name 'Ockamists'. By the end of the fourteenth century Ockham's views became generally accepted in the theological schools of Western Europe.

These Franciscans were among the most distinguished scholars in the history of medieval philosophy and theology. Their era was important for the future of religious belief because it opened wide the cleft between philosophy and theology. It was an era when theology was fashioned into the scientific system we possess today; it emphasised that the Christian revelation could not be rationally established, but explained by an act of faith in a Supreme Being. During this period, the Oxford Franciscan house was the brilliant centre of intellectual life in Britain, a position it held for more than a century. After these men, the intellectual leadership passed from the friars to the laymen of the universities.

The Oxford Dominicans also produced a number of celebrated scholars, like Robert Bacon, Robert Kilwasdby and John Darlington. Bacon, not to be confused with the illustrious Roger Bacon, was admitted to the order without going through a year's noviciate and was the first Dominican to become prominent in university matters. He was the first Dominican Regent Master and taught in Oxford until his death in 1248. Kilwasdby (d. 1279) was the most notable English medieval Dominican at Oxford. He was Regent in Theology at Oxford, Regent Master of the Dominican Order and became Archbishop of Canterbury in 1272 and a cardinal in 1278. Nicholas Trivet, the most versatile of English Dominican writers, in 1314 was Master of the Oxford Dominican School. He wrote voluminous commentaries on the Psalms and was an expositor of biblical text. Compared to the Franciscans, most Dominican English masters appeared less distinguished, as they held to the traditional thoughts on higher theology and concentrated on their devotional and teaching roles in the church.

There was a widening of the intellectual gap between the educated elite and their brethren who received very little education. Students who completed university training were established as qualified teachers of either philosophy or theology in their schools and were granted many privileges. Nearly all the leaders of their respective orders were university-trained friars, and the less well educated knew they had little chance of advancement and seldom rose to important posts within their house or order. This must have been a cause of resentment.

In the late fifteenth century, George Ripley, a friar of the Boston Carmelite community, was a noted alchemist who devoted much of his life searching for the philosophers' stone, the ability to turn base metal into gold.

As we have seen, friars' schools were in the universities, but were not part of them, and, as a result, they tended to be lax in their obligations towards the university corporations. As universities grew, it was inevitable that tension should increase between friar students and secular students, and between mendicant and university authorities. University hostility to the friars in the thirteenth and fourteenth centuries was partly due to jealousy of the friars' buildings and influence, and partly due to the friars' exemption from taking the Bachelor of Arts degree. The late fourteenth century saw the universities imposing their will, establishing freedom from ecclesiastical control, and limiting the powers of the friars.

The fifteenth century saw a marked growth of colleges in the universities, but friars no longer possessed the sharp edge of the spiritual and intellectual life they had had in their prime. The late fifteenth and early sixteenth centuries were the darkest period for the friars. They were affected by what David Knowles called 'The strangle paralysis and hardening of the arteries that affected for a time the intellectual life of North West Europe and particularly evident in England in the fifteenth century'. The friars were losing their grip on the universities and ceased to produce anywhere near the same volume of students as they had hitherto. Friars were no longer indispensable to the academic well-being of the universities, and, with their decreasing academic influence, they retired more and more into the background of university life.

Despite the number of friar's houses in Scotland, there was no university foundation there prior to the foundation of Aberdeen, Glasgow and St Andrews universities in the fifteenth century. Members of Scottish religious orders seeking higher education had to go to Oxford, Paris or one of the other Continental universities. Due to the close links between Scotland and France, most students tended to go to Paris University, where they were financially supported by the various Scottish chapters of their orders, who required a continual supply of trained men.

In 1411, Bishop Wardlaw obtained a charter of incorporation and privileges for St Andrews University from Pope Benedict XIII, and in 1413 the Pope issued a papal bull for the foundation of 'A university of study for the faculties of theology, canon and civil law, medicine and the liberal arts'. Benedict XIII was an Avignon Pope, and Scotland, at that time, recognised popes of the Avignon obedience. In 1430, St Andrews University suppressed all private houses of teachers in the city and consolidated the accommodation into a single teaching centre which formed the core of the university. The need for such an institution soon became evident from the numbers of students attending.

The Bishop's decision to establish a university in his cathedral town was due to the hazardous journey to France during the Hundred Years War between England and France. The dangers of the sea journey between Scotland and France were highlighted when, in 1406, James I was captured while on a voyage to France and held to ransom by the English. It was also difficult for Scottish students to travel to Oxford during the Hundred Years War because they could have been classed as allies of France and enemies of England.

Glasgow University was founded in 1451 by William Turnbull, Bishop of Glasgow. The infant university was first situated in Glasgow Cathedral, but after a few years it was sited in a house used by clerics in the diocese.

Bishop Elphinstone, who had taken a great interest in education in Scotland, founded Aberdeen University at King's College, Old Aberdeen, in 1494, with the aim of creating a class of administrators in Scotland.

By the end of the fifteenth century, Scotland had three universities, one more than England, but the Scottish universities were small and did not attract foreign students. The majority of teachers and students in these new universities were, at first, members of religious orders, but by the end of the fifteenth century this influence had declined.

The Irish friars had difficulty in obtaining higher education studies due to there being no universities in Ireland. When funds were available, most Irish student-friars came to Oxford or Cambridge universities, while a few of them went to Paris University.

8

MEDIEVAL BELIEFS AND PRACTICES

By the middle of the fifteenth century the friars were leaders in both teaching and, unfortunately, embellishing the beliefs and practices of the medieval church. Whereas in earlier times the mendicant friars had revived the church by their zeal and devotion to the faith, later they encouraged new and diverse observances. They left the simple truths of bygone days, introducing and encouraging practices which strayed into fantasy and confused allegory with reality. They changed the faith so much that one doubts if either St Dominic or St Francis would have recognised the message they proclaimed.

When looking at some of the later observances of the medieval church as they were practised during the late medieval period, we do not propose to compare the doctrines and traditions then with today's beliefs and practices. It is the province of theologians to debate the teachings of the church.

PURGATORY

As we have seen in a previous chapter, the ongoing effects of the Black Death made people keenly aware of the imminence of death and there was a preoccupation with mortality and the hereafter. By late medieval times, the faithful were no longer engulfed by the fear of hell; rather they trembled in fear at the prospects of a prolonged time of suffering in purgatory, and their fear of purgatory and its consequences led them into extremes.

The church taught that souls survived the death of the body, and the doctrine of purgatory rested in the belief that there was a transitional period between death and the ushering of believers into the presence of God. Though God forgave sins, nothing defiled could enter heaven and very few people died in a state of perfection that would fit them for the immediate enjoyment of God's Kingdom.

There were, according to theologians, two consequences of sin – guilt and punishment. Guilt removed the sinner from a desirable relationship with God, and punishment must take place, either in this life or in purgatory, to expiate sin. The church considered that the doctrine of purgatory was supported by such Scriptures as 'It is a holy and wholesome thought to pray for the dead that they may be loosed from sins' (II Maccabees 12:46).

Those who professed the Christian faith were promised that when they had ended their earthly pilgrimage, they would be united with God in heaven. The souls of the faithful had already achieved salvation and nothing could imperil their final union with God, but amends must be made in the afterlife, where amends were not made in this life, before such enjoyment could take place.

Purgatory, which comes from the Latin *purgare*, 'to purge', was perceived as a place, or stage, of spiritual cleansing where the souls of those who died in a state of grace, but were not free from imperfection, underwent a limited amount of suffering to expiate their venial (lesser) sins and became purified of the remaining effects of mortal sin, before entering the presence of God. Purgatory was a place where the soul underwent a period of suffering to remove the last imperfections remaining from their mortal existence and 'made good' to God for the offence caused to Him. The teaching of purgatory was defined at the 1274 Council of Trent, and, as an article of faith by the 1439 Council of Florence.

The church stressed the horrors awaiting sinners in purgatory and how sinners could reduce the time spent there. The dogma that sinners, by their acts of repentance in the form of masses and indulgences, could mitigate the sufferings of purgatory was accepted by the educated and influential in society.

Thomas More (1478–1535), scholar and Lord Chancellor of England, in his *Supplication of Souls* made the suffering dead cry out to the living for more prayers and masses, and stressed the claims of the dead in purgatory to have their souls remembered by the pious living.

In 1532 or 1533 Hugh Latimer, who was burnt at the stake as a heretic in Oxford in 1555, preached in the Bristol Dominican church against purgatory and other hitherto accepted doctrines of the church. John Hilsey, the prior of the house, who later became one of Cromwell's visitors to the friars' houses, preached a reply to Latimer's sermon.

OBITUARY MASSES

There was a fundamental conviction in all classes of people that spiritual benefits could be obtained by frequently offering the most holy thing in Christendom – the Mass. From this grew the widespread belief that the more masses said for the souls of individuals, the less time they would spend in purgatory. Funerary arrangements made for the dead included a Requiem Mass to plead Christ's sacrifice for the repose of the dead person's soul, and those who could afford it made arrangements for a series of obituary masses to be said for them after their death and, thereafter, on the anniversaries of the death.

In 1215, the Lateran Council decreed the offering of masses for the departed. The teaching that trentals of masses (masses for the dead sung on 30 consecutive days) alleviated or terminated the suffering of the souls in purgatory became very popular in the late Middle Ages. The purchase of such masses was meant to shorten the time spent there and hasten the penitent's journey to heaven. The saying of private masses is mainly due to the friars' teaching based on Divine Justice and came into popular use during the fourteenth century.

Priests were not allowed to celebrate private masses at the high altar of churches, and friars could not have coped in their churches with the enormous number of additional obituary masses they were asked for. There were two results of the vast increase in the number of masses. There was a proliferation of side altars in nearly all churches, be they cathedrals, monastery churches, parish churches or friary churches, for the provision for soul masses. For instance, Salisbury Dominican church was said to have had 12 altars, besides the high altar. Many churches were either enlarged or the side aisles were subdivided in order to provide space for additional side altars. Also, an army of priests were employed in the churches, including friars' churches, for the sole purpose of saying obituary masses. They did not consider themselves as priests performing a service in the church, but as soul-priests performing masses for the souls of the departed. Most endowments for chantries were small, and men of lower ability tended to seek employment as soul-priests.

People valued the friars' prayers and were willing to pay fairly handsomely for trentals of masses and anniversary masses to be said on behalf of their souls, while the poorer and less well off members of society usually left funds for a few masses to be said for them in the weeks following their death.

Wealthier individuals made provisions for a series of obituary masses to be said regularly for a period of months, years, or even in perpetuity, following their death. Friars eagerly took part in celebrating these masses, and the stipends paid for them became a valuable source of income for their houses. However, the purchase of such masses introduced an element of commercialism into saying prayers for the dead.

In 1484, Richard III paid 12.5 marks to the Richmond (Yorkshire) Franciscan friars to say a thousand masses for Edward IV. In 1487, James IV bestowed an annuity of 40 marks to the Edinburgh Dominican house on condition that they celebrated a daily Mass for the soul of his consort, Queen Margaret. Henry VII endowed a chantry in the Carmarthen Franciscan church in 1504 for a Mass to be sung daily for the soul of his father, Edmund Tudor, who was buried in the church. He also ordered 10,000 obituary masses to be said for his own soul, at the rate of sixpence a mass.

The purchase of masses, although not on this royal scale,

was repeated many times by people who left money in their will for perpetual, or a series of masses for the repose of their souls and for the souls of their family and ancestors. By the fourteenth century, people tried to outdo each other in their bequest for such masses.

In 1319, Sir Robert Ughtred granted the Scarborough Dominican friars a plot of land on the understanding that two friars would daily celebrate masses for him and his family. In 1354, Thomas Lucy gave the Thelsford Trinitarian friars land at Charlecote, so that the friars would celebrate Mass for the souls of the donor and his wife. In his will of 1498, Edmund Lucy made provision with the same house, that for 22 years on the anniversary of his death, 11 poor men should be given black gowns and hoods and carry tapers in procession around the area and, 40 shillings be spent on masses for his soul and for the relief of the poor.

In 1361, John Barford left funds to provide for six priests to say Mass for his soul for a year, four priests for the second year and two priests to say Mass for the third year after his death. The will of John de Rynger, who died in 1369, made financial arrangements for the Aylesford Carmelite friars to celebrate a daily Mass for his, his wife's, his children's and his friends' souls. At the end of the fifteenth century, William Harewell left £10 to the Warwick Dominican friary for the repair of the church, on condition that one of their friars sang a daily Mass between nine and ten a.m. at the altar of St Peter of Milan, for himself and his wife. In his will dated 1393, the Earl of Arundel ordered his executors to have particular care for the friars' houses in Arundel and Guildford, as they were pledged to pray for the souls of his father, his mother, his wife and himself. Generations of the Earls of Crawford were finally laid to rest in Dundee Franciscan church. In 1481, the Dowager Countess of Errol gave a gift of £100 to the Dundee Franciscan church for the friars to say a daily Mass for the Countess, her son and her deceased husband, for ever, at the high altar of the church. In 1506, John, Earl of Crawford also made arrangements for a daily Mass to be said at the high altar of the Dundee Franciscan church, for the souls of his father, wife, elder brother and himself, with a daily absolution to be said at the memorial, or cenotaph, of the Earls of Crawford. The Earl fell at Flodden Field. Henry Pisford, who was buried in Coventry Franciscan church in 1522, directed that soon after his decease, five trentals of masses should be said for him.

The numerous private masses became a mere arithmetical arrangement of payment in return for a period of remission from the punishment of purgatory, and, as we have seen, provision was made by the faithful for such masses to be said in mendicant churches and within chantry chapels in them. It did not seem to have occurred to people that God might prefer fewer masses, said in a more dignified manner and with all the pomp of the medieval church, to masses which were rushed in an unseemly manner. They went for quantity in masses, rather than quality.

During the fifteenth century, a large number of side altars were funded and endowed by trade and religious guilds. Altars for the more affluent guilds were richly endowed in order that priests could be employed to say masses for departed members, thus increasing the number of masses said for an individual.

Churches kept obituary calendars of such anniversaries, and if friars failed to mark the anniversaries of deaths by vigils and masses for which they had received funds, the heirs of the deceased had the right to enter the house and take away goods to the value of 20 marks.

The commercialisation and multiplication of masses led to the abuse of what should have been an act of holy observance, by an army of illiterate and ill-disciplined mass-priests. This brought both the mendicant friars, and the Mass itself, into disrepute and was a prime cause of the debasement of the medieval priesthood.

In an age when society was increasingly articulate and educated, reformers demanded biblical evidence for the medieval church's belief in the multiplication of intercessory masses. They laid the charge of 'trafficking in masses' at the door of the late-medieval church.

INDULGENCES

An indulgence is a pardon, a remission of some, or all, of the temporal punishment which still remained because of sin after the guilt had been forgiven. Indulgences had devolved over the centuries from the earliest practice of penance. Instead of fasting or enduring some other mortification of the flesh, a penitent sinner was allowed to subscribe money to some worthy cause, such as contributions towards the repair of a church, a pilgrimage or crusade. An indulgence was not permission to commit sin, neither was it a pardon for sins already committed.

By the ninth century, popes and bishops frequently concluded their letters with an absolution grant, a solemn prayer asking God, through the intercession of Christ, to absolve the sinner from all penalties incurred by him.

Indulgence grants first appeared in the eleventh century. The practice of absolving the penitent before he had fulfilled his penance became established in 1095 when the Council of Clermont, under Pope Urban II, proclaimed that taking part in the crusade would be deemed a substitute for all other penances. In time, indulgences were gained by contributions given to church building, hospital work and pilgrimages. By the beginning of the thirteenth century, there was a general understanding that those who had been granted an indulgence for going on a crusade or pilgrimage and died during such an undertaking would have the indulgence carried over into the world to come.

Popes based their power to grant penances and indulgences on the authority of the Keys granted to St Peter, when Christ said to Peter 'And I will give unto thee the keys of the kingdom of heaven: and whatsoever thou shalt bind on earth shall be bound in heaven: and whatsover thou shalt loose on earth shall be loosed in heaven' (St Matthew 16:19). Popes claimed the authority, as Christ's vicar on earth, to secure from Christ the remission of punishment, even for souls in purgatory.

A change in the character of indulgences occurred when the

church accepted the teaching of Hugh of Saint-Cher (1200–63), a Dominican theologian and biblical scholar who became the first Dominican Cardinal. He wrote, 'The source of the indulgence grant was related to the church's treasury of merit and good works stored up by Christ, the Blessed Virgin Mary, and the saints of the church, both living and dead.' This was approved by the 1343 jubilee bull of Pope Clement VI.

Indulgences confirmed a reduction of the time the faithful departed had to spend in purgatory, and came to be seen as payment for this remission. That is why indulgences became so popular and people eagerly collected them. It was very much like the British Home Secretary remitting part of a prisoner's sentence.

When a church was built or restored, a new house of the Knights Hospitallers or some other order of mercy was founded, or when money was required for the upkeep of an establishment, instead of arranging a bazaar, concert or ball as some churches would do today, a grant of indulgences was applied for. Either the Bishop in his own diocese, or the Pope over a wider area, could grant the issuing of indulgences for church building work. Indulgences of 40 days were commonly given, 40 days being the length of time in Lent.

There are numerous references to indulgences being given in order to obtain funds for building or rebuilding friars' churches, as when a papal bull of 1246 granted an indulgence to all the faithful who contributed to the building of Glasgow Dominican church, which had just started. In 1248, the Bishop of Rochester granted a 40-day indulgence to those who contributed to the support of the new Aylesford Carmelite house, and in 1417 the Bishop of Rochester granted another indulgence of 40 days to those who contributed to the upkeep of the Aylesford Carmelites' new church and visited it on the day of its dedication, or through the eight-day festival following its opening. In 1274, the Bishop of Lichfield granted 20 days' indulgence to all who visited the Stafford Franciscan church on certain days and said the Lord's Prayer and a specified number of Hail Marys. The Archbishop of York granted 40 days' indulgence in 1300 to those who contributed to the building of Knaresborough Trinitarian church. The Archbishop of York also granted an indulgence to those who visited the York Carmelite church on 5 October 1304 and made an offering at the high altar, to cover the cost of lights and ornaments for the new church. The occasion appears to have been what we would call a 'gift day'.

In 1314, the Bishop of Lincoln granted indulgences to those who assisted in repairing the Boston Dominican church, and in 1330 he granted an indulgence to those who helped in the construction of a subterranean aqueduct from Bolingbroke to the Boston Dominican house. An indulgence was granted for the rebuilding of Berwick-upon-Tweed Dominican house following its accidental destruction by fire in 1436. In 1456, the Archbishop of York proclaimed an indulgence of 40 days to help the York Dominican friars, whose cloister and buildings, books, chalices and vestments were destroyed in a fire. The cost of repairing the Ludlow Carmelite house after it had suffered at the hands of Lancastrian soldiers in 1459 was secured by an indulgence.

By the late fifteenth century, the sale of indulgences was used to pay for secular schemes such as the repair of bridges, harbours and other such projects. The Bishop of Lincoln issued a letter granting a 40-day indulgence to all in his diocese who helped with funds to reopen the Fosse Dyke.

By the middle of the fifteenth century, 'pardoners' were licensed to sell pardons and indulgences in order to raise money for religious and semi-religious works. Due to their being free from parochial duties and being the Pope's men, most pardoners were friars. The remission of penance was for all who might '*Porrexerint manus adjutrices* – Lend a helping hand' to the pious work involved. Pardoners announced the indulgences, sought contributions and transmitted the funds to the charity concerned. They emphasised that the faithful should purchase indulgences either to increase their virtue or help to wipe out their sins. When pardoners first came into a town, they would firstly read lessons or sang in local churches in order to gain the people's attention to the sale of indulgences.

The method of dispensing indulgences proved successful in raising funds for the various charities; but money can corrupt, and the church in the late Middle Ages, while very rich, became greedy and used dubious practices to obtain more money from the faithful. By the early fifteenth century, indulgences were sold for quite trifling sums, and by the middle of the century could be bought for a few pence. This brought the clergy, particularly the friars, into disrepute.

The disparity between the authorative teaching of the church on indulgences and the way it was presented by the local clergy encouraged the faithful to eagerly avail themselves of this seemingly easy relief from the consequences of sin. It became an open abuse which undermined the idea of a physical penance as given in former times.

The sale of indulgences gradually became a scandal. In 1477, Pope Sixtus IV issued a papal bull which declared that indulgences for souls in purgatory could be retrospective. In 1507, Pope Julius II granted that plenary indulgences, that is, full and absolute indulgences, could be given. Within a short period of time plenary indulgences came into common usage and proved a most successful means of gathering funds for the papal treasury, for bishops, religious orders and individual parishes. Often, half the income from indulgences went to local causes and the other half went towards the building of St Peter's Church, Rome. The theologians had their explanations for indulgences, but ignorant people considered they were buying forgiveness for their sins, even for sins they had not yet committed. It was unfortunate that, for obvious reasons, as long as the money came in satisfactorily, the authorities in Rome were loath to scrutinise too intently the methods employed in the sale of indulgences.

The preachers of indulgences gained bad reputations because of the methods they used. Leaving aside the rights and wrongs of indulgences, the main problem was with the agents and intermediaries who sold them. As we have seen, the calibre of the friars of the late Middle Ages contrasted greatly with the friars in the thirteenth century, although this did not apply to all friars, as there were still many who endeavoured to follow the earlier ways.

Friars became the theme of satirists in literature across Western Europe. William Langland's poem *Piers Plowman* is a satirical allegory combined with social comments on human qualities in the professions. In a rendering of an archaic text, he wrote:

The pardoner [friar] brought forth a bull with the bishop's seals and said he could absolve them of falseness in fasting and broken vows. People came up to him kneeling and kissed the bulls. He thrust his brevet, his commission, in their faces and with tears in his eyes, gained rings and brooches by his charter. Thus, the people gave their gold to keep gluttons and put their faith in such worthless fellows.

He tells us that through the friars' flattery and their laxity as confessors, people lost their awareness of sin. A number of instances could be cited to support these assertions, but, equally, there is much evidence to suggest that however unpopular they may have been with writers, the intercession of the friars for the souls of the departed was particularly sought after.

The sale of indulgences and relics were the greatest factors that brought about the Reformation in Western Europe. Many people thought that the usefulness of the papal supremacy which introduced indulgences to the church was at an end and the time had come to return to the ideals closer to those of the New Testament and the early Christian era.

The breaking point came in 1517 when Pope Leo X appointed Johann Tetzel (1465–1519), a Dominican friar, as sub-commissioner in Meissen for indulgences granted to those who contributed to the rebuilding of St Peter's. Tetzel, who had been preaching in parts of Germany for a number of years, plied his trade of selling plenary indulgences by working on the feelings of the people and threatening them with dire punishment from God for their evil deeds if they did not buy indulgences. As a result, he did such a good trade that his preaching in Juterbog attracted many from nearby Wittenberg.

Martin Luther, an Austin Observants friar, was already hostile to indulgences because of the 129,799 years of indulgences obtained by the faithful for venerating Frederick the Wise, Elector of Saxony's collection of relics. Luther protested against the idea of indulgences and on 31 October 1517 he affirmed his position on the reform of the church for all to see, by nailing his 95 articles to the door of Wittenberg Cathedral. Most of the articles were not opposed to traditional church doctrine but he insisted some theological matters needed reformation.

On the same day, Luther wrote to his archbishop:

I regret that the faithful have conceived some erroneous notions about indulgences. They believe that if they buy a letter of pardon, they are sure of their salvation: souls fly out of purgatory as soon as money is cast into a chest, in short, that grace conferred is so great that there is no sin which could not be absolved. They believe that indulgences free them from all guilt of sin.

In June 1520, Pope Leo X condemned Luther's propositions, but his condemnation was not accepted or regarded as the final irrevocable decision of the church, and a final decision on controversies concerning the faith was to be agreed by an ecumenical council. The Catholic forces of the Counter-Reformation rallied, and between 1545 and 1563, the Roman church held a series of council meetings in Trento, northern Italy. It marked a major turning point in the efforts of the Catholic Church to respond to the challenge of the Protestant Reformation. The council admitted the abuses surrounding the practice of indulgences and enacted disciplinary measures to correct them. It eliminated ambiguity as to what were the fundamentals of the faith and what were merely subjects of theological speculation. The council recognised that the medieval church had pushed the boundaries of the faith to extremes and it rectified a number of the abuses. It agreed that the elaborate system of penance and indulgences, in which almost every kind of transgression had been allotted a penance penalty or an indulgence in proportion to its odiousness, had to be reformed. It also removed the saints from the realm of magic and placed them once again at the heart of the life of the church.

The council of Trent resulted in a movement within the Catholic clergy and laity for a widespread religious reform and revival within the church.

IMAGES

Pope Gregory the Great remarked, 'What scripture is to the educated, images are to the ignorant'. In AD 787, the Second Council of Nicaea, dealing with the difficulties of venerating images, decreed that saints might receive reverence, and veneration might be shown to likenesses of Christ, the angels and saints, without fear of idolatry. All veneration shown to a likeness was received by the being whom it portrayed.

The veneration of images and statues grew slowly over the years. One generation would install images as a pious act, as sanctioned by Pope Gregory; a later generation would elevate them into a part of their worship; while later generations venerated the images as objects for their devotion. Such is the nature of man.

In an age when life was desperately uncertain, religious images not only became examples to them, but people began to hope that the saints represented by the images and statues would ensure good luck and health. The word 'image' is from the Latin *imitari* meaning 'to imitate', and a religious image was a visual likeness or expression of the saint. Wooden and stone images and statues of the saints began to appear in profusion in churches during the late Middle Ages. Many friary churches contained two, three, or even more, images, which were usually placed near side altars. The Dorchester Franciscan church had three great alabaster images, with six suits of vestments, some of embroidered blue velvet, to clothe them. The Melcombe Regis Dominican church had seven images at the various altars.

Images were used as aids to worship by giving visual representations, through symbolic art, of the persons to whom the faithful directed their prayers. Veneration of images was an act of honour or reverence to Christ or the saints, through some representative of them in symbolic art. The church did not consider them to be graven images, but symbolic representations of saints who were deemed worthy of honour.

Saints, as we have seen, were those who during their lives had borne witness to God through their sanctity. Although images of saints had appeared in churches in previous centuries, the veneration of them became more prevalent during the fifteenth century when friars, through their preaching and teaching, became the chief exponents of the use of images as aids to worship. Under the influence of the Renaissance, it became the practice to adorn images in brocades and jewels and illuminate them with votive candle lights.

Abuse and excesses crept in over a long period of time as stories grew around the various images. By the fifteenth century, the idolatry and superstition surrounding them became widespread and people began to attribute to them supernatural qualities. People addressed their prayers to images, which became the centre of devotion for many of the faithful. Unfortunately, by the fifteenth century the original purpose of images had been lost and images of Mary and the saints became the focus of idolatry and image worship.

RELICS

Martyrs of the church were those who had endured persecution and suffering for the love of Christ, and thus, at their death, attained glory in paradise and eternal life. The veneration of relics arose from the natural instinct for the church to honour the mortal remains and mementos of those who had died for their faith and to preserve them with care and respect, going back to the second century AD, to a time when Christians paid the supreme sacrifice of martyrdom for their faith. After the martyrdom of St Polycarp, Bishop of Smyrna in AD 166, his body was burnt by the civil authorities to discourage veneration by the Christians in Smyrna, but his remains were gathered from the ashes and the place where they were buried became an early site for pilgrimage.

Between the third and sixteenth centuries, the veneration of relics was a normal part of Christian life and worship. As we have seen, the Christians in Rome showed their respect for the remains of the martyrs by celebrating Mass on their tombs on the anniversaries of their deaths.

Many of those who died for the Christian faith were canonised as saints and their places of burial became major Christian shrines. Most of the larger ancient churches were built over the burial place of a saint, as it was thought that those whose blood had been shed for the Christian faith should be associated with an altar where Mass was celebrated. A number of Britain's cathedrals and abbeys, such as St Albans, St Andrews, Chester, St Davids, Durham, St Edmunds, Glasgow and Malmsbury, began as shrines to saints.

St Thomas Aquinas, writing about holy relics, stated, 'The saints belonged to Christ and were the sons of God and as a consequence served as intercessors with God for the living. Every relic was a record of the saint'. The church considered that the saints had performed more than was required, or expected, of them and that their merits could be transferred to others. The body of a saint deserved honour for itself and relics deserved more veneration than images.

It was believed that God worked miracles through relics because they had a direct relationship with the saints, with Christ and with God. The relics were but representations of the saints, who were the objects of honour, and though their bones were divided, they nevertheless remained a source of spiritual life. This resulted in the bones of the saints being fragmented and distributed widely to many churches. A large number of churches had a bone, limb or some object owned or worn by a saint, which became their treasured possession. Bones or limbs of the saints were sealed in altar tables, others were kept in reliquaries and displayed to the faithful on special occasions.

By the late Middle Ages, the veneration of relics became a normal element of Christian worship and no large church was without them. The chief importance of relics, other than venerating the saint, was in the popular belief that they contained some power to cure the sick. Always prey to natural calamities, illnesses and sudden death, medieval people needed to feel there were certain places to which they could go to find those specific channels through which divine grace might flow and where they could come closer to God.

A number of notable relics were given to the friars, such as the right hand of St Mary Magdalen given to the York Dominican house in about 1385 by Sir Brian Stapleton, who brought it from France. The Dominican friars in Bangor were said to posses the 'holiest relic in North Wales', which they took with them when they went out to procure alms.

Undoubtedly, many relics were spurious, being brought home by credulous pilgrims or crusaders returning from the East. Little attempt was made to check the authenticity of relics. The most convincing test was that of miracles; if a sick person was cured, then the relic was genuine. However, relics attracted large numbers of pilgrims.

Relics were usually taken out of safe keeping on specific days of the year and paraded around the town as crowds thronged the streets to pay homage. The cult of relics became so popular that in times of pestilence or danger they were taken in procession through the streets and the saint's help was invoked in order to avert disaster.

The popularity of relics became so great that by the fifteenth century their significance had become blurred and a trade in counterfeit relics developed, which became a scandal. The fourteenth-century Italian storyteller Boccaccio tells of a friar who used to exhibit a feather shed by the Archangel Gabriel after the annunciation, and how some students sought to embarrass him by secretly burning it and leaving the ashes in the reliquary. The friar proved equal to this; he claimed that a miracle had taken place and Gabriel's feather had been transformed into the ashes of St Lawrance, who had been burnt on a gridiron.

What started as pious acts to remember the saints and martyrs of the church had turned into blatant commercialism which contributed to the growing criticism of the practices of the church.

By the sixteenth century, the abuse of relics had become one of the main condemnations made against the church. We don't know if friars followed the trend on relics, or whether they were in the forefront of expounding on the pious use of relics. However, they received much of the criticism about the relic cult.

PILGRIMAGES

The church had a natural desire to honour the memory of martyrs and preserve the sites of their martyrdoms. Pilgrimages to such sites were for centuries a factor in the life of the church and, by the fourteenth century, actively encouraged. It was considered that pilgrimages heightened people's faith.

During the Middle Ages many people went on pilgrimages. Young and old, rich and poor, all tried to go on one at least once in their lives. People banded together to go on pilgrimages, considering them to be adventures as well as religious excursions. Others went to fulfil a vow or to carry out a penance. Some sought comfort in communion with relics of the saints, while others went to pray to a saint for healing. Others went on pilgrimages to secure indulgences; the further pilgrims travelled, the greater the number of indulgences they could claim.

Inevitably, more secular motives blended with the religious; the exhilaration of seeing famous shrines and the consequential enhancement of status in one's community must have played a part in medieval attitudes towards pilgrimages. However, most went on them as an act of faith.

As generations passed, the nature of pilgrimages changed from devotion to expectation that just by being near to relics of the saints, one could expect healing and that prayers would be answered. By the fifteenth century, many believed the relics themselves had some magical quality to perform miracles, and by the late fifteenth century, many thought of relics as lucky charms. Friars, along with the rest of the church, had unwittingly encouraged such expectations.

In Scotland, the property of burgesses who went on pilgrimages was protected during their absence by the law of the burgh, so important were pilgrimages to the people.

A church that contained the relics of a saint became a place of pilgrimage and attracted large numbers of people; consequently, some pilgrimage churches became extremely wealthy through the offerings of the faithful. The more pilgrims who visited a site, the more ornate the shrine became, and church buildings were enlarged to accommodate the increasing number of people.

St Peter's Church, Rome, was the most popular pilgrimage site. According to tradition, in the 90s Pope Evaristus built an oratory over the tomb of St Peter, which was close to the Circus of Nero and near where St Peter had been martyred. Constantine the Great built a basilica, which was consecrated in 326, over the site of the tomb. In 1447, work was started on the new St Peter's Church, on the site of the apostle's tomb.

The capture of Jerusalem by the crusaders in 1099 fired the imagination of Europe with zeal for pilgrimages to the Holy Land and to places associated with the life and crucifixion of Jesus. A pilgrimage to Jerusalem was deemed to be an adventure as well as a religious undertaking for young men of royal blood and scions of noble houses, many of whom made the journey. With the fall of Jerusalem to the Moslems in 1187, pilgrimages were still made to the Holy Land, but the journey became much more hazardous.

Pilgrims from Britain went considerable distances to Continental centres, such as along the Way of St James to the shrine of St James the Apostle at Santiago de Compostela, in Galicia, northern Spain, the third greatest centre of Christian pilgrimage. They also went to the Three Kings (Magi who brought gifts to Jesus) at Cologne. These centres were meeting places for people from across Europe.

The shrine of St Thomas à Becket, Archbishop of Canterbury, who was murdered in Canterbury Cathedral in 1170, was the most popular pilgrimage site in Britain. The Archbishop's death in his own cathedral had a marked effect on Christians, and large numbers of pilgrims went on the 60-mile pilgrimage from London to Canterbury. The cult of the murdered Archbishop grew tremendously, and income from the pilgrims became immense. The fourteenth-century nave and transepts, the south-west tower and the central tower were rebuilt from the pilgrims' offerings. In some years as many as 100,000 pilgrims left offerings at the Becket shrine. So great was the number of pilgrims that the large Trinity Chapel was built at the east end of the cathedral to house the relics and cope with the large number of pilgrims.

Some pilgrimage shrines were fashionable for a time and then interest in the shrine, or saint, waned, as new shrines became popular. For many years, pilgrims flocked to the shrines of St Oswald and St Wulstan in Worcester Abbey Cathedral. King John had no reverence for God, but revered the bones of St Wulstan and believed they possessed miraculous powers. Edward I went no fewer then eight times to pray at St Wulstan's shrine and to solicit the help of the saint. His son, Edward II, was murdered in 1327 and buried in Gloucester Abbey (Cathedral). This unpleasant king was popularly acclaimed a saint and martyr, although he was never canonised by the church. Large numbers of pilgrims went to Gloucester to pray beside his shrine and brought so many gifts that the Gloucester Abbey authorities were able to beautify the buildings from the proceeds of the gifts. It is not known how the Abbot of Gloucester Abbey persuaded people that Edward was a saint and martyr, but it had the result of diverting large numbers of pilgrims from the shrines of the two worthies, St Oswald and St Wulstan, in Worcester. After about 40 years, people lost interest in the power of the relics of Edward and returned in large numbers to the shrines of St Oswald and St Wulstan.

The shrine of St Edmund, at Bury St Edmunds, was visited by a large number of pilgrims, and many miracles were said to have been performed there. Legend has it that Edmund was a saint who was not to be trifled with, for if he was kind to those who asked his favours, those who denied his sanctity or in some way offended him were sure to be visited by his wrath.

As we have seen, the church has always had a deep affection

for the Blessed Virgin Mary. Statues and images of her appeared in all churches. By the fifteenth century, some statues of her took on a unique aura and became pilgrim sites of special devotion to her. Walsingham, where kings, nobles and a vast throng of people came to pray before the statue of Our Lady of Walsingham, became a major attraction to those who venerated her. There were a number of other pilgrimage sites to Our Lady, such as the notable shrines at Doncaster, Ipswich and Cardigan.

Those who were unable to travel long distances or who had neither the time nor financial means for journeys to distant pilgrim sites were attracted to numerous shrines of saints of local importance, such as the shrine containing the relics of St Duthac in Tain, about 45 miles north of Inverness. St Duthac was the local 'hero' who was said to have been born in Tain in about AD 1000, educated in Ireland and returned to become the chief bishop of Scotland.

There was a network of pilgrims' roads, leading to places of pilgrimage, which were kept in fairly good order due to the constant flow of travelling pilgrims. Some pilgrims made circular tours, going from one shrine to another and stopping at smaller shrines on the way.

Most pilgrims travelled with a water bottle and small bag containing a few necessities slung across their shoulder and took some means with them to pay for accommodation along the way. When excavations were being carried out at Worcester Cathedral in 1986, archaeologists found the remains of a pilgrim. He was dressed in woollen garments and knee-length boots; at his side lay a wooden staff and a cockleshell badge, indicating he had probably made a pilgrimage to the shrine of St James at Santiago de Compostela.

Some pilgrims, travelling alone or with a companion, were tempting targets for attacks from robbers. One such was a baker named William who set out from Perth to St Peter's, Rome, stopping at the shrine of St Thomas à Becket, Canterbury. When passing through Rochester he was murdered by his servant and was buried in Rochester Cathedral. A number of miraculous events were said to have taken place at his tomb and, as a result, he was spontaneously venerated and canonised by local consent in 1256. He was not canonised by the church.

Pilgrims usually travelled during the pilgrimage seasons of spring and summer and used the numerous inns along pilgrim ways, where they could be accommodated and fed. There were many pilgrim chapels along pilgrim routes where travellers could stop for their devotions. Kings and the nobility also went on many pilgrimages, and in 1446 Henry VI, in the course of a pilgrimage to Holy Places, lodged in the King's Lynn Austin house. In 1498 Henry VII also lodged at the Austin house on his way to Walsingham.

Time was not particularly important to pilgrims, and they would make new friends, listen to the latest gossip and hear of the wonders of previous pilgrimages. Well-to-do people travelled on horseback, while others travelled on foot; the long journey was considered to be part of the pilgrimage. The strolling pace of pilgrims on their way from London to Canterbury was known as the 'Canterbury gallop', which has passed into our vocabulary as the verb 'to canter'.

Most pilgrimage sites had hospices and hostelries which provided ample accommodation. Poorer men and women were given basic accommodation, while the better off were able to afford chambers at the lodgings. Celebrated visitors could command more salubrious accommodation, such as the New Inn, Gloucester, which was built for the pilgrim trade. It is now an excellent hotel.

The Aylesford Carmelite house was one of the important stopping places for pilgrims on their way to Canterbury, and, as we have seen, it had a hostel to accommodate them. Canterbury Franciscan house had a guest wing for pilgrims to the city and travellers on their way to Dover.

From Chaucer's *Canterbury Tales* we get a picture of some of the characters of the time, such as the friar travelling with a band of pilgrims from London to Canterbury. Friars were the ideal guides for pilgrims; they were not tied down by local church duties and were free to come and go as they pleased, subject to the approval, or at the behest, of their superiors. Many friars would have completed a number of pilgrimages as they led parties to their destinations, telling stories along the way to amuse them. They acted as, in modern parlance, 'tour guides'.

Pilgrims included clerics and friars who, being men of religion, felt the need to go on pilgrimages. Those wishing to go on long pilgrimages had to obtain a licence from their bishop or order allowing them to be away from their duties for the estimated period of the pilgrimage.

When pilgrims arrived at a pilgrim site they were struck by the richness and the magnificence of the shrine where the relics of the saints were displayed for veneration. They joined with throngs of pilgrims of every class, expressing their religious enthusiasm as they carried out their devotions. When they arrived at a shrine they would kneel before it and, if possible, touch it; after praying, it was usual for pilgrims to make a donation to the shrine. A number of records make reference to the emotion and unrestrained weeping of the pilgrims at shrines. Their devotion was intensified by reports of miraculous events, such as the healing of the sick, taking place around the shrine, or the miraculous preservation of the body of the saint from corruption.

Pilgrims often brought back metal badges to show they had been to a particular shrine. Each major shrine produced its own design. Very often the badge was a crude portrait of the saint concerned, but sometimes it took the form of an ampulla, a miniature flask containing Holy Water from the pilgrimage site. It was much the same as today's tourists taking home their souvenirs. The Walsingham badge was a pewter ampulla containing Holy Water, whilst pilgrims from Canterbury brought back an ampulla with scenes of the martyrdom of Becket. The St Andrews pilgrim badges showed the saint being crucified on a cross formed like the letter X. The Jerusalem badge depicted crossed palm leaves.

When the pilgrims arrived home after some weeks or months, their outlook would have been enlarged and their religious aspirations stirred with excitement as they recounted to their friends and neighbours the events of the journey.

9

FINANCIAL SUPPORT

Many towns in Britain gave regular payments out of public funds towards their local friars' houses. Shrewsbury is a good example of a town which prospered during the thirteenth and fourteenth centuries and it became one of the dozen or so richest in Britain. It has been estimated that in 1280 it had a population of about 3,000 and was served by four parish churches, St Mary's, St Chad's, St Alkmund's and St Julian's. There was also a Benedictine abbey near the town's southern crossing of the River Severn. Possibly the burgesses in this prosperous community considered that the abbey on their doorstep didn't contribute much spiritually to the town, due to the isolation of the monks from the population, and the ministry from the four parish churches must have left something to be desired. When the friars first settled in England the burgesses and tradesmen of Shrewsbury were willing to give substantial financial support to any houses of mendicant friars that settled in their town. As we have seen, in about 1232, the Dominican friars established a house in Shrewsbury, and in 1245, the burgesses actively encouraged the Franciscan friars to settle in the town. On the back of a rent list compiled in 1246, is a list of subscriptions made to pay for the settlement of the Franciscans. It shows that townsmen and gentry from the area gave quite substantial sums to the work of the friars. Individual offerings reached £49, the town bailiffs gave £10 and the Sheriff, acting for the King, contributed just over £40. In addition, a plot of land was given to the Franciscan friars for the erection of their buildings. In 1254, the burgesses of Shrewsbury petitioned the Austin friars to come to their town, which they did. The town of Shrewsbury continually showed a generosity to the friars. In 1537, on the eve of the suppression of the three houses, the town's corporation accounts show a payment of 10 shillings to the Dominican friars 'as a reward for the friars preaching and proclaiming the word of God'.

The picture of religious life in Shrewsbury in the thirteenth century was repeated in many other towns. In the smaller, and less prosperous, town of Cardiff there were two parish churches, St John's and St Mary's. As we have seen, Cardiff had a population of about 2,000 during the medieval period, of which about 400 were burgesses or freemen. Even though the town was small and relatively poor, the people supported a house of Dominican friars and a house of Franciscan friars. It is not known how many friars were housed in these two friaries in about 1300, but as both were medium-sized establishments, there would have been between 15 and 20 friars per house. Both Cardiff houses had to rely for most of their transitory financial support on the only town in their area.

Appleby-in-Westmorland had a population of about 2,000 in the thirteenth and fourteenth centuries, and, while the people of the town prospered during the period, they also knew turbulent times due to the town being in the forefront of Scots border raids into northern England. The town had one parish church, St Lawrence, and another church, St Michaels, just outside the town, in Old Appleby. In 1281, a community of Carmelite friars settled there but could not have established themselves in the town, nor survived until the suppression of the house in 1539, if they had not received ongoing voluntary financial support from the townspeople.

ALMS AND DONATIONS

During the later Middle Ages, wealth was spread among the nobility, landowners and merchant classes, who found in the mendicants a focus for their acts of charity. The good will of people towards the friars is shown by the people, who had to pay tithes to their local church and taxes to the King, willingly giving their support to the friars.

The friars' understanding of money in the community was summed up in a sermon given in the fourteenth century by Dr Bromyard: 'Men were not masters of their riches, since they were only guardians of it for a short time'.

Many friars' houses could not have financially survived without the confraternities of lay people, who were the devoted adherents to their respective orders and who championed the friars' cause by organising financial support and giving aid continuously. Though the zeal and freshness shown by the earlier brethren may have waned, the friars were still receiving financial support from the people. For instance, in the early part of the sixteenth century the Ayr Dominican house received many gifts and donations, but they were becoming progressively less frequent and the flow of funds failed in the 1530s, the years leading up to the Reformation.

In addition, organisations gave regular donations to the friars' houses, and the range of donations is illustrated in the records of the Oxford Franciscan house. The King was top of the benefactors and gave the house 50 marks (£33.40p), paid in equal portions at Easter and Michaelmas, every year from 1289 until the dissolution of the house in 1538. At the bottom of the list was a contribution of six pence a year from St Ebbe's Church, in whose parish the friars' house stood.

BEQUESTS

Gifts to numerous charities were a feature of medieval wills; friars' houses, in particular, were constant beneficiaries and a large part of their revenues was derived from bequests. In the Middle Ages, most men and women of every rank and status made their wills when near death, by which time many were moved both by a fervour for their faith and the fear of hell or purgatory. Friars, who were of the educated classes, were trusted by the testators to write their wills, as they made no attempt to gain possession of property.

Wills were solemn deeds that were remarkable for their

simplicity. Most medieval wills were invariably signed both by a friar and a member of the laity, before an altar and the relic of a saint or saints.

Bequests to the friars, in amounts ranging from five pence to £10, became common from people in all walks in life. Friars were content to be acknowledged by small gifts and legacies to their houses, in the same way we today leave small bequests to the trustees of wills. Such numerous small gifts of money became an important part of the finance of friars' houses.

About 44 per cent of the wills in medieval Norwich made bequests to the friars, and about one-third of all known wills made in Oxford in the fourteenth century contained bequests to the Franciscan friars in the town; but this fell to about one in six from the mid-fifteenth century and tailed off during the sixteenth century. The other houses in the town were also provided for in the same manner. The citizens of Cambridge also generously remembered the friars in their wills, and the London mendicant houses were frequently remembered in the wills of the rich and influential of the land.

In 1270, Boniface, Archbishop of Canterbury, bequeathed 40 marks to the Canterbury Franciscan friars, 15 marks to the Oxford Dominican and Franciscan houses and five marks to every Dominican and Franciscan house in the Province of Canterbury.

In 1356, Matthew de Redman, in what is a typical will of the period, bequeathed his body to be buried in the churchyard of the Dominican friars at Carlisle. He left his best beast as a funeral gift to his parish church and 20 shillings each to the Dominican and Franciscan friars' houses in Carlisle.

In 1454, Robert Sutton, a dyer and prominent citizen of Worcester, left 20 shillings to the Worcester Dominican friars for them to celebrate his memorial Mass, 40 shillings for the cloister of the same house, and 20 shillings to the fraternity of St James there.

Sir Thomas Dutton, in 1379, in the presence of two abbots and many noblemen, recorded his gift to the Warrington Austin friars. In return for the gift the Austins promised to say daily Mass, and in case of omission, the house would be fined three shillings and four pence.

Queen Eleanor, wife of Edward I, who died in 1290, left 100 shillings to each of the Dominican houses in England and Wales. The legacies were distributed to the houses by the Provincial of the English Order.

The will listed in the Oxford History Society (1913), of Richard Brampton, an Oxford butcher who died in 1362, shows the variety of donations this tradesman of limited means contributed towards charity and religion. He left:

Two shillings for the repair of All Saints' Church, where he hoped to be buried.

Six shillings and eightpence for the payment of any tithes or offerings which he had neglected or forgotten to pay.

One shilling to the parish priest and sixpence to the priest's clerk.

Ten shillings for distribution to the poor on the day of his funeral.

Ten shillings for distribution among the mendicant friars of Oxford.

Three pounds, six shillings and eightpence for a chaplain to say a daily Mass for his soul for a year.

The legacies left to the Austin friars at Canterbury are typical of a bequest left to a friars' house. In his will, proved in 1400, John Tyece ordered that his grange at 'Redyngate' and other arable land in Canterbury should be sold and the proceeds divided among the mendicant friars, nuns and other poor religious of Canterbury. In 1457, Richard Pargate bequeathed 40 shillings towards making a new gate for the Austin friars' house, and in 1504, Didier Bargier, Rector of St Andrews, left 'my little brevet mass-book covered with red leather' to the altar of St Didier in the Austin friars' house. In 1506, Elizabeth Hale left three shillings and four pence annually for ten years to cover the cost of a series of memorial services for her. In 1522, Sir John Fineux, Chief Justice of Common Pleas, expended more than £40 on repairs to the church, refectory, dormitory and walls of the friary. In return, the brethren agreed to provide a chaplain to celebrate a daily mass in the chapel of the Visitation of the Blessed Virgin for the soul of Sir John, the souls of his wife and others. There were numerous other such legacies left to the house over the years.

Other typical gifts to friars were those of John Langley of Siddington, near Cirencester, who in 1459 left two shillings and six pence to the Dominican houses in Gloucester and Warwick, the Franciscan houses in Bristol and Coventry and to the Carmelite house in Gloucester. In 1490, his grandson, Edmond, left six shillings and eight pence each to the Carmelite, Dominican and Franciscan house in Gloucester. Sir Thomas Maul, who fell at Floddon Field in 1513, made a will prior to going to war, in which he left £16 to the Dundee Franciscans. As late as 1530, John Morgan left five shillings each to the Franciscan and Dominican houses in Cardiff and 20 shillings to the Newport (Gwent) Austin house near his home in Basseleg.

There are a number of references of the friars going to court to enforce the payment of legacies.

BENEFACTORS

The baronial families maintained an intimate connection with houses founded or supported by their families. However, the patronage of wealthy families did not cover the running cost of the houses.

The Nevilles of Raby Castle and the Scropes of Bolton Castle were principal patrons of the Richmond (Yorkshire) Franciscan house. In 1400, Sir Richard le Scrope gave 20 shillings to each house of friars in Carlisle, Penrith and Appleby.

The Lossenham Carmelite house, founded by Sir Thomas Alcher in 1242, remained under the patronage of the Alcher family, who lived nearby.

In 1279 the Statute of Mortmain, known as the 'dead hand

statute', forbade further gifts of inalienable ownership of land to the church, except under royal licence, due to the church holding so much land in perpetuity. The land they acquired passed into dead hands, as it were, and ceased to yield feudal profits to its lords, much like the loss of death duties or inheritance tax to the state today would be. The law also aimed at stopping the flow of land to the church, which already owned a large amount of it. This affected possible gifts and legacies of land to the friars at a time when some orders would have agreed to accept such gifts.

The Austin friars at Penrith, who suffered from their remoteness, were not receiving adequate funds and were in difficulty with their finances. In 1360, the Bishop of Carlisle assisted the house by appointing the prior as priest in charge of the church of Newton Reigny, a few miles outside Penrith. The prior was allowed to discharge his duties to the church by appointing one of his friars to perform the parochial duties for him. Four years later, the sacrist of the Penrith house was appointed as priest to the same church for four years.

GIFTS IN KIND

Until the end of the thirteenth century, it was common for donors to give gifts of building materials, cattle, food, wine, clothing and provisions to the friars. The Berkeley family liberally provided wine and wheat out of their granaries, together with many other benefactions annually over the years to each of the three mendicant houses in Gloucester.

The Crown granted some houses exemption from certain dues, which helped them financially. The Carmelite and Dominican friars in Chester were granted, by Royal Charter, exemption from tolls in the city and town mill, due to their houses having suffered in the Welsh raids. In 1267, Henry III granted an unusual favour to Warwick Dominican friars when he directed all bailiffs and other officers on the route from Norwich to Warwick to permit the Warwick friars to carry their herrings and other supplies freely from Norwich, without toll or hindrance, until the following Easter. When the New Romney Franciscan house was founded in 1241, Henry III granted them £100 to buy clothes, out of the revenues of the Archbishop of Canterbury, but the house ceased in 1287. Also in 1241, the King gave the Lewes Franciscans 10 marks for vestments, and in 1253 he ordered the Sheriff of Sussex to give the Chichester Franciscans 26 tunics. In 1233 he ordered the Sheriff of London to buy 700 ells (the length from the elbow to the tip of the middle finger) of cloth for the London Dominican and Franciscan friars, and 100 pairs of shoes for the Dominicans. In 1253, he granted the Moatenden Trinitarian house the right to hold an annual fair.

The Canterbury Dominican friars were on good terms with the monks of Christ Church Cathedral-Priory (Canterbury Cathedral) and St Augustines Abbey and received doles of corn as well as other gifts, from them every year. David, Bishop of Moray, gave two cauldrons of best meal from the episcopal grange yearly to the Elgin Dominican friars. After the latter part of the thirteenth century, gifts of money were mostly given.

By the mid-fifteenth century, there were indications that the mendicants were having difficulty in maintaining their prosperity, and some houses were given pastures to help support their houses.

In 1447, Marlborough Carmelite friars were granted as much fuel from Savernake Forest as a horse could take in three days, going and returning, for the relief of their poverty. In small and poor houses in rural districts where voluntary alms were less plentiful, friars were given pastures to supplement their livelihood by a certain amount of agricultural activity. The Richmond (Yorkshire) Franciscan house had 16 acres to help support the house. The Hartlepool Franciscan house was said to have had the 'best Ribstone Pippin apples', while the Preston Franciscan friars owned a watermill, windmill and other farming interests. Rhuddlan Dominican friary had three acres of meadow land, three gardens and two orchards and possessed a few cows and pigs. The Brecon Franciscan house had six acres of grazing land and an orchard, while the

Dunwich Franciscan house had its own fishing boat, which was used to supplement their income. In 1538, the produce from the Bristol Carmelite house gardens was their only source of income. In 1505, Denbigh Carmelites' house was given 12 mares and a horse, and in 1536 they were given two rams. In 1491 the Llanfaes Franciscans, who had about 30 acres of land, were given a cow, a further cow in 1506 and another in 1537 by the local landowner. In 1511, the Denbigh Carmelites, the Llanfaes Franciscans and the Chester Franciscans were each given a bullock. These houses were among the poorer ones and it appears that the local people gave gifts in kind to enable them to support themselves.

THE KING'S BOUNTY

As we have noted, English and Scottish kings were the greatest benefactors of the mendicants, and successive kings gave substantial gifts to a number of friars' houses. Royal patronage was important to the friars, especially during their early history.

The Patent and Close Rolls show how much Henry III patronised the Dominican and Franciscan Orders. They contain entries of his benefactions to a large number of friaries, many paid over a long period. There was scarcely a Dominican or Franciscan house in England which did not owe something to the liberality of the King, as many houses received royal gifts of money either for building or for clothes and household expenses. Sometimes the money was paid direct from the treasury, but often by a sheriff or other officer held responsible for the payment.

Kings and members of the royal families made numerous journeys through England and often stayed in religious houses en route. From 1289 to 1338, Edward I, Edward II and, for a number of years, Edward III, gave a house of friars a pittance of a silver groat (a silver four-pence piece) a head for each friar in residence for each day of the King's stay, to cover the expenses of the royal visit. This indicates the number of friars in the house during the time of the royal visit.

In 1300, Edward I, an orthodox churchman who was anxious to pay his dues to God, stayed with the Boston Dominicans and gave the house 19 shillings and eight pence for food for his two days' stay. In 1312, Edward II gave the same house 12 shillings for one day's food, and Edward III, who stopped there in 1328, gave them nine shillings and four pence for one day's food. The 19 shillings and eight pence given for two days' stay, at four pence per friar per day, indicates there were about 30 brethren attached to the house in 1300. The 12 shillings for one day's stay in 1312 indicates there were 36 brethren. Again, the nine shillings and four pence given in 1328 was for the 28 brethren there at that time. In 1301, Edward I lodged at the Warwick Dominican house for three days on his way to Scotland and gave 37 shillings on leaving the house, which indicates there were 37 friars in residence. When Edward III stayed at the same house for one day in 1329, he left 10 shillings for the 30 friars. He continued this custom until 1338, when it was discontinued due to the start of the costly wars with France – it was never renewed.

However, the royal bounty was not so generous to friars' houses in Wales and there are very few entries of such gifts to Welsh houses.

There are numerous references to royal gifts by the Scottish kings to mendicant houses in their realm. The Scottish Exchequer records show payments at regular intervals to the Dominican houses in Scotland. During his invasion of Scotland in 1297, Edward I wrote to the Earl of Surrey instructing him to examine the rent rolls of ten royal burghs in order to ascertain that the amount of stipends paid by Alexander III and John Balliol to the Dominican houses in Scotland were still being paid from the Crown revenues of the burghs.

Robert the Bruce gave an annual sum of 40 marks to the Dumfries Franciscan house, to expiate his sacrilege of the friary kirk, and 20 marks to each of the other Franciscan houses in Scotland.

CORRODIES

So far had friars departed from the early ways, and such was their quest for funds to augment their decreasing income from other sources, that by the fifteenth century, some houses followed the monastic example of corrody, that is, private persons occupying lodgings located within a friary precincts in exchange for a sum of money or for the transfer of a parcel of land. The corrodies were usually elderly couples who had provided for their needs in their old age and wished to see their days out in the security of a friars' house, where they were assigned separate accommodation from the friars. When they died, the friars said masses for them and they had the privilege of being buried in the friars' cemetery.

A corrody was like an insurance policy paid to provide for the person's keep in old age. It was unfortunate for the friars if corrodies survived for a number of years because then this practice imposed a burden on the house.

In their constant struggle to maintain the financial viability of their houses, friars resorted to various means for their financial support. In order to understand the friars' approach to fund-raising, it should be borne in mind that they relied on transitory charity and the spontaneous acts of benefactors. The fact that friars did not have a guaranteed income from year to year was their early strength, but later became their greatest weakness.

Friars have been criticised for the methods they employed to raise money, but if they had not found ways of raising funds, they would not have existed for very long. If friars' houses had not been funded by the community, their valuable service to the community would have been lost, to the disadvantage of many. Although in theory they were poor, most houses received a constant flow of funds from one source or another.

During the latter part of their existence, more and more of their energy was directed to fund-raising, which diverted them from their spiritual work. By the sixteenth century, they had difficulty in maintaining the same level of services and charitable work as in the past. This could have been due partly to benefactors seeing how gifts of past generations to monastic houses were disappearing into the King's exchequer and fear that donations to the friars would go the same way.

By the late 1520s the flow of gifts and bequests had begun to dry up and the state of some friars' houses became piteous. Records show that many of their buildings became ruinous and decayed, presumably from lack of maintenance brought about by their financial problems. In 1538, for instance, the brethren of the Bridgnorth Franciscan house received only a few shillings in alms and three shillings from two small properties. They depended for their livelihood on the services they held in St Sythe's Chapel, a church on the south end of the River Severn town bridge.

The lack of adequate funds due to their past ideals of poverty and begging led the friars to search for other sources of income, and their ways of soliciting funds were to tarnish their image. As in all organisations, there were many good and honest brethren, but the inadequate and slothful gave the mendicants a bad name. I feel this happened to the friars, who, while doing a mountain of good within the communities they served, were tarnished by the way they solicited funds. Yet without sufficient funds, they could not have survived. They were caught in a vicious circle.

10

FRIARS AND NOTEWORTHY EVENTS

During the 300 years or so that the British medieval friars existed, there was a considerable amount of stability in the various houses. They lacked possessions and were, therefore, seldom involved in lawsuits. Consequently, there are few temporal records of them, and, as they were not liable to episcopal visitations, there are few ecclesiastical records.

Individual friars played their part in national affairs, going on errands or delicate negotiations for the King and holding important posts in the households of influential nobility. A number of friars were elevated to the office of bishop, where they were able to exercise considerable influence in their diocese. However, the mendicant movement as a whole was content to influence the church, and they kept out of politics as much as possible. As a result, the history of most of their houses, other than for their early starting-up days and the Reformation period, is obscure.

Some friars did get themselves into trouble with the authorities, but this was when they entered the realms of politics, rather than for religious reasons. There were occasions when some friars were in trouble with the civil authorities, but their only major conflict occurred during the period leading up to the Reformation.

The fifteenth century was spent almost entirely with Britain at war, but this did not affect the way the friars worked. In general they lived peaceful and uneventful lives as they continued with their ongoing duties to the communities they served.

PIERS GAVESTON

Piers Gaveston, notorious as a favourite of Edward II, had infuriated the barons, and in 1312 they formed a confederation to put an end to his influence. He was besieged in Scarborough Castle until, when his provisions ran out, he was induced to come out of the castle and confer with the Earl of Pembroke in Scarborough Dominican church. There, in the presence of the Host, with his hand on the Gospels, the Earl swore to Gaveston that the barons could either make peace and Gaveston be given a safe conduct to London, or he could return safely to his castle. On 10 June, while Gaveston was being taken to London, he was abducted at Deddington, near Banbury, by his implacable enemy, the Earl of Warwick, and taken a prisoner to Warwick Castle. On 19 June, he was taken from the castle and summarily beheaded. Dying excommunicated, he could not be buried in consecrated ground and it was left to some Oxford Dominicans to take his body to their church, where it remained for two years. In 1314, Gaveston's embalmed body was taken from Oxford and buried in the partly built King's Langley Dominican church, where the Last Rites were performed by Archbishop Reynolds of Canterbury, helped by four bishops.

QUEEN ISABELLA

In 1327, with the help of Roger Mortimer, Queen Isabella arranged the murder of her husband, Edward II. In the same year, they took her son, the boy King Edward III, to York and demanded quarters in the Franciscan house for the royal household, where they stayed for six weeks. The friars were ordered to keep their household separate from the royal party during the visit. One evening she gave a party for 60 courtiers and their ladies in the friars' dormitory. Three years later she fell from power and Mortimer was hanged at Tyburn. In old age, she suffered a change of heart and took the habit of the nuns of the Order of Poor Clares. She died in 1358 and was buried in the London Franciscan church.

RICHARD II

In 1384, John Latimer, a Carmelite friar, informed Richard II that his uncle, John of Gaunt, was plotting the King's murder. It seems the King believed him and condemned Gaunt as a traitor, without further enquiry. Gaunt defended himself and the lords present in Parliament persuaded the King to stay his hand and have the friar committed to prison while the matter was investigated. On his way there, however, the friar was intercepted by a band of Lancastrian knights and put to death. The truth of the threat to the King was never resolved publicly. When John of Gaunt died in 1399, Richard was deposed by his cousin, John of Gaunt's son, Henry Bolingbroke, who ascended the throne as Henry IV. Richard was either murdered or starved to death in Pontefract Castle, we are not certain which, and his death was announced in February 1400. Richard was secretly buried in King's Langley Dominican friary.

Word went round that Richard had escaped, and a statute was passed declaring it to be high treason to spread the rumour that he was still alive and waiting for his time to come.

The sympathies of the Leicester Franciscans were with the deposed Richard II, whom they recognised as their rightful king. Roger Frisby, the warden, and his friars were tried for conspiring against Henry IV by trying to get men to go and search for Richard II in Scotland. In 1402, the warden and seven friars at the same house were arrested and charged with treason for having organised an armed revolt to restore Richard to the throne. After two juries had failed to convict them, a third jury found them guilty and they were hanged at Tyburn. Two others escaped, but as two Franciscan friars were executed in Leicester about the same time, it is possible they were recaptured.

In 1402, a friar from Aylesbury Franciscan house was also accused of spreading a report that Richard was still alive. He was brought before Henry IV and, after being questioned by the King, was hanged and then beheaded.

LONDON

No town, not even London, which was by far the largest town in Britain, had more than one house of any mendicant order in it. However, the London friars' houses were large and well patronised.

London had 19 religious communities and Londoners were very generous to them, though they disapproved when the friars advocated tolerance towards the city's Jewish community. All the London mendicant houses had numerous burials in their churches, where some of the most powerful in the kingdom were laid to rest.

The London Austin, which was destroyed by a German bomb on 10 October 1940, was 284 feet in length and 83 feet wide. In comparison, Exeter Cathedral is 70 feet wide and Winchester Cathedral is 80 feet wide. The nine large windows in the church were regarded by many as the most beautiful in London. They owed the rebuilding of their church in 1354 to Humphrey de Bohun, Earl of Hereford, and the house doubtless benefited in 1361 under the will of the Earl, who left 300 marks for masses to be sung by friars of the order.

In 1381, the 13 Flemish men who had taken refuge in the church were dragged out and killed by rioters, but the hostility of the mob did not extend to the friars.

The London Carmelite house was 260 feet in length, the nave 80 feet wide and the chancel 25 feet wide. It was sited on land outside the city wall south of Fleet Street running down to the River Thames by Bouverie Street and Whitefriars Street. As we have seen, it was a *studium* with, at times, up to about 100 friars accommodated in a large residential block. The site probably left much to be desired regarding hygiene, for in 1290 many friars died because of the insanitary conditions. About 1350, the Earl of Devon had the church rebuilt, and in 1420 the Carmelite Bishop of Hereford added a steeple to the church. Being near to The Temple (the law school), the house was used for a number of church and royal councils during the fourteenth and fifteenth centuries and many of its friars were employed in political business.

In 1221, Hubert de Burgh gave the three Dominican friars who remained in London a site in Holborn. In 1276, the corporation of London granted them the abandoned Baynard's Castle. The friars demolished the castle and in 1306 they started to build their new house in the walled precincts of the castle. Hubert de Burgh was buried in the Holborn church in 1243, but when the friars moved to Baynard's Castle, they took the remains with them and buried them in their new church. The church was 260 feet long, the same length as the Carmelite church, the nave was 66 feet wide and the chancel 35 feet wide.

As previously noted, in 1225 the Franciscans were first given land in Newgate Street on the corner of Stynking Lane, so called due to the smell from the blood of slaughtered animals; it must have been one of the most unpleasant parts of the city. From the start, the citizens and nobility were very generous to the Franciscans. When work on the new church built on the site was started in 1306, Queen Margaret, second wife of Edward I, and the nobility financed the building work and the large church was built in just 21 years. Building work on the choir was paid by Queen Margaret, a wealthy citizen paid for erection of the spacious nave and another citizen paid for the domestic buildings. The 36 windows were provided by various donors, mostly notable London citizens and members of the nobility. Queen Isabella expended over £700 to complete work on the church. It was a large and attractive building which measured 300 feet long and 83 feet wide. In 1420–21, Sir Richard (Dick) Whittington paid for a library to be built over the north alley of the great cloister and bequeathed most of his books to it.

The Friars of the Sack settled in Aldersgate, London, in 1257, and in 1271 Queen Eleanor, wife of Henry III, gave them land in Coleman Street for their house. The site was near a synagogue and, in 1272, the friars complained about being disturbed at their devotions by the noise from the synagogue. As a remedy, Henry III gave the friars the synagogue and the Jews built another.

The house of the Crutched Cross friars was opposite St Olives

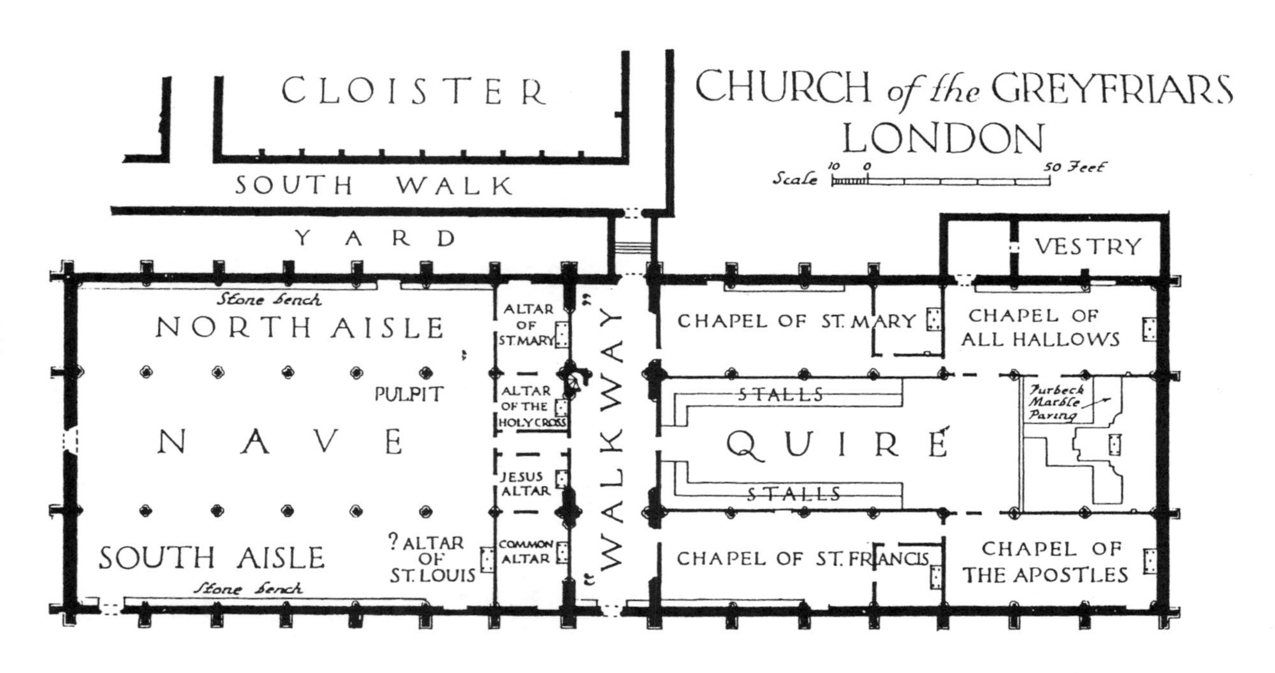
CHURCH of the GREYFRIARS
LONDON
Scale 10 0 50 Feet
CLOISTER
SOUTH WALK
YARD
VESTRY
Stone bench
NORTH AISLE
PULPIT
NAVE
SOUTH AISLE
? ALTAR OF ST. LOUIS
Stone bench
ALTAR OF ST. MARY
ALTAR OF THE HOLY CROSS
JESUS ALTAR
COMMON ALTAR
WALKWAY
CHAPEL OF ST. MARY
CHAPEL OF ALL HALLOWS
STALLS
QUIRE
STALLS
Purbeck Marble Paving
CHAPEL OF ST. FRANCIS
CHAPEL OF THE APOSTLES

Church, Hart Street, and Crutched Friars Street. It was founded in about 1298 by two men who later became friars of the order. It appears the house was popular with foreigners who lived nearby. The Fraternity of the Holy Blood of Jesus and the Brotherhood of St Katharine were founded there in the latter part of the fifteenth century. Both were of German origin.

PARLIAMENT

Parliaments were held in a number of friars' houses over the years, probably due to the larger houses having substantial accommodation and facilities. Henry III summoned a Parliament in the Oxford Dominican house in 1258, when the Provisions of Oxford were approved, which were major reforms of government. A Parliament was held in Lincoln Franciscan house in 1301; in 1316 another Parliament was held in Lincoln, at first in the Deans Hall and then in the Lincoln Carmelite friars' church. In 1388, a Parliament was held in the Cambridge Dominican house and the friars were awarded 20 marks as compensation for damage and inconvenience. In 1414, a Parliament assembled in the Leicester Franciscan house, when it passed a statute against heretics and Lollards and in 1449, a Parliament met in the London Dominican house.

ANCHORITES

Throughout the ages, a number of men and women have taken vows to live solitary lives of prayer and contemplation, most of them becoming recluses by a process of personal spiritual development. They sought spiritual insight and wisdom that found ultimate fulfilment in living a life of solitude, silence and prayer, away from the cares and distractions of the world. Such a life was common before the Reformation, when men and women dedicated to religion often lived in a room beside a church, where many people came to them for comfort and advice. Other solitary hermits, often clad in goatskins or other such garments, went about the country barefooted and carrying T-shaped staffs as a symbol of protection and salvation. In medieval times, such people were regarded as perfect expressions of the ideal of poverty and piety.

'Anchorite' comes from medieval Latin for 'retire into a space' and, in medieval times, numerous religious establishments had an anchorite or anchoress attached to them. These solitaries received popular respect, as the number of small bequests left to them show. Every large town would have supported at least one such person. Even in our own day there are a few people who live this life in Britain, but because of the nature of their calling, the public are not aware of them.

Richard Taylor, in his *Index Monasticus*, lists 38 anchorites in Norwich during the 1370s, including Lady Julian, the most famous English mystic of her day. She was a nun of Carrow Abbey and took her name from St Julian's Church, where she had a cell attached to the nave. She wrote *Revelations of Divine Love* and claimed that in 1373 Christ appeared and spoke to her on no less than 16 occasions.

Anchorites attached themselves to numerous friary churches as they considered a friary to be a place where they would be welcomed by holy men. These anchorites were not friars but 'lodgers' who were protected by the friars. But there are references to some friars professing the anchorite life and living in cells attached to friaries. Anchorites isolated themselves from the normal life by choice and were engaged in prayer, meditation and often in bodily affliction. Their guidance on religious matters was frequently sought, and people had access to them through small windows in the cells. Such cells were usually attached to the choir of the church and had an angled viewing squint, or lowside window, which allowed anchorites to see Mass being celebrated at the high altar without stepping outside their cell.

Two anchorites lived in the precincts of Norwich Franciscan church, two in the precincts of the Norwich Carmelite church and an anchoress lived in an enclosed cell outside the north side of the choir of Norwich Dominican church. One anchorite lived in the precincts of King's Lynn Carmelite church, while another lived in a hermitage built on the west end of Thetford Austin house. In 1402, John Bourne, an anchorite residing in a cell in Arundel Dominican house, found the place inconvenient and the house poor. He obtained a papal licence to move to a more suitable place, taking his clothes, books and other belongings with him. In 1507, an anchorite was living in the precincts of Walsingham Franciscan friary and was still there in 1526. An anchorite priest was living in a cell sited at the entrance of Northampton Austin church in 1538.

By a deed of 1388, recording the foundation of an anchorite's cell in Droitwich Austin house, the Earl of Warwick paid for a cell to be built on the south side of the choir, for the enclosure and habitation of Henry de Stokebrugge. It was a place where Stokebrugge could live the life of an anchorite to the honour of God and pray for the soul of the founder and Warwick's family. The Earl and his heirs had the right to nominate another person wishing to profess the anchorite life, following the death of the incumbent.

Following the death of an anchoress in the parish church of Richmond (Yorkshire) in 1490, an arbitration ruled that her goods should go to the Franciscan house in the town after her debts had been paid because she had taken her habit from the friars. Nomination to the Richmond anchorage was in the hands of the bailiff and burgesses of the town.

During the first part of the sixteenth century, two anchorites lived in small cells within the precincts of Canterbury Dominican church, and one, Robert Collens, was still there at the time of the dissolution of the house in 1538. An anchorite was still living at the Oxford Dominican house at the dissolution of the house. When the Bishop of Dover visited the Worcester Franciscan house in 1538 to close it, he appears to have had difficulty in persuading an anchoress living in a cell attached to the church to leave it. She is said to have built her house out of the ground and pleaded to be allowed to stay. There are references to numerous other such cells in friaries and other religious establishments.

WALES

The Cardiff Franciscan friars bore the mangled body of Llywelyn Bren for burial in their church after he had, in 1318, been dragged to a traitor's death through the streets of Cardiff for his part in the Welsh revolt in Glamorgan in 1315. The same church contained the tomb of Sir William Fleming, who, as the sheriff, carried out the harsh judgment on Llywelyn Bren.

In 1400, Owain Glyndwr, a Welsh patriotic leader in North Wales, was involved in a quarrel over land with Lord de Grey of Ruthin. This sparked a popular revolt in Wales against Henry IV, which did not wane until after 1406. The revolt was a time of acute trauma and distress which brought impoverishment to the mendicant houses in Wales.

During the uprising the Llanfaes Franciscan house was attacked in 1400 by Henry IV's troops, when the friars' goods were seized and the friars dispersed as rebels. However, the Provincial Minister took the matter up with the King, who then undertook some reparation, but by the reign of Henry V the house was ruinous. The King revived the house and made provision for an ongoing compliment of eight friars.

In 1403, Glyndwr fell upon Cardiff and burnt the Dominican house. He spared the Franciscan house as the Welsh Franciscans had been among Owain's most loyal supporters. However, prior to his attack on Cardiff, the Franciscan friars removed their books and valuables to Cardiff Castle for safe keeping. When Glyndwr captured the castle, he reproached the friars for their lack of confidence, saying that if they had kept the goods in their house, they would have been safe. It is not recorded whether or not the goods were returned to them. The revolt spread to Newport, where the Austin house was destroyed, but it was later rebuilt.

SCOTLAND

In March 1286, Alexander III held council in Edinburgh with

his lords. Later in the evening the King was returning to Kinghorn, on the north side of the Firth of Forth, where the Queen awaited him. The night was dark, but he was ferried across the rough waters of the Firth of Forth, and, on landing at Inverkeithing, he was separated from his two companions. As he rode along the cliff path towards Kinghorn, his horse missed its footing on the cliff-edge road and threw Alexander to his death on the rocks below. The King's two sons and daughter had died before their father, leaving a granddaughter, Margaret, the Maid of Norway. After a brief reign, she died in 1290, and with her death, Scotland was without a monarch. The right to the crown was disputed by 13 claimants. In their distress, the Scottish baronage agreed that Edward I of England be invited to arbitrate in order to prevent bloodshed. He chose between two, Robert Bruce and John Balliol, and he announced his decision in the great hall of Berwick Castle on 17 November 1292 in favour of Balliol, who was crowned King of Scots at Scone on the last day of November. Edward's ultimate aim was to make the King of Scots a vassal of the King of England and thereby take over Scotland. In 1296, Edward turned on Balliol, invaded Scotland and defeated him at the battle of Dunbar. Balliol was taken prisoner, stripped of his royal insignia, and, after three years, was allowed to retire to his estates in France.

During the reign of Alexander III, Berwick-upon-Tweed was a Royal Burgh, one of Scotland's most prosperous ports and an emporium of the northern trade. All four main orders of friars, as well as the Sack and Trinitarian friars, were established in Berwick-upon-Tweed while the town was under the Scottish crown and in the diocese of St Andrews.

When Edward invaded Scotland in 1296, he sacked Berwick, including the houses of friars, and massacred many of the inhabitants of the town. From that time Berwick, with its friaries, went from being an active and prosperous centre of trade into decline. When in 1333, the town was retaken by the English, Edward III instructed the Provincials of all the four mendicant orders to remove the Scottish friars from their Berwick-upon-Tweed houses, and they were sent to English houses south of the Trent in substitution for friars of English descent who could, by their sermons, lead the people into fidelity to the English king. During a temporary peace between England and Scotland in 1337, it was agreed by treaty that the border between the two countries should be on the Tweed–Solway line. However, during the medieval period, the border between England and Scotland was fluid and the town was to fall in the English–Scottish wars no less than 13 times, until it finally passed from Scottish possession in 1482. This had a devastating and impoverishing effect on the Berwick friaries. The friaries in the town are listed under English houses because the town was under the English crown at the time of their suppression.

Between 1296 and 1307 Edward I earned the title of Hammer of the Scots, but his hammering only served to force and temper a new sense of nationhood in the people he sought to subject. The common people were resolved in their dislike of the English, and the Scottish friars actively preached resistance.

On 10 February 1306, during the struggle for independence, Robert Bruce met John Comyn, one of the contenders for the crown of Scotland, in the Dumfries Franciscan church, hoping to resolve their differences. During their discussion, old enmities reasserted themselves and in a quarrel Bruce lost his temper and stabbed Comyn, who managed to stagger to the foot of the altar. Sir Roger Kirkpatrick, the dead man's uncle, was going to the assistance of his nephew when he was killed by a stroke to the head by Bruce's brother-in-law, Sir Christopher Seaton. This act of sacrilegious murder occurred before the high altar of the Franciscan church. Bruce straightaway made his way to Scone, where he was crowned on Palm Sunday 1306.

In 1309, an ecclesiastical council of bishops, abbots, priors and clergy of Scotland met in the Dundee Franciscan church to consider the Scottish church's view on the national crisis about whether John Balliol or Robert Bruce had the right to reign in Scotland. The council acknowledged and made fealty to Robert Bruce as their chosen king. Although the Dundee house had not been established long before 1286, it must have been substantially complete and large enough for such a meeting.

Alexander Stewart, Earl of Buchan, the brother of King Robert III, was known as the 'Wolf of Badenoch'. He served as justiciar for the north of Scotland and promised to defend Elgin Cathedral and its possessions. In 1388, he was removed from office and in 1390 the cathedral authorities decided that his services were too costly. As an act of revenge, in the summer of 1390 he went on the rampage against as many religious houses as he could find between Forres and Elgin, including the Elgin friaries, and sacked Elgin Cathedral. Buchan was excommunicated and was eventually forced to submit and make public penance in sackcloth for his deeds. After making reparation to the Bishop of Moray for the cost of repairs, he was absolved by the Bishop of St Andrews, in the presence of his brother the King, in the church of Perth Dominican house.

The Dominican house in Perth was an important place frequently visited by the Scottish kings, who used it as a royal residence when visiting Perth. The Dominican church and St John's kirk were the only buildings large enough in Perth to hold the King's general council meetings and Scottish parliaments. It is not known how these royal and other visits affected the running of the Perth Dominican friary and what effect it had on the spiritual activities of the friars, but it must have resulted in a considerable distraction from their religious duties.

In 1396, Robert III and his court used the Perth Dominican friary gardens to watch the 'Battle of the Clans', a brutal battle which took place on the North Inch, on the edge of Perth. The feud between Clan Chattan and Clan Kat was settled when 30 men were selected from each clan and armed with crossbows, battleaxes, sword and dirks, and fought to the death. Clan Chattan were the victors, but it was alleged that they used foul methods to win.

In restoring firm government in Scotland, James I (1394–1437) made many enemies, not the least being his own immediate family. The court, including the papal legate, was in

Perth for the 1436 Christmas festivities. James and his Queen, with her ladies, stayed in the royal lodgings in Perth Dominican friary and the rest of the court was dispersed in lodgings in the town. Sir Robert Stewart, grandson of the Earl of Atholl, was Chamberlain of the Royal Household and was in charge of the King's domestic arrangements. On the night of 20–21 February 1437, Robert, who had tampered with the friary door locks, laid planks across the fosse bordering the friary and, with eight conspirators led by the Earl of Atholl, entered the friary to assassinate the King. The King, alone with the Queen and her ladies, heard the commotion outside and was warned of the approaching danger. Catherine Douglas thrust her arm through the bolt loops of the door, while James managed to hide in the entrance of the privy under the floor in the closet. The assassins broke into the room and wounded the Queen and some of her ladies but could not find James. The King, thinking the assassins had gone, shouted to the ladies to haul him out of that unclean place, but the conspirators heard him and when they found him, stabbed him to death. The Earl's aim of placing his grandson, Robert, on the throne failed and James's six-year-old son succeeded him as James II.

The Gillten Arbour was an area in Perth between the North Inch and the Dominican friary. The ownership of the ground was disputed between the people of Perth and the friars to such an extent that the local people sowed the area with weeds and organised archery contests on it. In 1520, an incident, known as the Friars' Pot, took place when Alexander Chalmers and others broke into the Perth Dominican house, forced the locks, removed the doors and took a cooking pot from the kitchen, which they then paraded through the streets. The friars sought to find redress through the courts but could not find anyone who would take the case for them.

The Edinburgh Dominican friary had a large guest house which was used by the Scottish kings, prior to the erection of Holyrood Palace, as a place of entertainment for their royal and distinguished visitors. It was also used for a number of state purposes. On these occasions a special allowance was made by the Lord Chamberlain to the friars. After Henry VI's escape to

Scotland, following the defeat of his forces at the battle of Towton in 1461, he was provided with accommodation in the Edinburgh Dominican house. Perkin Warbeck (1474–99), when in Ireland in 1491, was persuaded to impersonate Richard, Duke of York, who, with his brother Edward V, had been presumed murdered in the Tower of London. After being acknowledged by Margaret, Duchess of Burgundy, Edward IV's sister, he was received by James IV as the Duke of York and was lodged in the Edinburgh Dominican friary during his stay in Scotland. Warbeck left Scotland in 1497. Accommodation for lady visitors was found in a house outside the friary walls, but it was the duty of the friar in charge of the guest house to make provision for their entertainment. The Edinburgh Dominican house also housed the Scottish exchequer officials. There must have been a lot of coming and going at the friary.

11

THE REFORMATION

The Renaissance revived the study of classical literature, and the educated classes started to express criticism of some of the teachings and many of the practices of the church. Reformers were looking at the teachings of the church anew and using the Holy Scripture as their guide. They claimed the church had moved away from the simplicity of worship of earlier times, had encrusted the apostolic faith with sub-Christian additions to dogma and had made a religion, which was essentially an inward faith, into a religion of the external. The beautiful simplicity of the faith had been undermined by the pomp of gaudy worship and vain ceremonies. The increasingly ostentatious ceremonies, and the codification of the faith, were done with the best of intention as the church attempted to bring the message of the Gospel to the uneducated masses. In doing so, the church showed an outward profession of faith, but had succumbed to a loss of spiritual substance, as it distorted the true principles of Christianity into fables and superstition. Nevertheless, the friars still stood high in the opinion of the laity.

Any organisation, be it secular or spiritual, would, over a period of 300 years or so, have lost its initial verve and so, by the late fifteenth century, the friars, except for the Franciscan Observants friars, remained undistinguished. It was a period when there was a general weakening of discipline throughout the church, and this affected the mendicant movement as much as other parts of the church. Friar B. Jarrett, in his *The English Dominicans*, wrote, 'Silent, dulled, asleep, the Dominicans took in the last century of their pre-reformation existence, hardly any place at all in the National life'. They were living on the kudos from the past. In most friaries sanctity and discipline were forgotten and their statutes ignored. Eminent people were still being buried in their churches, people were still leaving bequests to the friars and the populace was still flocking to their churches to listen to their sermons, but they had lost their hold of the heads and hearts of the people. In the lukewarm atmosphere of faith, as distinct from ceremonial, there were no sources of inspiration powerful enough to make friars or lay people feel passionately about the survival of the friars' houses.

Friars, and those who held to the old truths, emphasised the historical faith handed down to them from the early fathers of the church. They considered that it was their duty before God to defend the Christian faith as they saw it. They found themselves in opposition to the new learning and were identified with the old teachings which were being strongly challenged by the new thought. As they defended the church, and its traditional interpretations of the faith, they were accused of suppressing the spirit of enquiry.

Changes in the understanding of the faith had a direct effect on the future of the friaries and, by the late fifteenth century, friars were seen as mouthpieces of the Pope and upholders of the papacy, and that at a time when the primacy of the Pope was being questioned. The reformers said the friars had been guilty of teaching doctrines that were contrary to Scriptures and of obstinately defending and asserting the authority of the church. They accused the church of relying upon its accumulation of experience over the centuries, instead of using the authority of Holy Scripture. The reformers believed they were seeking the replacement of an infallible pope by an infallible book, and regarded friars as the most dangerous enemies of those who wanted a radical reform of the church.

The reformers considered that it was their duty to reform the faith in the manner they thought to be right. This can be said in a few words, but, in the mid-sixteenth century, it was the cause of a titanic religious struggle which swept away much of Catholicism in Northern Europe and was instrumental in the overthrow of the mendicant orders in Britain. The church in southern Europe was hardly touched by the new ideas which played such havoc north of the Alps.

If it had not been for the new learning coming from the Continent, the church in Britain would probably have gone on gradually reforming itself for some time, as did the church in the southern parts of the Continent.

WYCLIFFE

John Wycliffe (1330–84) became Master of Balliol College, Oxford, in about 1360. He had radical views on religion and was an outspoken opponent of the ways and doctrine of the church of his day, and waged an implacable war against monks and friars. Wycliffe was indignant at the corruption, as he saw it, of the church, and was the precursor of the Reformation. He criticised what he called the distortion of the true principles of the Christian faith, ecclesiastical abuses such as non-residence, pluralism of the clergy, and the acquisition of personal wealth by the church hierarchy. He argued that the church should not interfere in temporal affairs and claimed that canon law, that is, church decrees enacted to regulate morals and religious practice, had no force when they were opposed by Scripture. He attacked the claims to authority by the papacy and denied the doctrine of Transubstantiation. This denial of the real presence of Christ in the Holy Eucharist struck at the heart of Catholicism.

Wycliffe is best remembered as the first person to translate the Bible into the English vernacular. He called on people to put their trust in the Bible and believed that it was pre-eminent and should determine the doctrines, institutions and ceremonies of the church. Wycliffe's translation made its readers better equipped to argue the case for their views against the clergy, who quoted Scripture in support of the church's actions.

His sweeping assaults on many fundamentals of the church, and his reforming doctrines, spread rapidly and attracted many young students. He resolved to appeal directly to the people and organised his followers into bands of 'Lollard Preachers', very much like the early friars and later Methodist lay preachers. 'Lollards' derives from the Flemish *lollen* meaning 'mumblers' (of prayers).

Controversies were aroused by the views of John Wycliffe and the reforming campaign of the Lollards. Because they challenged accepted beliefs of the day, they were seen as a threat to the established order. Their preachers did not have the benefit of a long training in theology and many of them tended to propound extravagant opinions which earned them the hostility of both the temporal and ecclesiastical authorities. The friars were active and bitter opponents of Wycliffe's views and endeavoured to stamp out the Lollards. The Dominican and Carmelite Orders, in particular, played an important part in opposing Wycliffe's views. The Archbishop of Canterbury consulted the Dominican and Franciscan friars at the universities about Transubstantiation and, in 1382, went on to condemn Wycliffe's teaching. From that time, men turned away from him and there was little evidence of calls for reforms in the church in England until the latter years of Henry VIII's reign and in Scotland until the 1530s.

While Wycliffe's doctrines created such a stir in England, they made little impact in Scotland, which was hardly touched by the Reformation until the influence of Martin Luther reached there in the 1520s.

However, Wycliffe's views on the authority of the Pope spread to the Continent, particularly to Bohemia, where it was propounded by Jan Hus (1372–1415), the Czech religious reformer, and his followers. Hus was found guilty of heresy by the Council of Constance in 1415 for holding such views, which cost him his life.

ERASMUS

Desiderius Erasmus (1466–1536), the leading Dutch scholar of the Renaissance in northern Europe and an exponent of the new learning, worked to restore the Christian faith, as he saw it, to its basic simplicity, through study of the Scriptures. In his *The Handbook of a Christian Knight*, published in 1503, and *In Praise of Folly* published in 1509, he pointed out some of the distorted practices in the church. Satire can be damaging, and Erasmus's books on the abuses in the church of his day were widely read by the educated classes, who no doubt chuckled over them. He believed men could be mocked out of their superstitious religious ways and brought back to true religion.

Erasmus ridiculed the practices of indulgences and hoped reforms would come from within the church. He also had a profound distrust of the ways and methods of the reformers. He did not accept the doctrine of Justification by Faith, and thought both Luther and Protestantism were uncouth and destructive. For this, he was castigated by both sides and became ineffective in the Reformation struggle.

LUTHER

Martin Luther (1483–1546) received his Bachelor of Arts degree in 1502 and, in the shortest time possible, obtained his Master of Arts degree in January 1505. On July 1505, as Luther was returning home from his studies as a student lawyer, he encountered a severe thunderstorm during which a bolt of lightning threw him to the ground. In panic, he vowed to St Anne (Mother of the Virgin Mary) he would become a friar. In the same year he entered the Austin Order as a novice and, in 1507, was received into the priesthood. He received his Bachelor of Theology degree in 1509 and a Doctorate of Theology in 1512. During the next five years, as Professor of Scripture in Wittenberg University, he lectured on the Psalms and the Epistles to the Romans, Galatians and Hebrews. He was appointed sub-prior of the Wittenberg Austin friary.

Luther became obsessed with the problem of sin and, in view of the Great Day of Judgment, the means of attaining God's favour, and his meditations led him to stress the doctrine of Justification by Faith. He gradually became aware of the gulf between himself and the demands of God, as he saw them, in the Scriptures. In particular, his study of the Epistle to the Romans convinced him that it was justification by God that restored the sinner, by virtue of Christ's redemption. Gradually, a new understanding of the Scriptures came to him and he proclaimed that the religious vocation of an Austin friar had not brought him peace and reconciliation with God. He saw that his vocation had been part of the medieval system of salvation through good works, whereas he now believed salvation came only through faith. He stressed that conciliation with God was through justification by faith alone.

Other reformers took their cue from Luther's writings, and there was a growing agitation against the old faith. The medieval church was ripe for a radical reforming movement, which might have come from within the church if it had found the motivation, but events overtook it.

We may wonder if the Reformation would have taken off in the direction it did, or the church have split in the way it did, if Luther had not become a professor of theology and if he had not reacted so strongly to Tetzel's visit, but more about that further on.

Depressing Times

By the 1530s, friars had ceased to be an intellectual force and the new interest in biblical and classical learning was not pursued by them to any great extent. However, the new learning reached the Cambridge Austin house and, to a lesser degree, the London Austin house, where friars supported the reformers' aims and were in touch with the Reformation movement. In general, the Oxford friars resisted the new learning.

The first half of the sixteenth century was a depressing time for the friars, with their dwindling support and financial difficulties. They had fallen in popular esteem and lost many of their friends and admirers. Some friaries were still having major rebuilding work carried out, such as in 1514 when the St Andrews Dominicans were able to rebuild their church, and where a delightful chapel from this work still stands in the forecourt of Madras College. Much of the Gloucester Franciscans' church was newly built at this time and, in 1535, Henry Standish, the Franciscan Bishop of St Asaph, bequeathed £40 for the building of an aisle adjoining the Oxford Franciscan church, probably the south aisle, but it is almost certain it was never built.

However, building repairs were not being carried out at most friaries, due to lack of funds or the gradual loss of the friars' moral fibre. Most friary buildings were neglected in the 20 years or so prior to their suppression; this is borne out by numerous references to the poor state of friary buildings made at the time of the suppression of the houses. A typical description, made in 1538, was that the Newcastle-under-Lyme Dominicans' friary was in a very poor state, with the roof ready to fall in and everything old or inferior. The Shrewsbury Dominican buildings were described as ruinous, and only the choir and one aisle of the nave of the Chester Dominican church was waterproof. The Dundee Franciscan house became so impoverished that the brethren had to sell their sacred vessels and books to procure the necessities of life. In addition, the buildings of their house had become decayed because they were unable to carry out the necessary maintenance on them.

Robert Barnes

Dr Robert Barnes, who was born near King's Lynn about 1495, was an Austin Friar. He met Luther when he was on the Continent studying for his doctorate and became persuaded by his teachings. He was later made prior of the Cambridge Austin house, where some friars were supporters of the new theology then being hotly debated in the university. Barnes's influence was mostly with a group of prominent students who came together in the White Horse Tavern, Cambridge, where they studied the works of the German reformers. On Christmas Eve in 1525, he preached a sermon in St Edward's Church, in which he protested against worldly observances and festivals, criticising traditional religion on a number of points and dwelling on the ostentatious splendour of Cardinal Wolsey.

His sermon was considered offensive and he was arrested by Wolsey's agents and brought before the Cardinal, who privately interrogated him. After doing penance in the presence of the Cardinal and a host of bishops in front of St Paul's Cathedral, Barnes was released from prison and confined in the London Austin friary for a time, before being sent to the Northampton Austin friars' house. He later escaped to the Continent. In 1531, he was invited by Thomas Cromwell to return to his Cambridge house. Having been convinced of the value of Tyndale's New Testament, Barnes organised the sale of the proscribed book from his room at Cambridge Austin friary. It is not known if he was doing this with the knowledge and support of his brethren in the house, although he did not seem from his later activities to have been the kind of person to hide his light under a bushel. After preaching, in defiance of the ban on him, a sermon in which he begged Henry VIII to give the spoils of the monasteries to the poor, enforce reverence for Holy Matrimony and promote what was taught in the Scriptures, he was arrested and burnt at the stake at Smithfield in 1540.

DEFENDER OF THE FAITH

When Henry VIII ascended the throne in 1509, no churchman had cause to think that the King was other than a staunch upholder of the established religious order. Henry was fond of divinity from his youth and an admirer of Thomas Aquinas. In 1522, he completed his book *Assertio Septem Sacramentorum* (*The Assertion of the Seven Sacraments*), which refuted the doctrines of Martin Luther. The English ambassador presented the book, in a golden cover, to Pope Hadrian VI, who received it with extravagant acclaim and promised a ten years' indulgence to all readers of the King's book. The same year the Pope rewarded Henry with the title of Defender of the Faith (Latin: *Fidei Defensor*). Henry was proud of the title and all English monarchs since have borne it with honour. The title, Fid. Def. or F.D., is still stamped on British coinage.

HENRY VIII'S DIVORCE

The legal process of the Reformation in England and Wales began with the calling of the Reformation Parliament in 1529, the year of Wolsey's fall. The early measures of the Parliament were directed against the long-standing abuses in the church, papal impositions and appeals to Rome. They were later, at the King's bidding, to break the ancient links with the papacy and, between 1530 and 1539, Henry VIII made the severance with Rome final by crushing active opposition and seizing all the monastic lands in his realm.

The problems with Henry's marriage to Catherine of Aragon, who failed to produce a male heir to the throne, became complex. Henry and Catherine had lived contentedly together for about 12 years, but as she grew older the chances of her delivering an heir became less. She had a number of miscarriages and stillbirths, which accounted for all of her offspring apart from Princess Mary (Queen Mary Tudor), a weak and sickly girl. No man could have wished for a son more than the King, who saw the hand of God in his childlessness and recalled a verse in the book of Leviticus (20:21) in the Old Testament: 'If a man shall take his brother's wife, it is an unclean thing: he has uncovered his brother's nakedness; they shall be childless'. About 1525, Henry, who was a theologian and understood church doctrine and law, came to believe that his childlessness was due to his having married his dead brother Arthur's wife, and was God's punishment for breaking His law.

It was not only Henry's passion for Anne Boleyn that urged him to divorce; the question of the succession to the throne of England had for nearly a century, during the War of the Roses, filled England with confusion and bathed it in blood. Henry was trying to avoid a resumption of the struggle after his death. The years 1528–34 were critical in the history of England. Henry's daughter by Catherine, Mary Tudor, was in delicate health and, if she died, there would be no direct heir to the crown. This could have eventually plunged England into a dynastic war and Henry had no wish for his country to be torn asunder yet again because of the lack of a male heir. He probably considered that, even if Mary's days were prolonged, her title to the throne might have been in dispute because, to that time, no female sovereign had occupied the throne of England.

In 1527, Henry applied to Pope Clement VII (1478–1534) to annul his marriage to Catherine on the grounds that it had not been validly made, but Henry could not have chosen a worse time to submit his request. Emperor Charles V's troops had recently stormed the walls of Rome and had subjected the papal city to an appalling sacking and slaughter. The Pope was a virtual prisoner of the Emperor in Castel Sant' Angelo, Rome, and was not free to grant Henry's wish. The Pope recognised the danger of refusing such a request from a loyal son of the church, especially in days when the northern part of Christendom was in such ferment, but found it impossible to offend the Emperor. Clement VII, who had a troubled pontificate from 1523 to 1534, would no doubt have granted Henry his annulment if it had not been for the Emperor's troops being in Rome as an occupying army at the critical time. Popes had annulled other royal marriages. Pope Alexander VI granted a divorce to Louis XII of France, who was allowed to marry his brother's widow. Henry IV of Castile had been allowed to marry a second wife with the provision that if she gave him no children, he could return to his first wife.

The Pope's difficulty was to harmonise the desire of Henry VIII, who wanted a new wife who, he hoped, would produce a male heir, and the wishes of Emperor Charles V (Queen Catherine's nephew), who insisted that Henry's marriage to Catherine should not be annulled. It was not necessarily a matter of affection and loyalty to his aunt, but more a point of pride on the part of the Emperor, who was also King of Spain. In the sixteenth and seventeenth centuries the Spanish were easily offended when it came to matters of family honour. The Pope was in an impossible position; whatever action he took would offend one of the powerful parties.

We might wonder what would have happened if Henry's elder brother Arthur had not died a few months after his marriage to Catherine and Henry had become head of the church in England, as his father had intended! Then there would have been no question of a divorce to have divided the church and, perhaps, no Reformation in England and Wales. Had Catherine given Henry a male heir, would the Reformation, which in England was led by the King, have taken place? If the troops of the Emperor had not been in Rome at the critical period and the Pope had been free to grant Henry his annulment, would this have prevented the break with Rome and would England have remained a Catholic country, acknowledging the Pope as the head of the church on earth?

The break between Rome and England had been led by its king but the country was divided on the matter. The leaders of the country held the reins of power and had the means to direct the Reformation in the way they wished. However, after the break with Rome, Henry was hard pressed to halt the flow of Protestant beliefs that were flooding in from the Continent. The Reformation might still have come, as it did among the Germanic people, but the form and manner of it might have been different. During the short reign of Mary Tudor (1553 – 58) the Reformation was put into reverse, but when Elizabeth became Queen in 1558, she held the middle ground between Protestants and Catholics. In order to do this she rejected the authority of the Pope and the spiritual ties with Rome.

THE ENGLISH OBSERVANTS FRIARS

The Franciscan Observants friars had received special aid and royal patronage from Edward IV, Henry VII and Henry VIII from the time they were founded in England in 1482. Edward IV patronised the Franciscan Observants friars by giving them land for their friary next to his royal park at Greenwich. It was sighted next to the royal palace, as the King wanted a community of God-fearing, self-sacrificing men who would pray for his soul. The church of Greenwich friary was linked to the royal palace by a gallery so that the King could visit the friars' house at will. Their church was used for royal baptisms and marriages. Henry was probably christened in the church in 1491 and the marriage of Henry and Catherine of Aragon took place there. Princess Mary Tudor (Queen Mary) was christened there in 1516, Cardinal Wolsey being one of the godfathers, and Princess Elizabeth (Queen Elizabeth) was christened with great pomp and ceremony in the same church in 1533.

Henry VIII, who was well disposed towards the Observants, wrote to Pope Leo X in 1513 emphasising that he 'could not sufficiently commend the Observants Friars' strict adherence to poverty, their sincerity, charity and devotion. No group in the church stirred up the people in the faith or battled more assiduously against sin and none were more active in keeping Christ's flock'.

Although mendicant houses were exempt from episcopal visitations and disliked legative interference, Cardinal Wolsey insisted on his right to visit the Greenwich Observants house. The Pope went out of his way to stress the importance of the order in the battle against Luther and asked Wolsey to treat the Greenwich Observants friars with gentleness and tact. Wolsey assured the Pope that he would use such tact that no complaints would arise, but refused to give way on the visit. He commanded Friar John Forest, former Provincial of the Observants, to preach against his offending Greenwich Observants brothers at St Paul's Cross in January 1525, following their refusal to accept Wolsey's legatine authority to carry out a visitation to their house. He then appointed Henry Standish, Bishop of St Asaph and former Franciscan Provincial Minister, to carry out the visit at a time when there was a friction between the Conventual and Observants friars. A number of Greenwich Observants friars decided to sabotage the visit by having a mass walkout. However, Standish arranged a new day for the visitation and made it clear to the friars that those who did not attend would be expelled from the order. At length they submitted to Wolsey.

The Observants friars were frequently called upon by the royal court as preachers and confessors, and the better-off people, who were their principal supporters, were liberal to the Observants with their gifts.

In the early part of the sixteenth century there were six houses and about 200 Franciscan Observants friars in England.

The royal admiration was not to last and the conduct of the divorce proceedings brought matters to a head. The Observants friars first incurred the King's displeasure when Richard Risby and Hugh Rich, wardens of Canterbury and Richmond Observants houses, were seen to be among the chief supporters of Elizabeth Barton, the 'Holy Maid of Kent'. Barton was a young lady of a nervous temperament who had been greatly excited by the sufferings of Queen Catherine. The Maid was given to ecstatic and prophetic utterances, and in 1532 made widely known her prophecy: 'If Henry marries Anne Boleyn, in seven months' time there will be no king in England'. She varied her prophecy and announced in convents, castles and villages of Kent that 'Henry would fall and his subjects were already released from every obligation to him, because he had rejected God'. At length, Henry considered that the words of the Maid were a powerful means of arousing popular feeling against him and could cause insurrection among the people of Kent. He ordered that the Maid and her principal followers be arrested. A bill of attender was brought to the House of Lords against the Maid and her abettors on the plea that their conspiracy endangered the King's life.

Friars Risby and Rich were taken to Canterbury in November 1533, where they were made to do public penance. They stood with the Maid on the scaffold at St Paul's Cross when they were denounced by Dr Capon, Bishop of Bangor, for having encouraged their brethren to give perjured testimonies in the wicked quarrel of the Queen against the King. In April 1534, they were hanged at Tyburn with the Maid and others. The bodies of the two friars and the Maid were buried at the London Franciscan church.

The Canterbury Observants house suffered due to its support for the Maid of Kent. The King forbade the brethren to go out of their house and appointed John Arthur, from the Oxford Franciscan house, as warden. He treated the Observants friars with severity, due to their rebellion against the King and their loyalty to the Pope.

THE SUCCESSION AND ROYAL SUPREMACY ACTS OF 1534

The King, who had been amiable and a pleasure seeker until the time of Wolsey's fall in 1529, turned with great ferocity on those who opposed his will. The Act of Succession of 1534, which recognised the children of Henry and Anne Boleyn as heirs to the throne, also nullified Henry's first marriage. The Act declared that Henry's marriage to Anne Boleyn was undoubted, true, sincere and perfect and that their children should succeed to the throne. The wording of the oath of succession was not defined by Parliament, and Henry, availing himself of the omission, worded it as he pleased. The Act made it high treason for anyone to slander in writing, print, deed or words, the King's marriage with Anne Boleyn and empowered the King to demand from any subject an oath to maintain the provisions of the Act.

Officials and clergy were required to swear an oath which included the statement that the marriage of Henry to Catherine was illegal and invalid. He took care to obtain the oath from the clergy, which included the full recognition of his supremacy in the church and an assertion that the Bishop of Rome had no authority in his realm.

As we have seen, Henry's problems over his first marriage became so complex that he saw no satisfactory way of settling them other than breaking with the Pope. The dilatory measures of Rome over Henry's divorce infuriated the King. By an ever greater restriction of papal jurisdiction in his kingdom, Henry tried to bring a quick and favourable decision, a policy which ended in the Royal Supremacy Act of 1534. Henry and his Parliament argued that England was an empire subject to God and to no other external power. The Act of Succession was succeeded by the Act of Supremacy, which was also passed by Parliament in 1534. The Act declared that the King was the 'Only Supreme Head on earth of the Church of England'. Henry replaced the Pope as the head, under Christ, of the church in England and made it independent of Rome.

Those in religious orders in England and Wales were required to swear allegiance to Henry under the Act of Supremacy. Parish clergy mostly followed the lead of their bishops who had accepted the Act and thereby encouraged their flocks to accept the King's authority. Whereas most in religious orders, including the friars, accepted the Royal Supremacy without much demur, some steadfastly refused to acknowledge Henry as the supreme head of the church in England. John Fisher, the Bishop of Rochester, who had helped the Countess of Richmond, Henry's grandmother, to establish St John's College, was beheaded for refusing to acknowledge Henry's supremacy. Reginald Pole of the House of York, who as a young man was befriended by Henry, chose to go into exile on the Continent rather than accept the Royal Supremacy Act. In 1536, he was made a cardinal and remained in exile until the reign of Queen Mary, when in 1554 he returned as Papal Legate to England. Nearly all those in religious life accepted with great reluctance the Royal Supremacy Act.

When, in 1535, Archbishop Cranmer preached in Canterbury Cathedral against the authority of the Pope and in favour of the Royal Supremacy, the prior of the Canterbury Dominican house preached against him, maintaining that the Pope was head of the church. Cranmer, knowing that he was a man of influence in the neighbourhood, asked the King to take proceedings against him as an example to others who maintained the authority of the Bishop of Rome. However, the prior may have escaped, for nothing more was heard of him.

In May 1534 all mendicant provincials in England signed a declaration of fealty to the King, in which they acknowledged his marriage with Anne Boleyn, repudiated the Bishop of Rome and accepted Henry as Supreme Head of the Church in England.

In June 1534, John Hilsey, Prior Provincial of the Dominicans, and George Brown, Provincial of the Austin friars, were ordered by Henry VIII to visit the houses of the friars of the various orders in England and Wales, to ensure that all friars accepted the Royal Succession and to compel the friars to preach it to the people. As a reward, in the following year

Hilsey was appointed Bishop of Rochester. During Easter 1533, Brown preached at St Paul's Cross in favour of the King's divorce and asked the faithful to pray for Queen Anne. He was on friendly terms with Cromwell and was fully on Cromwell's side in the religious dispute of the time. He was later rewarded with the appointment of the archbishopric of Dublin.

Friars who failed to comply with the order faced a term of imprisonment or even death, but most friars accepted the Act without much dissent. Although the submission of the Bristol Dominican house was secured, most friars had abandoned the house and fled from England rather than acknowledge the Act, leaving only five brethren there. But as we shall see, most Franciscan Observant friars refused to accept the Act.

TREASON ACT, 1536

The scope of the treason law was enlarged in 1536 to include refusal to take the Oath of Supremacy. The Act abolishing the authority of the Bishop of Rome in England and Wales provided in one short clause that every layman and church official holding office should take an oath renouncing the Bishop of Rome and his authority. The Act imposed the penalties of treason on any cleric or lay official who refused an oath renouncing the jurisdiction of Rome. The King ordered that the word 'pope' should be obliterated from books used in public worship.

Even though Henry broke with Rome, he was no friend of the reformers and was still faithful to the old faith. His Statute of the Six Articles maintained that the actual presence of Christ was in the sacramental bread and wine, priests were forbidden to marry, the vows of chastity were to be observed and the Mass and auricular confession were indispensable. No doctrine was to be believed contrary to the six articles and no books against the Holy Sacrament were to be possessed by anyone.

FALL OF THE OBSERVANTS FRIARS

Franciscan Observants friars refused to accept the 1534 Acts of Succession and Supremacy on the grounds that the Act of Succession was contrary to divine law and the Act of Supremacy was aimed at undermining the Pope's authority and was contrary to the Rule of St Francis.

The annulment of Henry's marriage to Catherine brought the Observants friars into conflict with the King. On Easter Sunday 1532, William Peto, English Provincial of the Observants friars and confessor to Princess Mary, preached in the Greenwich Observants church, with Henry present, and warned him that he was endangering his crown, for both great and lowly were murmuring at his proposed marriage to Anne Boleyn. When Peto departed, the King ordered one of his chaplains, Dr Curwen, Bishop of Oxford, to preach a reply to Peto on the following Sunday in the same church. The Observants friars resented this, as it was against their practice to have outside preachers in their pulpits. Dr Curwen's sermon roused Henry Elstow, warden of the house, who remonstrated with Curwen in the King's presence. On the Monday, Peto and Elstow were brought before the King's Council, where they were given a severe reprimand and exiled. In the following year, the Greenwich and Richmond friars were still preaching obedience to the Pope and denouncing the King's marriage to Anne. In 1533, Elstow and Peto were in Antwerp, writing books against the King's marriage to Anne Boleyn. In 1557, Peto was offered the bishopric of Salisbury.

Thomas Lee, one of the King's chaplains, and Thomas Bedyll, clerk to the King's Council, were commissioned by Henry to visit the Greenwich and Richmond Franciscan Observants friaries in an effort to bring them to submission. On 16 June 1534, they visited Richmond and, meeting the whole house, tried to persuade the friars to affix their seal to the articles of supremacy, but they met with a resolute refusal. However, the brethren were persuaded to leave the matter with four senior members of their house. The commissioners arranged to meet the four members the following day in the

Greenwich Observants house and asked them to bring their friary seal with them. Next day at Greenwich, the commissioners met resistance from the Greenwich friars and the four Richmond representatives. They then went on to examine each friar in the Greenwich house separately. Nearly all of them refused to acknowledge the Royal Succession, as they considered that their first loyalty was to their faith and the Pope as the supreme head of the church of Christ on earth. Their refusal was a matter of religious conscience. Lee reported that the friars had professed St Francis's religion and would live and die in observance of it.

When their fearless and independent spirit was reported to Henry, he turned on them ferociously. There was one way, in his opinion, to deal with friars who refused to be convinced. The whole Observants Orders in his realm was speedily suppressed and, within a few days of Lee and Bedyll's visit, two cartloads of friars from the Richmond and Greenwich houses were taken to the Tower of London, where many of them died in chains. By the end of August 1534, the Obervants had been driven from their houses and all Observants houses in England were empty. The Observants friars were dispersed, generally to houses of Conventual Franciscans, who had orders to lock them up in chains.

The severity of their dispersion and treatment is shown in a list of 153 Observants friars from the six English Franciscan Observants houses. Of these: 30 fled to Scotland or the Continent; 36 were granted pardons and returned to the secular world; 31 died, probably in prison from hardship, and 56 remained in England. It is not known if the 56 friars were allowed to stay in friaries taken over by the Austin Order, or if they went into hiding.

Thomas Bourchier, a member of the Greenwich friary, who was later restored to the re-established Observants house by Queen Mary, related the incidents of several martyrdoms about this time. Among them was Anthony Brorbe, a distinguished Oxford theological scholar who was imprisoned and tortured for 25 days to such an extent that he could not turn in bed or lift his hand to his mouth. He was strangled with his own cord. Thomas Cortt, who had been imprisoned for preaching a sermon against the King, died in Newgate prison. A book written by a priest, Thomas Belchiam, which criticised the King, was found in the Greenwich Observants house. Belchiam was imprisoned and in August 1534 died of starvation.

William Sydenham, the new warden of the Greenwich Observants house, was sent to Bedford Franciscan house, where he was kept in confinement. Two Observants friars were sent to the Doncaster Franciscan house, where they died later from harsh treatment, three were sent to the Stamford Franciscan house, three to the Richmond (Yorkshire) Franciscan house and two were sent to the York Franciscan house, where the warden assigned one of them to the Beverley Franciscan house. There is a reference to an Observants friar in Carmarthen in 1537.

Friar John Forest, previously referred to, was a determined and courageous man who was prepared to give his life for what he thought was right. He was imprisoned in London in 1534 and, in 1536, he was transferred to the London Franciscan friary, where he was well treated and allowed considerable liberty. Suspicions soon arose that during the hearing of confessions he was inducing men to hold to the old faith. He was cast into Newgate prison, and after examination, was declared to be a traitor and heretic. He was burnt at the stake at Smithfield on 22 May 1538.

The Observants friars who fled were pursued across the country, but a number of them were able to escape to Scotland, Ireland or the Continent. Two Observants friars from Newark were pursued from Bristol, through Devon and Cornwall and on to Cardiff, where they unsuccessfully tried to smuggle themselves aboard a vessel bound for France. Dr John Hisley, who happened to be in Cardiff to ascertain whether the King's instructions on the Acts were being carried out, had them arrested by the town bailiffs. They were given a period of harsh imprisonment in London, but, following their pleas for mercy, were released.

The Newcastle-upon-Tyne Observants house, which does not

seem to have been affected by the controversy, reverted to the Conventuals. The Richmond house was emptied of its occupants and the Greenwich house was occupied by the Conventuals for a brief period. Friars of the Newark Franciscan Observants house were imprisoned and their house was occupied by Austin friars. The friars of the Southampton house were imprisoned and suffered privation and their vacated house was occupied by Austin friars for a few years. Some friars from the Canterbury Observants house fled abroad, others were dispersed and the house reverted to the Franciscan Conventuals for a few years.

In March 1537, the King, on hearing that some Observants friars who had been set free were still preaching against him, declared that the Observants friars were disciples of the Bishop of Rome and sowers of sedition, and ordered they should be arrested. Friar Hugh Payne, who in July 1534 had been cast into prison, received a pardon and obtained a living as a priest. He was denounced by Archbishop Cranmer for preaching against the King and imprisoned. In 1537, he wrote to the Duke of Norfolk urging that his trial be hastened as he was likely to die in prison of sickness and his irons. He died in prison shortly after.

CROMWELL

Thomas Cromwell (1485–1540), the son of a Putney blacksmith, was a person of great ability and possessed of a penetrating mind. He practised law and in that capacity he was employed by Cardinal Wolsey in suppressing some of the smaller monasteries. At the fall of Wolsey, he attracted the favourable attention of the King and rapidly rose in power. In 1531, he became Henry's closest adviser and, as Vicar General, was responsible for the dissolution of the larger monasteries. He drafted most of the Reformation legislation, including the Acts of Supremacy and Succession, securing their passage through Parliament. As a result he greatly strengthened the King's powers. The supreme power in England and Wales was now vested in the Crown, and many senior posts in the English Church were filled by men of Cromwell's persuasion, which was the principal reason why the break with Rome came about so easily in England.

Cromwell's fall was sudden. In April 1540, he was honoured with the Earldom of Essex as a reward for arranging the marriage of the King with Anne of Cleves, but the King found Anne unattractive and Cromwell lost favour. He was accused on a trumped-up charge of treason and executed in the Tower of London in July 1540. So ended the career of one of the most defamed men in English history.

SUPPRESSION OF SMALL MONASTERIES

At the beginning of the reign of Henry VIII there were almost 900 monastic houses in England and Wales, many of them only small communities.

On the grounds that discipline in the smaller monastic houses was lax and no longer served religion, and so that the revenues from them could be used for other good works, the papacy willingly accepted the closure of some religious houses in England. In 1497, the Bishop of Ely was granted permission to close the nunnery of St Radegund and appropriate the buildings and revenue to establish Jesus College, Cambridge. In 1505, the Bishop of Rochester, carrying out the wishes of the Countess of Richmond, mother of Henry VII and grandmother of Henry VIII, closed the Hospital of St John, a small Augustinian almshouse, and used the buildings and revenues for the new St John's College, Cambridge.

When in the 1520s, Cardinal Wolsey wanted to establish a school in his native Ipswich, and a college at Oxford, he secured a papal bull authorising him to suppress 21 lesser monasteries, which allowed him to transfer the income from them to support his new works. It was not a confiscation of church property for gain, but a redistribution of funds for ecclesiastical purposes. After Wolsey's fall in 1529, Henry VIII took over the monastic properties Wolsey had accumulated, and laid the foundation of Christ Church College, Oxford. Wolsey's project for St Mary Cardinal College, Ipswich, was never built. It seems that the suppression of the minor monasteries planted the idea of the suppression of all monastic houses in his realm in the King's mind.

VISITATIONS

The 1534 Act of Supremacy granted the King one-tenth of the church's annual income. In order to levy it on the church, Cromwell appointed commissioners to look into the extent of church revenues and property. Early in 1535, he set up a commission to enquire into the possessions of the church, diocese by diocese. The value of the church properties was assessed by the commissioners, who produced a survey of all ecclesiastical establishments. The 1534 *Valor Ecclesiasticus*, or survey of church revenues, was the result of the enquiry. It revealed in detail the property and income of the church in England and Wales.

As friars did not own their own property they were not included in the survey.

Also early in 1535, Cromwell appointed another commission to report on the moral and spiritual condition of the houses of religion, but this commission was held back until the enquiry into the church's possessions was over. The general visitation of the monasteries was begun in July 1535, when commissioners were despatched throughout the country to visit the monastic houses. They divided the kingdom into districts and appointed a couple of commissioners to each district. The commissioners asked similar questions to those visiting bishops had asked previously, but their visits were hurried and high-handed. The commissioners reported back to Cromwell six months later, giving him details of any alleged shortcomings in the monastic houses.

Visitors such as Dr London, Warden of New College, were not trained in the work and were described as grasping, worldly and without a trace of spiritual feeling. They were to be, albeit unconsciously, the principal agents in the most sudden and wholesale transformation that English social life had ever undergone between the Norman Conquest and our own day. It appears they were chosen by Cromwell because they knew what was expected of them and he knew that they would return with the kind of adverse reports he wanted. Historians have doubted the truth of a number of the visitors' reports.

On receiving the results of the survey, the King moved quickly, and in March 1536 he presented a bill to Parliament whereby all religious houses that had an income of under £200 a year, or those which had under 12 inmates, were to be converted to better use. Henry was not seeking to destroy monasticism at this stage, but to reform it. According to the *Valor Ecclesiasticus* returns, there were more than 300 monastic houses covered by the Act. The Suppression of Monasteries Act 1536 contained a clause reserving to the King the right to permit any house he selected to carry on, and 67 of the houses obtained exemption. This may have been partly due to accommodation problems, as there were many monks who wished to be transferred to other houses rather than take the dispensation to leave the religious life.

By the sixteenth century, popular opinion had swung away from the earlier enthusiasm for the religious orders to one of indifference. The suppression of the smaller monastic houses received little serious opposition in England and Wales, other than for the Pilgrimage of Grace in the northern parts of England.

PILGRIMAGE BY GRACE

The loss of the smaller monastic houses brought resentment in the north of England, where the Pilgrimage of Grace rebellion broke out to defend the institution of the monastic life. The motives of the movement were religious, namely that the dissolved monasteries be restored and Doctors Layton and Leigh, the two objectionable visitors to the monastic houses in the north of England, be punished for their extortions from religious houses and their abominable acts. The reaction in the northern parts of England revealed widespread concern about the suppression of the houses and a rebellion flared up in Lincolnshire from 1 to 12 October 1536.

During the short-lived rebellion, the newly elected prior of Grimsby Austin house and the warden of Grimsby Franciscan house rode into the camp of the insurgents and, under duress, offered them money. They were later given the benefit of the doubt and escaped punishment because the rebels had threatened to burn their friaries if they would not support the cause.

The main, and more serious, rising, from 8 October to 5 December 1536, affected Yorkshire, Lancashire and north-east England. The leaders of the Pilgrimage of Grace used the Doncaster Carmelite house for their negotiations with Robert Aske, a lawyer whom they appointed as the leader of the movement. Lawrence Coke, prior of the Doncaster Carmelite house, supported the movement and was later imprisoned in the Tower of London and condemned to be hanged by Act of Attainder. He was subsequently pardoned, but the pardon arrived too late to save him.

On 8 October 1536, a large crowd assembled on Westwood Green outside Beverley Franciscan house. The friars of the house generally did not support the movement and some rebels proposed to burn the friary and those in it. Thomas Johnson, an Observants friar who, on the suppression of his order, had been sent to Beverley Franciscan house, did a considerable amount of work in organising the rising and in persuading William Stapleton to become one of the leaders of the movement.

Robert Aske ordered a muster of the followers to take place on Skipwith Moor, about eight miles south of York, and by the middle of October they obtained possession of the city. Their leaders issued a proclamation in York that they had not assembled on account of taxation but because ill-disposed people in the King's Council sought to destroy the church and the whole body of the realm. They were entering, they contended, on a 'Pilgrimage of Grace', and their only objects were the maintenance of God's faith and the church militant, preservation of the King's person and purging the nobility of villainous and evil councillors. During the rising, the 'pilgrims' mustered under the banner of the Five Wounds of the Crucified Christ.

When Aske went to Doncaster to meet the Royal Commission, he and his followers were lodged in the Franciscan house, and the Duke of Norfolk's party used the Carmelite friars' house as their headquarters. On 6 December Aske presented the formal petition to Norfolk, who gave the leaders to understand that the King would consider it.

Norfolk persuaded the King to offer amnesty to the rebels; when they laid down their arms, he arrested the leaders of the rebellion. He sent Aske to the King, who sent him back to Yorkshire to be hanged in chains. Nearly 250 rebels were tried, hanged and quartered.

A great majority of the monks and friars, including the friars of the Beverley Franciscan house, which was in the thick of the rebellion, remained aloof from the movement.

Some of the Knaresborough Trinitarian brethren supported the Pilgrimage of Grace, but their ringleaders escaped to Scotland.

John Pickering, prior of York Dominican friary, took part in organising the Pilgrimage of Grace and composed a song beginning 'O faithful people of the Boreal region', which became popular among the insurgents. He was condemned for high treason and hanged at Tyburn in May 1537.

The penultimate prior of Northampton Dominican house fled, being unable to acknowledge the Act of Supremacy. John Pekock and William Gibson, two friars from the Burham Norton Carmelite house, were tried in 1537 for verbal treason after threatening insurrection in Norfolk. Pekock was executed in King's Lynn and Gibson was imprisoned for life. Also in 1537, two Franciscan friars from the Lewes house were punished for spreading the rumour that Henry VIII was dead.

SUPPRESSION OF THE MONASTERIES

The main reason for Henry's attack upon the monastic orders

was money. Although he inherited a large fortune from his thrifty father, Henry VII, he squandered it fighting pointless Continental wars. The nation was grateful for the order Henry brought to his realm, but lacked the enthusiasm to pay for the blessings of peace. So Henry had to look for a ready source of money to replenish his coffers, and the monastic houses seemed to be it. The religious houses were no longer regarded as power houses of prayer, which was the purpose for which their founders had endowed them, and Henry saw them as easy prey. The nobility, too, saw an opportunity for rich pickings from monastic properties.

Much has been written about the suppression of the monastic houses and there is no need to go into it here, other than to note that it was a precursor to action against friaries.

DISSOLUTION OF ENGLISH AND WELSH FRIARIES

During the 300 years or so of their existence, no houses of the four main orders in England and Wales, and few of the houses in Scotland, came to an end due to mismanagement or lack of support. However, most friaries in England and Wales were either dissolved during the second half of 1538, and the remainder in the northern parts of England were dissolved in the early part of 1539.

For a time it appeared that the friaries might be spared a similar fate to the monastic houses, for they had no landed property to tempt the Crown. But there were two factors working against them: they were the last bastion of allegiance to the Pope, and the people failed to support them in their hour of need. The tide of public opinion had turned against them.

Most friars were hostile to the new religious ideas but some were in the vanguard of the new thinking. In the popular mind, friars, along with the monastic houses, were identified with the old order of religion and were seen as bitterly opposing changes, and in this new religious climate they had to go. Even though Henry VIII had his reasons for suppressing the friars, if he had not suppressed them in 1538–39, they would probably have withered away, as they did in Scotland, overwhelmed by the growing tide of the Reformation sweeping in from the Continent. Henry unwittingly admitted the Reformation into his realm, but, in any case, whether he could have kept it out is another matter. The effects of the reforming ideas sweeping in from northern Europe could not be ignored in Britain because of its many close connections with the Continent. Away from the big towns, there was little demand for the radical changes being made in religion and people were reluctant to accept changes in what they considered to be a system that was both permanent and universally accepted.

In the early 1530s, there were about 175 friaries of the four main orders in England and 10 in Wales. In the time leading up to the Reformation, many of these houses were impoverished and had great difficulty in obtaining the necessities of life. The evidence of dissolution and suppression records relating to friaries is one of almost universal poverty, dilapidated buildings and leaking roofs, which told of neglect and privation. There was financial desperation in many houses and there were numerous cases of friars selling everything they could, their goods and plate, in order to subsist.

Rumours of the approaching dissolution of the friars' houses were rife in 1538. Many houses had fallen on such hard times that the few remaining brethren were waiting for the commissioners to enable them to surrender their houses and be released from their responsibilities. When the commissioners arrived at some houses, they found that most of the friars had left. Many friars saw that the end of the mendicant orders in England was in sight. Some went to Scotland, where they found an equally depressing situation, and others went to Ireland or to the Continent to continue their calling.

The Cambridge Austin house, where the friars had been the moving spirits of the Reformation, had practically dissolved itself. In some places, such as the Carmelite houses at Sele and Winchester, the commissioners found that all the friars had gone and abandoned their houses.

Ingworth described the Shrewsbury Austin house as being in

a ruinous state; the prior was nearly insane and there were only two other Irish friars. The church had been stripped of its furniture and vestments, it had no chalice for the Mass and the house provided a picture of general poverty, with no bedding, food or drink for the three friars living in dilapidated buildings. It was a house which had started nearly 300 years earlier amid great enthusiasm and, in better days, it had an average of 20 friars.

The Thetford Austin house was reported by the commissioners to have nothing in it but trash. They also found great poverty at the Droitwich Austin house. Ingworth wrote of the Austins' Clare house that the sale of implements would not pay their debts. The Austin house in Leicester was down to four friars, Lincoln down to four and Stamford down to six. The Canterbury Austin house was described as impoverished and had debts of £40 but, apart from some plate weighing 126 ounces, their movable goods were not worth £6.

In Gloucester, the Carmelite house had only three brethren in 1538, the Dominicans had seven brethren and the Franciscans had five. The friars of Gloucester Dominican house, which had been an important and well funded house with an average of 35 brethren in its heyday, had sold all its goods due to its penury. When the Salisbury Dominican house was suppressed it had debts of £80 and few assets. So great was the poverty of the four houses of friars in Norwich that the commissioners were able to raise only 49 shillings from them, and the Norwich Dominican house had previously sold its bell for £16 to the church across the road in order to survive. The Scarborough Franciscans had sold everything except some glass, stone and lead, and the Ipswich Franciscan house sold their altar plate as their only means of subsistence. In Bristol, the Austin house had eight friars, the Carmelites had four, the Dominicans had five and the Franciscans six friars, remaining to the end. The prior of the Bristol Carmelites had sold, in the three years previous to 1538, their altar plate and the timber that grew around the house.

In January 1539, the commissioners reported that friars in the Boston Austin, Carmelite and Dominican friaries were in such financial straits that they were piteously lamenting their poverty and did not know how to live until their house was surrendered. The devotion of the people in the town had gone, their plate and implements had been sold and they had nothing left but the lead from the roof, which they would have sold too, if they had not been prevented from doing so.

No doubt, the reason most of the members of the Grimsby Austin house had gone and the house was almost deserted by the time the royal visitor arrived in October 1538 was that the friars were afraid, following the cruel way the King had proceeded against the participants of the Pilgrimage of Grace.

There were eight Trinitarian houses in England before the Reformation but they were small, and other than at Moatenden and Hounslow, were in a poor state of repair. At the time of their suppression there were four brethren in the Thelsford house, and the prior and nine in the Knaresborough house. There were probably seven brethren in their Moatenden house. Their Easton house was burnt down and the hospital closed in 1536 and the Hertford house was abandoned by 1535. There were a prior and seven brethren in the Ingham house in 1534, but they refused to recognise Henry VIII as head of the church, and the commissioners found the house abandoned at the time of their visit in 1536. All the brethren, except the prior, had left the Newcastle-upon-Tyne house by 1539 when the commissioner came. The order was fading away.

The Crutched Cross friars, who had six small hospitals in England during the fifteenth century, had five struggling houses remaining in 1520. Their London house had only six friars, but shortly before it surrendered the prior was removed because of his outspoken remarks against the King.

The general dissolution of the friaries was dealt with under a separate royal commission to that dealing with the dissolution of monastic houses. In 1534, Richard Ingworth, who had been prior of King's Langley Dominican house and Prior-Provincial of the English Dominicans, was an active assistant to the King's visitors presenting the Oath of Supremacy to the friars. He was consecrated by Archbishop Cranmer as the

Suffragan Bishop of Dover on 9 December 1537, and was completely subservient to Cromwell for his own advancement. In February 1538, he was appointed Lord Visitor of the Friars under the Lord Privy Seal to all orders of friars. He was the only person to be so designated, but in a few instances he was deputised by other visitors, who took the surrender of a few friaries.

To illustrate his haste in taking the surrender of friaries, on 4 August 1538 Ingworth took the surrender of the Worcester Dominican and Franciscan houses, and on 7 August was in Lichfield taking the surrender of the Franciscan house there. On 9 August he was in Stafford taking the surrender of the Austin and Franciscan houses; on the 10th, in Newcastle-under-Lyne closing the Dominican house; then, on 15 and 16 August, he was in Chester taking the surrender of the three friaries in the town. He arrived in Rhuddlan on the 17th, when he took the surrender of the Dominican house and passed on to Denbigh, where he took the surrender of the Carmelite house on the 18th. Next day, 19 August, he took the surrender of both the Bangor Dominican and Llanfaes Franciscan houses. He was in Shrewsbury on 27 August, when he took the surrender of the Austin, Dominican and Franciscan houses in the town and went on to Woodhouse and Ludlow to close the Austin and Carmelite houses. He next moved on to Brecon, where he received the surrender of the Dominican house on 29 August, the Carmarthen Franciscan house on 30 August, Haverfordwest Dominican house on 2 September, the Cardiff Dominican and Franciscan houses on 6 September, the surrender of Newport Austin house on 8 September, and was in Bristol on 10 September, which must have been a busy day for him, as the surrender documents for the Bristol Austin, Dominican and Franciscan houses were dated that day. He probably closed the Bristol Carmelite house on the same visit and went on to Bridgwater, where he closed the Franciscan house. He then had a short break and in October resumed his destructive progress on the eastern side of the country.

In February 1539, Ingworth wrote to Cromwell that he

heard there were 20 mendicant houses still standing in the north, such as Scarborough, Carlisle, Lancaster and other places for which he would search. The Kingston-upon-Hull Austin and Carmelite houses, which were closed on 10 March 1539, were the last mendicant houses to be suppressed. The dissolution of the friars' houses in England and Wales was complete.

The surrender document presented to monastic houses for their signatures was in Latin, whereas the surrender document presented to the friars for their signatures was in English. It was a standard document which could be used for each house and stated 'We, the prior and convent of the (order and house) with one assent and consent and without any manner of coercion or council do give up our house into the hands of the Lord Visitor, to the king's use, desiring his grace to be good and gracious to us'. After recording the voluntary nature of the surrender, the document proceeded to say that the house was resigned into the King's hands in the conviction that those who signed it had been guilty of crimes and vices. In most instances the charges were false statements, but the friars had little choice but to sign the document.

There was no mention of 'surrender' in Ingworth's commission to the friars and he had no legal or parliamentary authority to forcibly suppress their houses; therefore their surrender had to appear voluntary, so he found any pretext to procure the surrender of house after house in rapid succession in the ten months of his visitations. It was Ingworth's custom on arriving at a friars' house to be accompanied by the town mayor or bailiffs, who acted as witnesses. He then assembled the brethren by ringing a bell. He took the same line in each visit, firstly saying his commission did not give him authority to evict them but, rather, to reform them so that they might continue in their house and keep their religion according to the King's injunctions. He read out their rules, and in each instance the friars could only agree that, under prevailing circumstances, they could not observe the rules of earlier times and at the same time maintain their house. Ingworth would then ask them if they would be reformed according to their early rules; if not, he would have to take the surrender of the house. He then confiscated the friars' chattels and that, together with their impoverished circumstances and their inability to accept the impossible conditions of reform, left them with no choice other than to sign the deed of surrender of their houses. In spite of his mild methods, he had little difficulty in obtaining the surrender of most houses he visited. The local bailiffs were then given the keys to the houses and assumed responsibility for the buildings until the King's pleasure for the vacated houses was known.

Although some surrender documents were not signed for some reason or other, this did not make any difference, as the houses were suppressed with or without signatures.

When Ingworth visited Aylesford Carmelite house in July 1538, he was told that two bogus commissioners had visited the house, claiming that the house had been given away and they had come with a commission to put the friars out. The friars then sold most of their goods to pay their debts, but Ingworth did not visit the house to take its surrender until the December of that year. A sham commissioner visited Norwich Carmelite house in 1538 but he was caught and punished.

Ingworth reported to Cromwell that when he visited the Canterbury Austin house, one friar named Stone said that he was 'ready to die that the king might not be head of the church in England, but it must be a spiritual father appointed by God'. Stone was arrested for his outspokenness and in December 1539 was hanged, drawn and quartered at Dane John, just outside the Canterbury city walls. He was beatified by Pope Leo X in 1886 and is included in the list of English martyrs.

One can imagine the distress and fear of the friars as the intentions of Ingworth were made known and they found themselves locked out of their houses at a time when most people had turned against them. Most friars were evicted from their houses in the autumn, and, with winter approaching, many of them had nowhere to go. They must have loathed the traitorous Ingworth, who enriched himself whilst carrying out his duties.

The instructions given to Ingworth were that the walls of the churches, towers, cloisters and other vacated buildings should be razed to the ground and left open to the elements to make the buildings uninhabitable. But demolition was expensive and Ingworth's commissioners contended themselves with defacing tombs, removing lead from the roofs and removing stairs, which resulted in the buildings gradually falling into decay.

Inventories were made of all the assets in the houses; glass, vestments, missals, organ, timber, chattels and other movables were auctioned on the spot to pay for any outstanding debts and for the expenses of the visit. The list of vestments and altar hangings taken at the time of the closure of Bristol Dominican church included six altar cloths, various hangings for the high altar and nine hangings for the low altars, 22 cloths to cover altars and images at the time of Lent and an unknown number of vestments.

Most houses were leaded and the lead often proved to be the most valuable asset of the house. It was ripped off the roofs and, with the bells and other removable metalwork, cast into manageable oblong ingots for transportation to the king's warehouses. The furnaces for such work were often stoked with the carved wooden furnishings of the friaries. Bell metal was reserved for the King's use for gun making. Ingworth himself took possession of any jewels, plate or ornaments, which he sent to the Jewel House, London, for the King to dispose of as he wished. Hardly any of the numerous chalices or altar vessels taken from the friaries have survived.

So it was, Ingworth annihilated institutions that had served the people for three centuries or so, with little regard for buildings that had been hallowed by worship of the living and were the repose of the dead.

In 1536, the King set up the Court of Augmentations to strengthen his finances and to take control of seized monastic properties. The properties and land of the suppressed friaries were transferred to the Court of Augmentations and remained royal property until they were either sold or handed over to laymen. The gentry, Catholic or not, bought friary lands on a commercial basis in order to expand their urban estates. Speculators thought that the quickest way to get a return on their outlay for leases on the vacated buildings was to demolish the buildings and sell the material. This was welcomed by the authorities as it prevented the friars from returning if there was a change of policy.

The Court of Augmentations seems on the whole to have accepted the terms on which a property was leased, without suspicion of sharp practice. The Duke of Norfolk gained control of the four friary sites in Norfolk.

There was a scramble for the spoils of the houses and nearly everywhere the process of decay was hastened by the townspeople using the buildings as sources of stone. The sites were urban properties and valuable. The dissolution of the houses made a great deal of cheap building material available, along with a number of disused but serviceable buildings. In most instances, church buildings were demolished and the domestic buildings rented out for a wide range of uses such as schools, granaries, workhouses or dwelling places. Whatever the use to which buildings were put, they gradually decayed and were pulled down.

Unlike monks, friars in England and Wales did not receive pensions when they left the religious life they had known for so long. Because they owned nothing of their own, they were put out by Ingworth without a penny for their immediate future. However, the visitors who deputised for him in closing a few houses gave the friars they expelled a small payment to help them on their way. Very little is known about the dispersal of the friars and the manner in which they were evicted from their houses. Due to the shortfall in recruitment in the period leading up to the suppression, the average age of friars would have been older than in previous times and therefore there would have been a number of old and infirm men among those who were evicted. Many friars sought to purchase capacities which authorised them to take up other religious duties, such as a chaplaincy or parish benefice, where they could carry out the functions of a parish priest. Capacities cost about £4 each and the required fee was often raised from relatives and friends. However, they faced strong competition from numerous friars and monks dispossessed at about the same time. Others returned to their families or sought alternative work, and novices were sent home. No provision was made for the sick and elderly brethren, who were put out on the street in a heartless way and probably took to secular begging for the rest of their days.

There were, doubtless, many heavy hearts as they passed through their friary gates for the last time and changed from their monastic habits to secular dress. These men who had for so long been familiar sights across the country and, despite their faults and failings, had performed an immense service to the community for so many years, now vanished from the scene and their houses went rapidly into oblivion.

We can only guess what became of the corrodians, the pensioners who had taken up residence in friaries. Most of them had given their funds to the friars so that they could have security in the closing years of their lives. There was not a large number of them, but in their advanced years they were turned out of the friaries at the same time as the friars.

SCOTLAND

In a matter of years a similar flow of reforming ideas from the Continent swamped much of Scotland, where religious life was in ferment. Whereas England at that time had a strong ruler in Henry VIII, James V, King of Scots, was ill. He died in Falkland Palace on 14 December 1542 following a physical and mental breakdown on hearing the news of the defeat of his forces at the battle of Solway Moss. He was succeeded by his infant daughter, Mary Queen of Scots, who in 1548 was sent to France for safety. In 1558 she married the heir to the French throne, who succeeded as Francis II in the following year. He died in 1560 and Mary returned to Scotland in 1561, after the Reformation had taken hold in Scotland. Mary Queen of Scots remained a loyal Catholic but, in 1567, she was overthrown by Protestant noblemen in favour of her young son, James VI of Scotland, who also became James I of England.

Henry VIII tried to persuade James V to adopt the same ecclesiastical policy as he was carrying out in England, but James would not consent to dissolving the monastic houses in his realm. The decline of monasticism in Scotland was a corollary of the teachings of John Calvin, who was opposed to the teaching of the confessional, praying for the dead and the authority of the Pope. The decline was accompanied by an indifference to the friars, and the public saw no reason for the continuance of their work in Scotland.

Nominations of commendam (temporary giving of an ecclesiastic post in trust) was originally given as a means of enabling a bishop to protect a monastery by recovering lands wrongfully occupied by a lay lord, or to tighten discipline that had become lax during the period of vacancy of a prior. For instance, in 1476, monastic life in the Fail Trinitarian house had deteriorated so much that John Mure, Provincial of the Scottish Dominicans, was granted the commendam of the house with the aim of overseeing its maintenance, repair and discipline.

In the reigns of James IV and V, the practice developed of conferring the income of the head of a monastic house during the period of a vacancy upon a beneficiary who was not in holy orders. Abbeys and other benefices were given in commendam to laymen, who enjoyed the revenues of the house and allowed the monks or friars a portion of it. This practice was developed further in order to secure an income for an individual and became an established and scandalous practice in Scotland. James V developed the system further by granting the office in perpetuity, and the recipient became an absentee abbot, or prior, for life. Five of James V's illegitimate sons were given the commendam of the richest abbeys in Scotland, in order to enrich the King and weaken the church financially. Many holders of commendams never showed an interest in the community from which they drew their income. It appears that contemporaries did not judge the kings too harshly for using this system for distributing the monastic wealth among friends. The practice of giving commendams was not instituted in England and Wales.

During the upheavals in the period leading up to the Reformation, a number of friaries in Scotland were put into the hands of secular commendams, who then assumed ownership of the friaries but had no interest in the continuance of the houses.

At the end of the fifteenth century there were 10 Carmelite houses, 15 Dominican houses, seven Conventual Franciscan houses and eight Franciscan Observants houses in Scotland.

In 1525, the Scottish Parliament legislated against the importation of Lutheran books and, in 1527, they legislated against persons disseminating Luther's opinions. However, by then, towns on the east coast of Scotland were hotbeds of the Lutheran concepts of the Christian faith. Patrick Hamilton, an illegitimate offspring of the Earl of Arran, was the first to suffer in Scotland for the Reformed cause. He was a student studying in Paris and enjoyed an income as commendam of Fearn Abbey, Rosshire. In 1528, he was arrested and charged at St Andrews with holding heretical views. Campbell, prior of St Andrews Dominican friary, was his chief accuser. On 29 February 1528, Hamilton was put to the stake in North Street, St Andrews. The executioner could not get the fire to burn properly and a bundle of straw was brought and thrown onto the fire, but a sudden gust of wind caused a flare that blew onto Prior Campbell, burning the front of his cowl.

English Invasion of 1544–45

James V died in December 1542. In 1543 the Earl of Arran, who was the Governor of Scotland, signed, on behalf of the infant Mary Queen of Scots, a treaty with Henry VIII by which Henry's son Edward would marry Mary and unite the kingdoms of England and Scotland. However, before the end of the year the Queen-Dowager, Marie de Guise, prompted by her adviser, Cardinal Beaton, repudiated the agreement. Henry retaliated uncompromisingly by renewing the English claim to the sovereignty of Scotland and started a campaign of 'rough wooing', by which he attempted to win the loyalties of the Scottish people by force. In the spring of 1544 he sent an army, under the command of the Earl of Hertford, to invade Scotland, with instructions to burn, destroy and put man, woman and child to the sword whenever resistance was offered.

In May 1544, the Earl's army landed near Edinburgh and for two days put Edinburgh and Leith to the torch before going on to devastate the countryside around the city. The monastic houses near the Firth of Forth and the Borders experienced the brutality of the Earl's expedition as he marched back to Berwick-upon-Tweed, leaving a trail of ruin behind him. In the following year Hertford again invaded and devastated towns and abbeys in the Tweed valley, leaving further devastation in his wake, and it was said that he left neither house, fortress, village, cattle, corn or other succour of man. In 1547–48, the English once again invaded Scotland, and further devastation was inflicted upon the people. Friaries and other monastic establishments in Scotland suffered terrible destruction at the hands of the English invaders, who claimed they came as reformers but, in their zeal, wantonly ruined many friaries which generations of pious people had built. The Franciscan friary at Haddington, which had been burnt by the English in their earlier invasion in 1355, was again destroyed by them during the 1544 raid. Roxburgh was destroyed during the 1545 raid and, following the destruction of the town, the friary was abandoned. Today, only a few scattered fragments of the town remain on Roxburgh hill near Kelso. The Jedburgh Franciscan Observant house was also sacked in 1545. The English invasions of 1544–48 effectively put an end to the activities of friars in Scotland.

End of Friaries in Scotland

There were seven houses of Trinitarian (Red) Friars in Scotland, but the order does not appear to have recruited brethren in sufficient numbers to sustain itself. In 1539, the Red Friars abandoned their Dirleton house and transferred the brethren to Scotlandwell to augment the numbers for divine worship there, and the Dirleton house was left in the care of a secular priest to pray for the soul of its founder. A small community of friars continued in the Aberdeen Trinitarian house until the Reformation, but their buildings were dilapidated. The Fail house, or Failford as it was sometimes known, had seven friars in 1528 and three in 1558. The house was destroyed by reformers in 1560.

By 1476, the Berwick-upon-Tweed Trinitarian house was in ruins and the brethren were transferred to their Peebles house. The small Dunbar Trinitarian house was annexed to Peebles in 1529. At the end of the fifteenth century the Houston house had three or four brethren, but this was down to just one in 1531 and the house was annexed to Peebles, leaving one secular priest, who later resigned to take up another benefice. This brought an end to the ministry of the house. Their Peebles house was destroyed by the English in 1548 but in 1556 there were five brethren remaining in the house and it was they who, on 27 January 1561, surrendered the keys of the house to the burgesses and dispersed. The church was used as the town parish church till 1784, due to the parish church in the town having been burnt down.

The first display of popular hostility to the friars in Scotland took place in Dundee in 1543 when the people welcomed George Withart and John Knox to their town. George Withart (1513–46) was a powerful Scottish Protestant preacher who fled to England in 1538. John Knox (1513–72), who at one time had been a priest, was influenced by Withart to work for the Lutheran reforms and joined the reformers in the defence of St Andrews Castle during the 1546–47 siege of the castle. The English fleet held the sea off St Andrews but, with the death of Henry VIII in 1547, it was withdrawn. In June 1548, 6,000 French mercenary troops landed in Scotland and took St Andrews Castle. Knox was captured and held prisoner until 1549, when he became a chaplain to Edward VI. Following the accession of Queen Mary (Tudor) in 1553, he fled to Dieppe and then to Geneva, where he was influenced by John Calvin. He returned to Scotland in 1559 and became a leader of the reformed Church of Scotland in 1560.

Following the preaching of Lutheran doctrines by Withart and Knox in Dundee in 1543, the Dominican and Franciscan houses in the town were sacked by a mob, and in 1548 both houses were burnt by the English. From then on, many other friaries in Scotland were subject to the tumults of the English invasion and the Reformation. In 1559 the people of Dundee declared for the Reformation and set about reorganising the church. When the Dundee Franciscan house lay in ruins, one of the brethren appears to have earned his livelihood by growing herbs and kale in the kirkyard.

In 1545, Withart was betrayed to Cardinal Beaton, Archbishop of St Andrews, and was convicted by a clerical court and condemned as a heretic. On 1 March 1546, when he was being taken to be burnt as a heretic, two Franciscan friars came to hear his confessions, but he refused to have them. Personal enemies of Beaton, and supporters of Withart, conspired against the Cardinal, and on 26 May they gained entry to the Cardinal's castle in St Andrews, killed him and hung his body from the battlements. Then, in the castle, they formed the first congregation of the Protestant Church in Scotland.

The Dominican friary at St Andrews, which had been rebuilt in 1514, was burnt by the followers of Norman Lesley (d. 1554) in July 1547, but the friars were not finally ejected from the house until 12 years later. Lesley then led the mob to St Andrews Franciscan Observants house, which they burnt. He was the Master of Rothes, Moray, and one of the leaders in the murder of Cardinal Beaton.

Queen Elizabeth acceded to the throne of England in November 1558, following the death of Queen Mary (Tudor), her half-sister. In 1503, Margaret Tudor, daughter of Henry VII, had married James IV of Scotland, and Mary Queen of Scots claimed the crown of England through her grandmother.

By the time of Elizabeth's accession to the throne the Reformation was almost complete in England and Wales, but Elizabeth's court paid close attention to what was happening north of the border, especially as Mary and her husband, Francis II of France, claimed the title of King and Queen of England. If Mary and Francis had gained the crown of England, they would have tried to overturn the Reformation in England and restore papal supremacy. It was in Elizabeth's interest that the Reformation succeed in Scotland, but she did not play a part in the final moves in the Reformation which were to have such a devastating effect on the Scottish friars.

The Scottish friars were caught in the religious upheaval that was sweeping through the land and fared worse than the monastic houses from the anti-Catholic violence, due to their houses being in towns and within easy reach of the mobs who hounded them. Many friars fled before the storm of the Reformation burst upon them, leaving the friary buildings to their fate.

In 1557, the reformist cause in Scotland was directed by the 'Lords of the Congregation', who signed a covenant to support the Protestant 'Congregation of God'. Their demands included the public exposition of the Scriptures.

The religious controversy in Scotland came to a head when, on 1 January 1559, notices were placed on the doors of friaries throughout Scotland calling on the friars to vacate their houses by Friday, 12 May, and make their buildings over to the poor and infirm.

On Thursday, 11 May 1559, John Knox preached his famous incendiary sermon in St John's Kirk, Perth, which aroused the mob to destroy images and other liturgical objects which they considered idolatrous. This led to an orgy of destruction which swept away religious images and sacred objects and the demolition of altars that had been polluted, as they thought, by the idolatry of the Mass, in churches in and around Perth.

John Knox later wrote about the happenings in Perth:

The multitude was so inflamed that neither the exhortation of the preacher or the commands of the magistrate stayed them from destroying the places of idolatry. The preacher had before declared how odious was idolatry in God's presence. When the sermon was noised abroad, a whole rascally rabble who found nothing to do in St John's, ran to the Grey Friars and Black Friars houses and not withstanding that they had a strong guard within them, the mob entered both houses and with an outburst of iconoclasm, proceeded to despoil the items and the altars which were considered idolatrous. After that, they permitted the spoils of the houses to be given to the poor. The preachers beforehand threatened all men that no honest man should be enriched by as much as a groat. The Perth Franciscan friars, Dominican friars and Carmelite friars houses and the Charterhouse Priory were destroyed by the reforming townspeople, the walls only remaining of these houses.

The destruction of images and altars had been commanded by the preacher, who said no harm should be done to the buildings, but John Knox was not the first to find how hard it is to control the results of an appeal to the fanaticism of a mob.

The Charterhouse priory, founded in 1429, was the last royal monastic foundation in Scotland and was the first monastery to be destroyed in the Reformation. Fifty or so friars and monks from the religious houses in Perth fled to the Regent, Mary de Guise, in Stirling for protection.

The Edinburgh Franciscan Observants house, which was partly burnt in 1544, was destroyed on 14 June 1559 by reformers, who Knox referred to as a rascal multitude. The Stirling Dominican and Observants houses were also destroyed by the reformers in June 1559. The Banff Carmelite house was set on fire on 20 July 1559 and the Aberdeen Carmelite and Dominican houses were destroyed on 4 January 1560 by the reforming barons of Kincardineshire. By 1559–60, most friars had deserted their houses. Dumfries Franciscan house had 12 brethren in 1427, down to seven in 1548 and six in 1557. Montrose Dominican house had eight brethren in 1531 and four in 1560. The Inverberie Carmelite house was down to two friars in 1556 and the Linlithgow Carmelites were down to four friars.

The Lords of the Congregation sent a summons to the backers of the Reformation to muster at St Andrews on 4 June 1559 to force the reforms onto the Archbishop. The sermon preached by John Knox in the parish church in St Andrews on 11 June aroused the congregation to action. The Provost and Bailies, as well as many of the people of the town, were provoked to expel the friars and remove all images and altars associated with 'popish' worship in St Andrews. The mob made the Dominican house a particular target for their fury, considering the Dominican friars represented the intellectual wing of the old ways. They then went to the Franciscan house; before sundown there was nothing left but bare walls. Both houses had been previously burnt by a mob in 1547. On 14 June 1559 the mob burst into St Andrews Cathedral, removed 'idolatrous material' and burnt it on a bonfire. From that time the days of the medieval church in Scotland were numbered. The cathedral was abandoned by the Archbishop, who considered St Andrews parish church sufficient for the new needs, and the cathedral was allowed to decay and became a quarry for stone.

In 1560, the Master of Huntley, who later became the Earl of Huntley, invaded Elgin with a mob that laid waste the cathedral and the Dominican and Franciscan Observants houses in the town. The Observants house was fired by Alexander Innes, grandson of John Innes, who had refounded the house in 1479, but the four walls of the roofless church survived to roof level. The buildings came into the possession of the Sisters of Mercy and, after restoration work, the building was reopened in 1898 as the church of their convent. Today the Elgin Franciscan church is the only Franciscan pre-Reformation church in Britain still in use for worship.

The Reformation Parliament met in Edinburgh in 1560 with over 100 minor lords and lairds among its members. The Parliament banned the celebration of the Mass, rejected the Pope's authority over the Scottish Church and accepted a reformed confession of faith. On 12 August 1560, the Lords of the Congregation in Edinburgh despatched instructions throughout the kingdom: 'Our trusted friends, after most hearty commendations, we pray that you take down the images in the kirk and take them to the kirk yard and burn them openly. Cast down the altars and purge the kirk of all kinds of monuments of idolatry. Fail not to do this, as you will do us singular pleasure and so commit you to the protection of God'. Archbishop Hamilton sat in the Reformation Parliament as

Primate of Scotland and concurred in the repudiation of the Pope and Mass. All Scottish monastic houses effectively came to an end with the abolition of the Mass on 24 August 1560.

It was only half a revolution. It was not until 1690 that King William of Orange established Presbyterianism as the official government of the church in Scotland.

The mob violence generated against the friars in Scotland did not bring about an immediate and sudden end, as did the actions of Henry VIII south of the border. By 1560, most friars had left their houses and many of them emigrated to the Low Countries. No single date can be given for the cessation of many of the friars' houses in Scotland, and the friars who remained were not dislodged but left to die out. Although some friars' communities continued until the death of the last of its members, their significance had come to an end, due to the lack of postulants entering the friars' orders to replace older men. The overpowering wave of Protestantism had drained the sense of vocation for the mendicant life. One by one, the Scottish friaries were secularised and their revenues made over to the burghs by Royal Charters, on the pretext that the revenues and sites granted of old had been Crown property.

In Scotland, monks and friars were not able to obtain posts in parishes or religious establishments, as they were seen as representing the old ways in religion. When they left their houses, unlike the English brethren, they received compensation, usually at the rate of £16 per annum, which was referred to as 'friars' wages'.

The social aspect of their work ceased with the passing of the friars and they were sadly missed by the poor and needy at a time when there were no other organisations to continue their social work. Friars would have also been missed for their lively and intellectual sermons, for preachers of the new religious ideas lacked the high standard of training the preaching friars had. Their preaching, too, was much more sombre than the friars' preaching. Society was immeasurably poorer for the loss of the friars and their dispersal struck the secular world more forcefully than any other aspect of the Reformation.

During the Reformation, iconoclasm took place in Britain on a greater scale than on the Continent. Many thousands of paintings, sculptures and wooden images were destroyed, resulting in a massive loss of medieval art. The emphasis in religion had turned from the visual arts to understanding the Scriptures.

APPENDIX 1

FRIARS' HOUSES IN BRITAIN

Austin Friars' Houses

England

Atherstone	1375	
Berwick-upon-Tweed	-1299	#
Boston	1317	
Bristol	1313	
Cambridge	-1289	
Canterbury	1318	
Clare	1249	
Droitwich	1331	
Gorleston	-1267	
Grimsby	1293	
Hull	1317	
Huntingdon	-1258	
King's Lynn	-1295	
Leicester	1304	%
Lincoln	1269	
London	1253	
Ludlow	1254	
Newark	1534	*
Newcastle-upon-Tyne	1291	
Northampton	-1290	@
Norwich	-1289	
Orford	1295–99	
Oxford	1266	
Penrith	1291	
Rye	1364	
Shrewsbury	1255	
Southampton	1534	*
Stafford	1343	
Stamford	1342	
Thetford	1387	
Tickhill	1256	
Warrington	-1272	
Winchester	-1300	
Woodhouse	1250	
York	1271	

Wales

Newport (Mon)	-1377

Scotland

Nil

Notes

It is possible the house was founded before the death of Alexander III in 1286.
% Possibly as early as 1254, although the first documented date is 1304.
* Austin friars took over former Observant Franciscan house.
@ There are references to the house in 1275 and 1290, although some authorities place the foundation date as 1323.
- A hyphen before a date indicates that this is the first recorded date of the house and that it was probably established at an earlier date.

Carmelite Friars' Houses

England

Appleby	1290–93
Aylesford	1242
Berwick-upon-Tweed	-1262
Blakeney	1304–16
Boston	1293
Bristol	1256
Burnham Norton	1242–47
Cambridge	1247
Chester	-1277
Coventry	1342
Doncaster	1351
Gloucester	-1268
Hitching	1317
Hull	1290–93
Hulne	1242
Ipswich	-1271
King's Lynn	-1260
Lincoln	-1260
London	1247
Lossenham	1242–47
Ludlow	1350
Maldon	1293
Marlborough	1316
Newcastle-upon-Tyne	1262
Northallerton	1356–57
Northampton	-1265
Norwich	1256
Nottingham	-1271
Oxford	1256
Plymouth	-1296
Sandwich	-1268
Scarborough	1319
Shoreham/Sele	-1317
Stamford	-1268
Winchester	-1268
Yarmouth	1276–77
York	-1253

Wales

Denbigh	1343–50

Scotland

Aberdeen	1273	
Banff	1321–24	
Edinburgh	1520	
Inverbervie	-1443	
Irvine	-1293	
Kingussie	*c.* 1500	
Linlithgow	*c.* 1401	
Luffness	-1293	
Queensferry	1441	*
Tullilum (Perth)	1262	

Notes

* It is possible that the house was first established in about 1330 and rebuilt in 1441.

\- A hyphen before a date indicates that this is the first recorded date of the house and that it was probably established at an earlier date.

Dominican Friars' Houses

England

Arundel	1253
Bamburgh	1265
Berwick-upon-Tweed	1240
Beverley	1240
Boston	1280
Bristol	1227–28
Cambridge	-1237
Canterbury	1237
Carlisle	1233
Chelmsford	-1277
Chester	-1236
Chichester	1280
Derby	-1239
Dunstable	1259
Dunwich	-1256
Exeter	1232
Gloucester	*c.* 1239
Guildford	1275
Hereford	1246
Ilchester	1261
Ipswich	1263
King's Langley	1308
King's Lynn	-1256
Lancaster	1260
Leicester	-1252
Lincoln	-1238
London	1221
Melcombe Regis	1418
Newcastle-under-Lyme	1277
Newcastle-upon-Tyne	1239
Northampton	-1233
Norwich	1226
Oxford	1221
Pontefract	1256
Salisbury	1281
Scarborough	-1252
Shrewsbury	1230
Stamford	-1241
Sudbury	-1248
Thetford	1335
Truro	1259
Warwick	1263
Wilton	1247
Winchelsea	1318
Winchester	-1234
Worcester	1347
Yarm	*c.* 1266
Yarmouth	1267
York	1226

Wales

Bangor	-1251
Brecon	-1269
Cardiff	-1242
Haverfordwest	-1245
Rhuddlan	*c.* 1257

Scotland

Aberdeen	1239–40	
Ayr	*c.* 1242	
Cupar	1348	
Dundee	1521	
Edinburgh	1230	
Elgin	1233–34	
Glasgow	-1246	
Haddington	1471	
Inverness	-1240	
Montrose	-1275	
Perth	1231	
St Andrews	1274	#
St Monan's	1471	
Stirling	1233	
Wigtown	1267–87	?

House of Dominican Nuns

England		*Scotland*	
Dartford	1356	Sciennes (Edinburgh)	1517

Notes

There are some doubts about the thirteenth-century foundation dates. The house appears to have become impoverished and dilapidated and was refounded at the latter part of the fifteenth century.

- A hyphen before a date indicates that this is the first recorded date of the house and that it was probably established at an earlier date.

Franciscan (Conventual) Friars' Houses

England

Aylesbury	1380		Hartlepool	1240	
Bedford	-1238		Hereford	1228	
Berwick-upon-Tweed	1231		Ipswich	-1236	
Beverley	*c.* 1267		King's Lynn	-1230	
Bodmin	-1260		Leicester	1230	
Boston	-1268		Lewes	-1241	
Bridgenorth	-1244		Lichfield	*c.* 1237	
Bridgewater	1245		Lincoln	1230	
Bristol	1230		London	1224	
Bury St Edmunds	1263		Newcastle-upon-Tyne	-1237	
Cambridge	1226		Northampton	1226	
Canterbury	1224		Norwich	1226	
Carlisle	1233		Nottingham	1230	
Chester	1236–38		Oxford	1224	
Chichester	-1232	*	Plymouth	1383	
Colchester	-1237		Preston	1260	
Coventry	*c.* 1234		Reading	1233	
Doncaster	*c.* 1284		Richmond (Yorks)	1257–58	
Dorchester	-1267		Salisbury	-1230	
Dunwich	-1277		Scarborough	1239	%
Exeter	1240		Shrewsbury	1245	
Gloucester	1230		Southampton	1235	
Grantham	-1290		Stafford	1274	
Grimsby	-1240		Stamford	-1230	

Walsingham	1347	
Ware	1338	
Winchelsea	1242	
Winchester	1237	
Worcester	1226	
Yarmouth	1271	#
York	*c.* 1230	

Wales

Cardiff	1280	
Carmarthen	-1282	
Llanfaes	1240	

Scotland

Dumfries	1234	
Dundee	-1289	
Elgin	1281	+
Haddington	-1242	
Inverkeithing	-1346	
Kirkcudbright	1449–56	
Lanark	1328–29	
Roxburgh	1233	

Franciscan (Observants) Friars' Houses

England

Canterbury	1498	@
Greenwich	1482	
Newcastle-upon-Tyne	1498	@
Newark	1507	
Richmond (Surrey)	1499	
Southampton	1498	@

Scotland

Aberdeen	1469
Ayr	1488–97
Edinburgh	*c.* 1463
Elgin	1479
Glasgow	1473–79
Jedburgh	*c.* 1505
Perth	1488–96
St Andrews	1463–66
Stirling	1494

Houses of Franciscan (Poor Clare) Nuns

England

Bruisyard (Suffolk)	1366
London (Aldergate)	1293
Denney (Cambs)	1342
Waterbeach (Cambs)	1294–1348

Scotland

Aberdour	1486
Dundee	1502

Notes

* The exact date of the arrival of the Franciscans in Chichester is unknown but it was

probably shortly before 1232. The original site was found to be too restrictive and in 1269 they were given the site of the old castle.
% The 1239 settlement was opposed and the Franciscan friars did not return to Scarborough until about 30 years later.
# The Yarmouth house was probably founded soon after 1224 when Franciscans settled in Norwich; however, the earliest known mention of it occurs in 1271.
+ The Elgin settlement of the friars must have been only temporary and the house has no history. It was refounded as an Observants house in 1479.
@ Transferred from Conventual to Observants houses in 1498.

- A hyphen before a date indicates that this was the first recorded date of the house and that it was probably established at an earlier date.

Minor Orders That Existed Up To The Reformation

Crutched Cross Friars' Houses

Barham	1293		Kildale (Yorks)	1307	#
Berwick-upon-Tweed	1240–48		London	1298	
Colchester	-1235		Oxford	1342	%
Donnington	1376		Welnetham	1274	

Trinitarian Friars' Houses

England

Berwick-upon-Tweed	-1240	
Easton (Wilts)	1261	+
Hertford	1261	$
Hounslow	-1252	
Ingham	1360	@
Knaresborough	*c.* 1252	
Moatenden	1224	
Newcastle-upon-Tyne	1361	
Oxford	1286	*
Thelsford	-1240	
Totnes	1271	

Scotland (Red Friars)

Aberdeen	-1273
Dirleton	N/K – 15th C.
Dunbar	1240–48
Fail	-1335
Houston (Lothian)	*c.* 1270
Peebles	1296
Scotlandwell	1250–51

Notes

The house was short-lived and had closed by 1313.
% House abandoned by 1362, perhaps due to the result of Black Death.
+ Destroyed by fire in 1493.
$ Abandoned before 1535.
@ Abandoned in 1536.
* Ceased to exist sometime after 1362 due to the ravages of the Black Death.

Minor Orders that were Abolished in 1274

Pied Friars' Houses

	Year Founded	*Year Ceased to Exist*	
Cambridge	1273	1319	
London	1267	-1317	
Norwich	1307	1307	

Sack Friars' Houses

	Year Founded	*Year Ceased to Exist*	
Berwick-upon-Tweed	1267	1285	
Bristol	-1266	-1317	
Cambridge	1258	1307	
Canterbury	-1274	-1314	
King's Lynn	1258	-1317	
Leicester	1274	-1300	
Lincoln	1266	1307	
London	1257	1305	
Newcastle-upon-Tyne	1267	1307	*
Northampton	-1271	-1303	
Norwich	1258	1307	#
Oxford	1261	1309	@
Rye	1263	-1307	
Stamford	-1274	-1317	%
Worcester	-1272	-1317	
York	*c.* 1260	1312	

Notes

* Site given to the Newcastle Carmelites in 1307.
# Site given to the Norwich Dominicans in 1307.
@ Site given to the Oxford Franciscans in 1309.
% Austin friars occupied the site in 1343.

APPENDIX 2

AGGREGATE NUMBER OF FRIARS IN FRIARIES

For some 50 years up to 1338, when English kings stayed at a house of friars they gave the friary alms of one groat for each member of the community for each day of their stay. From this we can list the number of brethren in the houses at the time of the royal visit. Many of the deeds of surrender signed when friaries were being closed contain the number of friars in the house, and from these we can list the number of friars in the houses at that time; but there is very little other information on the number of friars in friaries in England and Wales during the medieval period. Where the figures for more than one date under the various year headings are known, the aggregate number during the period is given. These tables therefore give a general idea of the number of friars in the various houses during the period. However, very little information on the numbers of friars is known for the period following the Black Death. The following information has been gleaned from various sources.

Austin Friars

	1270–90	**1291–1310**	**1311–30**	**1331–48**	**Other**	**1538–39**
Berwick		6	12	15		
Boston			20			
Bristol						8
Cambridge	20	70	43		49 (1377)	4
Canterbury			8	18		
Clare		29		30		
Gorleston	19					
Hull			16		18 (1500)	
Huntingdon			20			
King's Lynn		20	30		46 (1446)	11
Leicester		20	27	24		4

	1270–90	1291–1310	1311–30	1331–48	Other	1538–39
Lincoln	33	29	32	36		4
London	60	51	65			12
Ludlow		20	35		30 (1446)	4
Newcastle-Tyne		26	25	30		14
Northampton			21	30		9
Norwich	15		37			17
Oxford	40	52	43		49 (1377)	
Penrith		8				
Shrewsbury	20	18			6 (1456)	3
Southampton						6
Stamford				12		6
Thetford		6				3
Tickhill		18	20	24		8
Warrington						9
Winchester		13	20			
York		34	31	36	20 (1440)	14

Carmelites

	1270–90	1291–1310	1311–30	1331–48	Other	1538–39
Aylesford				20		
Berwick			4	15	14	
Boston			18	22		
Bristol						4
Burnham Norton		An average of 15			16 (1505)	4
Cambridge		An average of 50				2
Chester						10
Coventry						14
Denbigh						4
Doncaster			18			8
Gloucester				31		3
Hitchin						5
Hull		15				8
Hulne						10
King's Lynn		14			30 (1377)	11
Lincoln		28	30	34		
London			55			13
Ludlow						5
Marlborough						5
Newcastle-upon-Tyne		27	24			10
Northallerton						11
Northampton						9
Nottingham						7
Oxford			45		57 (1377)	

	1270–90	1291–1310	1311–30	1331–48	Other	1538–39
Plymouth						6
Sandwich		15				
Stamford		20	26			7
Winchester			6			
York			26	38		13
Dominicans						
Arundel		22	20			5
Bamburgh		10		8		
Bangor						2
Berwick-upon-Tweed		6	15	18	20 (1366)	
Beverley		33	42	30	14 (1500)	
Boston		29	28			
Brecon						10
Bristol		An average of 30				5
Cambridge	58	59	55		50 (1489)	16
Canterbury	50	31	30	34		
Cardiff						7
Carlisle		16		20		
Chelmsford	30		34			
Chester	24					5
Chichester		34	21			6
Derby		30	26			6
Dunstable	18	30	28			13
Dunwich	24					
Exeter		36				
Gloucester	30		33	31		7
Guildford		12	24	17		7
Haverfordwest						7
Hereford		Average of about 30			(12 in 1352)	8
Ilchester						7
Ipswich	22	40				
King's Langley			45			
King's Lynn	40	45		45		12
Lancaster		30				
Leicester		32	30	18		10
Lincoln		45	38	48		
London	80 (1243)	90	72	90	34 (1466)	16
Newcastle-Lyme	20		12			
Newcastle-Tyne		33	38	30		13
Northampton	31 (1244)	40	36	33		
Norwich	40		53			

	1270–90	1291–1310	1311–30	1331–48	Other	1538–39
Oxford	80 (1255)	96	90		70 (1377)	14
Pontefract		36	27	30		7
Rhuddlan	25	23				6
Salisbury	57	50		42		14
Scarborough			30			
Shrewsbury		31				
Stamford		42	38	38		9
Sudbury		30				
Thetford						6
Truro						11
Warwick		37	30			8
Wilton		(2 or 3)				1
Winchester	28 (1239)	32	46	36		6
Yarm		30	33	28		12
Yarmouth	35		33	28		
York	70	53	48	55		11

Franciscans

Aylesbury		Average of between 12 and 15				7
Bedford						13
Berwick-upon-Tweed		6	15	15		
Beverley		36	28	26		
Bodmin						9
Boston			30	35		
Bridgwater						8
Bristol						6
Bury St Edmunds		40				
Cambridge	58	70	61			24
Canterbury	60	39	36			
Cardiff	18					9
Carmarthen						14
Chester						7
Chichester	26 (1243)					7
Coventry						11
Doncaster		30	28	18		10
Dorchester		32				8
Exeter						10
Gloucester				31		5
Grantham		20				
Grimsby						9
Hartlepool						19

	1270–90	1291–1310	1311–30	1331–48	Other	1538–39
Hereford						14
King's Lynn						10
Leicester						8
Lewes		24				
Lincoln		53	40	37		
Lichfield						3
Llanfaes						4
London	80 (1245)	70	90			27
Newcastle-Tyne		34	24			11
Northampton		34	50			
Norwich	50 (1230)					
Nottingham						8
Oxford	40 (1233–80 1243)		84	40	103 (1377)	28
Reading	13 (1243)					11
Richmond						15
Romney	14 (1243)					
Salisbury	20 (1243)					10
Southampton	30 (1243)					
Stamford		40	28	36		10
Walsingham						3
Winchelsea						7
Winchester	33 (1243)		28			3
York		52	49	45		21

APPENDIX 3

DISTRIBUTION OF THE FOUR MAIN ORDERS OF FRIARS IN THE VARIOUS TOWNS

(A) Austin – (C) Carmelite – (D) Dominicans – (F) Franciscan

England

Town	A	C	D	F
Appleby		C		
Arundel			D	
Atherstone	A			
Aylesbury				F
Aylesford		C		
Bamburgh			D	
Bedford				F
Berwick-on-Tweed	A	C	D	F
Beverley			D	F
Blakeney		C		
Bodmin				F
Boston	A	C	D	F
Bridgnorth				F
Bridgwater				F
Bristol	A	C	D	F
Burnham Norton		C		
Bury St Edmunds				F
Cambridge	A	C	D	F
Canterbury	A		D	F
Carlisle			D	F
Chelmsford			D	
Chester		C	D	F
Chichester			D	F
Clare	A			
Colchester				F
Coventry		C		F
Derby			D	
Doncaster		C		F
Dorchester				F
Droitwich	A			
Dunstable			D	
Dunwich			D	F
Exeter			D	F
Gloucester		C	D	F
Gorleston	A			
Grantham				F
Grimsby	A			F
Guildford			D	
Hartlepool				F
Hereford			D	F
Hitchin		C		
Hull	A	C		
Hulne		C		
Huntingdon	A			
Ilchester			D	
Ipswich		C	D	F
King's Langley			D	
King's Lynn	A	C	D	F
Lancaster			D	
Leicester	A		D	F
Lewes				F
Lichfield				F
Lincoln	A	C	D	F
London	A	C	D	F
Lossenham		C		
Ludlow	A	C		
Maldon		C		
Marlborough		C		
Melcombe Regis			D	
Newcastle-Lyme			D	
Newcastle Tyne	A	C	D	F
Northallerton		C		
Northampton	A	C	D	F
Norwich	A	C	D	F

(A) Austin – (C) Carmelite – (D) Dominican – (F) Franciscan #

England

	A	C	D	F
Nottingham				F
	C			
Orford	A			
Oxford	A	C	D	F
Penrith	A			
Plymouth		C		F
Pontefract			D	
Preston				F
Reading				F
Richmond (Yorks)				F
Rye	A			
Salisbury			D	F
Sandwich		C		
Scarborough		C	D	F
Shrewsbury	A		D	F
Shoreham/Sele		C		
Southampton	A			F
Stafford	A			F
Stamford	A	C	D	F
Sudbury			D	
Thetford	A		D	
Tickhill	A			
Truro			D	
Walsingham				F
Ware				F
Warrington	A			
Warwick			D	
Wilton			D	
Winchelsea			D	F
Winchester	A	C	D	F
Woodhouse	A			
Worcester			D	F
Yarm			D	
Yarmouth		C	D	F
York	A	C	D	F

Wales

	A	C	D	F
Bangor			D	
Brecon			D	
Cardiff			D	F
Carmarthen				F
Denbigh		C		
Haverfordwest			D	
Llanfaes				F
Newport	A			
Rhuddlan			D	

Scotland

	A	C	D	F
Aberdeen		C	D	
Ayr			D	
Banff		C		
Cupar			D	
Dumfries				F
Dundee			D	F
Edinburgh		C	D	
Elgin			D	F
Glasgow			D	
Haddington			D	F
Inverbervie		C		
Inverkeithing				F
Irvine		C		
Inverness			D	
Kingussie		C		
Kirkcudbright				F
Lanark				F
Linlithgow		C		
Luffness		C		
Montrose			D	
Perch		C*	D	
Queensferry		C		
Roxburgh				F
St Andrews			D	
St Moman's			D	
Stirling			D	
Wigtown			D	

Notes

Franciscan Observants houses are not included in the list.
* The Carmelite Tullilum house is listed under Perth, as it was on the outskirts of the town.

The Newark Austin house has not been included as it lasted only from 1534 to 1538.

BIBLIOGRAPHY

Abbeys – Yorkshire's Monastic Heritage, English Heritage.
Alexander, Matthew, *Guildford, A Short History*, Ammonite 1992.
Archaeologia Cambrensis, 1855. *Llanfaes Friary and its Mystery Monuments*.
Bede, Venerable, *History of the English Church and People*. Dorset Press.
Bingham, Caroline, *Kings & Queens of Scotland*, Penguin 1955.
Bourne, Rev. Peter & Quin, Mabel, *Shrines and Pilgrimages*, Virtue & Co 1965.
Brown, J.F., *'The Blackfriars of Guildford', SURREY ADVERTISER*, 13.9.52.
Burton, Janet, *Monastic and Religious Orders in Britain 1000–1300*, Cambridge U.P. 1994.
Butler, A., *Lives of the Saints*, Studio Editions 1990.
Butler, Lionel & Given-Wilson, Chris, *Medieval Monasteries of Great Britain*, Michael Joseph 1979.
Bryce, W. Moir, *The Blackfriars of Edinburgh* 1911.
'Carmel in Britain', Essays on the Medieval English Carmelite Province, vol. 1, *People and Places*. C.E. Institutumm Carmelitanum 1992.
Catholic Truth Society – various booklets.
Comfort, Nicholas, *The Lost City of Dunwich*, Terence Dalton 1994.
Cooper, Janet, *Medieval Oxford, A History of the City*. A reprint from the *Victorian History of the County of Oxford*, vol. IV.
Cotton, E., *Greyfriars of Canterbury*, Manchester University Press 1924.

Coventry Leisure Services, *The Story of Whitefriars,* Coventry.
Cowan, Ian, & Easton, D., *Medieval Religious Houses of Scotland*, Longman 1976.
Dartford Priory – The History of the English Dominicanesses, by Dominican nuns of Headington. Blackfriars, Oxford 1945.
Deanery, Margaret, *History of the Medieval Church* – 590–1500, Methuen.
Dickinson, J.C., *Ecclesiastical History Guide of England – The Late Middle Ages.*
Doyle, E., *Canterbury and the Franciscans*, 1924.
Dyer, Alan, *Decline and Growth in English Towns.*
Faraday, M.A., *Ludlow – 1085–1660*, Phillimore 1991.
Froth, Rev. F. OSA, *The English Austin Friars 1249–1258*, Augustinian Historical Institute, New York 1966.
Fullbrook-Leggatt, L., *Anglo-Saxon and Medieval Gloucester*, John Jennings 1952.
Gloucester Blackfriars, English Heritage guidebook.
Gumbly, Fr W., OP, *The Cambridge Dominicans*, Blackfriars, Oxford 1938.
Hamilton, Bernard, *Religion in the Medieval West.*
Hill, Sir Francis, *A Short History of Lincoln*, Lincoln Civic Trust 1979.
Hinnebusch, W.A., *The Early English Friar Preachers*, Rome 1951.
Hinrlebush, W.A., *Studies in Thirteenth Century Dominican History* – Part II.
Hutton, Edward, *The Franciscans in England – 1224–1538, 1926.*
Inverness, Local History & Archaeology Guidebook No. 4, 1982.
Jacob, E.F., *The Oxford History of England – The Fifteenth Century*, Clarendon Press 1976.
Jantzen, Grace, *Julian of Norwich*, SPCK.
Jedin, Hubert, ed., *History of the Church* – vol IV, *From the Middle Ages to the Eve of the Reformation*, Burns and Oates 1980.
Jewell, Helen, *English Local Administration in the Middle Ages.*
Knowles, David, *Bare Ruined Choirs*, Cambridge U.P. 1959.
Knowles, David, *Religious Orders in England* – Part 3, *The Tudor Age*, Cambridge U.P. 1959.

Lawrence, C.H., *Medieval Monasticism*, Longman 1984.
le Goff, Jacques, *History of European Society – The Medieval World*, Collins and Brown 1990.
Leighton, Wilfrid, *'The Black Friars, Now Quaker's Friars, Bristol'*, in *TRANSACTIONS OF THE BRISTOL AND GLOUCESTER ARCHAEOLOGICAL SOCIETY*, vol. 54.
Little, A.G., *Greyfriars in Oxford*, Oxford Historical Society, 1892.
Lodwick, Malcolm & Edith, *Story of Carmarthen*, revised by Joyce & Victor Lodwick, St Peter Press 1972.
Lynch, Rev. E.K., Carm, O., *The Scapular of Carmel*, Carmelite Press 1955.
McIntosh, H.B., *Elgin Past and Present*, Moray D.C. 1995.
Martin, A.A., *Franciscan Architecture in England*, Manchester University Press 1937.
Martin, A.R., *'Dominican Priory of Canterbury', ARCHAEOLOGICAL JOURNAL* LXXXVI (2nd series).
Maxwell, Alexander, *Old Dundee Prior to the Reformation*, William Kidd 1911.
McCann, A. & T.J., *Chichester Greyfriars and Priory Park*, Chichester Museum 1988.
Mackie, J.D., *The Oxford History of England – The Earlier Tudors*, Clarendon Press 1978.
McKisack, May, *The Oxford History of England – The Fourteenth Century*, Clarendon Press 1963.
Merle d'Aubigne, J.H., *The Reformation in England*, Banner of Truth 1962.
Midmer, Roy, *English Medieval Monasteries – 1066–1540*, Heinemann 1979.
Milnes, Robert, *The Blackfriars of Perth – THE CHARTULARY AND PAPERS OF THE HOUSE*, 1893.
Monastic Shropshire, Shropshire Libraries 1982.
Moorman, John R.H., *The Grey Friars of Cambridge*, Cambridge U.P. 1952.
Moorman, John R.H., *History of the Franciscan Order*, Oxford U.P. 1968.
Morgan, Dennis, *The Cardiff Story*, D. Brown and Sons 1991.
Mosheim, J.M., *Ecclesiastical History – Ancient and Modern*, Vol 3 1819.

New Catholic Encyclopedia, Library of Congress 1966.
New, Anthony, *A Guide to the Abbeys of Scotland*, Constable 1988.
Nicholson, Ranald, *Scotland – The Late Middle Ages.*
Nineham, Dennis, *Christianity – Medieval & Modern.*
Monastic Britain, North and South sheets, Ordnance Survey map.
Oxoniensia (Journal of the Oxfordshire Architectural and Historical Society) – 1976 and 1977.
Platt, Colin, *The Abbeys and Priories of Medieval England*, Chancellor Press 1995.
Ponsford, M.W., *Excavations at Greyfriars, Bristol*, Bristol Museum 1975.
Powicke, Sir Maurice, *The Oxford History of England – The Thirteenth Century*, Clarendon Press 1970.
Richards, Paul, *King's Lynn*, Phillimore 1990.
Russel, Percy, *The Good Town of Totnes*, The Devonshire Association 1984.
Smith, Martin, *The Story of Stamford* Alden Press 1994.
Smith, Philip, *The History of the Christian Church During the Middle Ages*, John Murray 1885.
Soulsby, I., *Towns of Medieval Wales*, Phillimore 1983.
Southern, R.W., *Western Society and the Church in the Middle Ages*, Pelican 1970.
Sparks, Margaret with Tatton-Brown, Tim, *'The Blackfriars in Canterbury', MEDIEVAL ARCHAEOLOGY*, vol. 15.
Stavert, Marion L., *Perth, A Short History*, Perth & Kinross District Libraries 1991.
Sutermeister, Helen, *The Norwich Blackfriars, City of Norwich*, City of Norwich Library Service.
Taylor, Pauline, *Greyfriars Convent, Elgin.* Booklet containing an extract from *The Northern Scot*, which was published by permission of the Moray and Nairn Newspaper Co.
Thorold, Henry, *The Ruined Abbeys of England, Wales and Scotland*, Harper Collins 1993.
Tugwell, Simon, O.P., *Early Dominicans – Selected Writings*, SPCK 1984.

Tugwell, Simon, O.P., *Early St Dominic and the Order of Preachers,* Catholic Truth Society.
Wakeman, H.O., *History of the Church of England*, Rivingtons 1899.
Walsh, Michael, *The Popes*, Marshal Cavendish 1980.
Wheater, William, *Knaresborough and its Rulers*, Richard Jackson 1907.
Wiltshire Archaeological Magazine, vol. 18, 1879.
Victorian County Histories of England (VCH), 'Religious Houses' section – Most books in this series.
Young, Douglas, *St Andrews*, Cassell 1969.